The Whole Works of the Rev. Oliver Heywood

Now First Collected, Revised, and Arranged
Including some Tracts extremely scarce, and
others from unpublished manuscripts:

With Memoirs Of His Life

In Five Volumes

Volume 2

containing

Heart Treasure

and

The Sure Mercies of David

Soli Deo Gloria Publications
... for instruction in righteousness ...

Soli Deo Gloria Publications
P.O. Box 451, Morgan, PA 15064
(412) 221-1901/FAX 221-1902

*

The Works of Oliver Heywood was first published in 1825. This 1997 Soli Deo Gloria reprint is taken from the 1825 edition published in London by John Vint. Printed in the USA.

*

Volume 2 of *The Works of Oliver Heywood*, "Heart Treasure" is ISBN 1-57358-063-5

CONTENTS

OF

THE SECOND VOLUME.

                                                      Page.

Editor's Preface - - - - - - - - v

HEART TREASURE.

Mr. Chester's Recommendatory Address - - - - xxi
Dedication of the Author - - - - - xxiii
CHAP. I. The Introduction - - - - - - 1
     II. On the Nature of a Treasure - - - - 6
     III. On the Christian's Treasure - - - - 12
     IV. On the laying out of Heart Treasure - - 20
     V. On the great Necessity of laying up this Treasure - - - - - - - - 29
     VI. On Self-examination relative to this Treasure 47
     VII. Neglect of Heart Treasure reproved - - 57
     VIII. Instructions for the Destitute to obtain a Treasure of Good - - - - - 79
     IX. Directions relative to good Thoughts - - 99
     X. Truths which a Christian should treasure up - 128
     XI. The Graces which a good Man should cherish and cultivate - - - - - 138
     XII. Experiences which should be collected - 149
     XIII. Comforts, as a Treasure, should be laid up in the Heart - - - - - 159
     XIV. On the Preservation and Increase of a Christian's Treasure - - - - - 170
     XV. Directions for bringing forth good Things out of the Believer's good Treasure - - - 191

CONTENTS.

	Page.
CHAP. XVI. The Excellency and Advantage of having a Treasure in the Heart	202
XVII. Some Objections answered, and Exhortations urged	228
APPENDIX. Concerning Meditation, with some Helps to furnish the Thoughts with suitable and profitable Subjects	246

SURE MERCIES OF DAVID.

Preface	285
CHAP. I. Introductory Remarks	293
II. Mercies of the Covenant	300
III. The Way in which Covenant Mercies are made sure	315
IV. The Manner in which Covenant Mercies are confirmed	321
V. The Medium through which the Sure Mercies of David are conveyed	333
VI. The Sure Mercies of David furnish a Confutation of Errors	347
VII. The Sure Mercies of David considered as contributing Instruction	360
VIII. These Sure Mercies supply Materials for Self-Examination	381
IX. Covenant Mercies tend to produce Conviction	408
X. These Mercies deserve Consideration, and should excite in all a Solicitude to obtain them	432
XI. The Sure Mercies of David suggest various Directions	447
XII. The Sure Mercies of David are calculated to encourage Believers, and to excite their Gratitude	495

EDITOR'S
PREFACE.

THE preaching of the gospel is the primary and most efficient agency appointed and employed by infinite wisdom for the conversion of men and the edification of the church. But the circulation of books characterized by a tendency to promote the interests of religion, must be regarded as auxiliary means. There have indeed been times when the auxiliary means have taken the place of the principal, and books have become almost the sole dispensers of religious knowledge.

Before the apostles and evangelists had finished their course, persecution raised his ferocious and infernal visage, and blighted the hopes which had been entertained by the first followers of Jesus. The preachers of truth were driven into corners, or immured in dungeons, or suffered at the stake; but prior to the termination of their career so highly distinguished for its usefulness and importance to the church of God, the Gospels and Epistles, together with the Acts of the Apostles, and the Revelation of John, were, under the direction of the Holy Spirit, composed for the general benefit of every succeeding age. Those sacred writings were also transcribed by many a hand with unwearied perseverance, and the copies were distributed amongst the various societies of Christians for their edification and comfort. In their circumstances of persecution, we may easily conceive that the records of truth would be held as precious indeed.

Passing over the instances which exhibit a similarity of situation to that of the primitive Christians, and in which the value of religious books would be estimated at a singularly high rate, the Editor would introduce the case of about two thousand congregations that were at once,* by the Act of Uniformity, deprived of the ministers, who had dispensed among them the word of life, and whom they esteemed very highly in love for their works' sake. Their ministers, however, were not formed of such materials as to cause them to sink into a state of inactivity. If they were not permitted any longer to officiate in their former places of worship, or to address the people when summoned together by the " church-going bell," after embracing every opportunity of preaching which presented itself, they retired to their studies and employed their leisure hours in writing, in order to promote the spiritual welfare of the people around them.

In such a state of seclusion, and even when the strong hand of power has shut up the witnesses to the truth within the walls of a prison, some of the most valuable literary productions have originated. When

* Aug. 24, 1662.

Luther was confined in the castle of Wartburg, which he was accustomed to denominate his *Patmos*, he composed several theological tracts, which displayed the energies of his powerful mind, and contributed greatly to confirm the resolution of those who had attached themselves to the cause of the Reformation—which also had a mighty influence in gaining adherents to this cause, as well as establishing those who not unfrequently wavered in their trying and precarious circumstances. But the most of his solitude he employed on a translation of the Scriptures into the language of his native country. This German version, the result of his confinement was of the highest importance. "The different parts of it," says Mosheim, "being successively and gradually spread abroad among the people, produced sudden and almost incredible effects, and extirpated root and branch, the erroneous principles and superstitious doctrines of the church of Rome, from the minds of a prodigious number of persons." Bunyan is another extraordinary instance of successful toil, when prevented from discharging in a public manner the duties of the ministerial office. In a jail at Bedford, torn from the scenes of active life, cut off from all the ordinary intercourse of society, his whole library consisting of his Bible and Fox's Martyrology, he sketched the Progress of his Pilgrim, and even in this world procured for himself an immortal name.

> Ingenious dreamer, in whose well told tale
> Sweet fiction and sweet truth alike prevail;
> Whose hum'rous vein, strong sense, and simple style,
> May teach the gayest, make the gravest smile.—COWPER.

The popular Author of Pilgrim's Progress, the venerable Oliver Heywood, and their contemporaries who embarked with them in the same cause, had their lot cast on evil times; but whilst enduring the most harassing treatment, and the most painful privations under the edicts of a faithless monarch, their days of trial and suffering did not pass unimproved. The consequence of their ejectment from their places of worship, and their condemnation to silence was, that during the period between the Restoration and the Revolution, a far greater number of religious books issued from the English press than had ever, in the same space of time, been published in any age or any country. Before that period, those authors who made a figure in the republic of letters through the whole of Europe, generally wrote and published in the Latin language; but as the principal object of the Nonconformist writers was not to engage the attention of the learned merely, nor to challenge them to enter any arena of controversy either at home or abroad, and as they duly estimated the imperious claims of their fellow-countrymen at large, and especially the people to whose service they had dedicated themselves, and from the charge of whom they had been forcibly driven with unrelenting severity, the compositions which they prepared for the press were in their native language, and were chiefly intended either to promote the spiritual welfare of those who had believed through grace and possessed genuine piety, or to arrest the attention of such as were in danger of perishing for lack of knowledge, and lead them to a consideration of their eternal interests. Accordingly the age of our forefathers witnessed the publications of Owen and Baxter, Goodwin and Flavel, Howe and Charnock, Manton and Bates, and many others, whose names only would fill several pages of this Preface.

To ascertain what degree of moral influence, their productions had on the minds of those among whom they were first circulated, or on the generation that succeeded, would be difficult or rather it may be said impossible. There can, however, be no doubt but that they operated imperceptibly, and that the impressions they made were favourable to the interests of truth and morality. It is true that not many years after the Revolution, when the civil and religious liberties of Britain had been secured, religion could no longer boast of the pious zeal which distinguished her confessors of a former age: her stated ministers, generally speaking, began to have less and still less concern, for the spiritual and eternal interests of men; a frigid indifference at length seized possession of their minds, and then an awful stillness both within and without the pale of the established church, seems to have reigned over the population of the country. In these circumstances, however, a new description of Nonconformists appeared within the walls of the Establishment— Whitfield and Wesley and others, broke loose from the prescribed routine of ecclesiastical office, and went out into the streets and lanes of our towns and cities, and into the high ways and hedges of our country, to publish the glad tidings of salvation to the people, who almost in every place crowded to attend on their extra-parochial ministry. But is there not reason to believe, that their hearers in numerous instances had experienced some peculiar excitement, which prompted them to listen to the doctrines advanced, and that their minds were in some measure prepared to receive cordially the message of the gospel? When in the year 1755, Mr. Whitfield preached at Birstall to an assembly of fifteen thousand hearers, and at other places in the same district to similar multitudes, the fields may be said to have been white unto harvest—but had there been previously no tranquil cultivation? had not the thorns and briars in many instances been eradicated? had not the soil been insensibly imbibing the dews of heavenly truth? were not the seeds of religion sown here and there, according to our Lord's expression, in "honest and good hearts?"* The circulation of our Author's works was probably local rather than general. As Bernard Gilpin was esteemed and justly designated the Apostle of the North, so Oliver Heywood may be denominated the Apostle of Yorkshire, on account of his unwearied labours in this populous and important division of the kingdom; for annually he travelled in every direction many hundreds of miles, and dispensed the word of life to a population but partially favoured with the means of grace. And whilst he was thus employed under the guidance of Providence, *to make ready a people prepared for the Lord*,† wherever he travelled he was welcomed, and hailed as a messenger of God. In such circumstances,

* Luke viii. 15. † Luke i. 17.

no wonder that his publications bearing the impress of his piety and zeal, were esteemed and read with pleasure ; and as a great book has been reckoned a great evil, the smallness of their size too would ensure for them a preference to the ponderous folio, among the generality of readers.

The Treatises of our Author published at different intervals during the course of forty years, are sixteen in number, and they no doubt had a considerable circulation ; for unless their publication had been sanctioned by the constant patronage of the friends of religion, it can scarcely be supposed that he would have continued to publish through such an extended period of his life. If we should suppose then, that each copy of his circulated Treatises found a few readers in a family, that they were read through the space of 50 or 100 years, and that only a portion of the many thousands of his readers experienced improvement of character from their perusal ; and if we should suppose also that every individual who had experienced some excitement of feeling from their moral influence, and had in consequence become in any respect a better man—should either directly or indirectly meliorate in some slight degree the moral circumstances of those with whom he was brought into contact in the common intercourse of society ; who on summing up these considerations could calculate the mighty effects of such publications as our Author's in a religious point of view ? and if from these premises an inference may be drawn that their circulation has already had an extensive moral influence, may we not cherish a hope that their republication will not be unproductive of good?

In the village in which the Editor resides he has ascertained that there are two of Mr. Heywood's Treatises: one of them, entitled *Heart Treasure*, he found in the course of its transit from family to family, in which holy progress it had been proceeding for 158 years; but almost all the copies of his works have finished their course, and it has been with very great difficulty that copies have been procured to complete this republication: of the smallest of his publications (*Job's Appeal*) only one printed copy is known to exist, and some of the others are exceedingly scarce. The Treatise on *Closet Prayer* is the only part of his Works, so far as the Editor knows, which has hitherto been re-printed. Dr. Fawcett, indeed, published *Life in God's Favour*, but it cannot, with strict propriety, be called a re-publication of the venerable Nonconformist's work, for as the Doctor, with the best intentions, seems to have resolved on doing what he could to secure public approbation by modernizing the phraseology, and interweaving with the original many additional observations, (calculated, as he justly thought, for usefulness) it became, in his hands, what may be denominated a paraphrase or an improvement.

In presenting the whole Works of the Reverend OLIVER HEYWOOD to the Public, the Editor acknowledges that he has had some hesitation, not because his respect for the memory of the Author has wavered, nor because he ever considered the subjects discussed and illustrated by him as unimportant or uninteresting, nor because he judged the Author or his Work unworthy of ceaseless fame. No; but he is aware that the taste of the age in which we live is very different from that which prevailed in the days of our ancestors, and he has apprehended that the language of the seventeenth century would have but few attractions in the nineteenth. That quaintness of expression which characterized almost all the literary productions of the writers who flourished before the revolution, tinges everywhere the style of our Author; his language may often be considered as of a homely description, and forms of sentences are frequently occurring, in which words are introduced to rhyme with each other, which were, doubtless, regarded by him, and probably by a majority of his readers, as beauties of composition, but which will appear as blemishes to those who are accustomed to the polished periods of this refined age. But then there are many redeeming qualities. The medium of his thoughts is, in general, very transparent; perspicuity, the first excellence of all language, invariably distinguishes his compositions. Seldom will you find an intricate or involved sentence; in the formation of his periods he does not, like some of his contemporaries, conduct you into a labyrinth, from which, with great difficulty only, you can find your way. His numerous comparisons, though they may in some instances be liable to the charge of coarseness, are taken generally from common life, and are very often striking and happy. An unaffected simplicity is a prominent characteristic of his writings; an indescribable something which the French have denominated *naïveté*, which springs from the amiable and undisguised feelings of the writer, and which engages and often charms the attention and feelings of his reader, runs through every page. And above all, the Works which now, for the first time, make their appearance in a uniform edition, are rendered interesting by the evident solicitude and earnestness of the Author to promote the spiritual and eternal welfare of his fellow-men.

After what has been said, it may be unnecessary to observe, that the graces of eloquence are not to be expected to ornament these Volumes, and neither do learned or metaphysical disquisitions characterize their pages. Piety is the grace which must recommend them, if they obtain any cordial reception at all, but with this recommendation there may be hope that they will succeed; for piety, like the poet's beauty,

" ―――― is when unadorned, adorned the most."

It must be acknowledged that piety, as here attired, appears a little in the antique style—her garb is according to the fashion of other times, but even at the present day the fashion of antiquity has had its admirers. A singular confirmation of this remark has lately occurred; a preacher and author,[*] who has been ambitious to convert our sermons and discourses into orations and arguments, has attempted to revive

[*] Rev. E. Irving.

the obsolete phraseology of our forefathers, and his popularity has been great; but if the copy has not been without its attractions, the original ought certainly to be received with still greater favour.

To the reader the Editor would say, you will not see here the master-hand of Owen—you will not perceive the giant-grasp of Howe—nor will you be gratified with the harmonious periods of the "silver-tongued Bates;" but if you can be pleased and edified with the plainness, simplicity, seriousness, and pathetic admonitions of Flavel—or if your religious feelings are excited by the pious solicitude of Baxter and his earnest appeals to the consciences of men, there is reason to believe that the affection, faithfulness, and zeal perpetually discoverable in all the productions of our Author, cannot fail to engage your attention, and make those impressions which mark the progress of religion in the heart. The state of that man's mind must be far from being what it ought to be, who should read the *Subjects of Thought and Meditation* on daily occurrences, prescribed at the close of the Treatise, entitled *Heart Treasure*, or the advantages of assurance, stated in the eleventh Chapter of the *Sure Mercies of David*, and who, when he has finished the perusal, does not feel a disposition to say, " Let my soul be as the soul of Oliver Heywood—let me die the death of that righteous man, and let my last end be like his."

The state in which the Editor found the original copies, has occasioned him far more labour than he had contemplated. The errors of the Press were innumerable; in not a few instances too, there appear to have been slips of the pen, not to be wondered at in the Author's circumstances; in consequence of which, heterogeneous sentences sometimes occur which he, unquestionably, would himself have corrected if an opportunity had presented itself; and in those copies, there are also words which custom has long banished from the language, and which would now be unintelligible to many. Errors of the press, or the pen, the Editor has corrected,* and instead of obsolete words, he has substituted others sanctioned by modern use; but this has been done very sparingly, and in every case of this description, the sense of the Author has been most religiously preserved—in several instances, the antiquated terms have been retained, and their signification given at the bottom of the page.

In these Volumes, Oliver Heywood appears in his own dress, in the costume of his age, and if the Editor has taken the liberty of brushing off a spot or two which had rather an unsightly appearance, he hopes he will not be condemned for officiousness; indeed, he is more apprehensive that he may be blamed for not

* The passages quoted from Justin Martyr, Irenæus, Clemens Alexandrinus, Tertullian, Cyprian, Augustine, and others, have been collated, and the errors in them, of which there were not a few, have been corrected with care. In two or three instances, the passages adduced were in such a state, that they were beyond the possibility of being corrected, without collation. The Works of Bernard, from which several quotations are made, the Editor does not possess.

taking such liberty more frequently than he has done. If, in this publication he had chiefly proposed to himself, as the scope of his labours, the gratification of the antiquary, he would not have ventured on any alteration whatever, he would not have suffered the shield of Scriblerus to have its rust in any particle disturbed by a furbishing operation, but he had a more important object in view, and he has therefore departed a little, and but a little, from antiquarian punctiliousness in the direction of his course.

Our revered Author by his publications erected for himself a monument which has perpetuated the remembrance of his name upwards of 150 years; but it has suffered from the ravages of time, its parts have been dislocated, and the fragments have been scattered about, in danger of being for ever lost. They are, however, now collected, and if Providence should spare the Editor a little longer in this precarious state of things, they may be expected to be replaced and beautified with some additional ornaments, to give permanence to the memory of a venerated man. But it was not posthumous fame to which he himself aspired as the prize of his Christian race; in the performance of his ministerial services often laborious and fatiguing, amidst the sufferings he endured in his Master's cause, and when publishing the productions of his pen, he sought, principally, the approbation of heaven. It was sufficient for him, as it was for the Apostle of the Gentiles, that Christ was magnified either by his life or by his death; " whether he lived, he lived to the Lord, or whether he died, he died to the Lord, so that whether living or dying he was the Lord's."

So far as the Editor has proceeded, he has, himself, reaped no little advantage from the occupation in which he has been engaged. The strain of fervent piety which pervades every production which came from the Author's pen, the artless simplicity with which the genuine feelings of a Christian are often described, and the unwearied zeal manifested for the immortal interests of men, have not been reviewed without some correspondent impression. Dr. Doddridge in his Preface to Archbishop Leighton's Commentary on Peter, expresses himself thus: "The preparing of these Volumes for the Press has generally taken up a little of my time, in the intervals of other business, daily for several months, but I am far from repenting the labour I have bestowed upon it. The delight and edification which I have found would have been a full equivalent for my pains, separate from all prospect of that effect they might have upon others." Similar language I can adopt; after having been for a considerable time employed on the Works of my Author, which bear a strong resemblance to those of the pious Archbishop, the experience which I have myself had, encourages me to hope that the circulation of this Edition will, under the blessing of God, contribute to the spiritual improvement of many.

WILLIAM VINT.

Idle, near Bradford,
May 2, 1825.

HEART TREASURE;

OR,

AN ESSAY

COMPRISING THE SUBSTANCE OF A COURSE OF

Sermons,

PREACHED AT COLEY, NEAR HALIFAX,

YORKSHIRE.

MR. CHESTER'S

RECOMMENDATORY ADDRESS.

Reader,

So soon as thine eye views the Title of this Treatise, do not slightly cast the Treatise itself away, but spend some time in the serious perusal of it. If any value is to be put on my poor judgment, I do assure thee I esteem it a choice Treasure. In it thou wilt find a most useful subject treated on, namely, the furnishing of the heart with a spiritual treasure, an argument necessary for these times, wherein we cannot ensure outward treasures. The pious, learned Author, in handling this subject, hath approved himself a most experienced Christian, and a workman who needeth not to be ashamed.

Among the variety of good books, which through divine indulgence are yet to be bought, it will be thy wisdom to buy those that are of general use, and such is this book which I commend to thee. Buy it, read it oft, meditate on it seriously, and lift up thy heart to God for his blessing, and thou wilt find much cause to admire his good providence in handing this book to thee, and wilt be incited to do what many professors are too remiss in, namely, getting a heart treasure, which will greatly support thee under present and future trial.

In the *Appendix* thou wilt meet with excellent helps for the discharge of the necessary and much neglected duty of meditation, whereby thou mayest get much treasure for holy thoughts, and so prevent what is the burden of many gracious souls, namely, vain thoughts; while thou wilt be fitted for duty, and enjoy much of heaven on earth.

The good Lord bless these papers, and the labours of all his faithful ambassadors to the good of his church, so prayeth,

The meanest of Christ's servants,

And thy soul's Friend,

JOHN CHESTER

July the 12*th,* 1667.

AUTHOR'S

DEDICATION.

TO MY VERY LOVING AND DEARLY BELOVED FRIENDS
AND NEIGHBOURS,

THE INHABITANTS OF COLEY,

And the Places adjacent.

MY DEARLY BELOVED IN THE LORD,

GOOD books are not the least part of the church's treasure and furniture, but there is not any book to be compared to that Book of books, the Holy Bible, or book of canonical Scripture, which was indited by the immediate dictates of the blessed Spirit—penned by holy men of God—which contains the whole of man, and opens God's heart to the sons of men. This precious Book is the common magazine of the saints, the greatest treasure of heavenly wisdom and science (saith a good Divine) that the whole earth hath in keeping. He that peruses and digests this Book cannot but be in a thriving state—he that digs in these golden mines cannot but be rich—and he that makes this Book his main study must needs be learned, holy, and happy. The best men have delighted most in the word of God, and they that have delighted most therein have become the best men : of some famous men it is recorded, that they read every day fifteen Chapters in the Bible, many years together ; of others it is said, they read it above twenty times over in their lives, with special observations ; of others, that by long and assiduous meditation on the Scriptures, their breasts became libraries of Jesus Christ. And, indeed, it is the duty and property of a gracious soul to meditate in God's law day and night, and to set a higher estimate upon it than upon the richest treasures of gold and silver, pearls, or precious stones. " It were better that all other books were burnt, (as Luther said) than that they should abate Scripture study: yet subordinately, the choice treatises of eminent divines in all ages are no mean part of the church's treasure, as helps to understand and improve the treasures of knowledge contained and couched in those sacred pages. These are as so many Philips to the studious eunuch to take the uncertain and inquiring passenger by the hand, through the deeper fords of Scripture studies; these as tender nurses, feed the children of God with milk or stronger meat, as they are able. These are those mineralists that dig out of this precious quarry such gold and silver ore, that if it have the stamp of God upon it, will much enrich the souls of spiritual merchants; only let the spiritual man, who judgeth all things, try the spirits, and distinguish betwixt the dross of error, and the solid gold of saving truth; let no poison, dropping from the pen, infect the eyes, and so bewitch the heart. It is a blessed thing to have a solid judgment, and an honest heart, to prove all things, and to hold fast that which is good. Blessed be God for good books, which are a better treasure for the church than the Romish stock of merits and indulgences; they are as so many sweet reflections from the sun of Scripture upon the dark and doubting soul, they are as pipes to convey the streams of salvation from those blessed fountains to private houses, and troubled hearts: and there is an advantage in writing; when preachers are dead or cannot speak, books may remain and instruct their surviving people, and what is wanting to the ear may be compensated to the eye, (which some have called the learned senses) and through the eye the heart may be affected, and why may not life be conveyed through the eyes to the heart? as death came in that way, so God can by his Spirit make pen and ink characters, to leave lively impressions, not on paper and parchment, but on the fleshly tables of the heart.*

* 2 Cor. iii. 3.

This in part is my apology for putting my sickle into this harvest, and taking such pains in composing this Treatise; whether it shall ever have the advantage of publication through the Press, I know not, but if the Lord will make any further use of it, for the good of his church, I shall accept of such opportunity, and leave myself and these poor labours to the service of that God, to whom I have devoted myself and all that I have or can do. I look upon myself as the weakest and unworthiest of all those that wait at God's altar, yet as the Lord hath put me in trust with the gospel, so I have desired in my measure to be faithful to the Lord and to your souls, and having obtained help of God, I continue a mirror of Providence to this day. I am not worthy to preach, much less to print any thing on these glorious mysteries. I rather wonder that God hath had patience with me thus long in his work; my God hath humbled me amongst you—you know how I have served the Lord with many tears and temptations which have befallen me many ways,[*] yet God is faithful, who hath not suffered me to be tempted beyond that strength he hath supplied me with, and hath, at last, made a way to escape.[†] Let God glorify himself, whatever become of this vile, wretched worm; the good of your souls lies near my heart—God is my witness how greatly I long after your spiritual welfare; it much grieves me to think of leaving any of your souls without a saving treasure, after all my soul-travail over you, and serving two full apprenticeships amongst you. Let not my sins or sufferings blemish my doctrine or practise, or be a stumbling-block before any of you. What you have seen good in me, imitate—what hath been amiss, cover with the skirt of love, and beg a pardon from heaven for me. Some may think better of me than I deserve, and others worse, but while I consider man's judgment of little importance, both have tended to humble me, because I do not answer the apprehensions of the one, and my corruptions exceed any grounded censures of the other; it were but a sorry business to undertake a vindication of myself, except wherein the gospel is concerned. O that you and yours may be and do that which is good, though I should be as reprobate and unapproved. Let

---

[*] Acts xx. 19.   [†] 1 Cor. x. 13.

Christ live, though we die—let souls be enriched, though we be impoverished;* would to God poor souls did reign as spiritual kings, for though they should seek to exclude us as means thereof, yet we also would reign with them as sharers therein, and in thankfulness to God for their mercy.† Let people be truly rich in grace, and we must be full of comfort; yea, our people's faith should comfort us in all our affliction. O how much would our people's spiritual gains countervail our temporal losses! It is better, infinitely better that you be rich with our wares, than we with yours; our greatest treasure, as Ministers, lies in your soul's riches—we seek not yours, but you, and it will be transcendently more comfort, if you give up your souls to Christ, than if you should give all your estates to us. We shall get riches enough if we make you rich, as Constantius said once. This is one of Paul's paradoxes. O that it might be verified in our success also, as poor, yet making many rich.—2 Cor. vi. 10.

Concerning the birth and bulk of this Treatise I must tell you, that the occasion of it was this: I heard a godly Minister preach a sermon upon this text, and I was much affected with it, and resolved, when I came home to search into it; I studied and preached three sermons, as I remember, upon it, with which some were so affected, that several entreated me to give them copies thereof, which I set myself to; but as I wrote, it swelled in my hands to this magnitude at last—and when some had perused it, they entreated me to let it be printed, and some would be at the charge. It was a sudden, and, to me, a strange motion, for I never yet judged any labours of mine to be of so much worth as to be exposed to public view, yet I did not know what hand and end the Lord might have in this motion. I sought God about it, and desired him to search my heart, and and purge it from the leaven of vanity and ostentation, which, God knows, I found too much working in me—then I told my friends I would communicate it to some Reverend Ministers, and should be ruled by their judgment and advice. I did so, and four or five eminent men in these two Counties of Yorkshire and Lancashire have moved me to publish it; and if Providence

* 2 Cor. xiii. 7. † 1 Cor. iv. 8.

clears the way, I freely consent: the Lord do with me and it, as seems good in his eyes.

The subject, I am sure, is of great importance, nor have I ever seen any Treatise of this nature; if it were profitably handled, it might be of singular use—with respect to what is merely of man, I hope God will pity, and pardon the unworthy instrument, and what proceedeth from his blessed Spirit, may that, through the help of the Spirit, reach and teach the spirit; as this occupation hath been, in a measure, painful, so hath it been very pleasant and delightful to me; and this I can say, I I never found such variety of matter flowing into my mind at any time, as I have experienced in writing this book; if the Lord do good by it, I have my end.

Devout Bernard begins an Epistle to a great man with this text, " A good man out of the good treasure of the heart bringeth forth good things;" and towards the close of that Epistle, he hath these words, " Truly, for myself, I read myself in thy letters, not what I am, but what I would be, and what I am ashamed that I am not." Just so may I say in this case. I have written on the Heart's Treasure, but alas, how little have I attained of that whereof I have written! The Lord grant that my own Book may not rise up as a witness against me; but it is the desire of my heart to have such a treasure as is here described—if it make our souls long and pray for it, some good is done.

I shall not any longer detain you in the porch, I entreat you to read deliberately, and practice what you read and find backed with the Scripture of truth, and God forbid that my preaching or this writing should rise up in judgment against you; God forbid that any of you should be found without this Heart Treasure of saving grace, at death or judgment.

My dear Friends, pray for me, who have *you* much upon my heart, when I am upon my knees; pray for me, that utterance may be given unto me—" that I may make known the mystery of the gospel. Pray, that I may come unto you with joy by the will of God, and may with you be refreshed, for the perfecting of that which is lacking in your faith," * that so you may have a treasure of grace in your hearts laid up in you, and a treasure of glory in the heavens laid up for you, which is the constant prayer of

 A sinful Worm,

   That desires to continue with you,

     For your furtherance and joy of faith.

        OLIVER HEYWOOD.

From my Study, at Coley-Hall,
 June 14, 1666.

    * Ephes. v. 19. Rom. xv. 32.

HEART TREASURE.

MATTH. XII. 35.

A good man out of the good treasure of the heart, bringeth forth good things.———

CHAP. I.

THE INTRODUCTION.

OUR blessed Lord and Saviour Jesus Christ, like a skilful alchymist, extracts the pure gold of wholesome doctrine from common objects and occurrences: as from material water, he proceeds to discourse on spiritual water of life;* from common bread, he ascends to soul-nourishing conferences on his own flesh and blood, that living bread that came down from heaven.† As he passed through the vineyards, he takes occasion to speak of the true vine himself, and of those saints that are really grafted into him, and bring forth proportionable fruit. ‡ Christ could preach an excellent sermon from any text; but here he takes an occasion of uttering precious medicinal truths, from the poisonous blasphemies of the Scribes and Pharisees; distinguishing the fruit of the lips into good and bad words, which evidence the nature of the root to be either good or bad. The occasion of the words was this,—when our soul-saving and body-healing Redeemer had cast out a blind and dumb devil, that glo-

* John, iv. 10.   † Ibid. vi. 27.   ‡ Ibid. xv. 1.

rious miracle had various effects: upon the possessed person, it wrought soundness; (ver. 22.) upon the people, amazement; (ver. 23.) upon the Pharisees, madness and blasphemy (though that was only accidental) whereby they charge God himself with imposture. (ver. 24.) To these last, Christ speaks by way of apology for himself, and confutation of their impudent slander; his answer consists of three members.

1. He refutes the calumny by clear arguments, demonstrating his divine power in the miracle, from ver. 25—31.*

2. He detects the heinousness of the slander, calling it an irremissible blasphemy, ver. 32.

3. He exhorts them to repentance, by a severe and serious challenge, urging them to conceive more soundly and soberly of divine works; and to speak more spiritually and profitably, since they must give an account of every idle, much more blasphemous expression; from whence there will be drawn sufficient matter of their condemnation: this exhortation he directs to the Pharisees, ver. 33 and 34. parabolically; and to all, 35—37. properly and doctrinally.

Or our Lord Jesus shews, that thoughts are the first-born of the heart the fountain of expressions, words are the echo of heart-language; much may be in the heart that is not vented with the lips, but there is nothing comes out, but what was first within; "for out of the abundance of the heart the mouth speaks," ver. 34. This is illustrated by two similitudes,

Of a *tree*, ver. 33. and a *treasure*, ver. 35.

There is much ado amongst expositors to determine what is meant by tree; but it is clear, by tree is meant a man or woman, who must be good before good can be done: but the latter resemblance of a treasure, is

* Vide Pareum in cap.

our present subject, which consists of two parts; relating, the first, to good men, and the second, to bad men.*

In both which, are—layings up, called a **treasure,**—and layings out, expressed by bringing forth.

But to explain a little.

A good man—there is good, 1. Absolutely; so there is none good but God, that is, essentially, perfectly, originally, independently. 2. Comparatively; so godly men are truly good, that is, sincerely, if compared with profane men, or hypocrites. It is said of Barnabas, that he was a good man, and full of the Holy Ghost and faith, Acts xi. 24. There are also good men, as compared with froward, 1 Pet. ii. 18. or choice instruments, compared with persons of an inferior rank, Rom. v. 7. as David was worth ten thousand of the people. This good man in the text is to be taken in the former sense, in opposition to wicked men.

Good treasure.—This is a metaphorical expression, and alludes to the husbandman and tradesman laying up in store what must be used in aftertimes;† or provision laid up for the whole year by the mistress of a house. This crosses not Christ's prohibition, Matt. 6. 19. " Lay not up for yourselves treasures upon earth," for that is in opposition, this in subordination to the true treasure and divine providence, as Joseph's hoarding corn was; and it is called a *good* treasure in opposition to treasures of wickedness, Prov. x. 2.

Of the heart.—The heart in man is the first mover of the actions of man,‡ even as the first mover car-

---

* Bonus est, non qui talis videtur, sed qui intus habet cor bonum, id est, à malitiâ naturali, Spiritu Dei, repurgatum et regeneratum.—*Par. in locum.*

† Θησαύρος, παρὰ τὸ εἰς αὔριον τίθεσθαι, quod in crastinum reponitur. ‡ Weems's Portrait. page 26.

rieth all the spheres of heaven about with it; so doth this little thing in the little world of man, animate all his operations. By heart I understand the rational soul, with all its faculties of understanding, memory, will, and affections; the chief part of man. The Jews compare the heart, 1. To the Holy of holies, or oracle, whence the Lord gave his answers. 2. To Solomon's throne, as the stateliest place where the King of heaven sat, as his throne of residence. 3. To the two tables of stone in Moses's hands, in which the Lord wrote the law of wisdom; and I may add, 4. The heart of a Christian is the storehouse of the choicest treasures, and cabinet of the most precious jewels.

Bringeth forth,—emits or sends out suitable emanations, for his own soul's comfort, and the supply or profit of others. This is drawing off the fountain into several channels, an educing the habits of grace into various acts, the exercise and improvement of what has been laid up, a stirring up the gift of God, a trading with the talent, required of every soul that hopes to give a good account at the last day.

Good things.—There are some things good only materially, good civilly, but these are good things spiritually, both as to matter, manner, and end; pleasing to God, profitable to man, and comfortable to him that brings them forth; these are streams flowing from the spring of true grace in the heart, through the banks and bounds of a divine command to the infinite ocean of God's glory.

The sum of all is this: every man is, and acts as principles are found in his heart; we judge of the heart by outward acts, but God judgeth of outward acts by the inward frame of the heart; and hence that of Luther is a great truth, that good works do not make good men, but first they must be made good men, before they can do good works,* for habits must be before acts; yet good acts make good men better, as evil actions make bad men worse; for acts strengthen habits, as we see by experience.

The doctrines are these:

1. Men's layings out are according to their layings up.
2. Every sincere Christian is truly good.
3. Every gracious soul hath a good treasure.
4. True grace is a Christian's treasure.
5. A saint's treasure is in heaven, and in his heart.
6. A treasure in the heart vents itself in the life.
7. A treasure truly good, will send forth good things; the heart, so far as it is sanctified and doth act like itself, produces gracious acts and exercises.

But I shall comprise all in this one observation:

That a good treasure in the heart, is necessary to good expenses in the life. No man can do good, except he first be good; there must be first a laying in, before there can be a laying out.

The Dutch have a proverb, "That a good saver, makes a well-doer." I am sure it is so in a spiritual sense; he that lays in spiritual provision, is only fit to lay out in the exercises of religion.

I shall give but this one proof for the general doctrine, Matt. xiii. 52.—"A scribe" or minister "instructed unto the kingdom of heaven," that is, prepared to declare the mysteries of the gospel, "is like a householder" or steward, for so ministers are called, (1 Cor. iv. 1.) "which bringeth forth out of his treasure things new and old;" a plain allusion to a housekeeper's old store which makes a daily standing dish,

* Bona opera non facere bonos, sed prius oportere bonos esse, quam faciamus bona: sic propriè mala opera non facere malos, sed malos facere mala.

and a new supply from the market upon special occasions. This scripture clearly holds forth, that he had laid up what he now lays out. Joseph laid up abundance of corn in the seven years of plenty, else there could not have been a supply in time of scarcity, Gen. xli. 47—49. But this is only for a hint in general; for a more clear explanation and confirmation of this truth, I shall now endeavour to discover,

1. What laying up a treasure is.
2. What this treasure in the text is.
3. What laying out implies.
4. Why laying up is thus necessary.

CHAP. II.

ON THE NATURE OF A TREASURE.

A TREASURE imports the laying up of things for necessary use in aftertimes, and holds forth these seven particulars, all which suit with the laying up of spiritual provision in general.

First,—Laying up a treasure, implies carefulness, anxious thoughts, solicitous endeavours; it is easy to scatter, but it requires some industry to gather, yea it is easier to gather by filching and cheating than by trading or working; and things easily got by evil means, are as quickly lost by strange ways, Prov. xiii. 11. "Wealth gotten by vanity, shall be diminished," that is, an estate procured by base shifts, devices, and juggling tricks, comes to nought; "but what a man gathereth by labour shall increase," and in time become a treasure. Experience tells us, that

* Malè parta, malè dilabuntur.

they that would get a great estate, take pains in the day, and plan in the night, and desires to get and keep their abundance, will not suffer them to sleep :* it is so in spiritual things, there is hard tugging to get abiding provision ; spiritual goods are not got with a wet finger ; they drop not into the mouth of a careless loiterer; the choicer any thing is, the hardlier is it attained ;† a harvest-man's labour is hard toiling. O think not to get heaven by laziness ; the kingdom of heaven is taken by violence, Matt. xi. 12. A resolute Christian as it were storms this uphill city ; as soldiers run to get the prey, or racers to obtain the prize.

Secondly,—It imports choiceness in the things laid up. It is not all labour that obtains a treasure; "they labour in the very fire, that weary themselves for very vanity."‡ Men may lay out money and labour for that which neither doth profit nor satisfy ; ‖ there are many things better slighted, than sought and gained ; stones and straws make no good treasure; no wise man will account himself rich with toys and trifles. A Christian's treasure consists in spiritual things, which only are of worth and value; gold and silver are but yellow and white clay, called thick clay,§ because solid bodies ; but compared with divine things they are but dross. Spiritual blessings only make believers blessed ; ¶ nothing can be accounted a treasure, but what comes from, and leads to heaven: *bona throni*, the good things of the throne, are a saint's treasure ; *bona scabelli*, the good things of the footstool, are the portion of wicked men, and they may have a large measure, yea, a treasure of them ; their bellies are filled with hid treasures ;** yet these do not make them happy ; all under-moon comforts are but sorry trifles to make

---

* Eccl. v. 12.   ‡ Hab. ii. 13.   † Difficilia quæ pulchra.
‖ Isa. lv. 2.   § Hab. ii. 6.   ¶ Eph. i. 3.   ** Ps. xvii. 14.

a treasure of; the whole world cannot counterbalance a grain of grace. We account of things by their worth, not by their bulk; a little box of precious ointment is of more value and virtue, than whole tuns of ordinary liquor; only heavenly riches make up a soul's treasure.

Thirdly,—Suitableness of the things stored up. No man will lay up what he shall never need, and account it as his treasure; every tradesman lays up that which is fit for his calling; clothiers, staplers, tanners, husbandmen, have all their peculiar provisions, suited to their vocations: that may be a cumber to one, which is a treasure to another: kings have their peculiar treasure, that is, that which none but kings have;* so all God's kings have their peculiar treasure, which as it is different from all others, so in some respects different one from another. Moses had a treasure of meekness, Job of patience, Solomon of wisdom, John of love. As the child of God is to come behind in no gift, so is he to excel in that which he is more especially called to exercise.† It is a great duty and mystery in religion to be wise in observation, and prudent in provision; let Christians lay up supplies suitable to the several ages, estates, sexes, offices, burdens, duties, relations, places, trials, or temptations, through which they may have to pass, in the whole course of their lives; so shall they not be unprovided or unfurnished, but which way soever the Lord leads them in this uneven world, still their feet shall stand in an even place, and go straight to heaven.‡

Fourthly,—A treasure imports sufficiency. Store hath no lack; it is abundance that constitutes a treasure; the granary of Egypt afforded plenty of corn:

* Eccles. ii. 8. † 1 Cor. i. 7. ‡ Psa. xxvi. 12.

a scant *modicum* makes not a treasure. Spiritual goods are a Christian's riches, and he ought to be rich in these riches, rich in faith, and rich in good works.* What a full expression is that of St. Paul? (Ephes. iii. 19.) where he begs to be filled with all the fulness of God. What, Paul, can thy narrow vessel contain an infinite ocean? Though he cannot hold all, yet he would have all divine fulness; he would know the love of Christ, which passeth knowledge; that is, to furnish his intellectual faculty with a treasure of heavenly knowledge;† and he would be filled with all grace, as the richest treasure of his will and affections; yea, nothing less than fulness will suffice. Nay further, the fulness of God; yet higher, even all the fulness of God, let the vessel be filled to the brim, and let it be made more capacious to receive larger incomes; never hath the believing soul grace enough, till grace be perfected and crowned with glory. A gracious heart hath an insatiable appetite after heavenly delights and dainties; nothing so good as grace, and the more a soul hath of it, the better.

Fifthly,—It implies secresy. A treasure is not exposed to the common view of all men; it was Hezekiah's pride and weakness to lead the Babylonian messengers through his treasures. Treasures are usually hid in secret places; hence we read of treasures of darkness, and hidden riches of secret places, and a treasure hid in a field.‡ So this good man's treasure is said to be in his heart;|| which St. Peter calls the hidden man of the heart, none can see into this, but the heart searching God, he that knows all

* James ii. 5. 1 Tim. vi. 18.
† Scientia quæ Spiritus Sancti magisterio, non ingenii nostri acumine discitur.—*Marl.*
‡ Isa. xlv. 3. Matt. xiii. 44. || 1 Pet. iii. 4. Ὁ κρύπτος τῆς καρδίας, Occultus ille, id est, cordis homo.

things, only is the anatomist of this close and hidden man. Men see the face, but they see not what lies within; hence it is that the greatest and best part of a Christian's treasure, is invisible; as the roots of a tree under the earth, or the bottom of a ship under water; or rather as a merchant's goods in his warehouse. So it is with a saint's treasure; he is a Jew inwardly, his circumcision is that of the heart, in the spirit and not in the letter, whose praise is not of men, but of God. Rom. ii. 29. The regenerate soul is the King of heaven's daughter, who is all glorious within, though some sparklings of grace appear without. The best and the worst of a soul is hid from the view of men; happy were it for a Christian if he had no more corruption than appears outwardly, and wretched were he also, if he had no more grace than others can take notice of.

Sixthly,—It is a treasure for its safety. This treasure being out of men's views is therefore secured from men's reach and touch: treasures lie not loose, but are under lock and key: those at Rome are now laid up in the impregnable Castle of St. Angelo. Treasure-cities are always well fenced, guards are appointed to attend them; dragons were fancied to wait on treasures; hence come dragooners, say some. But sure I am, the treasure of a Christian is safe; grace and peace are a saint's freehold that men and devils cannot deprive him of; grace is an incorruptible seed, and God hath engaged himself to maintain it; Mary's better part cannot be taken from her; as soon, saith one, may they pluck Christ out of heaven, as grace out of my heart. Nay the treasure of joy can no man take from the believing soul,[*] for this pure stream of spiritual joy, grows stronger and sweeter, till it be

[*] John xvi. 22.

swallowed up in the vast ocean of our Master's joy in eternal bliss. A Christian's treasure is locked up in his heart, which is a cabinet that none can wrest open: Christ's heart was pierced, that a Christian's might remain untouched; hence it becomes impenetrable, and invulnerable. A lively emblem whereof was the heart of John Huss, which remained entire, even when his body was consumed in the flames. The heart may be pulled out of the bosom, but not a saint's treasure out of his heart.

Seventhly.—In a treasure there is readiness for a present supply, it is but giving a turn with the key, and taking out provision, and making use thereof, which is as soon made ready as Abraham's feast for the angels, or Jacob's venison for his father Isaac. He that hath a treasure of food, hath it not to seek when he should use it; as the man in the Parable, that ran to call up his neighbour, to borrow three loaves because he had nothing to set before his friend that came unexpectedly;* but the well-furnished Christian can make God welcome in all his visits, in mercy or displeasure, and own him as a friend, whether he come by day or by night; a well-stored soul hath something in readiness for his honourable guest. A notable resemblance hereof we have in the parable of the wise and foolish virgins;† the oil in the lamp is the treasure of grace in the heart; and though the virgin Christian may slumber as to the exercise of grace, yet he is ready upon a sudden alarm for the bridegroom's entertainment; but the foolish virgin is the treasureless soul, the graceless sinner, that hath no oil at all, but while he goes to buy, is shut out of the presence-chamber. But of this more hereafter; only observe, in general, that he

* Luke xi. 5, 6. † Matt. xxv. 1—11.

that hath a treasure will be quickly furnished with all accommodations, on all occasions.

CHAP. III.

ON THE CHRISTIAN'S TREASURE.

THE second general head is, what is the treasure that our Saviour speaks of here? I conceive it is principally intended of the thoughts of the heart, which are called the possessions of the heart,* (Job xvii. 11.) because these are the first-born of the soul, and enjoy the inheritance of it. You cannot turn off the thoughts from their freehold, you may suspend the tongue from speaking, the hand from acting, but you cannot suspend the soul from thinking, while it is a rational soul; for this is the essential property of it, while it is itself. Good or bad thoughts are every man's treasure and possession; and these centre and settle in the heart; these are the spring and source of actions and expressions. Now it is said of a godly man, "The thoughts of the righteous are right," (Prov. xii. 5.) that is, judgment, law, measure, as the word imports;† the meaning is, a gracious person thinks as he is, according to the rules of rectified, sanctified reason; his thoughts run in a right channel, to right objects, for right ends, and are therefore very precious, and may well be called a treasure; hence David's exclamation, Ps. cxxxix. 17. "How precious also are thy thoughts unto me, O God!" that is, say some, how rare and dear

* מורשי לבבי Hæreditarias possessiones cordis mei, a ירש jure hæreditario possedit.

† משפט Lex, statutum, mensura, sive enim secundum normam et rationem, vel in judicio.—*Pagnin.*

are the thoughts I have of thee to my soul! This may be probable from what follows, "When I awake, I am still with thee," in thoughts and heavenly meditations, ver. 18. Certainly a godly man's holy thoughts are a precious treasure; if his tongue be as choice silver,* what are his thoughts that furnish the tongue with profitable discourses?

Now, as the thoughts feed the tongue and hand, so there are four springs that feed and furnish the heart with holy thoughts; these are like the four streams of the river of paradise,† they water the divine garden of a Christian's soul, and being followed to the head, will certainly lead the believer to the heavenly paradise.

Those thought-nourishing streams are—Scripture truths—spiritual graces—large experiences—lively comforts.

The first of these, Scripture truths, is like the river Pison, which compasseth the whole land of Havilah, where there is gold. So this taketh in the large territories of the holy Scriptures, where there is such choice gold of divine truths, as are able to make the soul both wise and rich, unto salvation; it is a choice mercy to have the understanding furnished with a treasure of saving knowledge of gospel mysteries. Hence the command is to buy the truth,‡ to search the Scriptures, to seek for wisdom as for silver;|| to search for knowledge as for hid treasures. That is a notable passage, "Let the word of God dwell richly in you." Cor. iii. 16. [πλουσίως] copiously, abundantly, the word notes two things,§ 1. The measure, and so it is rendered plenteously. 2. The worth of the knowledge of the word, and so it is otherwise ren-

* Prov. x. 20. † Gen. ii. 10. ‡ Prov. xxiii. 23.
|| John v. 39. Prov. ii. 4. § Leigh Crit. Sac.

dered richly. And surely a great stock of Scripture-knowledge is a precious treasure. O what a blessed thing it is to have a man's breast the library of Jesus Christ! The sacred Scriptures are the treasures and pleasures of a gracious soul:* to David they were better than thousands of gold and silver. A mountain of transparent pearls heaped as high as heaven, is not so rich a treasure as these; hence that good man chose these as his heritage for ever, and rejoiced in them as in all riches. A covetous miser could not take such delight in his bags, nor a young heir in a large inheritance, as holy David did in God's word. † All the saints are priests unto God; now of Levi it is said, Mal. ii. 6. "That the law of truth was in his mouth, and his lips kept knowledge as a storehouse. So it is or ought to be with God's spiritual priests; they have the law of God graven on their hearts, and in their tongues is the law of kindness and holiness. The word law, comes from a root that signifies to try as merchants that search and prove the wares that they buy and lay up; hence also comes the word for gems and jewels that are tried, and found right. ‡ The sound Christian is the wise merchant, seeking goodly pearls, he tries what he reads, or hears, by the standard and touchstone of Scripture, and having found genuine truths, he lays them up to the great enriching of this supreme, and sovereign faculty of the understanding.

2. Another spring that feeds holy thoughts is spiritual graces, the fruits of the Spirit, which exceedingly help the fruit of the lips; if the will and affections be

* Sacræ Scripturæ sunt sanctæ deliciæ et divitiæ animæ.
† Psal. cxix. 72. also 14. and 111.
‡ Rad. תור Explorare, scrutari: hinc תורה Lex, Statutum, et תורם Gemmæ, margaritæ.

sanctified with a principle of true holiness, the lips and the life will bring forth heavenly expressions and actions in the conversation: hence "The fear of the Lord is a fountain of life," Prov. xiv. 27. A gracious habit streams freely and fully into all acts of spiritual life, and at last is swallowed up in the ocean of eternal life. It is said of Jesus Christ, the origin of all grace, that the fear of the Lord is his treasure; and we may say also, it is a Christian's treasure: a head full of notions will not make the soul rich, without a heart full of grace; it is grace that ennobles the soul with heavenly excellencies, and enables the soul to bear burdens, and do duties. Without a principle in the heart, there can be no holiness in the life; all works of piety, charity, and sobriety, must flow from a pure heart, a good conscience, and faith unfeigned;† all which do contribute their influence to every good work. Obedience (saith one) respects the command of a superior; love, the kindness of the lawgiver; faith, his bounty and reward: ‡ the first swayeth the conscience, the second inclineth the heart, the third giveth encouragement; sure I am, without these there can be no spiritual actings in an evangelical manner. He only hath a gospel frame of spirit, that hath the law written in his heart, and the works thereof in his hand; whose life is a continual transcript of this blessed copy; for he that doth righteousness, is righteous; yea, it is he that moveth heaven-wards, from a living treasure of gracious principles, and not from external compulsion, as clocks and such dead, artificial, yet self-moving engines do: hence the church and a believing soul saith, "My soul made me like the chariots of Amminadib," ‖ or of a willing people. Song vi. 12. Though some say

* Isa. xxxiii. 6.   † 1 Tim. i. 5.   ‡ Manton on Jude, v. 1.
‖ עם Populus et נדב Sponte moveri.

they are the words of Christ, yet they are applicable to every gracious soul, that is acted by a new and living principle towards God, and goodness. Christ's people are volunteers in the day of his power, in the way of duty, being acted by a free and princely spirit, the renewed will being the great engine that moves the soul in a Christian course; their own spirits make them willing for God.*

3. Another spring that feeds holy thoughts is well gathered experience: the Christian's breast is to be a treasury of experimental observations, which may be improved as good props to uphold a tottering faith. It is said of those mentioned in Luke i. 66. that they laid up all the strange passages concerning John, in their hearts. And thus we find several saints carefully gathering, and seasonably recollecting their former experiences, as Jacob, David, Paul, Samuel, Manoah and his wife. Time would fail me to recount all the instances of this nature; recording the time, place, and manner of divine discoveries, hath been of singular advantage to believers. Experience begets hope;† we lose much through neglect thereof: signal memorials of received mercies help to present duties, and quicken faith in the greatest future difficulties. All artists gather knowledge, by recording experiments; and he is the wisest Christian, that in this respect with Solomon, hath his heart filled with experience of wisdom and knowledge;‡ experience is the best instructor, and helps a man best in instructing others; an experienced physician or lawyer, is seldom *non-plust;* an expeperienced soldier comes off with honour. O Christians! lay up in your hearts, what you have seen with your eyes, and felt in your souls, of the vanity of

---

* Exod. xxv. 2, and xxxv. 21 and 29.
† Rom. v. 4.   ‡ Eccles. i. 16.

wordly, and the excellency of heavenly attainments, and enjoyments. You cannot be too young to collect experiences; you cannot be too old to recollect and improve them; if your green heads would use diligence, your grey hairs would arrive at large experiences; by which means, the works and loads of old age would be easy, which were almost intolerable in your younger years.* A young carpenter is long with a little, and makes many chips, that an experienced workman dispatcheth, both more quickly, and more neatly: it is so in religion, experience facilitates every work of it. And how doth experience feed thoughts? Thus; when a soul is at a pinch, and the heart struck dead with a sudden surprisal, so that the thoughts are puzzled, experience comes in to bring relief, and represents the matter as feasible, since it calls to mind as arduous a case, which yet was not insuperable; and why mayest thou not get through as well as formerly, saith experience? And thus it marshals the soul's faculties in their proper ranks, and brings it through the present attempt with order and victory, whether the undertaking be of doing duty, or enduring trial.

4. The last refreshing stream that supplies the heart with heavenly thoughts, is from the wells of consolation; this like the last, yet not the least river of Paradise (Euphrates) doth as the name has been thought to import, refresh the heart with cheering incomes and influences. This makes the soul both cheerful and fruitful; in the midst of terrifying thoughts, these comforts delight the soul, Psal. xciv. 19. O the joy that these beget in the midst of sorrow! Nothing can make sad, if divine comforts make glad. These

* Seniores sunt saniores, incipientes insipientes; quæ laboriosa fuere juventuti studia, ea sunt jucunda senectuti otia.

bright beams of light chase away the dismal mists of darkness, and disconsolate horror; these pure streams of comfort wash away the bitter effects of despairing thoughts. These comforts infinitely exceed wine, which philosophers have called the chief allayment of men's miseries,* but the sense of this love is better than wine; one drop of these divine joys would even mitigate hell torments. This is a treasure indeed, which, as it is of great efficacy, so it is the satisfying result of the forementioned provision; saving truths, savoury graces, and sensible experiences, beget solid peace. But besides those, there are two clear streams that much promote the soul's comfortable thoughts; which are,

Precious promises,—and a clear conscience.

(1.) Promises are the storehouse of comfort, the charter of our privileges, the conveyances of our heavenly inheritance. Promises are the breasts of consolation, the *evangelica mulctralia*, the milk-pails of the gospel; the great receptacles of that ἄδολον γάλα sincere milk of the word, stored up for babes in Christ. The promises, saith a good divine, are bills of exchange given you, that you may draw your estate into another country.† Nothing can cheer up the heart so much as a word of promise. Hence David desires to "hear the voice of joy and gladness,"‡ that is, in a promise. There is a *probatum est*∥ upon this means of spiritual comfort, whether it concern life or godliness, present or future enjoyments.§ It is said of the Duke of Guise, that he was the richest man in France, though not in lands, yet in bills and bonds, and great friends: so is a right Christian, he is the richest man in the world, in possession and reversion, for he inherits all

---

* Miseriarum humanarum μαλάκτικα.
† Manton on Jude, page 152.   ‡ Ps. li. 8.
∥ It has been tried and approved.   § 1 Tim. iv. 8.

things, and he is heir to a glorious crown at death.* The exceeding great and precious promises may cheer up the heart of a drooping saint, if it were as low as hell; for they were made and confirmed with an oath, that the heirs of promise might have strong consolation. † It is strange if the bucket of faith do not always draw up the water of consolation out of the wells of salvation. God hath ordered in nature our feeding to be with pleasure; so in spiritual things, our application and improvement of promises is with sweetness and delight. This is the first means to beget a treasure of comfortable thoughts on the believing of soul-enriching promises.

(2.) Clearness of conscience, also is a help to comfortable thoughts. Yet observe, that peace is not so much effected as preserved by a good conscience, and conversation, for though joy in the Holy Ghost, will make its nest no where but in a holy soul, yet the blood of Christ only can speak peace, "being justified by faith, we have peace," Rom. v. 1. An exact life will not make, but keep conscience quiet; an easy shoe, heals not a sore foot, but keeps a sound one from crushing. Walking with God according to gospel rules, hath peace entailed upon it, and that peace is such a treasure, as thereby a Christian may have his rejoicing from himself, Galatians vi. 4, 16. His own heart sings him a merry tune, which the threats and reproaches of the world cannot silence. The treasure of comfort is not expended in affliction; death itself doth not exhaust, but increase and advance it to an eternal triumph. O the excellency and necessity of it! Paul laid it up for a death-bed cordial: " Our rejoicing is this, the testimony of our conscience," 2 Cor. i. 12. And Hezekiah dares hold it up to God, as well as cheer

* 1 Pet. v. 4.   † Heb. vi. 17, 18.

up himself with it on approaching death.* A conscience good in point of integrity, will be good also in point of tranquillity: "The righteous are bold as a lion; they have great peace that love and keep God's commandments."† And saith the apostle, "If our heart condemn us not, then have we confidence towards God,"‡ and I may add also, towards men. O! what comfort and solace hath a clear conscience! A conscientious man hath something within, to answer accusations without; he hath such a rich treasure as will not fail in greatest straits and hazards. I shall conclude this with a notable saying of an ancient. "The pleasures of a good conscience are the Paradise of souls, the joy of angels, a garden of delights, a field of blessing, the temple of Solomon, the court of God, the habitation of the Holy Spirit."||

CHAP. IV.

ON THE LAYING OUT OF HEART TREASURE.

HITHERTO the laying up of a treasure of good thoughts by the accession of truths, graces, experiences, and comforts, has been considered. The third head propounded, is how this treasure is expended, brought forth, and improved, for that treasure is in a sort useless, that is not made use of. Now this treasure is employed four ways, that is,

By the heart *in meditating*, the lips *in speaking*, the hands *in doing*, and the back *in enduring*.

I. By the heart in divine soliloquies, and heavenly

---

* Isa. xxxviii. 3.   † Prov. xxviii. 1. Ps. cxix. 165.   ‡ 1 John iii. 2.
|| Lætitiæ bonæ conscientiæ Paradisus animarum, gaudium angelorum, hortus deliciarum, ager benedictionis, templum Solomonis, aula Dei, habitaculum Spiritus Sancti.—*Bern.*

meditations, in cheering sentiments, and elevating emotions; these keep the Christian good company, so that he is never less alone than when alone,* as a very heathen could say. Scripture truths are sweet and satisfying companions in all conditions, places, and stations: " When thou goest, it shall lead thee; when thou sleepest, it shall keep thee; and when thou awakest, it shall talk with thee," Prov. vi. 22. And what can we desire more than a guide in our way, a guard around our beds, and a sweet companion in our solitudes, and serious retirements? Such are divine truths. A Christian may live upon this treasure in a wilderness, in prison, *(etiam in inferno)* even in hell itself, saith Luther. God's statutes were David's songs in the house of his pilgrimage:† Isaac went out into the fields for recreation, and took his treasure along with him, getting a solitary and savoury repast, of meditation. Gen. xxiv. 63. When a man is shut out from ordinances, " his soul may be satisfied with marrow and fatness, when it meditates on God in the night watches;" ‡ yea, when dull and discouraging thoughts discompose the spirit, this treasure helps as a holy spell to raise the spirit of the believer, and drive away the evil spirit of deadness and distraction.|| Meditation is a kind of deliberate extacy; the harmonious melody of the soul's faculties within itself by a mutual and musical concert; it is the soul's self-conference heard only by itself: it is a restoring of meat formerly taken down, and diffusing it into the several veins and arteries of the soul; meditation, in a word, is a holy concoction and digestion of divine truths, which meetens and ripens the soul for heaven. O the ravishing nature of a close and fixed meditation! It is

* Nunquam minus solus, quam cum solus. † Ps. cxix. 54.
‡ Ibid. lxiii. 5, 6. || Ibid. xxxix. 3. Ibid. xlii. 5.

a God-enjoying, and self-profiting exercise; the devout soul, that is thus furnished with a treasure, can expatiate upon all things, and like the laborious bee, fetch the honey of some comfort out of every object and subject. When grace is in the heart, knowledge in the head, and truth in the memory, the Christian through divine assistance will make good work of every condition and dispensation. It is both the character and the honour of a Christian to meditate on God's law day and night;* he that talks much with his own heart by meditation, and takes frequent turns in Paradise by contemplation, doth far transcend the rate and pace of ordinary Christians: "for," saith a great divine,† "commonly we are transformed into the dispositions and manners of those whose company we frequent." And if we keep company with a holy God, by meditation, we shall be more exactly holy in all manner of conversation.

II. This treasure of the heart vents itself by the lips in heavenly communications, and that two ways.

1. A treasured soul doth discourse profitably with men. This, I think, is the chief design of the text; a bringing forth good things in talking to men's edification. A gracious heart freely pours out holy expressions; Solomon saith, "the heart of the wise teacheth his mouth."‡ That inward spring feeds these sweet streams, and tips the tongue with divine rhetoric; so Cant. iv. 11. "Thy lips, O my spouse, drop as the honey-comb, honey and milk are under thy tongue." Not like vain-glorious, empty scholars, or conceited, formal professors, that have got some scraps of confused notions, then set open the pack, and expose all to open view, but are quickly exhausted; no, no, these well-furnished souls have an overflowing

* Ps. i. 2.   † Dr. Hall's Solil. iii. p. 8, 9.   ‡ Prov. xvi. 23

treasure of holy matter, to produce upon occasion, and can speak a word in season upon any subject, to any soul. It is said of Plato and Ambrose, that bees swarmed in their cradles, as presages of their future eloquence : so the honey-comb of Scripture truths distinguishes the Christian; his speech is seasoned with salt, because his heart is seasoned with grace;* his discourses, like honey at once become salutary, and please the sanctified auditor.† When the well-guided tongue is an interpreter of a cleansed heart, it is food and physic to him that improves it; " for the tongue of the wise is health," Prov. xii. 18. The same word in the Hebrew that signifies tongue, is also used, joined with another word, for a wedge of gold : ‡ the truth is, a treasured heart finds a precious golden tongue; and nothing more cordial to the fainting heart, than the fruit of such choice lips.

2. This treasure is exercised in religious duties and holy performances. The root of grace in the heart, brings forth these fruits of the lips in prayer and praise.‖ The spirit of prayer sends up to heaven this divine incense : such a soul that hath this lively liturgy in his heart, needs not to be prompted by men; the Spirit can help both to affections and expressions.§ A treasured soul hath a stock of prayers, as an able minister hath a stock of sermons, though he may be without a stock of written notes; I mean the body of divinity in his head, which makes a ready scribe. The more treasure a soul hath within, the more ready will it be to every good work; yea, and the more raised to God in the work: such a one is helped very much against distractions, the great complaint of pious souls.

---

* Colos. iv. 6.   Ephes. iv. 29.   † Prov. xvi. 24.
‡ ולשן זהב lingua auri, Joshua vii. 21.   ‖ Heb. xiii. 15.
Zech. xii. 10.   § Rom. viii. 26.

It is a notable expression of a good author, "He that hath store of gold and silver in his pocket, and but a few brass farthings, will more readily, upon every draught, come out with gold and silver, than with brass farthings."* So he whose heart is stocked with holy thoughts, will not find carnal cogitations so rife and frequent. If the heart have indited a good matter, the tongue will be as the pen of a ready writer;† if the heart be filled with grace, it will make melody to the Lord, and music to good men.‡ A treasured soul is ready to trade with God in duty. Yet take this caution: a true Christian having a large measure of habitual grace, is not always in an equal actual capacity for duty; David's heart may need tuning as well as his harp; the key of this treasure may be lost or rusted; hence the treasure of that man after God's own heart, was locked up in a great measure, for the space of nine months, till God sent the key by Nathan to open the sluice of repentance, and draw out the seeds of grace.

III. The treasure in the heart is also drawn out with the hands, in the works of piety towards God, charity to men, and sobriety with respect to ourselves; so the apostle distributeth good works, Tit. ii. 12. It is not enough for the believer to have the axe laid to the root of the tree, in sound conviction and gospel-humiliation but he is to bring forth fruits meet for such repentance,‖ in a gospel-conversation. We must not only believe with the heart, and confess with the mouth,§ but faith must work by love;¶ upwards to God, by the obedience of faith; inwards in the heart, by purifying it; and downwards to men, by doing good unto all, but especially to the houshold of faith. Here is a large field of matter for my pen, and the Christian's hand; but the

---

* Cobbet on Prayer.   † Ps. xlv. 1.   ‡ Col. iii. 16. Eph. v. 19.
‖ Matt. iii. 8.   § Rom. x. 10.   ¶ Gal. v. 6.

furnished Christian is unreserved in obedience, shuns not the hardest and most hazardous duties, will not serve God with that which costs him nothing: and this is a grand discriminating characteristic betwixt a treasured saint, and a treasureless hypocrite. The carnal person loves a cheap religion, and is loath to be at any cost or pains for God, in a way of commanded duty. But to a child of God, the more spiritual a duty is, and the more opposite it is to carnal ease and profit, the more freely doth he close with it; he is willing to cut off a right hand of a beloved lust, pray for enemies, forgive wrongs, give to the poor,* as knowing that all these are essential parts of our religion; therefore, when the heart is full of grace, the hands, Dorcas-like, will be full of good works, which are called fruits of righteousness.† It is the Christian's duty and dignity to be fruitful in every good work,‡ which cannot proceed from any other root than this heart treasure. A willing heart will find a liberal hand to relieve the poor; the merchandise of penitent Tyre is treasured up for the supply of God's holy ones.‖ This liberal soul deviseth liberal things, and will not make use of carnal reasonings, as danger of poverty, unworthiness of the poor, hardness of the times, and the like, which the prophet calls the instruments of the churl;§ but the largeness of a saint's inward treasure will make him carefully to seek, and thankfully to embrace objects and occasions of charity; yea, in some cases, he stretcheth beyond his power, whereby the freeness of his heart enhanceth the mite into a pound, in true worth and God's account. Thus the readiness of the heart compensates the weakness of the hand.¶

* James i. 27.   † Phil. i. 11.   ‡ Col. i. 10.   ‖ Isa. xxiii. 18.   § Isa. xxxii. 7, 8.   ¶ On this subject of Alms-giving, see Morning Exercises at Cripplegate, Serm. xi. p. 240—278.

But I must fix bounds to this discourse. Yet a treasured saint hath no stint of desires and endeavours to be acting for God, and the good-will of his heart adds new vigour to his fainting hand. Naturalists observe, that when the heart more inclineth to the right side, the spirits are more lively and apt for contemplation and action; hence that of Solomon's, " A wise man's heart is at his right hand."* I am sure when a Christian's heart boweth God-wards, his hand is full of activity in the ways of God, and works of godliness; when the soul is filled with grace, the hand is fitted for acts of religion.

IV. This inward heart-treasure helps the back and shoulders to bear the Christian's burdens. The time of affliction is a spending time; if there be any grace within, tribulation will draw it out. Hence it is said to work patience;† not that it creates what was not in the soul before, but educeth and evidenceth that which before lay hid in the heart. The fiery furnace will prove and improve the soul's spiritual strength; for if it faint in the day of adversity, its strength is small, and treasure poor. Now, shall it be clearly known, whether the conscience be sound or will founder, whether it will pace well or not, in rough ways. Twice is it repeated in the Revelation, when mention is made of Antichrist's tyranny and ruin, " Here is the patience, here is the patience and faith of saints;‡ that is, here is the trial of it, here is room for it, here is the root and fruit of it, even Antichrist's desolation, which they have been so long waiting and praying for: surely a glorious sight worth beholding,—Rome flaming, saints triumphing,—yet, in the mean time, they have need of faith and patience. For immediately before both these passages, we have a description of

---

* Eccles. x. 2.   † Rom. v. 3.   ‡ Rev. xiii. 10. & xiv. 12.

Rome's rage; the devil will come down with the greater wrath when he hath a shorter time;* and the last bitings of this dying Beast will be the fiercest, which may bring forth all the saint's graces, and all little enough in times of trial.† We have great need of patience after we have done God's will, that we may also endure his will, till promises be performed.‡ We must buckle on the armour of God, that we may be able to withstand in an evil day; and having done and endured all, to stand on the field as conquerors.|| In personal conflicts, all our stock of suffering graces may be put to it; poverty will try our faith, disgrace our self-denial, sickness our patience, delay of return of prayers for a long expected mercy will try our hope,—and all these graces must have their perfect work, that the Christian also may be perfect and entire, wanting nothing, James i. 4. He should have the whole heritage § of a Christian, the complete accomplishments of a saint, every grace in its height and due proportion. Job, David, Eli, and Hezekiah had laid in a large stock of bearing graces, and they found enough to do with them in affliction; they had no more than they needed. Love bears and breaks through all things; faith holds up the head and heart above discouragements. Nature hath furnished the camel with a bunched back, to bear huge burdens, and a tractable bowing of his knees to the ground, that he may be the better loaded: so will the well-taught and accomplished saint meekly stoop to take up, and cheerfully carry Christ's cross, during his pleasure. That is a sound-hearted Christian indeed, that like the

* Rev. xii. 12.
† Morientium ferarum, violentiores sunt morsus.
‡ Hebrews x. 36. || Ephesians vi. 13.
§ Ὁλόκληροι ex ὅλος totus, et κλῆρος sors, hereditas tota sorte constans.

nightingale can sing most sweetly when the thorn is at his breast; that like spices, the more they are bruised, the better is the savour of their graces. But a carnal man wanting this treasure of grace, kicks at, yea, kicks off his burden; yet though it be possible that the spirit of a man (as of a man of a masculine temper naturally, or from acquired magnanimity) may possibly sustain his infirmity, and not succumb under outward burdens of sorrow, yet there is a vast difference betwixt a gracious and graceless heart in enduring afflictions, both as to their carriage thereunder, and advantage thereby: hear Austin elegantly discovering the difference: "There is, saith he, a dissimilitude of sufferers in a similitude of sufferings, and though they be under the same torment, yet is there not the same virtue and vice; as under one fire gold brighteneth, chaff smoketh, and under the same flail stubble is crushed, corn is purged. Hence also the lees mingle not with the oil, though pressed together; so one and the same onset proves, purifieth, and sweetly melteth the good—condemneth, wasteth, rooteth out the bad. Hence in the same affliction the wicked hate and blaspheme God, the godly pray and praise. So much is it of importance not what things a man suffereth, but of what a spirit is the sufferer: for with the same motion may the channel smell abominably, and the ointment most sweetly."* Such

* Manet enim dissimilitudo passorum in similitudine passionum, et licet sub eodem tormento, non est idem virtus et vitium. Nam sicut sub uno igne, aurum rutilat, palea fumat, et sub eadem tribula stipulæ comminuuntur, frumenta purgantur, nec ideo cum oleo, amurca confunditur, quia eodem præli pondere exprimitur; ita una eademque vis irruens bonos probat, purificat, eliquat; malos damnat, vastat, exterminat. Unde in eadem afflictione mali Deum detestantur, atque blasphemant; boni autem precantur, et laudant. Tantum interest, non qualia sed qualis quisque, patiatur: nam pari motu exagitatum et exhalat horribiliter cœnum, et suaviter fragrat unguentum.—*August. De Civit. Dei. lib.* i. *cap.* 8. *p.* 16.

is the language of Austin, with which I shall conclude this head.

CHAP. V.

ON THE GREAT NECESSITY OF LAYING UP THIS TREASURE.

At last we come to the confirmation of this doctrine, *That a good treasure in the heart is necessary to good expences in the life;* and the

First ground is taken from nature and reason, which furnish us with those undoubted maxims, That a thing must first be, before it can act—Nothing can give what it hath not—Such as the cause is, such are the effects—Of nothing, nothing can be made,† without a miracle of creation; and we cannot expect to be fed by miracles where ordinary means are proposed, and supposed to be used. If we wilfully neglect to lay in provision while we have a season for it, we are guilty of groundless presumption if we conceit we can lay out in a necessitous condition. How can any expect liquor from the still, meat from the cupboard, garments from the wardrobe, where none of these were laid in? What madman would think to reap without sowing, or to teach others when he hath no learning himself? Was there ever a bringing forth without a conception? Is it not fond dotage in a shop-keeper to think to sell wares that hath none? And is this preposterous in natural things, and can it hold in spiritual? Joseph could not supply the country with corn without a store. A tree cannot bring forth good fruit, except it be good. The Scripture saith, "Can a fig-

† Operari sequitur esse. Nihil dat quod non habet. Qualis causa talis effectus. Ex nihilo nihil fit.

tree bear olive-berries, or a vine figs?" James iii. 12. And can we think men can act graciously without a principle of grace?

A *Second* reason is drawn from the offices of Christ. The second person in the sacred Trinity was filled with treasure, that he might fill the saints with a treasure of grace. " In him are hid all the treasures of wisdom and knowledge. The fulness of the Godhead dwelleth bodily in Christ." * And for this very end hath God stored Christ, that he might supply his members, " that of his fulness, we may receive, and grace for grace," John i. 16. " The plain, simple sense of which text," saith Calvin, " is that, what graces God heaps upon us, they all flow from this fountain; therefore are we watered with the graces that are poured upon Christ.† For observe it, this is the nature of the gospel dispensation; what spiritual good things the saints receive, they have them not now from God as Creator, so much as through the hands of Jesus Christ as the great Mediator of the new covenant; he is the channel or cistern, or rather fountain of all grace, that our souls expect or receive; he is our Aaron anointed above his fellows, that the oil of grace might in its proportion fall from the head to the members. Hence it is that he is called Christ, and we Christians, from this holy unction. For this end was the Lord Jesus advanced to be the head of the church, that he might fill it with all gracious supplies; and hence it is that the church is called "his body, the fulness of him that filleth all in all," Eph. i. 23; that is, the effect of Christ's fulness, who filleth all the saints, in all ordinances and means of

* Col. ii. 3, 9.
† Simplex sensus esse videtur, quascunque in nos gratias cumulat Deus, peræque ex hoc fonte manare: rectè ergo sentiunt qui nos irrigari dicunt effusis in Christum gratiis.—*Calv. in loc.*

conveyance of gracious influences. Truth of grace is from him, growth and strength of grace are from him; both the least measure and a large treasure are to be had in him: "I came that they might have life, and that they might have it more abundantly," John x. 10; that is, the essence and abundance are both from him. So then we see Christ is designed to be our Joseph, to furnish our souls with a treasure; and therefore he that neglects to stock his heart from this storehouse doth undervalue the great office of Christ, and doeth what he can to frustrate the object of God, in soul's supply.—This is horrible ingratitude.

A *Third* reason is drawn from the end and design of all providences and ordinances. They are given to be helps to promote this heart treasure. God puts a price into our hands, that we may have grace in our hearts: he gives us a summer season to lay up for this pinching winter. Naturalists say, that while the bird called halcyon sitteth on her nest there is calmness and serenity upon the sea: such halcyon days of tranquillity and gospel opportunities have we enjoyed in this tempestuous sea of the world, not to feather our nests below, much less to hatch the cockatrice eggs of sin; but to warm and ripen the brood of grace in our souls, and to lay up a precious treasure for the evil days of old age, sickness, or persecution, and for the long day of eternity. When God affords a season, he expects things should be done in that season; and if man neglect it, his misery will be great upon him. The very ant lays up for winter, and reads a lecture to man of good husbandry. Gathering in summer is a token of wisdom, but sleeping in harvest is a sinful, shameful, beggaring practice.* God expects that we should work

* Eccles. viii. 6, 8; Prov. vi. 6. Prov. x. 5. Formica, apis, et ciconia, sunt verè laicorum libri.

in the light, and walk in the day, while this day of grace lasts, John xii. 35. It is a sad astonishing thing, that God should hold men a candle for them to play by; especially when time is short and uncertain—death and eternity are so near, and of such vast consequence. O what a confounding question will that be one day— "Wherefore is there a price in the hand of a fool to get wisdom, seeing he hath no heart to it?" Prov. xvii. 16. Observe it, God takes a strict account of our helps and of our hoard, and expects a due proportion. O what a sad reckoning will many make, whose negligence will be condemned by the diligence of brute creatures, and heathen philosophers in moral studies;* yea, by the light of their own consciences!

Fourthly, Another reason is taken from our heart's natural emptiness of a treasure of good. "In me, (saith Paul) that is, in my flesh, dwells no good thing," Rom. vii. 18. This barren soil hath the more need to be manured, this empty house to be well furnished; lest the heart continue still destitute of all saving good, and the soul depart out of this world as naked of saving grace as it entered. 'Tis a pity so brave a house should stand empty of inhabitant and furniture. The souls of God's people are vessels that are to be well fraught with all saving graces, that they may be fitted for, and filled with, eternal glory, Rom. ix. 23. The Christian is to be holily covetous of those riches of glory, that amends may be made for his natural vacuity. Oh, the vast chaos of an unregenerate heart! A long time and great pains must go, to the replenishing of it. There are many waste corners to be filled, even after the truth of grace is planted, before the soul be enlarged to a due capacity of service here, and for heaven

---

* Nullus mihi per otium exit dies, partem etiam noctium studiis vendico.—*Senec.*

hereafter. "The soul of a believer," saith one,* "is a house well built, where faith lays the foundation, hope helps up the walls, knowledge sets open the windows, and love covers the roof; and this makes a room fit for Christ." And I add, there must be every day a sweeping, and watching, and decking of this house, with further degrees of grace; embellishing it with divine ornaments, and furnishing every room, I mean every faculty, with a rich treasure of heavenly blessings. It will be some cost and toil to hang every room of the heart with lively pictures of the Divine image; for it is altogether empty of that which is truly and spiritually good, or may be called a treasure. But that is not all, for

Fifthly, The soul is by nature filled with an evil treasure. "The heart is desperately wicked," Jer. xvii. 9. "Every imagination of the thoughts of man's heart is only and continually evil," Gen. vi. 5. The mind, will, and affections, are stuffed with a world of blindness, hardness, and wildness. The soul is naturally propense to evil, averse to good; and therefore a treasure of good is necessary, to preponderate and exclude this treasure of wickedness—to season and seize upon the soul for God, as sin did for Satan. The love of God is to be shed abroad into those veins and channels of the heart where sin did run with a violent current†—the Christian is to be sanctified in the most polluted part. And certainly it is not a little grace that will obstruct the active movements of sin; for though grace be of greater worth, yet it is disputable whether it attain to greater strength than corruption, even in the hearts of the sanctified, in this life. But certainly, the greater measure of grace and treasure of sanctifying truths, the more power against corruption: the whole

* Mr. Goodwin. † Rom. v. 5. Rom. ii. 29.

armour of God (which is also the saint's treasure) resists inward lusts and Satan's assaults, Eph. vi. 12—14. The Spirit is compared to wind;* now some have called the winds, "the besoms of the world."† But I am sure, the spirit of grace with the fruits thereof, are choice besoms to sweep the filth of sin out of the soul, and also to adorn it with divine jewels, and assist it with notable antidotes against corruption. These are as water to wash the heart from filthiness: the smallest measure helps against sin; but the more grace, the less sin in the heart. Grace is a principle of life, and opposeth dead works, which otherwise would lead the soul to the chambers of death; therefore this treasure is of absolute necessity; and the same might we say of the word, which being hid in the heart,‡ helps against sin in the life.

Sixthly, Another reason is taken from the inbred motions of human nature. All men on earth seek after a treasure; it is the harmonious inquest of all rational creatures, Who will show us any good, any thing to make a treasure of? Man hath a capacious soul, an active and laborious spirit;∥ the whole world is not a morsel big enough for his rapacious swallow. "Our covetous desires," saith one, "are a long sentence without a period." Finite things are dry meat to a hungry soul; they sooner glut than fill: nay, they put on this busy bee to buzz about one flower after another, till it hath wearied itself in vain, and sit down in utter despair of comfort and satisfaction. Only interest in the God of heaven, and the image of the God of heaven, make up all defects: See Psalm lxxiii. 25, 26. A Christ alone to justify, and a Christ within to sanctify,

---

* John iii. 8.   † Scopas mundi; because they serve to sweep the air and the world clean from infectious vapours.

‡ Psalm cxix. 11.   ∥ Homo est ζωόν ἐπίπονον.

make the soul completely happy; for Christ within is "the hope of glory."* A glorified and a gracious Redeemer is the Christian's only treasure—his all in all.† God hath furnished man with an immortal soul; learning may expand it, but grace fills it: nothing else will reach its large dimensions. Man is a little world himself, nay, bigger and better than this greater, by Christ's own verdict,‡ who is truth itself. The soul itself is better than the world, and it must have something better than itself to be a treasure for it. Philosophy seeks, Christianity shews, the sound believer only finds true happiness, which the wise merchant has fetched out of the field of the gospel into the cabinet of his own heart. ||

Seventhly, Whatsoever men have or love, they desire a treasure thereof. No man but would have a large treasure of a precious commodity—he that hath gold and silver would heap it up to a treasure—he that hath wisdom and learning would still have more. Men join house to house, and field to field, to procure for themselves and heirs a fair domain—a large estate. How many rich men are still as eager for more as if they had not enough to purchase a meal's meat! Yet these seek for earth, as if abundance thereof would purchase heaven: like the partridge, they sit close on these eggs, though they hatch them not,§ nor are ever likely to bring them to their desired maturity. O the unhallowed thirst after filthy lucre!¶ Many think to fill their souls with wealth, whereas they cannot fill one of the least members of their body, the eye,†† which yet a nut shell will cover. The world at the best is like

* Col. i. 27. Phil. iii. 8, 9. † Col. iii. 11.
‡ Homo est universi orbis epitome, et abbreviata mundi tabella, Matt. xvi. 26. || Matt. xiii. 44—46. § Jer. xvii. 11.
¶ Auri sacra fames! †† Eccles. i. 8.

Pasotes' banquet, which when the guests began to eat vanished into nothing. And shall so many men set their eyes, and hearts too, on that which is not;* and shall not God's children make a treasure of that which is enduring substance? Shall men think to make a treasure of coals, and chaff, and empty shadows? and shall not the Christian gather store of pearls and jewels for his treasure? Shall the children of the world be more wise and wary for earth, than the children of light for heaven? God forbid. Surely the Christian hath as great reason to heap up as any; these commodities are more rare, rich, and necessary than any other; and why then should he not get a heart treasure? For with these reasons I would both convince the judgment and sway the affections; these are the chief motives I have: for I would spend most time in direction.

Eightly, This and only this doth discriminate betwixt persons and persons: my meaning is, this heart treasure puts a difference betwixt saints and sinners, betwixt weak and strong Christians. As the treasure in the heart is, so is the professor's state; as Solomon saith in another case, Prov. xxiii. 7. "As he thinketh in his heart, so is he:" not as he speaks with his lips. Formalists will speak God as fair as any; they honour him with their lips, and flatter him with false and fawning attentions,† as though he were an idol. But the heart-searching God is not pleased, except the heart be upright with him. It is the upright in whom he delights; not in a person merely, as he acts with his hands, or walks with his feet, in many passages of his life. A man may, with Ahab, walk softly—with Herod do many things—with Simon Magus make large professions of faith; yea, it is possible a man may suf-

* Prov. xxiii. 5. † Isa. xxix. 13. Psalm lxxviii. 36, 37.

fer many troubles, and even death itself, in a good cause; yet except he have a heart treasured with grace, he is rejected, and may go to hell at last. God judgeth of the fruits by the root; though men judge of the root by the fruits; a heart after his own heart is better than the tongue of men and angels. The distinction of persons is in respect of inside principles and workings. A good man may sometimes do an evil work, and a bad man may do a good work; but how are their hearts? The best conferences or performances are not current coin with the God of heaven, except they issue out of the mint of a heart where God's image is stamped.* A little good is accounted much when there is a treasure within—much seeming good is looked on as nothing when there is no treasure. This also makes the difference betwixt a strong and weak Christian; let their gifts and outward seemings be what they will, yet the greater or lesser degree of real grace distinguisheth their attainments; and accordingly these measures have different influences upon their lives, duties, comforts, or preparedness for death.

Ninthly, This treasure doth assimilate the soul to God. The great Jehovah is the only self-existent and self-sufficient good; he is an absolute, complete, and independent Being, and needs no accession of creatures or created powers to make him happy. Nothing can add to, or detract from, his infinite and incomprehensible blessedness—he is a treasure of all good,† in and to himself, and needs neither gold nor silver to make him rich. Parallel to this, in some proportion, is the saint's sweet and secret heart treasure, and solitary re-

* Pius homo numisma est a Deo cusum, impius adulterinum, non a Deo sed a Diabolo effectum.—*Ignat. Epist. ad Magnes.*

† Et Deum ipsum verum recte dicimus divitem, non tamen pecuniâ, sed omnipotentiâ: dicuntur pauperes pecuniâ carentes, sed interius divites si sapientes.—*Aug. de Civit. Dei, l. 7. c. 12. p. 395.*

cesses. The Christian is a little world, and is purely independent upon the creature to make him happy :* he can, through grace, live comfortably without the world, though not without but upon God; yea, God is so much in him, as well as to him, that he can live comfortably when other things are dead. "A good man is satisfied from himself," Prov. xiv. 14. that is, he shall have sufficient content from his own conscience. There is but one word there for a backslider, being filled with his ways of sin and guilt, and a gracious soul's satisfaction from the sweet result of his own heart; to shew that a man's own conscience is either his heaven or hell, his greatest comforter or tormentor. The world cannot alter the joy or sadness of the heart; a thorough-paced, well tried child of God hath his rejoicing in himself alone, and not in another, Gal. vi. 4. It is a pedling beggarly life to wander abroad for morsels; but that is a noble kind of living, when a man hath all within doors, and needs not creatures' sorry contributions. I speak not of the fancied familistical deification, which is nothing less than blasphemy; but certainly the sound Christian in a sound sense bears some resemblance of the Divinity in this [$αὐταρκεῖα$] self-sufficiency: and the more treasure, the more like God; for such a soul is elevated above the creature, and placed in a higher orbit, which storms and tempests cannot reach. Nay, a soul whose conversation is in heaven, hath no dependence upon, nor intercourse with the creature, in order to complete his felicity; no more than the sun needs the glimmering light of the stars to make day: who then would not have this treasure? I might also add, herein is the Christian's re-

* וישבע Satiatus est, abundavit; quidam conferunt cum שבע, septem, quod septem sit numerus plenitudinis: that is, what he hath within, shall be as seven witnesses, or many.

semblance to the infinite Jehovah, because he hath a principle of motion within himself, and not from without; for as God is a free agent, yea a pure act, so in a sense are the saints, acting from an inward principle. Hence those Scripture expressions, of a man's spirit making him willing; and the heart smiting a man, or witnessing for him, or with him.* And in the exercise of repentance, it is said of Lot, " he vexed his righteous soul;"† or put himself upon the rack. Wicked men are dead, but grace is a principle of life, and resembles the Author of it: "for that which is born of the Spirit is spirit," John iii. 6. The decayed liberty of the will is in part by grace restored; and so far as the soul is spiritual, the soul of a saint is a flame of fire ascending to and acting for God; and the greater treasure of this a man hath in his breast, the more he resembles God.

The *Tenth* argument, to evince the necessity of this heart treasure, is drawn from the profit and advantage in having it; and that principally in facilitating the hardest duties of religion, and furnishing the soul for every good work.‡ And here I shall keep close to the treasure of holy thoughts, fed with those four streams of—truths, graces, comforts, and experiences; not only a saving principle, but such a measure thereof as will make up a treasure.

Now the frame of a treasured soul for duty is— ready—sincere—uniform—and perpetual.

1. A treasured heart is ready for duty. Like a well stored housekeeper, you cannot take him unprovided— a well accomplished scholar, that is never *non-plust*— and a watchful soldier, that is always fit for service. The Christian hath prepared materials to build the

* Exod. xxxv. 21.   2 Sam. xxiv. 10.   Rom. ix. 1.
† 2 Pet. ii. 8.   ψυχὴν—ἐβασάνιζεν.   ‡ 2 Tim. iii. 17.

house, and wants nothing but its setting up in actual performance; yea, the house is built and furnished, in some degree, for the entertaining of this royal guest—"Let my beloved come into his garden, and eat his pleasant fruits," Canticles iv. 16. The bow is strung, the heart fixed, the fire glowing in the embers upon the hearth, and one blast of the Spirit's breathing heightens it to a flame. Yet suppose the heart be not in actual readiness, still habits are sooner educed into act than new habits infused; and this the foolish virgins knew by sad experience.

But observe it, the more of this treasure, and the more readiness. The reason why we are not so free to prayer, conference, and meditation, is because we are not so filled with grace; otherwise gracious acts would flow from us as naturally as streams from the spring. Had we a treasure, we should never want suitable matter, and lively affections; we should not need to force ourselves to offer sacrifice, as Saul in another respect, nor with main strength to bind the sacrifice to the horns of the altar; but we should come off freely, cheerfully, delighting in God's ways as in our proper element, and running with enlarged hearts. The glorious angels, and glorified spirits of the just made perfect, have a perfect treasure of divine faculties, and are therefore ready prepared to do God's will. Now we pray that God's "will may be done on earth, as it is done in heaven;" and that will never be, without this living treasure. But, O how quickly shall we hear a command, and how swiftly shall we obey, if we have a treasure! A good soul is like the centurion's servant—half a word will make him run. When God said to David, "Seek my face," his heart quickly echoed, "Thy face, Lord, will I seek."* His warrant carried the

* Psalm xxvii. 8.

force of an argument—he needs no persuading when he knows his Master's pleasure. This is one choice advantage of having a treasure.

2. A treasured soul is sincere and serious; not complimental and forced. Israel of old made covenants, and seemed very religious; and God himself attested that they had well said, but adds, " O that there were such a heart in them!"* We have a strange passage in Jer. v. 2. " Though they say, the Lord liveth, surely they swear falsely." Why, is not that a truth? Yes, a great truth. God alone is the living God; but when they say so, their heart gives the lie to their lips; they say it with a deceitful heart, and that they may deceive; though it be a truth in itself, yet they speak it not as a truth, wanting a heart to assert the same. It is but a fond and frolic ostentation to invite a friend to dinner, when nothing is prepared. It is a mocking of God to bring Cain's sacrifice, a body without a heart, a carcase without spirit—it is as if a Jew had brought the skin of a beast for sacrifice, and no more. But where the treasure is in the heart, there the essentials of the service are made up—the work is filled up, or complete before God,† Rev. iii. 2; that is, it is not lame or defective in any considerable constitutive part thereof—it is such as may be truly called a real good work. This is the chief thing that God expects; and if a good heart be wanting, the work is as undone still. But a sincere Christian finds his prayer in his heart, which he utters with his lips: " Thy servant hath found in his heart to pray this prayer," 2 Sam. vii. 27. He found it not only in his book, but in his heart; he fetcheth his prayer from a treasure. Such a man will pray a prayer, as David here, and not only say a prayer, when he finds it in his heart. What cares God for

* Deuter. v. 28, 29. † Πεπληρωμένα.

a little lip-labour. He may say, "Who required these things at your hand? Did I not require them of your hearts? A mock feast or fast will not content me; I shall not be put off with an empty show: I will have your hearts, or nothing; and I must have a treasure in your hearts, or all you bring is worth nothing." The truth is, God takes principal notice of the heart, and observes how that stands affected. If idols be set up in the heart, God takes no notice of a people's prayers;[*] therefore we had need look to the frame of the heart.

3. A heart treasure makes the Christian uniform, and without reserve, in the duties of religion. He takes a christian course as it lies, carries on religion before him without halting or halving—he practiseth all righteousness at all times. There is a sweet harmony and exact symmetry in a saint's performance of duty. Some can frame[†] to some easier duties, not to more difficult; but the treasured soul can frame to any thing which God in the word hath made his duty; and hence it is, that he is "complete in all the will of God,"[‡] Col. iv. 12. The law of God in his heart carries an aspect to every part of his will in the written word; graces and duties are concordant one to another, like "a company of horses in Pharaoh's chariot—their cheeks are comely with rows of jewels, their necks with chains of gold," Song, i. 9, 10. That is, the soul of a believer is handsomely adorned with a comely train of graces and duties. Yea, such a person will at all times act like himself, so that one part of his life will not cross another, as a liar's tales and hypocrite's carriage do. He doth not serve God by fits and starts, in good

[*] Ezek. xiv. 3, 4.
[†] In the dialect of Yorkshire and Lancashire, "to frame," signifies to set about a thing properly, or to proceed in the performance of any thing with readiness and like a workman.—Ed.
[‡] Πεπληρωμένοι εν παντὶ θελήματι τοῦ Θεοῦ.

moods and motions, so as to be off and on in religion; but he hath a constant, settled spirit, which David prays for, and the translators call "a right spirit;*" (and truly so it is)—disposed for God, fitted for duty, bringing forth good fruit in due season; like a constant good housekeeper, that is never so suddenly surprised, but can make a prudent shift to treat his friend according to his degree. The truth is, man in his fallen estate is uncertain, intricate, and multiform in all his ways; you cannot tell where to find him, "gadding about to change his way," Jer. ii. 36. But being renewed, he is in part, and in some proportion, reduced to that original rectitude, simplicity, and stability of spirit and practice that was in Adam; so that according to the degree of grace received, he hath a constant, uniform frame and tenor of spirit, and holds one straight, direct, and even course towards heaven. In all this suitable to the motion of the wheels in the Prophet Ezekiel's vision, chap. i. 17. "When they went, they went upon their four sides;" *there* is their squareness and suitableness to all God's will: "and they returned not when they went;" *there* is their constant, permanent, and unchanging motion. That will lead us to the next head: only consider what an excellency and beauty there is in uniformity in religious duties. When works of nature or art are uniform, what lustre they have! We are much taken with a building that is compact and proportionable. A garden drawn exactly, an army marshalled in complete ranks and postures, are comely sights—just such are the fruits of holiness, proceeding from a well treasured heart. And indeed without this treasure there can be no such harmony in holy performances; but the actings will be like the legs of the lame, very unequal.

* Psalm li. 10. רוח נכון Spiritus constans, firmus, dispositus.

4. A treasure makes holy duties constant and perpetual: though there may be some temporary intermissions, yet never a total cessation, in acts of religion. Will a hypocrite pray always? Job xxvii. 10. No, verily. The water riseth no higher than the spring, and waters fail that have no spring, like Job's snow-water, which, when it waxeth warm, vanisheth away;* but a little brook supplied with a constant spring holds out in winter and summer: just such is the difference betwixt the performances of a treasured and treasureless heart. Two men perform duties, the one from gifts, the other from grace; the former in time withers, the latter daily increaseth. The King of France showed Spain's Ambassador his rich treasures: the Ambassador looks under the treasure chests, saying, "Have these a spring?—my master's treasures have:" meaning both the Indies. Just so it is here: let natural men's attainments be never so excellent, you may come to see an end of all their perfections; their eye of knowledge may be darkened, and their arm of natural and acquired abilities clean dried up. For, how can a well be always giving out water that receives none? How can a rose keep its freshness without a root? But they that are "planted in the house of the Lord, shall flourish in the courts of our God; yea, they shall bring forth fruit in old age," Psalm xcii. 13, 14. For the seed of God is a lively principle, that will never die; and this spring of grace is fed with supplies from the fulness of Jesus Christ, who is the fountain of gardens and well of living waters. Hence he saith, "He that believeth in me, out of his belly shall flow rivers of living water,"† John vii. 38. That is, he shall have

* Job vi. 16, 17.

† In summa, hîc tam perpetuitas donorum Spiritus, quam affluentia nobis promittitur.—*Marl. in loc.*

a perpetual supply of grace, and shall send forth constant emanations of gracious acts. A well furnished Christian shall never be drawn dry; his Saviour and treasure ever live, and because Christ lives, the saints and their graces shall live for ever. O friends! what would you give in these backsliding times to hold out to the end, that you may not make shipwreck of faith and a good conscience? Behold, I shew unto you an excellent way;—heap one grace upon another, till you possess a treasure—tie a chain of these pearls together, and lay them up in the closet of your hearts, and you will never be spiritually impoverished—be holily covetous after all graces that are attainable—" add to your faith virtue, to virtue knowledge, temperance, patience, godliness, brotherly kindness, charity;" for if you have these you will not be barren or unfruitful in duties, and if you perform duties according to that treasure, you shall never fall, 2 Pet. i. 5—11. These form a chain that link the soul to God, and reach as high as heaven. But do not think you can endure to the end without a treasure; for he that " hath not root in himself, dureth but for a while," Matt. xiii. 21. No wonder if many drop off like leaves in autumn—they have not any thing to bear them out; they spend upon themselves, as the spider, which spins her webs out of her own bowels, and they are swept away as the spider's web. But the gracious soul hath no less than an infinite God to supply the treasures of grace; so that let a Christian fall off to many acts of sin, carelessness in duty, and a course of dissipation, yet this treasure will work it off:—as a spring clears itself from mud in time, so he shall be brought back to God. There is something in the heart of a backsliding saint that makes him restless in that estate, and moving towards the centre. David saith, " I have gone astray like a lost sheep;" *there* is his acknowledgment: "seek thy servant;" *there* is his request: "for I do not forget thy commandments;" *there* is the argument to enforce it. As if he had said, There is yet something in my heart that owns thee; though I be fallen far, yet not so far but that I am still reaching after thee, and I am not fallen below thy reach. The truth is, a child of God hath more hold of God in his lowest ebbs than another sinner hath. As the spinster leaveth a lock of wool to draw on the next thread, so there is something left in the heart, the seed of God, that springs heaven-wards. Though a saint be in a very dead frame, yet he is not twice dead, as wicked men are; there is yet the root of the matter in the heart, that by the scent of water, (the heavenly dew of divine grace) will sprout again, and bring forth fruit: I dispute not how far men may fall, and whether a true saint may not be brought back to the bare habits of grace as they were at first infused, and lose degrees of grace obtained; but sure I am that Christ prayed for Peter, (and so for all believers) that his faith should not fail, Luke xxii. 32. and God always heareth him;* therefore our Divines have determined, that the seed of regeneration, with those fundamental gifts, without which spiritual life cannot subsist, are kept safe and entire; for the same Holy Ghost that infused that seed of grace, hath imprinted in it an incorruptible virtue, and perpetually cherisheth it and maintaineth it;* Mary's better part shall not be taken away. This fear in the heart, keeps them from departing from God, Jer. xxxii. 40. They have [*constantiam in proposito, et*

* Vid. Suff. Brit. de quin. Artic. thes. 6, p. 189. In sanctorum cordibus secundum quasdam virtutes semper manet Spiritus. Secundum quasdam recessurus venit, et venturus recedit. In his virtutibus, sine quibus ad vitam non pervenitur, in electorum suorum cordibus permanet.—*Greg. Moral.*

perseverantiam in opere] constancy in their hearts, and perseverance in their hands. Holy resolutions produce successful performances; and thus doth the treasured Christian hold on in a christian course, till these smaller measures of grace end in the vast ocean of glory. Thus much for the reasons of the point.

CHAP. VI.

SELF-EXAMINATION RELATIVE TO THIS TREASURE.

Now for a more close application of this to our own souls; is it so, that a good treasure in the heart, is necessary to good expences in the life? then

1. It stands us all in hand to try ourselves, and dig into our own hearts to see if we can find a treasure there, both in respect of sincerity and degree of grace. Know it, you are beggarly souls unless you have truth of grace; graceless souls are the only treasureless souls, and I fear there are more than a good many, that could never experimentally distinguish betwixt nature and grace, and therefore are increasing guilt, and treasuring up wrath: O Christians! see whether you have the true riches, try what proficiency you have made for grace, and in grace; you have long had a day of grace, and you must be accountable for all opportunities. Cheat not yourselves with counters instead of gold; Bristol-stones may make as fair a show as pearls; true grace is a rare and rich commodity. Thousands that are empty, conceit to themselves a treasure; proud, conceited professors are apt to boast of their attainments, whilst some self-denying humble souls, are apt to bear false witness against themselves, by denying what they have: Solomon saith, " There is that maketh

himself rich, yet hath nothing; there is that maketh himself poor, yet hath great riches," Prov. xiii. 7. Sounding vessels are often empty, and still running waters are usually deep; vapouring tradesmen jingle their money in their hands, whilst sober chapmen keep it in their chests; you shall find more of a merchant's goods in his warehouse, than in his shop window. So it is with a sober, serious, and judicious Christian; his glory and treasure is most within, whilst vain-glorious mountebanks in religion set all upon the stage. I entreat you, read those books that lay down marks of true grace, hear and attend the most heart-searching ministry, take much pains in descending frequently into your own hearts, and the God of heaven make you serious in a thorough search.

More particularly that I may help you in a discovery whether you have laid up a treasure of holy thoughts, proceeding from truths, graces, comforts, and experiences, ask, I beseech you, your own hearts these four questions—*How came you by it? How do you value it? How do you use it? How do you increase it?*

1. Let me ask you, and do you ask yourselves, if you pretend to such a treasure, *How came you by it?* Men usually know how they get a treasure. "The hand of the diligent maketh rich," Prov. x. 4. that is, "the blessing of the Lord" upon diligent endeavours, ver. 22. Men that would be rich ply the oars, run to markets and fairs, travel from city to city, to "buy and sell, and get gain;"* they travel by sea and by land, compassing the world to possess a small portion of it. Why, now, what do you in spiritual things? Where are your thoughtful cares and painful hands? Though labour will not get this treasure, (it is a free gift,) yet it will not be had without labour. God's ordinance

* James iv. 13.

must be honoured; it is the immutable decree of Heaven since the fall—"In the sweat of thy face shalt thou eat thy bread," Gen. iii. 19. Yea, this holds good for the soul: "Labour for that meat which endureth to everlasting life, which the Son of man shall give unto you," John vi. 27. Mark it, man's endeavours are very consistent with God's free grace, and Christ's dear purchase. God will be found in his own way; he ordinarily conveys the first grace in and by his own institutions, but seldom will a soul grow up to a treasure without a long trading in the royal exchange of holy duties; and diligence hath the promise of increase— " And unto you that hear shall more be given," Mark iv. 24. Well, sirs, hath the care of your hearts put labour into your hands, and travel into your feet, to repair to the markets and fairs of public, private, and secret performances, to get a solid treasure? Have you both digged and begged for it? Where are your sweat and agony? Hath Jesus Christ sweat blood to fit you for heaven, and have not you gone through a bloody sweat to get interest in him, and possession of his grace? O the pangs of conscience, and sad pantings of a convinced sinner, to obtain a portion in these riches of grace! Never did a poor labourer toil so hard for his day's wages as an humbled soul to be filled with Christ. A treasure of money is got with sweat and blood; or to be obtained from alms, with weary steps and loud cries:* but if thou be too idle to dig, and too proud to beg, thou art without a treasure, and mayest pine away in everlasting poverty.

2. *How do you value this treasure?* " Where the treasure is, there will the heart be also," Matt. vi. 21. The thoughts, cares, and affections will centre upon a

* ⃞ ꜆ Proprie est sanguis, sed apud Chaldæos notat pecuniam, quia sanguine ac sudore pauperum paratur.—*Byth.*

man's treasure; for he accounts his treasure the best thing he hath, yea worth all his other possessions. No man would willingly part with his treasure. So Naboth did tenaciously adhere to his hereditary possession. The wise merchant parts with all to purchase this.* Paul accounted his gain to be no better than loss for Christ, nay, as dung,† in comparison of his sweet and satisfying Saviour. All the world is a prejudice to a Christian, when it obstructs or obscures the grace of Christ. Is it thus with your souls? Do you account your spiritual portion your only riches? The truth is, the riches of the soul, and the riches in the soul, are the very soul of riches. I confess, that is a meretricious love that prizeth receipts from Christ more than the person of Christ.‡ But here I understand Jesus Christ to be the marrow and treasure of this treasure, and all these as ensuring evidences of interest in him; for all that the soul hath is wrapt up in him. Well, then, let me question the most dark and doubting, if sincere, Christian. What sayest thou, poor soul, wouldst thou quit thy share in Christ and spiritual treasures, for a crown and kingdom? wouldst thou not answer, No? Wouldst thou cast away thy trembling hopes of acceptance with God, to be delivered from the infamy, poverty, and persecution which sometimes attend the zealous profession of Christianity, that thou mayest live in honour, pleasure, and worldly delights? Surely thou wouldest answer, No. Wouldest thou change thy present low, afflicted, and conflicting state, with thy former carnal, but confident condition, or with the pompous, prosperous state of graceless sinners? I dare say thou wilt answer negatively. Yet, again, art thou not willing to part with thy dearest

---

* Matt. xiii. 44.   † Phil. iii. 8.
‡ Meretricius est amor, plus annulum, quam sponsum amare.

bosom lust and earthly enjoyment, for a true immortal treasure in heaven and in thy heart? I am confident an upright heart will answer, Yes. And if I mistake not, this if not only, yet chiefly, is the very parting point betwixt a sound Christian and a rotten hearted hypocrite; the one chooseth Martha's many things, the other Mary's one thing needful. This is indeed a discriminating mark; for a gracious soul will cry out, " None but Christ, none but Christ; give me Christ, or else I die; give me Christ and I shall live—Christ is my life, my crown, my joy, my all;* if I may have him I have enough, without him I have nothing." When one asked Alexander where his treasure was, he answered, "Where Hephæstion my faithful friend is." Just so will a good soul say—" Christ is the chief of ten thousand."† I prize him above my life, who loved me unto the death; I account that of great value that doth evidence my interest in him. As the marigold opens to the sun in the firmament, so doth the heart of a sincere Christian to the Sun of Righteousness: take an instance in Moses, who chose the bitterest cup of affliction, rather than the sugared cup of sensual pleasures, that he might enjoy Jesus Christ. See Heb. xi. 25, 26. Observe the strange disparity that appears to carnal reason in that choice; on the one side there was suffering, on the other enjoying—affliction on the one hand, pleasures on the other—the despised people of God were companions on one side, ruffling gallants in Pharaoh's court on the other—yet on the one side it was for a season, and but for a season, and that *but* turned the scales in his choice: those were pleasures, but treasures may perhaps prevail, with which Christ was last tempted.‡ No, good Moses esteemed the reproach of Christ greater riches than the treasures of

* Christus meus est omnia.   † Song v. 10.   ‡ Matt. iv. 8, 9.

Egypt. The worst of Christ is better than the best of the world. The noble Marquis Galeacius Caracciolus, in imitation of him, being tempted with large offers to depart from Zion to Babylon, resolutely replied, "Let their money perish with them, that account all the treasures of the world worth one hour's communion with Jesus Christ." If all the mountains were gold, the rocks pearls, and the whole world filled with the sweetest delights of the sons of men, and these offered to the Christian to be his proper inheritance for ever, he would, with a holy scorn, trample upon them, and look on them as not worth one glance of his eye, in comparison of one taste of the love of Christ, and a grain of saving grace in his heaven-born soul. But a carnal heart sees no such beauty in Christ, wherefore he should be so desired, nor is he taken with the comeliness and excellency of grace; a sad yet lively emblem whereof we have in the hopeful young gentleman that bade fair for heaven, yet when he saw it would cost him so dear as to part with all, he would rather go without it than forego his estate for it.* O, sirs! this is a pinching point, look to it—this one thing employed for examination will pierce betwixt joint and marrow, and a day of trial will discover what you account a treasure.

3. *How do you use and improve this treasure?* Habits of grace are no otherwise known than by their acts. What is a man better for that he useth not? A talent of grace of the right stamp will not be confined to a napkin, though gifts may—exercising is as necessary and evidential as having sincere grace. Things that are not, and things that appear not, are both alike.†
He is a wicked man that boasteth of his heart's desire, and he is a fool that trusteth in his heart. Yet many

* Matt. xix. 21, 22,
† De non entibus et non apparentibus eadem est ratio.

will say, "I have as good a heart as the best, though I do not talk so well with my tongue, or work so much with my hands—I have as good a meaning as any of them all, though I cannot make so great a show—I love to keep my religion to myself; none knows how good I am." It is not denied, but degrees of modesty, fears of vain-glory, and jealousies of apostacy, may restrain some Christian's profession, yet there may be a temptation on that hand also; let such know, that where fire is, it will betray itself, by heat or smoke—it is impossible grace should be hid or stifled; though there be only a smoking flax,* (even the wick of a candle, that affords little light and much offensive smell,) yet it will appear. Truths and graces in the heart will be (as the word was to Jeremiah) as " a burning fire shut up in the bones"† and bosom, that cannot be concealed. He that is full of matter is constrained, by the internal workings of the Spirit, to vent it; else it is like Elihu's new wine that hath no vent, and bursts the new bottles.‡ The truth is, it is as natural for a gracious heart to talk and walk holily, as for a living creature to breathe and move, so far as gracious; thus it cannot be otherwise, and also, observe it, it must not be otherwise. Your treasure within ought to be laid out; what have you it for else? Profession with the mouth is as necessary, in its kind, as believing with the heart, Rom. x. 10. Our light must not be " hid under a bushel," but " shine before men," that it may produce comfort to ourselves and have influence upon others, as well as have approbation from the Lord. So then, if thou hast a treasure within, thou dost witness a good confession, and thy conversation will be suitable to thy profession—thy trading will answer thy stock. The text tells you, " A good man, out of the

* Isa. xlii. 3. † Jer. xx. 9. ‡ Job xxxii. 18, 19.

good treasure of his heart, bringeth forth good things." And I told you the manner of laying out was, in holy meditations, savoury expressions, suitable actions, and patiently bearing, and profitably improving of afflictions. Why, now, lay judgment to the line, and compare your own course of life with these practices of religion. How do you trade with heaven, and for heaven? What do you more than others? Where is the life and power of religion? Do you indeed exercise yourselves to godliness? What large expences do you lay out for that God from whom you have such liberal incomes? When we see rich men lay out abundance of money in household goods, housekeeping, building, and recreations, we guess, certainly, such have a good stock beforehand, a great yearly revenue. Thus it is here; though many make a great show of what they have not, yet a ready, real, uniform, and constant performance of duty—a serious, sensible course of walking with God—and exercise of grace in all conditions, do evidence a suitable inward treasure. What say you to these things? Can our hearts witness for us, "that in simplicity and godly sincerity," by the assistance of grace, "we have had our conversation?"* Can our relations and neighbours witness for us, that we have served the Lord with all humility of mind, with many tears and temptations? Can our closets, chambers, shops, and fields testify our secret groans, meditations, self-examinations? Have we performed our relative duties with all care and conscience—as magistrates, punishing sin—as ministers, faithfully preaching at all seasons, suitably to all persons—as householders, instructing, correcting, and leaving a good example—as husbands, wives, parents, children, masters, servants? That man is not good at all that is not good in all re-

* Cor. i. 12.

lations. Doth the treasure of grace and truths prompt our tongues, employ our hands, guide our feet? Do those sentiments in our heads, and that principle in the heart, dictate to us our duty, and assist us in doing it? Are we fruitful in good works, words, and meditations; and are we useful in our generation? Let us not deceive ourselves, it is not a conceit of some good meanings within, that will serve our turn; but the Apostle tells us roundly and plainly, "He that doth righteousness is righteous," 1 John iii. 7. Acts do evidence the state, and a man cannot be good, unless he do good.

4. *How do you increase this treasure?* "To him that hath shall be given." Truth of grace is the prologue to growth in grace; and growth in grace arrives at full strength of grace—the saints "go from strength to strength," Psalm lxxxiv. 7. The true Christian, like his Master, "increaseth in wisdom and stature, and in favour with God and man," Luke ii. 52. These waters of the sanctuary rise up to the ancles, knees, loins, neck, till the soul come to the head, Christ, and so be swallowed up in the unfathomable ocean of glory. It is monstrous in grace, as well as nature, to grow none, but continue as a dwarf. It is a sad shrewd sign you have no grace, if you think you have grace enough. He was never good that desires not to be better;[*] they are hypocrites, and sure to be apostates, that are contented with a taste: the true believer is unsatiable, still hungering and thirsting after righteousness, daily adding one cubit after another to his spiritual stature, that he may be a tall man in Christ, and at last attain to the "measure of the stature of the fulness of Christ," Eph. iv. 13.[†] That is, not so much with respect to

[*] Minime bonus est qui melior fieri non vult.—*Ber.*

[†] Habet enim augmenta sua fides, habet suam infantiam, habet ætatem virilem, habet senectam.—*Mar. in loc.*

the complete stature of our bodies at the resurrection, proportionable to Christ's full age upon earth, as some expound it, though that may be true; but we must be increasing, till Christ's mystical body grow to ripeness and perfection, both in respect of all the members to be added thereunto, and also particular members' growth in grace, till they advance to a full maturity in knowledge and hol ness. What say you to this? are you any better than you have been? are your last works more than your first? What light of knowledge in saving truths, what heat and warmth in sanctifying graces, what heart-refreshing experiences and comforts have you laid up? Are you grown more solid, humble, holy, watchful, faithful and fruitful? Do you get more power against your lusts, and more ability to walk with God? Do you forget what is behind, and press forwards to perfection?* Are you stirred up more to holiness, and strengthened with all might by his Spirit in the inward man?† Are you still sensible of defects, craving for more spiritual riches, as a beggar for alms? I confess I have sometimes wondered at this strange paradox in Christianity, that there is nothing doth so fill the soul as grace, and yet nothing makes the soul so hungry for more grace as a principle of grace; nothing contents but a dram of grace, yet a dram of grace will not content. Believers desire more knowlege, more faith, more love, and accordingly they are still perfecting holiness in the fear of God.‡ So that, as the apostle saith of some, their faith groweth exceedingly, and charity aboundeth even till it become a treasure; ‖ for observe it, this spiritual treasure is made up, and increased by accumulation, by adding more graces, or strengthening graces already conferred.

* Phil. iii. 13, 14.
† Eph. iii. 16.
‡ 2 Cor. vii. 1.
‖ 2 Thess. i. 3.

Several good Divines* have done worthily in satisfying scrupulous souls in this important case about growth in grace. Let such as doubt of sincerity read them, it would be a digression here to speak fully to this point: only take this observation, the more life you have added to your light, the more humility to your graces, the more watchfulness to your lives by your experiences; and the more tenderness of conscience, and cheerfulness in holy performances by your comforts, the more have you grown in grace and increased your treasure: and thereby have given a clear evidence that you have a spiritual treasure in your hearts.

CHAP. VII.

NEGLECT OF HEART TREASURE REPROVED.

If it be so necessary to have a heart treasure within, that a Christian may be fitter to walk, speak and act holily, then this falls with weight upon the head of four sorts of persons, namely—

Careless loiterers, vain-glorious boasters, impious offenders, and unprofitable Christians.

I. Careless loiterers, that sleep out a fair summer's day of grace, and forget the day of their visitation. Many poor ministers have cause to weep over their dear people, as Christ over Jerusalem, and say, " If thou hadst known, at least in this thy day, the things that belong to thy peace! but now they are hid from thine eyes," Luke xix. 41, 42. If any soul be without

* See Symonds' Deserted Soul's Case and Cure, *p.* 416—421. Manton on Jude, v. 2. *p.* 122—127. Barlow's Sermon, 2 Pet. iii. 18.

grace, under precious means of grace, let such tremble at present providences, lest they lead on to the loss of ordinances: if thou hast sat under the droppings of the sanctuary, and art yet barren, be afraid, lest God either command the clouds to rain no rain on thee, or the curse of the barren fig-tree be pronounced against thee,—" Let no fruit grow on thee henceforward for ever," or else, " cut it down, why cumbereth it the ground?"* Oh sirs, have your souls been till now empty of grace, amidst ordinances which are the channels of grace? have you lived thus long in Goshen, and are you yet in Egyptian darkness? where is the fault, what can you say for yourselves? Suppose God should put you to it, to bring forth your strong reasons, (as he expostulated with the man that wanted the wedding garment†) and should say, friend, (for so wilt thou needs be accounted, and as such thou wast invited) where hast thou lived? in my Church? and didst thou not there hear of a rich wardrobe provided for naked souls, even the fine white linen of Christ's perfect righteousness? Was there not a well-furnished shop and storehouse of the gifts and graces of the Spirit to fill and adorn the house of thy heart? How comes it then that thou art so devoid and destitute of what is good? Hadst thou lived in Turkey or India, where I did not set up such an office of mercy, thou mightest have more to say, but now what apologies canst thou make? What fig-leaves canst thou find to cover thy shameful nakedness, or colour thy wretched negligence? How camest thou hither? *quâ fronte?* What canst thou say to excuse thy brazen impudence, that darest approach such a presence in so sordid a habit, or rather miserably naked? The truth is, though witty sinners can find shifts enough to put off

* Matt. xxi. 19. Luke xiii. 7. † Matt. xxii. 12.

ministers' arguings, and silence the clamours of conscience, yet how can their hearts endure, or hands be strong, when God shall deal with them? Their mouths shall be muzzled up in speechless, yet self-condemning astonishment; they must needs be condemned out of their own mouths. Oh consider, if yet thou be without a treasure of grace, and rather ask thyself some heart-awakening questions, than that God should put to thee such alarming interrogatories: as thus, say to thy soul, My poor pining soul, how is it with thee? What hast thou been doing, and what wast thou sent into the world for? what must become of thee? what provision hast thou made for an eternal state? where must thou lodge, if thou die this night? And let me propose to you these considerations—

1. If thy soul be yet without a true treasure of a gracious principle, thy condition is miserable; for thou hast no assurance of any more means to obtain it, nor to live another day to hear another sermon, or to hear of grace to make the means effectual for thy soul's good. Remember Esau; hast thou stood out so long, and dost thou now presume upon a longer day? Must the earth be forsaken for thee? and shall God leave his ordinary road to do thee good, step aside to meet with thee? God sometimes doth so, but what ground hast thou to expect it, that hast abused grace so long?

2. Is not this emptiness of good a dreadful sign of rejection? Solomon saith, " He that hath a froward heart findeth no good.* Nothing doeth him good, neither word nor rod. But he saith, " the heart of the prudent getteth knowledge;"† may not you sadly fear judicial hardness, to punish wilful negligence? One would have thought, if any good had been intended for you, that you should have been possessed of it

* Prov. xvii. 20. † Prov. xviii 15.

before this; it is a black brand of reprobation to live long under melting ordinances, and be still hard and dead.

3. Wilful neglect is an act of disingenuousness towards God, cruelty to your own souls, and the ready way to banish ordinances from posterity. What? must God always hold you the candle to play by? " Wherefore is there a price in the hand of a fool, when there is no heart to improve it?"* Be sure, if Satan find you idle, he will set you to work. Negligence is a sad prognostic, and preparative for eternal torment; and so much ease now, so much torment hereafter. Shall the God of Heaven always heap kindness upon offending, grace-abusing and refusing wretches? No, no; when love hath said its errand, justice will act its part: and,

4. Your lost advantages will prove your bitterest torment; all men must be judged according to their receipts, and wilful loiterers shall be punished according to their contempt of gospel opportunities. Gospel despisers shall account poor heathens comparatively happy, though their companions in eternal misery. Their bright sun of gospel grace shall set in thicker darkness, and greater treasures of wrath shall be poured into those vessels, that shut out treasures of grace.

II. Another sort to be reproved, are empty and vainglorious boasters, gilded hypocrites that pretend to a great treasure, but are sorry beggars. Some rigid Papists there are, who will tell you they have merit enough, both for themselves and others, that out of the abundant treasure of their good works, they can furnish defective souls on earth, and deliver tormented souls out of purgatory: but believe them not—they

* Prov. xvii. 16.

would make merchandize of souls, and draw them to delusions and damnation. Jesus Christ is our only treasury, there is nothing like merit in a mere creature. Angels in heaven stand by grace, having their confirmation by Christ; sure I am, they have no merits to spare; the wise virgins could not furnish others, but a boasting friar pretends he can, though the most of his seeming good works will rather prejudice himself, than profit others, since they generally spring from that vain will-worship, which is coined in the mint of a superstitious brain, and so would make the commands of God to be of none effect, and provoke the Lord's wrath against the promoters and practisers thereof. But suppose a man could obey positive commands, in practising all Scripture duties, and avoid all prohibited sins, yet wherein hath he to glory? Is he not still an unprofitable servant? Doth he give God any thing but his own? Is it not due debt? and is it by his own strength, or by the strength of God? And can he do what he doth, perfectly, without the least tincture or stain of imperfection, or of defect? Let any mere creature shew such good works as these, and let him climb up to heaven upon Acestus's rotten ladder, we are resolved to ascend on Jacob's ladder; let others trust their own merit, but let true Christians depend on grace.* I hope we shall be so wise as to choose Bellarmine's *dying safe way*, rather than his *disputing politic way* to heaven; to repose all our trust in the mercy of God and merits of Christ, rather than' the tottering foundation of man's best righteousness, which is *but a filthy rag*, and will rather defile than cover our nakedness.† But I principally design to lash such persons, as hypocritically and histrionically act the

* Quærant alii, si velint meritum, nos gratiam studeamus.—*Bern.*
† Col. ii. 7. Isa. lxiv. 6.

part of kings and emperors, but are despicable upstarts, that pretend upon the stage of their fair profession to coffers of gold, and precious treasures of grace; but alas! follow them into withdrawing-rooms of privacy, and you shall find them wofully destitute of all saving good; these poor souls conceit with counterfeit graces to purchase heaven! and by making lies their refuge to be secured from wrath: but alas, the God of heaven sees their false coin and self-flattering hearts; " All the ways of man are clean in his own eyes, but the Lord weigheth the spirits," Prov. xvi. 2. Oh, how many hearts and ways would be found light and wanting, if weighed in an even balance, even in the balance of the sanctuary? At the last day it will be seen that there are wonderful self-cheating conceits and confidences; there are many false hearts under fair vizors, but when these vizors are plucked off, all shall appear in their own colours; and O what strange sights will then be seen! When wicked men's foul insides are turned out, certainly they will be very abominable; though now every cunning hypocrite carries so closely that none can detect him, or say black is his eye, yet a time will come that shall bring every secret thing to light, and discover the guile of the deceitful usurer in religion, who thinks to truck for heaven with his stolen wares.* Oh, how much better is a poor soul than such a self-deluding richling, that thinks he is something, yet he is nothing, and so deceives his own soul, plays the sophister, and puts a false syllogism upon himself, as the Apostle James speaks. How many are in a golden dream, that build castles in the air, and fancy they are kings; but when they awake out of their frantic dreams do find them-

* איש תככים Signifies both a deceitful man and a usurer. See Prov. xxix. 13. *Marg.* For usurers are commonly fraudulent.

selves miserably mistaken! Solomon saith, "Whoso boasteth himself of a false gift, is like clouds and wind without rain," Prov. xxv. 14. That is, he that pretendeth to give or receive what is not real, but counterfeiteth either, renders himself ridiculous among men and odious to God. Our Lord Jesus " cursed the barren fig-tree," to manifest his displeasure against hypocrisy: hypocrites are the most hateful of all persons; they are hated of wicked men for seeming good, they are hated of God and good men for *but* seeming, and not being truly good. As hypocrites' fruit is like the apples of Sodom, that look fair with a beautiful skin, but touch them and they are dust; so the end of hypocrites will probably be like that of Sodom, which God overthrew as in a moment: yea, these must be patterns to others of a peculiarly dreadful destruction; hence the phrase of " appointing a portion with the hypocrites."* But here comes in a carnal, sensual sot, and applies all this to the zealous professor, and will needs condemn him for a hypocrite, because he makes so great a show, and he accounts himself a sincere saint because he conceits his heart to be good. The former censure is contrary to Scripture, and this latter conceit is contrary to the very sense and experience of mere pretenders to religion; for they may find, and God's children do feel, that the heart is the worst part of the whole man; it is a man's ignorance of it that makes him imagine it is the best. The truth is, no man will commend this common cheater, but he that knows it not; for it is known to be " desperately wicked, and it is deceitful,"† or a supplanter, (as the word imports,) that would trip up the heels of the Christian, and cheat him of his prize and reward. If ever thou be undone, it is thy heart that will undo thee: thou dost brag of

* Matt. xxiv. 51. † Jer. xvii. 9.

thy heart; alas, poor soul, thou hast cause to bewail it, and be afraid of it; and if conviction open thee a window to look into it, thou shalt see a monstrous, dreadful sight, that will make thee out of love with thyself, and cause thy heart to ache, if it do not break, with godly sorrow. As for the children of God whom wicked men condemn, for making so great a show, I shall say but this, that it is the most unreasonable uncharitableness in the world, to judge contrary to what we see; yea, it is a blasphemous assuming to a man's self the property of God's omniscience, to pretend to search the heart, and to say, the thoughts of the heart are opposite to the professions of the lips, and practices of the life. The Lord rebuke such railing Rabshakehs, as condemn all the generation of God's children, and that because of their holy, world-condemning conversation. These moles cannot endure the light of saints' paths; hence they say, " I warrant you, these precise walkers are no better than their neighbours; if the truth were known, they are a company of dissemblers, and are rotten at the heart; Pharisee-like, they make clean the outside of the cup, and condemn others as profane;" and then they bind it with an oath that they are as bad as themselves! And if a professor slip into an open sin, then they are confirmed in their censures, and conclude, " they are all alike—a pack of dissemblers!" And now the holiest saint (that hates sin, and mourns for it as his greatest burden) shall have his brother's miscarriage dashed in his teeth for ever. But if a man might argue with these sottish, yet censorious souls, in a rational way, what could they answer? Are not they themselves worse than the loosest professors, and how far short do they fall of close-walking Christians? Should all be condemned for the sake of one? and should we not judge according to what we see, or can attain to the knowledge of? Is not the tree known to us by its fruits, and not by its roots, which are invisible to us? Lord, set these vain boasters a work in searching their own hearts, and examining their "ownselves, whether Christ be within them," as Paul directs the Corinthians in this very case,* and this will cure their censorious spirits, and find them work enough to do at home; for as the eye that looks most abroad sees least within, so the most uncharitable censurers are the most empty, unprofitable professors: whereas a Christian that hath most grace himself, judgeth best of others; and observe it, they that groundlessly judge others to be worse than they see apparent cause, will be judged by others in like manner in this world,† and are in danger of a sad and just censure and sentence at the dreadful day of judgment. "What then is the hope of the hypocrite, though he hath gained, when God taketh away his soul?"‡

III. Another sort to be reproved are, impious offenders, impenitent sinners, that verify the latter part of the text, and run a course directly contrary to the good man:—"An evil man, out of the evil treasure of his heart, bringeth forth evil things." How should it be otherwise? Men must needs act as they are. It was a proverb of the ancients, "Wickedness proceedeth from the wicked," 1 Sam. xxiv. 13. Such as the fountain is, such must needs be the streams; the fruit is answerable to the nature of the root and tree: the working forge of men's wicked hearts doth sparkle forth suitable imaginations.|| Why are men so wicked in their lives? It is because they have more naughty hearts; for the cause hath more in it than the effects.

---

* 2 Cor. xiii. 5.   † Matt. vii. 1, 2.
‡ Job xxvii. 8. || James iii. 10, 11. Gen vi. 5.

Oh, how many vassals of Satan and vessels of sin are replenishing and preparing for wrath! For as a good man's treasure prepares him to do the more good, so too many are filling their souls with guilt, and harden their hearts by custom in sin, that they may be vile with less remorse, and swallow down iniquity as the fish drinks in water; they cauterize their consciences, and twist a strong cord of customary sinning, that they may draw iniquity with cart-ropes, and do evil with both hands earnestly, so that their hearts may not smite them with a sense of remorse. As the scholar that Dr. Preston speaks of, who had committed such a scandalous sin, that he could not rest by reason of terrors of conscience, the devil having instigated him to commit that sin again, in order to obtain quiet; he did so, and afterwards could sin without remorse: just so do many persons, who have imprinted an impudence on their foreheads by constant sinning, so that at last they are " past feeling, having given themselves over to all lasciviousness, to work all uncleanness with greediness," Eph. iv. 19.* The word "past feeling," imports remorselessness, senselessness, like that of a member benumbed, seared; and this comes with custom in sinning, according to that—*Consuetudo peccandi tollit sensum peccati:* that is, the custom of sinning takes away the sense of sin. We are apt to wonder at the horrid abominations that break out, but if we do consider the prodigious wickedness of an atheistical heart, we may rather wonder that there is no more profaneness in the world. If the tongue be a world of iniquity,† how many worlds of wickedness are there in a wicked heart? The thousandth part of corruption breaks not out, of

* Ἀπηλγηκότες μηκέτι θέλοντες πονεῖν, qui non amplius laborare volunt aut possunt.—*Vide Hein. Excercit. in loc.*

† James iii. 6.

that which is within. Surely, did not God set bounds to men's raging lusts, the world would not be habitable for the saints: God restrains that wrath which will not turn to his praise, and saints' advantage;* and when wicked men have belched out as much rage as they can, there is a remnant yet behind. We are fallen into the dregs of time, and iniquity doth abound; there is a world of atheism, pride, uncleanness, swearing, drunkenness, gluttony, blasphemy, Sabbath-breaking, contempt and scorning of religion; men break out, and blood toucheth blood: but were there a casement or perspective whereby a man might look into a carnal heart, O what a filthy sink of unheard-of sin, and full nest of odious vipers, might he behold! certainly it would be the dreadfullest sight in the world, far worse than to see the devil in the ugliest hue. We may stand wondering at the fathomless, bottomless depth of wickedness in the heart of man; " it is," saith Luther, "the treasure of evils, the fountain of poison, the head and original of all iniquity."† Every man hath that in his heart which he cannot believe is in him, but yet may and will break out in its season, upon occasion, as in the known instance of Hazael.‡ The truth is, the seed and spawn of all heresies, impieties, and blasphemies, are in our nature. The Rev. Mr. Greenham saith, "That if all errors and the memorials of them were annihilated, by the absolute power of God, so that there should not the least remembrance of them remain, yet there is enough in the heart of one man to revive them all again the next day;" and I may add also, as to profane practices: so that the wickedness that is in the world doth not proceed from

* Psalm lxxvi. 10.
† Cor est thesaurus malorum, fons venenorum, caput et origo omnis iniquitatis.—*Luth. tom.* 4. *fol.* 335.   ‡ 2 Kings viii. 13.

imitation of Adam's first sin, (as Pelagians dream,) at least not from thence only, but also and chiefly from the propagation of original corruption to all his posterity; for there is an habitual pravity entailed upon us and transmitted to us from our first parents, which hath its regency in the heart, and activity in the life. The fifth chapter of the Epistle to the Romans will stand firm against all Pelagian and Socinian adversaries, proving that both Adam and Christ our second Adam, do communicate to their seed that which is their own, both by imputation and propagation; only the first Adam distributes impurity, guilt, and death; the second gives grace, righteousness, and eternal life.* It will remain as an undoubted maxim and sad experience, that there is an habitual depravation and deviation of our whole nature from the law of God; so that there is a universal corruption of the whole man—understanding, conscience, will, affections, and all the members of the body. Now this propagation, Divines commonly say, is two ways :—

1. By divine appointment and designation, that whatsoever Adam received or lost should be not only for himself but for his posterity, being a public person; so God leaves the soul in respect of his image, and hence follows defect of original righteousness: this he doth not as author of sin, but as a righteous Judge.

2. By natural generation. As sweet oil poured into a fusty vessel loseth its pureness, being infected by the vessel, so the soul created good, and put into the corrupt body, receives contagion thence. This putting

* Vide Calvin Instit. lib. 2. cap. 8. sect. 5, &c. See M. Perk. Exp. on Creed, fol. 162. Adamus fuit humanæ naturæ non modo progenitor, sed radix, ideo in illius corruptione merito vitiatum fuit hominum genus.—*Calvin ubi supra.* Conferas hac de re *Baron. de orig. Anim. Excer.* 2. *Art.* 6, 7, 8. *p.* 91—104.

of a pure soul into a corrupt body is a just punishment of the sin of all men in Adam; so some. But this is generally agreed upon, that original sin is not in some men more, in some less, but in every man equally, as all men do equally from Adam participate the nature of man, and are equally the children of wrath; and the reason why some are more civil, others outrageous, proceedeth from God's bridling some and leaving others: and, truly, restraining grace is a choice mercy, in its kind, else what would not men do? The truth is, the origin of sin is within: " Every man is tempted when he is drawn away and enticed of his own lust," saith the Apostle; *there* lust is the father: " and lust when it hath conceived bringeth forth sin;"* *there* lust is the mother too. "Hence," saith one, " there is no sin but might be committed if Satan were dead and buried: original sin is virtually every sin; and could one kill the devil, yet you cannot name the sin that original depravity would not entice a man to: suppose it possible for a man to be separated from the contagious company of wicked men, and out of the reach of Satan's suggestions, nay, to converse in the midst of renowned saints, yet that man hath enough in himself to beget, conceive, bring forth, and consummate all actual sins."† Well then, sirs, let all men behold the foul face of their hearts in the pure glass of the law of God, and they will see a strange and astonishing spectacle, which would end either in evangelical repentance or final despair; as one saith—

> ——— If apparitions make us sad,
> By sight of sin we should grow mad.—HERBERT.

There is a necessary and profitable sight of sin, which

* James i. 13—15. See Capel on Tempt. p. 38—43. and p. 65—70, where it is excellently and fully handled.
† Reynolds' Sinf. of Sin, p. 151, &c.

drives the soul out of itself to Jesus Christ. O labour for that! Take the candle of the word, and go down into the dark dungeon of your hearts—search yourselves, lest the Lord search you as with candles—know and acknowledge the plague of your own hearts—be not afraid to know the worst of yourselves. It is better we should set our sins in order before us while there is hope of pardon, for our humiliation, than that God should set them in order before us at the great and last day, for our eternal condemnation. We may say of an impenitent soul as the prophet of his servant,* "Lord, open his eyes," and surely he shall see a troop of lusts. The mountain of his proud heart is covered with monstrous armed sins, that fight against the soul. O that the thoughts of your hearts may be discovered, pardoned, and purged out, lest, by wilful sinning, you heap up "wrath against the day of wrath,"† and your souls perish for want of a treasure of grace, and by reason of this dreadful treasure of sin and guilt.

IV. The last sort of persons that fall under the lash of a sharp and just reproof are, unprofitable Christians, who, though they be sincere for the main, and have the root of the matter, still have not yet gained this treasure. Alas, sirs! there is none of us but we have too much bad, and too little good treasure in our hearts. We cannot but know all the wickedness that our hearts are privy to, and cannot our consciences discover an emptiness, and vacuity of good? O what a chaos of confusion is in our hearts! And whence comes this? Have we not had means of gathering a large treasure? What have we done with all our ordinances, sermons, sacraments, mercies, afflictions? If we had been diligent, we might have furnished our souls with truths,

* 2 Kings vi. 17.   † Rom. ii. 5.

graces, comforts, and experiences. What could have been done more for us? And have we a treasure proportionable to our enjoyments? Whence then are we so unfit for, and untoward in, duties—so slight, dead, and trifling in performances—so unprepared for, and unprofitable under, ordinances—so unthankful for mercies, discontented under crosses—so weak in resisting temptations, subduing corruptions—so unwilling and unprepared for the communion of saints? Oh, whence is it, that we are so apt to sit loose from God—so little fit for fellowship with him, and so much at a distance from him? Certainly the reason is obvious—we have not such a treasure as becomes saints. Especially the great reason why we are so little skilful in the heavenly duty of meditation is, the want of a treasure of holy thoughts; when we are alone we cannot fix our minds upon a heart-affecting subject, or, at least, cannot pursue it, till our hearts be deeply affected; but our thoughts are off and on, very inconsistent, incoherent, independent, like the rambling discourses of a madman, or the ranging motions of a spaniel, or like "the eyes of a fool, that are in the ends of the earth."* We run from object to object in a moment, and one thought looks like a mere stranger to another; should our thoughts be patent, or an invisible notary acquainted with them, write them down, and repeat them to us, how should we blush and be confounded in the rehearsal! As it is recorded of Dr. Potter, that hearing the fellows of the college talk of trivial things, said nothing; but after they had done talking he thus bespake them—" And now, my masters, will you hear all your extravagant discourses, for I have strictly observed and marked what you said; and he told them every whit."† So suppose some should present to our

---

* Prov. xvii. 24.   † Mr. Clark's Life of Dr. Potter, p. 393.

ears or eyes a relation of our wild imaginations in one hour's time, what a strange medley of nonsense would there be! We may say, "The Lord knoweth the thoughts of man, that they are vanity," Psalm xciv. 11. When we have summed up all the traverses, reasonings, and discourses of the mind, we may write this at the bottom as the total sum—"All is vanity, nothing but vanity; yea, vanity in the abstract." And what is the reason of all this, but a want of the fore-mentioned treasure—a stock of truths, graces, comforts, and experiences.

I shall propound these four considerations, briefly for the saints' conviction and humiliation:—

1. Are not these spiritual things worth hoarding up? Look about you, through the whole creation, and see if you can find any thing better to make a treasure of. David saith, "I have seen an end of all perfection," Psalm cxix. 96. All outward enjoyments are a scant garment, that cannot cover us, or rotten rags, and are soon worn out; but one part of this treasure, that is, God's commandment is of a large extent; hence saith that good man, "Thy commandment is exceeding broad,"—it reaches from heaven to earth, from great to small, to all sorts of sinners, to all the faculties of the soul, to and through all eternity. Thus long and broad is the Christian's treasure; where then can you mend yourselves for a treasure? Spiritual blessings have all dimensions of perfection—these are the cream and flower of all blessings; no other treasures avail in the day of wrath. If heavenly things be not worth looking after, what are? Should not spiritual persons set their hearts on spiritual riches? Are not these most suitable to your immortal souls, and spiritual principles? Have you not been married to Christ, and can you be content to be without any

part of your dowry?* Are not you risen with Christ, and should you not then seek after things above?† Are not the things of God *magnalia*—great things of eternal concernment? And did you not prize them at a high rate at your first conviction? And was not this your motto, *Non est mortale quod opto*—I seek not, I pursue not mortal things, temporary, fading enjoyments? And are not these as much worth inquiring after now as formerly? Yes, certainly, these do not decay through age; it was the matters belonging to the old covenant, or legal dispensation, that decayed and waxed old, and so by degrees did vanish away.‡ New covenant mercies are the "sure mercies of David,"‖ and they are always fresh and green; hence saith the church, in Cant. i. 16. "also our bed is green:" that is, our mutual delight in each other is lively, sweet, and satisfying, never glutting, as earthly delights are. "He that drinks of these living waters shall never thirst,"§ that is, after muddy waters of earthly comforts, but shall more ardently thirst and pant after the living God. Well, sirs, look to it; there is nothing worth desiring but this heavenly treasure: if you can find any better, take it, much good may it do you; yet brag not of your bargain till you see the issue.

2. Are you in any danger of having too much of these things? Surely there are no superfluities in the internals of religion. In the outward part too much may be done, (though not if a man keep to the rule,) so that in some respects one may be "righteous overmuch;"¶ that is, in either a self-willed, superstitious way, or else in an unseasonable or unmeasurable performance of religious duties, to tire out a tempted soul,

---

* Rom. vii 4. † Col. iii. 1, 2. ‡ Heb. viii. 13.
‖ Isa. lv. 3. § John iv. 14. ¶ Eccles. vii. 16.

and run the Christian off his legs: but for inward graces, sanctified knowledge, and real holiness, there can never be an overplus or excess—whilst you are on this side the line, you will be short of perfection. Let Festus-like sots say, that "much learning makes professors mad;"* let *us* study to increase and abound more and more in knowledge, faith, love, humility, experience; as Paul pressed forward, if by any means he might attain to the resurrection of the dead, forgetting what was behind, and reaching forth to what was before.† Moses's ark had staves for removing further, Jacob's ladder had rounds for ascending higher—Christians must sing the song of degrees in this world, and should seek to be renewed day by day. We must not sit upon, and be satisfied with, our measure,‡ but work hard to make it a treasure; we must strive both for fulness of grace and fulness of joy. It is possible a Christian may attain to a full assurance; yea, to that joy which is unspeakable, and peace which passeth all understanding; and he may even think he hath enough; as I have heard of a good soul that enjoyed such an abundant tide of comfort, that he desired the Lord to stay his hand, lest the vessel should break, (though this is not ordinary for every believer, nor at all times for any,) so that some may possibly have as much comfort as they can desire; but I never read or heard of any saints that had too much grace, or so much as they desired—all have bewailed their defects, living and dying; and the best men have been most covetous of divine things, young and old. It is said of good Mr. Herbert Palmer, when he was of the age of four or five years, "that he would cry to go to his lady-mother, that he might hear something of God." And of old Grynæus

---

* Acts xxvi. 24. † Phil. iii. 11—14.
‡ Χοινικι μη επικαθησο, was Pythagoras's motto.

(that savoury German Divine) it is recorded, that when some persons were discoursing by his death-bed he lift up himself, saying, " I shall die with more comfort if I may die learning something for the good of my soul." Now, sirs, who or what are you? Are you wise enough, good enough? Are you afraid of being too like God, or of having too much of God in and with your souls? Are you loth to get too ready for, or too readily into, heaven? Alas, alas! you may call your estate into question, if you say, you have grace enough, or are good enough, or if you slacken your endeavours to get more grace, upon a conceit you have enough.* It is as natural for a living saint to call for grace as for a lively child to cry for food; insatiable desire after grace, is a clear test of the truth of grace. O shame thyself, then, for thy neglect, and humble thy soul for thy nonproficiency.

3. Do you certainly know what treasure you may need? When you go a journey you take money enough, because you cannot tell but you may be put to extraordinary expences; and truly, in your journey to heaven you may be put to unexpected charges. You little know what a day may bring forth; it may bring forth a burden for your back; God may call you to sharp service, in a way of duty and difficulty: you are sure to go through a purgatory to glory; the way to heaven is strait and narrow, and you must crowd hard to get in, and thrust through—" through manifold temptations and tribulations you must enter into heaven." It is an irrevocable decree of Heaven, that " he that will live godly in Christ Jesus must suffer persecution." We have had fair weather hitherto, but the greater storm is behind; we have not yet " resisted to blood," but we may be put to it. Be you sure, as long

* Si dixisti satis est, periisti.

as the devil is in hell, and Antichrist on earth, there will be persecutions raised against the Church, in some part of it or other; yea, and the dying blows of the latter may prove the heaviest to the Reformed Churches.* Woe to those that are unprovided for that sharp day! Oh; what piteous shirking will there be to save the skin, and damn the soul! O Christians! get furnished for this encounter; we little know whom it may reach, or how long the storm may last. You had need get "strengthened with all might, unto all patience and long-suffering, with joyfulness,"† lest, if your patience be short and sufferings long, you fail in the way, and fall short of your crown. What a sad plight are those seamen in that have made but a scant provision, and meet with a long voyage. It was a good saying of the Rev. Mr. Dod, "That this is the difference betwixt a Christian that is provided for troubles, and one that is not; that to the one they are but blows on the harness, but to the other they are blows on the flesh."‡ Ælian saith, "That in Lybia men slept with their boots on, because of the scorpions, that they might not sting them." We had need also be well "shod, or booted, with the preparation of the gospel of peace;"‖ that is, with a disposition and resolution to walk in the most thorny way, and stinging company of wicked men, that we may "follow the Lamb which way soever he goeth." We had need to count the cost in the profession of religion, we do not know what God may call us to do or to endure. Great services require great strength; that we may neither be weary of, nor weary in, the Lord's work; we must lay *in* much, that we may lay *out* much for God; we know not what God will call

---

* Contra quos deinceps, bellum geretur, hodieque durat nec finietur, donec, bestia in exitium ierit.—*Mede Com. in Apoc.* p. 198.
† Col. i. 11.   ‡ Mr. Clark in his Life.   ‖ Eph. vi. 15.

us to use. When Israel was to go out of Egypt, Moses would take the cattle, and not leave "a hoof behind; for, saith he, we know not with what we must serve the Lord, till we come thither," Exod. x. 26: therefore must they also borrow jewels,* to be thoroughly furnished; "and the Egyptians were more willing to lend them," saith a learned man, "because themselves were decked with jewels, that they might be more acceptable to their fine-decked deities."† So you do not know with what sort of graces or truths you must serve the Lord; only let us get furnished with all instituted qualifications, that we may be so adorned and armed that the Lord may take pleasure in us, and that we may get through services and sufferings with glory to God, credit to religion, and comfort to our own souls. Those are unwise Christians that lose their time, and are not furnished for the tempests of their sea-voyage, since no man knows what he must need.

4. Neglect herein is a dishonour to God, and disparagement to the treasures of grace. "Why art thou being the king's son, lean from day to day," said Jonadab to Ammon, 2 Sam. xiii. 4. So say I, whence proceeds this leanness? Is there not meat enough at your Father's table, store sufficient in your Master's treasury? Do you not disparage the means of your supply, and bring an ill report on the good land? God is not a hard master, but distributes liberally an abundant dole of grace: why then are your souls no better liking in religion? The reason is not in God, but in yourselves: "you are not straitened in him, but in your own bowels,"‡ as Paul in another case; now, as a recompense of his love and munificence, be ye also enlarged. Indeed, it doth (as it were) ease God's

* Exod. xi. 2.   † Dr. Lightfoot Glean. on Exod. p. 24.
‡ 2 Cor. vi. 12.

heart to be communicating of his goodness; it did please him infinitely from eternity, to think of expending riches of grace upon sinners in time :* but he can be perfectly and perpetually happy without you; it doth chiefly concern you to fetch all from him, that you also may be happy in the enjoyment of him. Are you afraid of being happy? who, but foolish man would forsake his own mercies?† Shall God set up an office of grace in Christ, and will indigent souls take no notice of it? You cannot grieve him worse than to neglect his infinite condescension and tender affection. If a mighty king should open his treasure, and bid men come and bring their bags, and take as much as they desired, do you think they would neglect this occasion of enriching themselves? Surely not; they would rather fetch bag after bag, (for scarce is any one weary of taking money) and with the poor woman in sacred story, borrow vessels that may contain larger treasures. The God of heaven hath made a glorious proclamation of scattering precious treasures; do you question whether he intends as he speaketh? God forbid: or, do you fear being welcome? Why, you are most welcome when you come for the greatest share. Do you fear unworthiness will hinder you? I say, sense of unworthiness will help you to be capable of greater receipts. Do you fear these treasures of heaven will be exhausted by the myriads of souls that are supplied therefrom? Know it, sirs, the royal exchequer is as rich this day, as it was when Christ was first promised, or the first man saved; these riches of grace are an inexhaustible spring. Distribution doth not impair its fulness, no more than the sun's shining doth rob it of its innate and native light. Oh then, why are our souls so poor and pining? The

* Prov. viii. 31. † Jonah ii. 8.

Lord humble us because we have no more, when there is so much to be had in our all-sufficient treasury.

CHAP. VIII.

INSTRUCTIONS FOR A GRACELESS HEART TO OBTAIN A TREASURE OF GOOD.

A THIRD use is of direction, how a poor soul may be furnished with a rich and suitable heart-treasure. Now, this is useful to sinners and saints, and it is the latter to whom I shall principally address myself. But because the treasure of true grace is absolutely necessary, I shall lay down some few directions for the graceless soul, that it may have a right principle, without which it cannot bring forth one good thought, word, or work. This is the habit without which there can be no gracious acts; this is the root, without which there can be no fruit to God; this is that stock to trade with, without which there can be no transactions with God, or true heaping up of the fore-mentioned treasure of sanctifying truths, spiritual graces, heart-melting experiences, or heart-cheering comforts. I know the School-men* have long disputes about the generating, acquiring, or infusing of habits, as whether any habit be from nature? or be caused by acts, or by one act? or whether habits be infused by God? But we must distinguish betwixt inferior habits, that are merely natural, and spiritual, gracious habits, that are supernatural; these are of a heavenly extract and origin. Yet we are to wait upon God in

* Aquin. Sum Prim. Sec. Qu. 51. Art. 1—4. Qu. 109. Ubi videas decimas questiones de gratia agitatas.

the use of his appointed means; so saith the Apostle—"Work out your own salvation with fear and trembling; for it is God which worketh in you both to will and to do, of his own good pleasure," Phil. ii. 12, 13.* This text both confuteth the speculative free-willer, and convinceth the practical loiterer, that grace is to be had from God in his way, though it is not purchased by man's working. I purposely wave the schoolmen's voluminous disputes concerning grace, and shall propound these seven directions to poor graceless souls; and they are plain and practical duties.

1. Withdraw from the world. At some times learn to sequester yourselves from the cares, affairs, comforts, cumbers, and company here below. Do not think you can hoard up in a crowd. Satan loves to fish in troubled waters, but so doth not Christ; the noise of Cain's hammers, in building cities, drowned the voice of conscience. A man will best enjoy himself alone; solitary recesses are of singular advantage, both for getting and increasing grace: "Through desire a man having separated himself, seeketh and intermeddleth with all wisdom," Prov. xviii. 1. In this you may and must be separatists: let me advise you (and, Oh, that I could prevail at least thus far) to treat and entertain yourselves by yourselves. He is a wicked man, and resolves to continue so, that dare not entertain himself with discourses about spiritual subjects and soul affairs: it were more safe to know the worst, before you feel the worst. Let your solitary thoughts be working about things of eternity; accustom yourselves to secret and serious pondering. I have read, that the father of a prodigal left it as his death-bed charge, unto his only son, to spend a quarter of an hour every day in

* What persons may do towards their own conversion, see Morn. Lect. Case of Consc. p. 33.

retired thinking, but left him at liberty to think of what he would: the son having this liberty to please himself in the subject, sets himself to the performance of his promise; his thoughts one day recall his past pleasures; another, contrive his future delights; but at length becoming inquisitive to know what might be his Father's end in proposing this task, he thought his father was a wise and good man, therefore surely he intended and hoped that he would some time or other think of religion; when this had leavened his thoughts they multiplied abundantly, neither could he contain them in so short a confinement, but was that night sleepless, and afterwards restless, till he became seriously religious.*

> By all means use sometimes to be alone,
>   Salute thyself; see what thy soul doth wear;
> Dare to look in thy chest, for 'tis thine own,
>   And tumble up and down what thou find'st there.
> Who cannot rest till he good fellows find,
> He breaks up house, turns out of doors his mind.†

Oh, sirs, you little know what good effects a serious consideration may produce! God propounds it, and men have practised it, as the great expedient to begin and promote repentance. Consider what you came into the world for—whither you must go if you die this moment—what a state you were born in—what is the need and nature of regeneration—what the worth and price of your immortal souls, and, through God's blessing, these thoughts may leave some good impressions.

2. Be at a point concerning your state. Be exact and impartial in searching your hearts, to find out your state. Trifle not in this great work of self-examina-

---

* Morning Lect. at Crippl. Consc. p. 9.

† Herb. Church-porch, p. 6.

tion; be not afraid to know the worst of thyself; make a curious and critical heart-anatomy; try whether "Jesus Christ be in you;"* do as the goldsmith, who brings his gold to the balance, so do you weigh yourselves in the balance of the sanctuary; judge not of your state by the common opinion of others concerning you, but by Scripture characters, and bring your virtues to the touchstone; pierce them through, to try whether they be genuine graces or moral endowments; see whether your treasure be that " gold that is tried in the fire," that is, in the fiery furnace of affliction and persecution. Oh, how many are deceived with imaginary felicities, and empty flourishes! Take heed of being put off with gifts, instead of grace; conviction, instead of conversion; outward reformation, instead of saving sanctification; which is the damning and undoing of thousands of souls. Why will you not use as much diligence for your souls as you do for your bodies, or estates? If your body be in a dangerous disease, or your estate at hazard in an intricate suit, you will run and ride, and make friends, and pay any money, to know what shall become of them, or to secure them: and are not your souls of more worth than a putrid carcase, or dunghill estate? Sirs, pose yourselves with serious questions:—Heart, how is it with thee? Art thou renewed? What life of grace is in thee? Are thy graces of the right stamp? Whither art thou going? And get distinct and positive answers to such questions as these. Let not thy treacherous heart dally with thee; be not put off with general hopes and groundless conjectures. A man is easily induced to believe what he would have to be true; but rest not there, try further, make it out how it comes to be so, detect and answer every flaw in thy

* 2 Cor. xiii. 5. δοκιμάζετε, πειράζετε.

spiritual estate. If thou canst not do this thyself, make thy case known to some able Minister, or experienced Christian; tell them how things are with thee, beg advice; ask them how it was with their souls, and thou shalt find much help this way. Yet after all, suspect thine own heart; call in aid from heaven; desire the Lord to search thee;* and be willing to be sifted to the bran, searched to the bottom. David is so intent upon it, and so afraid of a mistake, that he useth three emphatical words, in that challenge he makes for his soul's inquisition, Psalm xxvi. 2. " Examine me, O Lord, and prove me, try my reins and my heart." The first word imports a viewing us as from a watch-tower; the second word imports a trying, or finding out a thing by questions, or an inquiry by signs or tests; the last word imports such a trial, as separates the dross from the gold, or the dregs from the wine; so the Christian would be tried and purged, that grace may appear true, sincere, solid; and indeed it is as much as your souls are worth; therefore take the most effectual course to clear your state to yourselves, and be not put off with any answer, but what will be accepted by God at the great day.

3. Mourn over your empty hearts: if you find things not right in your own hearts lament your state, cry out with a loud and bitter cry, as Esau did when the blessing was gone; lament and say, woe and alas that ever I was born! that I have lived thus long without God in the world, at first entrance into it a bankrupt, and ever since a spiritual beggar. Oh what will become of me, if I die in this estate? there

* Psalm cxxxix. 23.

† בחן probavit, exploravit, tentavit; נסה signo agnoscere, conflavit; צרף defæcavit. Met. probavit; inde Sarepta, civitas metallica, nomen habet ab officinis quibus metalla excoquuntur.

is but a step betwixt me and death, and the next breath I breathe may be in everlasting burnings. It is a wonder I am not hurled into hell before this, what shall I do to be saved? Is there any hope for such a wretch as I am? O that I could bathe myself in briny tears of evangelical repentance! O, how shall I believe in Jesus Christ, that I may receive remission of sins! Truth it is, sirs, you will never be filled till you be sensible of soul-emptiness; spiritual poverty is the prologue and preparative to true soul-plenty; gospel sorrow expands the soul, and so capacitates it for grace; the oil of grace is poured only into a contrite heart; the kingdom of God belongs to the *poor in spirit*, and we know, the best benefits of this kingdom are internal, as "righteousness, peace, and joy in the Holy Ghost;"* and these as a rich treasure replenish the penitent soul, for it is the sorrowful soul whom God doth replenish, Jer. xxxi. 25. Therefore, you are to endeavour to discover the nature of sin, and danger therein, the wrath of God hanging over your heads for it: if you were pricked in your hearts with a pinching pain, you would be restless till you had obtained an interest in Jesus Christ; if your souls were weary and heavy laden, you would not be content till you had laid the stress of all upon an infinite Saviour. If the Lord would help graceless sinners these two steps, to see that they are yet graceless, and to discern their misery in being so, that were a hopeful gradation towards conversion: did you see your state, you could not but bewail it, and make out for a change; and did you see the precious nature of the soul, and that grace which is to fill it, you would not be another day without it.

4. Empty thy heart of all corruption; oh, cleanse

* Deus oleum non infundit nisi in vas contritum.—*Bern.* Matt. v. 3. Rom. xiv. 17.

that filthy source of all sin, purge thyself from all filthiness both of flesh and spirit. Shake hands with that sin which forbids the banns of marriage betwixt Jesus Christ and thy soul: lay aside every weight, and the sin which doth so easily beset thee, and then lift up thine eyes and heart to Jesus Christ.* " Cleanse your hands, ye sinners; purify your hearts, ye doubleminded."† Empty this dirty house of thy heart, that the King of Glory may enter in; throw out the devil's household stuff, and make room for a new inhabitant. The vessel must be emptied, or it can never be filled with saving good; for that which is within, hinders any thing else entering:‡ and alas, the heart is full of vain conceits, and worldly thoughts, and impure lusts, which keep off good emotions and keep out good dispositions. Now, if a man purge himself from these, he shall be a vessel unto honour, sanctified, and meet for the Master's use, and prepared unto every good work, 2 Tim. ii. 21. Let me entreat you for the Lord's sake, and for your own soul's sake, to search and sweep every dusty corner of your defiled heart. Let not this train of graces and treasure of truths be always waiting your leisure, whilst you are wallowing in the puddle of sin, and swallowing down the devil's sweet, but dangerous pills of soul-murdering temptations. Oh, be willing to make this blessed change, to part with thy base lusts for a precious Christ, to forego soul-damning corruptions for soul-gladdening dispositions: if you cannot put off the whole body of sin, yet you are to cut off the members thereof, you ought indeed to stub up sin by the roots, but you may lop off its branches; you may abate sin in part by contrary actings; knowledge doth remove ignorance, as light doth

* Heb. xii. 1, 2. † James iv. 8.
‡ Intus existens prohibet extraneum.

darkness; grief abates pleasure, and fear, boldness in sinning; patience daunts passion, and fasting tames unruly lusts: these you may do, and these may be good preparatives for this treasure. Because, as one saith, when the strength of a fever is abated by physical means, a man is disposed towards health; * and ploughed ground is at least materially prepared for seed, though God is not bound then to sow the seeds of saving grace, yet thou hast encouragement, that thy labour shall not be in vain. Use these means and try the issue; endeavour "to cast off these works of darkness, and to put on the armour of light; yea, labour to put off the old man, and to put on the new;"† at least do what you can to wash your hearts from filthiness, that your vain thoughts may not lodge within you, Jer. iv. 14. that you may have a saving treasure of holy meditations.

5. Be gleaning in God's field, be filling your sacks in the divine granary of ordinances. The way for Ruth to be well laden was to glean in Boaz's field, among the sheaves near the reapers;‡ the Patriarchs must have recourse to Joseph's storehouse for provision; and where may we expect supply, but in gospel ordinances? those [*canales gratiæ*] channels of grace; the door-posts of wisdom, the garden where such precious spices grow, the orchard where the soul may be loaded with the fruits of righteousness. Ordinances are the Lord's camp, where this heavenly manna falls; they are the green pastures, where we may fill and feast our souls, the galleries where the king of heaven takes his walks,* and here the Christless may meet with him; this is like Solomon's house of the forest of Lebanon, built for an armory, where the

---

* See Morn. Lect. *p.*41. *Ser.* 2. † Rom. xiii. 12. Eph. iv. 22, 24.
‡ Ruth ii. 8. 17. ‖ Song vii. 5.

naked soul may be furnished with shields and spears; offensive and defensive weapons to fortify the soul against the fiercest onsets of the great Abaddon. If your souls be sick of love, here you may find flagons of precious liquor to revive your fainting spirits, dispensed by the Lord's stewards. If you sit under this apple-tree, you shall be under its shadow with great delight, and the fruit thereof will be sweet to your taste. O then seek Christ in the broad ways of public ordinances, and "go forth by these footsteps of the flock."* Search this pearl in the field of gospel-dispensations, and your souls shall be truly enriched thereby: it is by these ordinances, through which, as by golden pipes, that precious oil is conveyed to us from the fruitful olive, Jesus Christ.† O do not leave off ordinances, as some conceited professors that boast they are above them; for if you set the cistern above the cock, it will never be full; and therefore you must have a reverent esteem for the Lord's appointments. Prepare yourselves, and frequent soul-filling ordinances—live still within the sound of Aaron's bells, and beg of God that Aaron's rod may bring forth the buds of grace in your immortal souls. "The rod of Aaron," as one well observes,‡ "may signify the ministry, effective, as to the effects it produceth, by the blessing of God, bringing forth buds, blossoms, and ripe nuts, all at once: that is," saith he, "precious buds of grace, blossoms of heavenly joy, and holy fruits of righteousness and new obedience." Only let me entreat you to wait upon a heart-searching ministry, that the secrets of your heart may be manifest, and conscience may be pricked. Be not afraid of a Boanerges, but gladly welcome the sharp rebukes of your soul's

---

* Song ii. 5. verse 2. iii. 2. i. 8. † Zech. iv. 12
‡ Mr. Lee on Solomon's Temple, *cap.* 9. *p.* 266. Num. xvii. 8.

friends; it may be fittest for your sleepy or seared conscience. It is said of the almond tree, of which Aaron's rod was,* that the rind thereof is bitter, but the kernel is very delicious, and the oil pressed out of it very physical and of much virtue: just such are the chastising words of a round-dealing ministry; bitter at present, but profitable afterwards. And, observe it, they are ordinarily the soundest Christians that are trained under the most plain and piercing preaching; therefore, I entreat you, lay yourselves directly under the hammer of the word, to be framed by the Lord according to his will.

6. Study and improve free grace. Oh, let your thoughts dwell much upon God's infinite condescension and unlimited invitation of poor sinners. See what you derive from Isaiah lv. 1, John vii. 37, and Rev. xxii. 17. "Whosoever will, let him take the water of life freely;" there is no bar to your admission, but what yourselves make; Christ Jesus includes you in gospel tenders; Oh, do not exclude yourselves. The great Shepherd calleth his sheep by name, John x. 3. How is that, but by speaking expressly to their case? as if he should strike the troubled heart upon the shoulder and say, Here is comfort for thee; what if thy name be not there, yet the proposition is universal —" he that believeth shall be saved." Thousands of poor sinners have ventured their souls upon such a word, and never any miscarried that cast themselves into the arms of Christ; you have no reason to suspect acceptance if you come to him, you have all the grounds of encouragement imaginable. A physician offereth cure to all that will come, it were madness to stand off and say, I know not whether he intendeth it for me or not. If men were ready to perish in deep

* See Mr. Lee on Solomon's Temple, *cap.* 9. *p.* 266.

waters, and a boat should be offered to carry to land them that would come into it, it were an absurd thing to dispute whether it be for us. If a pardon come from the king for a company of condemned prisoners, and they shall all have benefit by it, if they will but accept of it, what madman would refuse it, and question whether the prince intend him particularly, when his name is included in the general grant. Surely men would not so fondly cast away themselves in temporal things, and who would be such a fool in the everlasting concernments of his precious soul? The way here is not to dispute, but believe. Is not Jesus Christ our souls' physician, and are not we sick? Is not the gospel-design of grace a plank after shipwreck, and are not we drowning? Are not we condemned malefactors at the bar of God's justice? and doth not God graciously tender to us the redemption so dearly purchased by our precious Saviour? and why then should we forsake our own mercies—why will you be cruel to your own souls? If it were in temporal things, you would put out the hand and be very ready for receiving: if you sit at a feast, and there stand a dish upon the table that is agreeable to your palate, though all the company be free to make use of it, yet you say, Here is a dish for me, and you think it good manners to feed heartily upon it, without scruples and disputes of being welcome, since you were freely invited by your generous friend.—Our Lord Jesus hath made "a feast of fat things,"* and hath bidden his guests; he invites you to eat and drink abundantly: O do not you make apologies for your absence from this gospel feast;

* Isa. xxv. 6. Prov. ix. 1, 2. Cant. v. 1, 2. The porch of the Temple was open and without doors on all sides, to shew the open heartedness of God's grace under the Gospel.—*See Mr. Lee on Solomon's Temple, cap.* 9. *p.* 210.

when he invites, do not you question whether he means as he speaks, but fall to, and make a long arm, and take your share of this provision; I can assure you, he hath not an evil eye, he doth not grudge you this heavenly manna; nay, rather than your souls shall famish, he freely gives you his flesh and blood, to nourish your poor immortal souls. Oh, you that have torn his flesh with the teeth of cruel persecution of himself and his members—you, that have trampled upon his blood with the feet of an odious and abominable conversation—*you*, he calls to " eat his flesh and drink his blood," by faith in him, and improvement of him, that your souls may live—you that have despised riches of grace, treasures of grace are opened for *you* —you that have fought against Jesus Christ all your days, with all your might, he invites *you* to be his soldiers, and he will graciously entertain you as if you had never been in rebellion against the King of kings! Will not this melt aud move you to yield yourselves unto your dear and loving Lord? I beseech you, take these things into your serious thoughts, and accept of Jesus Christ; only presume not by dreaming of application of Christ, without separation from sin. Take a whole Christ, to sanctify thy heart as well as justify thy person, to purify conscience as well as pacify wrath —take Christ aright, mistake him not, lest you be wofully mistaken to your eternal undoing. You need a whole Christ, and a broken heart will not be content with a divided Saviour; it is the whorish heart that will divide; a sincere soul must have all, he needs grace as well as peace. Indeed, there is nothing of Christ useless; every part of this Lamb of God is of absolute necessity to the indigent soul, and true faith takes him in all his mediatory latitude; it is as dangerous to divide Christ believed on, as the heart believing; therefore stir up yourselves to a due consideration of free grace, and application of it in the right gospel way of *believing.*

7. Be humble petitioners at the throne of grace; beg hard at the gates of mercy, for a large dole of heavenly riches. *Ask;* if that will not do, *seek;* if *seeking* avail not, *knock,* and you shall be sure to prevail. The choicest riches of heaven may be had for asking, and if they be not worth that, they are worth nothing. God loves importunate beggars; there is liberty of petitioning in the court of heaven; it is no bad manners there to heap suit upon suit; the oftener you come the welcomer you are: " He will give the Holy Spirit to them that ask him;"* and that is a good thing in God's account, and should be in ours, for it enricheth the soul with an abundant treasure. O beg the Spirit of God! "open your mouths wide, and he will fill them." We should think ourselves made for ever, if we might but have what we can ask: but the truth is, we cannot ask so much as God is able and willing to give us, Ephes. iii. 19, 20. Therefore, sirs, stir up your hearts to desire grace; open these windows of your souls; lift up yourselves to God upon these wings of desires, and fetch a treasure from heaven into your hearts. Strong desires are real prayers,† and shall prevail; for they not only capacitate the soul for grace, but lay it directly under the promise, Matt. v. 6. Desire forms the soul's pullies, that wind it up to heaven; and it is the soul's stomach that receives heaven into the Christian: therefore, pray hard. Do not you see and hear the pathetical cries of poor beggars, backed with rhetorical arguments of sores and nakedness, at your doors and in the road? Go you

* Compare Matt. vii. 11, with Luke xi. 13.
† Mens orat, lingua loquitur.

and do likewise; fill the ears of God with mighty cries; take no denial, give God no rest, till you have your share in spiritual blessings. Tell God you will not be put off with the transient good things of this wicked world; tell him he hath better things than these to bestow upon children; crowns and golden mines are but crumbs cast to dogs—tell him thou comest to him for a child's portion; and if he will but give thee a treasure of grace in thy heart, and reserve a treasure of glory for thee in heaven, thou wilt refer matters of the world to him, and he shall do with those things as he sees good, whether he give thee less or more of the " Mammon of unrighteousness," any thing or nothing. Tell the Lord, he hath entrusted these talents of grace with unworthy creatures and great sinners, and if thou be worse than any that ever yet partook thereof, yet tell him, he doth not sell these precious commodities to men deserving, but give them to necessitous sinners, and thou art one that needs as much as any—tell him, thou never yet heardest that he refused to give them to any that sought them for Christ's sake, with a broken heart, above worldly treasures—tell him, that himself hath *promised*, his Son hath *purchased*, his Spirit will *freely convey* these gospel riches into thy heart, and if he "will but speak the word," the thing shall be quickly done. Tell the Lord, yet once again, what a monument he will thereby raise to his own glory; if he will fill thy soul with this treasure, he will thereby " make known the riches of his glory on a poor vessel of mercy."* And whereas now thou art a useless vessel, wherein the Lord can have no pleasure, by whom he can have no profit nor honour; yet if he will be pleased to own and crown thy soul with saving grace, he may then take delight in thee and rest in his

* Rom. ix. 23.

love towards thee; and when he "hath blessed thee with spiritual blessings in heavenly things," then thou wilt be "to the praise of the glory of his grace," Eph. i. 3, 6. Thus come, thus pour out your hearts like water before the Lord, lie day and night at the throne of grace; it is worth all this pains in seeking. Will not you do as much as Esau for his blessing? He took pains to hunt for venison, that Isaac's soul might bless him, and missing of it, he lift up his voice, and "cried with a great and exceeding bitter cry," redoubling his request with an affectionate echo, "Bless me, even me also, O my father!"[*] The words are very remarkable, and have as notable an emphasis as almost is to be found in Scripture; and will you be worse than profane Esau? O sirs, if you knew your soul's want, and the worth of divine things, your prayers would have another accent, and be put up with more fervency than usually they are, and you might have hopes to speed. So saith the wise man—"If thou criest after knowledge, and liftest up thy voice for understanding; if thou seekest her as silver, and searchest for her as for hidden treasures; then shalt thou understand the fear of the Lord, and find the knowledge of God," Prov. ii. 3—5.

Before I break off this subject, let me press a little upon you the wholesome counsel of our dear Saviour. "I counsel thee to buy of me gold tried in the fire, that thou mayest be rich," &c. Rev. iii. 18. Consider

First,—What is your estate naturally, and without Christ; you may imagine great things, but God knows there is no such matter, as he saith to this self-conceited church of Laodicea, "Thou sayest I am rich—and knowest not that thou art wretched, miserable, poor, blind, naked," verse 17. He heaps up many words to

[*] Gen. xxvii. 34, 38. ויצעק צעק גדלה ומרה עד־מאד.

aggravate their beggarly state. The graceless soul is, 1. *Wretched*,* that is, pressed with sickness, misery, and calamity, overwhelmed with reproach, overthrown in conflicts, cannot stir hand or foot for God, being always overborne by his master, Satan. 2. He is *miserable*;† that is, though he stand in absolute need of divine help and mercy, yet he is unworthy and destitute of it; God will have no mercy on this woful object, so that the forlorn soul may be called *Loruhamah*.‡ 3. The sinner is *poor*;‖ that is, in extreme necessity, hath not a bit or morsel of brown bread, but begs from door to door; these poor souls are ready to famish and pine, and shall have no relief. 4. *Blind*;§ this is a sad aggravation, when a man must wander for bread to relieve his soul, yet knows not whither to go, nay, knows not that he needs to go; is miserable, and knows it not; yea further, he is 5. *Naked*;¶ exposed to the injuries of weather, and lashes of men. Thus is the poor sinner destitute of the wedding garment—Christ's righteousness, having only a naked skin to shield him against the wrath of God, the curse of the law, and tormentings of conscience; and what can this avail the wretched miscreant? Let a man be the richest potentate under heaven, yet if he be graceless, he is thus wretchedly poor; no tongue can express the misery of an unregenerate person. There are seven words in Hebrew, that signify poor, and they are all applicable to a poor creature without Christ and grace. 1. He is straitened†† in the abundance of outward sufficiency, with a

---

* Ὁ ταλαίπωρος, à ταλαω suffero, et πῶρος luctus.

† Ὁ ἐλεεινός. ‡ Isa. xxvii. 11. Hosea i. 6.

‖ Πτωχὸς, qui ostiatim petit eleemosynam. § Τυφλὸς.

¶ Γυμνὸς, à γυῖα μόνα ἐχων, solam cutem habens.

†† עני pauper.

griping conscience and avaricious grasping after shadows. 2. His goods are diminished,* and he is become a bankrupt in Adam, vain inventions have wasted a fair estate, and daily weaken the relics of natural light. 3. He is oppressed † with intolerable labour, grinding in the devil's mill, toiling in worse than Egyptian thraldom, without any relief for his famishing soul. 4. He is of a dejected ‡ mind, like the serpent, going with his bellow on the dust, a degenerate plant, the worst part of the creation, the basest of creatures, the tail, and not the head. 5. Besides all this he is afflicted || spiritually with suits, hatred, exile, imprisonment; God himself commenceth suit against him, hates him, banisheth him from his presence, delivers him over into Satan's hands, by whom he is led captive at his pleasure. 6. He is always needy, § desires all things, but hath nothing; cannot be content, snatching on the right and left hand, yet is never satisfied; unbridled in motion towards a wrong object, that increaseth his thirst. 7. He is empty ¶ of virtues, which are the riches of the mind, for though he may have some moral accomplishments, yet they are but [*splendida peccata*] mere splendid and shining sins, without grace; and also he is destitute of the world; for having a curse and not God's blessing therewith, it doth him no good; nay, it is his bane, being both a snare and a poison, aggravating sin, and increasing his torment, having a sadder account to make another day. This and much worse is the condition of a graceless heart, from which it is counselled! Oh, who would tarry one hour in such a wretched state? The Lord be merciful to you, and pluck you out of the Sodom of unregeneracy, lest you perish eternally.

* דל perditus.   † דך attritus.   ‡ מר attenuatus.
|| חלכה afflictus.   § אביון egenus.   ¶ דק vacuus.

Secondly,—Consider the state to which you are counselled; for this end observe, 1. Who is your Counsellor,* Jesus Christ, who indeed is the only Counsellor, the wisdom of the Father, who best understands the law of heaven, and what will stand you in stead in the court of God; he that might command you into hell, doth counsel you for heaven; he that died for you, opens his heart to you; he that will speak to the Father for you, entreats you to make use of him as your only Advocate. 2. Consider what and who you are and have been, that are thus counselled; enemies to his grace, in whom he might glorify his justice, and cast you headlong into the pit, and there is an end of you; persons that have been a provocation all your days, that have resisted, quenched, grieved, vexed his Holy Spirit, trampled Christ under foot, served Satan and yourselves; behold he pours out his words unto you, yea, he offers to pour his Spirit into you :† it is the voice of an infinite God, to mortal, sinful man—" Unto you, O men, I call, and my voice is to the sons of men," Prov. viii. 4. And, 3. Consider what he counsels to—it is to a rich and precious purchase. O ye great purchasers, here is a bargain for you! not of a piece of land, but a kingdom—not an earthly, but a heavenly kingdom—not a fair house to live in here, but eternal mansions in the heavens. Come, strike up the bargain, bid freely; but what must you give? money, or money's worth?† No, worldly treasures are dross here; money has no ascendancy; the price is fallen to just nothing—shall I say nothing? You are to give away your sins, and give God yourselves; yet that is no price, because it bears no proportion to such

---

* Isaiah ix. 5.   † Prov. i. 23.

‡ Isaiah lv. 1, 2. Jubet emere non pretio, sed mendicorum more, precibus emendicare apud Deum.—*Par. in loc.*

receipts. Grace and glory are God's gifts, yet God puts this honour upon such as honour him by believing, as though they buy what they enjoy. Let every soul make this cheap purchase. But if it be so cheap, is it not of little worth? Will it not prove accordingly? What is the purchase, and what is it good for? That brings in four things, namely, the things purchased are absolutely necessary and beneficial—1. *Gold.* 2. *Raiment.* 3. *Eye-salve.* 4. Every one accomplisheth a notable end to make rich cloth and recover sight: we cannot be without any of these. I cannot enlarge, take a specimen. 1. This *gold tried in the fire*, is Scripture truths; and we must by all means buy truth, by no means sell it;* and "the words of God are as silver tried in a furnace of earth, purified seven times;" therefore David loved the word "above fine gold."† I told you, we must make a treasure of this refined gold of Scripture truths; but I rather understand this of the tried gold of precious graces, especially faith,‡ which being tried in the furnace of affliction, is much more precious than gold that perisheth. This indeed makes the soul truly rich; as money answers all things, so this will bring us through all conditions; and this is to be had of Christ,∥ therefore buy or beg it of him, and believe in him for obtaining more of the riches of grace. 2. *White raiment* is the robe of Christ's righteousness, the garments of our elder Brother, fine linen, clean and white; for whiteness is a token of purity, and here is an allusion to the Roman candidates, that, seeking dignity or magistracy, came forth conspicuously into the assembly, thereby signifying that integrity which became those honourable offices. So the saints

* Prov. xxiii. 23.   † Psalm xii. 6. . Psalm cxix. 127.
‡ 1 Pet, i. 7.
∥ Hoc μονοπώλιον est Christi, extra quod nulla est salus.

must have the upper garment of imputed righteousness, and closer raiment of inherent holiness, of both which it is said, (Rev. xvi. 15.) "Blessed is he that watcheth and keepeth his garments, lest he walk naked, and they see his shame," that is, the filth and guilt of sin. 3. *Eye-salve;* an ointment that purgeth away the rheum and dimness of the eyes. This grace banisheth the dark mists from the soul, and makes it see clearly the state of our hearts, the evil of sin, and excellency of the things of God. A right understanding of divine mysteries is a mercy worth praying for and prizing. This is the only learning of importance; book learning and brain knowledge are not worth naming in comparison of this; for this "anointing will teach you of all things," 1 John ii. 27.

Well, sirs, I am loth to leave this subject, till I have prevailed with you to make it your main business to look after this divine treasure. O that Jesus Christ were formed in your hearts, and the life of grace were begun in your souls! If that be wrought, you will be fit for all conditions, without it you will be fit for nothing, and nothing can suit you; you will make no shift in a hard time, and you know not how to improve happy times; a day of affliction will swallow you up —temptation will overthrow you—mercies will increase your guilt—judgments drive you to despair— you cannot buckle to the easiest duties, nor apply the sweetest promises, and how will you come off in the great day of accounts—" whither will you go for help, and where will you leave your glory ?"

CHAP. IX.

DIRECTIONS RELATIVE TO GOOD THOUGHTS.

My principal design is to lay down a directory for the the people of God; and because this is a business of great moment, consequence, and concernment, to have, keep, use, improve, and increase a heart-treasure, I shall be the larger upon it, and rank what I have to say under these four topics or heads, viz:—

I. By what means shall a soul be furnished with a treasure of good thoughts?

II. In what way shall a Christian lay up truths, graces, comforts, and experiences?

III. How may a Christian preserve and increase this treasure?

IV. How he must draw out, and make use of this treasure.

To begin with the first, which is this: What course shall a Christian take to hoard up a treasure of holy thoughts? This is the *good treasure* chiefly intended in the text, and I shall be the larger upon this head. To this end I shall propound these ten directions:

1. Work upon your hearts the reality and rarity of the things of God: get thoroughly convinced that there are such things to be had, and that they are worth laying up. You must look upon divine things as infallibly certain, and incomparably excellent. Those were accounted sensual and brutish Philosophers, that (following Epicurus) placed man's chief happiness in matters of sense, such as profit, pleasure, and honour. But those were the most sublime, and in a sort, divine, that placed the *summum bonum*, or chief good, in what is

above, or opposite to sense—as in the good things of the mind, and moral virtue. Can heathens, by the light of nature and reason, see a reality and excellency in things invisible to sense? and shall not Christians much more? It is a shame for a saint enlightened by the Spirit, to be so blear-eyed, as not to see afar off, or view spiritual objects.* It is the duty and property of a Christian to overlook things that are seen, and intently to behold things not seen.—2 Cor. iv. 18. O, sirs, could you as really see with a spiritual eye, spiritual good, as you can with your natural eyes behold corporeal objects, what an advantage would it be to you! Could you make gospel-mysteries and mercies as attractive to yourselves as a rich man's bags and lands are to him, what an exceeding help would it be! This made Moses forsake the visible glory of Egypt, and endure intolerable things in the wilderness, for he saw him that was invisible.—Heb. xi. 27. Thus Christians are to realize divine things, and account highly of them, for no man will treasure up that which he accounts not as most excellent. The making light of gospel-grace, is the great reason why so many go without it; so it is said in Matt. xxii. 5. the bidden guests made light of it; or, as as the word† signifies, they would not take it into their care and thoughts; they looked upon it as not worth looking after. I am persuaded that unbelief, or want of a thorough, settled and effectual persuasion of the truth of the gospel, and of what real good is contained in the promises, is the root of that gross atheism and wilful neglect existing in the world. You are to give your full assent to the things of God; to venture your souls upon Scripture principles. God's *ipse dixit*‡ must be instead of all the

* 1 Cor. ii. 10. 2 Pet. i. 9. † 'Αμελήσαντες, curam non habentes.
‡ "Thus saith the Lord."

demonstrations in the world. You must centre and anchor yourselves upon that impregnable rock, *scriptum est*, it is written—and though you cannot find a reason of the things believed, yet this is to be accounted a sufficient reason for your belief, namely, God hath spoken them, and you may safely trust your souls upon his word; for he cannot lie. He is wiser than to be deceived—and he is more righteous than to deceive. You may safely lay the stress of your souls upon his word. O, that I could persuade you to this! Do not put off these things with a slight notion and conjectural opinion, but advance " to the riches of the full assurance of understanding."* That is a high word, but you cannot be too sure about these things. Your strongest confidence may be battered; your persuasion may stagger; and, therefore, get as well-rooted as you can, for according to the degrees of your affiance, will your graces and duties ebb and flow, rise or fall. And you must not only believe the truth of them, but urge them upon your own hearts. As Paul saith, so say you: "What shall I say to these things?"† Are they true, or are they not? Are they worth thinking of, or are they not? Have I an interest in them, or have I not? O, my soul! let me press thee to the serious view of heavenly objects. They are choice things and deserve our study; rare things, wherein few have actual interest, yet absolutely necessary, wherein all must have a share, or they are undone for ever.

2. Reserve thy heart for, and resign it up wholly to, God. He calls for it, " My son, give me thy heart," Prov. xxiii. 26. Let not thy dearest comforts, relations, or companions have a predominating influence in thy soul. This is the chief tribute that is due to God. Rob not God of any part of it. Clip not the King of

* Col. ii. 2. † Rom. viii. 31.

heaven's coin; but you may and must direct your hearts solely and wholly to God, and things above, as the lines go to the centre. David had set his affections on the house of his God, and therefore his thoughts were vehemently carried out after those things, that made him offer so much, and offer so wilingly.* The same man of God prays, Psal. lxxxvi. 11. " Unite my heart to fear thy name." The word† imports a making his heart one. He would not have a heart, and a heart. A divided heart is no God-fearing heart. He that would patch up a contentment both with God and the creature, shall go without a solid treasure, for the creature cannot, and God will not fill such a heartless heart. Besides, love, saith one, is for one object; like a pyramid, it ends in a point; affection is weakened by dispersion, as a river by being turned into many channels. You cannot serve two masters. He that would have a treasure of any thing intends that only; he contracts his affairs into a narrow compass, and makes that [τό ἔργον] his only work. So must you knit your thoughts together, and fix them upon this sole object. It is a dangerous thing to divide the affections betwixt God and the world, like Judah, that sware by the Lord,‡ and by Malcham, or their king. But God doth make account, that that soul is not at all for him, which is not *altogether* for him. Those nations feared not the Lord that joined their serving idols, with fearing the true God.—2 Kings, xvii. 33, 34. There can no more be two chief delights in one heart, than two suns in one firmament; those spirits are winding and crooked, that are like that haven we read of, Acts, xxvii. 12. lying directly towards two opposite points of heaven.‖ Cyrus took

* 1 Chron. xxix. 3.   † יחד unicum fac.   ‡ Zeph. i. 5.
‖ Mr Burrough's Heart-div. p. 7.

Babylon, by dividing the river. The devil soon surpriseth us if he can but divide our hearts. If our hearts be divided, we shall be found faulty.* O let us take heed of being voluntary cripples, to halt between two opinions.† Let us not dismember ourselves by being half and hollow-hearted. God is infinite; Christ is complete; spiritual things are most excellent; and these deserve the whole heart. Therefore, resign up yourselves unto God resolvedly, unreservedly, and universally. Fear not, as he findeth his life that loseth it for God, so he only receiveth his heart as good, and worth having, that giveth it to God, for he takes it to make it better, as even a heathen could say to his scholar, that had nothing to give him but himself.‡ Give God your hearts, and he will furnish them with a treasure. Commit your souls into his hands, and he will both commit a treasure to you, and will also keep that which you commit to him, till the great day of his illustrious appearing.‖ He will preserve both the case and the jewel, soul and body; the least atom of dust shall not be lost. How much more will he graciously preserve that good work of grace, and those fruits of the Spirit, that he hath committed to you; therefore, I beseech you take my counsel in this: keep no corner of your hearts for a stranger, but yield yourselves to the Lord. Deliver the keys of your hearts into his hands. Let the King of glory enter in, and his glorious train will fill the temple of your souls.§ He is a treasure wherever he comes. Christians are called God's house, his temple;¶ it is, therefore, gross sacrilege to rob him of his house, or to keep him out of doors. "The soul of a believer," saith an ancient, "is the

---

* Hosea x. 2. † 1 Kings xviii. 21.
‡ Eâ conditione te accipio, ut te tibi reddam meliorem.—*Socrat.*
‖ 2 Tim. i. 12. § Isa. vi. 1. ¶ Heb. iii. 6. 1 Cor. vi. 19.

true temple of Christ; adorn and furnish that—offer gifts to that—receive Christ into it."* Herein consists the sum and marrow of our religion, namely, a heart totally dedicated unto God; and that is the second help to get a treasure in the heart.

3. Live by faith upon Jesus Christ. The lively acting of faith upon the Mediator of the covenant, will fill your souls with saving and savoury incomes. God hath appointed Christ to be the storehouse of his church. Now faith is the hand to fetch supplies from Christ to the heart. By faith is the soul engrafted into this true olive, and sucks fatness from it.† Christ dwells in the heart by faith, ‡ and still more of Christ is fetched in by faith. All the means of a Christian's life is by the exercise of faith; therefore is the righteous said to live by his faith, because it lives and feeds the soul upon Christ. Faith empties the heart, and so makes room for Jesus Christ, and then lays hold of him and compels him to turn into the heart. And our dear Saviour is willingly conquered with the strength of faith. Faith is the key that opens the chest where treasures lie, and the hand that brings them into the heart. Faith opens the heart to receive riches of grace, and that man hath a closed heart that hath not the key of faith.‖ O, get a great measure of faith! for the more faith you have the richer you are; for faith itself is a precious treasure, and it doth all for enriching the soul. Truths cannot be a treasure in our minds to profit our hearts, except mixed with this precious ingredient, faith. § All graces of the

---

* Verum Christi templum anima credentis est, illam exorna, illam vesti, illi offer donaria, in illâ Christum suscipe.—*Hieron. ad Paulin. tom.* 1. *p.* 105.   † Rom. xi. 17, 20.   ‡ Eph. iii. 17.

‖ Cor clausum habet, qui clavem fidei non habet.

§ Heb. iv. 2.   2 Pet. i. 5.

spirit attend this queen and sovereign grace of faith. Experiences cannot be gathered or improved without faith, and that comfort is but a fancy that is not ushered in by the assurance of faith. Faith is the great bucket to draw water out of the wells of salvation, and the more faith you bring, the more you receive.* Well then, would you have your hearts stored with a treasure? strive to increase your faith, and let the Lord Jesus be the direct object of your faith. It is he alone that hath the key of David, that doth both open heaven to us, and a heavenly treasure for us.† Since the fall we have no converse with God, or communication from him, but through a mediator. " It is a terrible thing," said Luther, " even to think of God out of Christ." You must " honour the Son as you honour the Father," and as you believe in God, so must you also act faith upon Christ God-man ;—that as our nature in Christ's person is filled with all that poor souls can want, so from that fulness we may receive all things needful for our being and well-being in grace. O, stir up and awake your faith ! Come, poor soul, reach hither thy hand of faith, " and thrust it into thy Saviour's pierced side,"‡ and there thou mayest feel, and thence fetch abundant fruits of love : " Be not faithless but believing." Do not dam up the channels of grace by unbelief. Do not forsake thy own mercies, by being shy and fearful to venture ; thou canst lose nothing,—thou mayest get much by one single act of faith. O, sirs, one pure act of a lively faith will bring you in more treasure, than many hours tugging and struggling in duties and performances. Nothing in the world doth shoot a bar, and bolt the door betwixt Christ and the

* Quantum illuc fidei capacis afferimus, tantum inde gratiæ inundantis haurimus.—*Cyp. Epist. ad Horat. p.* 108.
† Rev. iii. 7.   ‡ John xx. 27.

heart, but unbelief; if thou canst believe all things are possible, but unbelief hinders the working of miracles* and operations of grace. Away with all distrust, set afoot the precious grace of faith,—break through the quarrelings of thy unbelieving heart,—lie low under the sad sense of thine insufficiency, and sweet apprehension of Christ's all-sufficiency. Humbly stretch forth the trembling hand of thy weak faith, though thou hast many misgivings of spirit,—yet say, with tears, " Lord, I believe, help thou mine unbelief." I am no more able of myself to put forth one saving act of justifying faith, than I am to fulfil all righteousness, and keep the whole law;—but the grace of the gospel hath undertaken to do that which it requireth to be done. Lord, I roll myself upon thee. I come to thee by faith. Do not cast me off. Do not cast me out as a broken vessel, wherein there is no pleasure, but fill this empty vessel of my broken heart with abundant incomes, which will redound to thy glory, and my soul's abundant comfort. This do and prosper,—thus believe, and be thou filled, poor, wanting soul, " For whatsoever you ask believing, you shall receive."— Matth. xxi. 22.

4. Cherish in your hearts the grace of love. That noble grace is of an expatiating and extensive nature. Heaven is the fittest room for its exercise, and eternity for its duration. He that loves much will not be content with a little, and God will not put him off with a scanty portion. The more the soul is filled with love, the more it is filled with God, " for God is love,"† and can a man have a better treasure than God himself? Now if you love God, " he will come in unto you, and make his abode with you," John, xiv. 23, and can you wish a better treasure? Love makes room in the

---

* Mark vi. 5.   † 1 John iv. 8.

heart for more grace. He that loveth much, because much is forgiven him, shall have more given. Indeed, that expression in 2 Cor. v. 14, seems to denote the contracting nature of love, " The love of God constraineth us," [συνέχει]* straiteneth, keeps us in; but that is from other things, that the soul may have freer scope for God. This love diverts the affections from running in any other channel but towards Jesus Christ. It captivates the soul for Christ, and forceth it to do and endure, any thing for him whom the soul loveth. The grace of love widens the arms to embrace Jesus Christ, enlargeth the heart to entertain him, and spiriteth the hands to act for him. Christ Jesus rides in a glorious triumphant chariot. Whether it refer to his personal character, or mystical body,†—his flesh and human nature, or his church, which he fills with his presence, I dispute not; but sure I am, the midst thereof is "paved with love," Cant. iii. 10. Certainly, a soul decorated with the sparkling gems of love is the fittest receptacle for Jesus Christ. He that is love itself doth most freely commit the largest treasure to a loving disciple, as he bequeathed his dear mother to John,‡ when he was breathing out his last upon the bitter cross, and after his death entrusted him with the Revelation; ‖ yea, him only, with a description of the state of the church to the end of the world. O, how freely do a loving Saviour, and loving soul, open their hearts to each other! Like entire and ancient friends meeting,—who let out themselves in ample evidences, and reciprocal acts of love. So here, the pure flame of a saint's love mounts up to Christ, and there meeting with that hea-

* Ut non possint non velle extrema quæque pro Christo perpeti.—*Aret. in loc.*

† See Ainsworth on the place, and Brightman.

‡ John xix. 26. ‖ Rev. i. 1.

venly element of perfect love, brings more down into the soul, and still these continued sallies of love to God, bring in successive incomes and increases of grace. Every act of love exhales away some corrupt vapours, and dilates the soul's faculties, that it may be fit for the reception of more grace. Yea, love sets the soul on edge for more, and makes it as insatiable as it is unwearied in painful endeavours. "Faith worketh by love," that is, as by its hand to act for God; and, indeed, love, in a sort, worketh by faith, as its hand to fetch all from God. Faith sets love on to crave, and love engageth faith to derive more grace from God; and as love helps the soul to a treasure of graces, so of truths. Love to truths makes the soul look upon them as a precious depositum; to think much of them, and thus rivet them and clench them fast in the heart by meditation. Love makes a man " contend for the faith" by disputing and dying, if God call him to it. Hence it is, that love is one of those hands that " hold fast the form of sound words."—2 Tim. i. 13. But " he that receives not the truth in love,"* will never make it a treasure, but will sell it for a lust, and embrace a lie; therefore, sirs, I entreat you work up this grace,—stir up your hearts to think of the love of Christ. Blow up this spark to a flame. Content not yourselves with a low degree of love to God. Love him with an intensive, extensive, appreciative love. Let your measure of love to him be beyond measure. Let your hearts ascend to him in this holy flame of entire love. Love him more than your enjoyments,—more than your relations,—more than yourselves.† I shall say no

* 2 Thess. xii. 10.
† See this subject handled in Mr. Williams' transcend. of Christ's Love, on Eph. iii. 19, pp. 73 — 145. " Plus quam tua, plus quam tuos, plus quam te;" vid. ibid. p. 114, very fully. Morn. Lect. Serm. 9, p. 186. Dr. Reynolds on Psal. 110.

more on this ordinary, yet very necessary subject; because many have done so worthily herein. Read them.

5. Walk humbly with your God. A hint may be given respecting a close walk with God, but I shall speak most of that soul-enriching grace of humility. O Christians, the best means of edification is a holy conversation. God communicates secrets, and solace to them that walk with him. A man of a well-ordered conversation shall see God's salvation.* A master will entrust a faithful, careful, painful servant with a larger talent,† for such a one is a credit to his master, and promotes his designs. Bringing forth much fruit glorifies God and edifies man, and surely the Lord will dignify such fruitful vines with more care in dressing, and yet more of his blessing to help their abundant fruit-bearing; those shall have more clear discoveries of God's will, who carefully do it; and such as do his commandments have right to the tree of life,—that they may come to it when they please, and eat abundantly, and live for ever. There is an incomparable advantage in close-walking. In keeping the commandments there is this reward, that every act of obedience doth increase ability to obey. Every step reneweth strength. Saints go from strength to strength, for the way of the Lord is strength to the upright. Nothing evidenceth and increaseth grace so much as holiness; therefore, as he that hath called you is holy, so be you holy, in all manner of conversation; and let me persuade you to be very humble. God gives more grace to the humble; humility is not only a grace, but a vessel to receive more, the high and holy God fills the humble and lowly heart. The King of heaven loves to walk upon this blessed pavement. " Blessed are the

* Psal. L. 23.   † Matth. xxv. 21.

poor in spirit, for theirs is the kingdom of heaven,* and such a soul is the fittest receptacle for the precious riches of this heavenly kingdom. Much of the riches of the ancients consisted in their garments, and a Christian's treasure lies much in his vesture, some whereof is his larger upper coat; that is, Christ's righteousness imputed, which covers all defects and imperfections. Some are closer garments, girded to the soul by the girdle of truth and sincerity. These are the garments of sanctification; one choice part whereof is humility, 1 Pet. v. 5. " Be clothed with humility."† Some think the word imports what as a string or ribband ties together the precious pearls of divine graces; these adorn the soul, and if this string break they are all scattered. Humility is the knot of every virtue,— the ornament of every grace. Hence I have read a quotation out of Basil, who calls humility [θησαυροφυλάκιον παντος αγαθου] the storehouse or magazine of all good. Would to God we were all humble and holy walkers, and we should quickly have our hearts furnished with a treasure! Consecration in the time of the law was by filling the hand, and he that is consecrated to the Lord shall have his heart filled, especially they that are emptied of all self-conceit, shall be filled with much of God's fulness. Valley-souls are usually covered over with a rich harvest of precious fruits.‡ Humility is likewise a fit disposition for entertaining divine truths, these choice grafts will like best in a low ground.‖ A meek soul will bid truths welcome; for an humble heart looks upon every truth of God as infinitely above

* John xv. John vii. 17. Rev. xxii. 14. Psal. xix. 11. Psal. lxxxiv. 7. Prov. x. 29. Jam. iv. 6. Isa. lvii. 15. Mat. v. 3.

† Τὴν ταπεινοφροσύνην ἐγκομβώσασθε, humilitatem animi vobis infixam habete: *Eras.* on κόμβος, a knot, vid. *Leigh Crit.*

‡ Psalm lxv. 13. ‖ Jam. i. 21.

itself, and, therefore, falls down under it, and saith, "Speak, Lord, for thy servant heareth." An humble soul owns the authority of God in his word, wherever it finds it, whoever brings it, so that even a "little child may lead him"* any whither with a twine-thread of Scripture discoveries. But proud men and truth can never hit it, for they think scorn to put their necks under the yoke of truth, and it will have the victory where it lodgeth. Those were proud men that would not obey truth in Jeremiah's mouth,† and therefore must that prophet take down their crests before they could be right disciples of truth, Jer. xiii. 15. " Hear ye, give ear, be not proud." And observe this, a proud man is always on the losing hand, both in the account of God and man, and in his natural or acquired accomplishments. The more a man conceits to himself some imaginary attainments, the more he loseth. The stomach may be so stuffed with noxious things that a man cannot eat; or swelled with flatulency, which may prove dangerous. This, however, is not a right fulness, but a disordered state. Just thus is it with men's souls. The swelling disease hinders health by either truths or graces. O, therefore, be you humble, self-denying souls; sensible of your own defects. Be nothing in your own eyes, and you shall be a temple for the God of all grace to abide in, and to walk constantly in; yea, he will fill you with abundance of grace here and glory hereafter.

6. Be much in secret prayer. Pray much and pray in secret: a word on both. O, pray without ceasing! ‡ that is, keep a constant praying disposition, and lay hold on every fit season for that duty. While prayer standeth still, the trade of religion standeth still, and there is nothing got. All comes into the soul by this door.

* Isa. xi. 6. † Jer. xliii. 2. ‡ 1 Thess. v. 17.

It is good for a Christian to keep up set and stated times of prayer. Daniel and David prayed three times a day, in extraordinary cases seven times a day.* It is not lost labour to be much on our knees. We cannot go to God too often. I am sure not oftener than we shall be welcome if we pray aright, for the holy of holies is ever open, and our High Priest ever lives to make intercession for us; prayer was made in the Jewish temple service morning and evening, and we must be constant and instant in prayer, † as the hunting dog that will not cease following the game till he have got it; so must we pursue the Lord, and persevere with strength, till we have obtained what we want. There is a kind of omnipotence in prayer; as it was said of Luther, he could do with God, even what he would. At present I would advise all Christians to keep up a constant set time of prayer. What if thou gettest little thereby? yet, wait on God still. Tradesmen will go to markets and fairs, and set open their shop doors and windows, though there be little to be done or gotten many times; so let the Christian keep this market of holy duties, and go upon the exchange to spy what good bargain he can meet with for his soul. Learn to maintain commerce with heaven still, lest you lose your custom. Keep canonical hours as it were of prayer, though your hearts be often out of frame. Venture upon duty, and try what the Lord will do with you. It is the folly of our trifling spirits to put off duty, when our hearts are not in tune, with expectation that they will be in a better frame another time. But do we think that one sin will excuse another? or that we

* Dan. vi. 10. Psal. lv. 17. Psal. cxix. 164.

† Rom. xii. 12. Τῇ προσευχῇ προσκαρτεροῦντες, in oratione perdurantes.—*Beza.* Continue with strength: ἀ καρτεῖν, id est, fortiter tolerare.—*Leigh's Crit. Sac.*

shall be better fitted by a present neglect? No, certainly. We ought to stir up ourselves to take hold on God, for why should Satan be gratified by a total forbearance? Will not disuse make us lother to go to God another time? Yea, have we not found it in Scripture and experience, that a dead and discouraged entrance upon duty hath increased to sweet enlargements, and ravishments of spirit? Search and see. Usually a heart-engagement hath ended in a heart-enlargement, and God-enjoyment. God will bring an engaged heart nearer himself.—Jer. xxx. 21. None ever lost their labour in struggling with their untoward hearts. Oh, Christians, be sure you be found in prayer, though you come hardly to it, and have much ado to keep at it, and have more hazard to get something by it; though with Jonathan and his armour bearer you clamber up the hill on your hands and knees, and fight when you mount the top; yet, you shall get the victory, and the spoils of such a conflict will be the most enriching. One Pisgah-sight of Christ in a promise will quit the cost and hazard a thousand-fold. The evidence and advantage of such a performance will be the best, and worth all the rest; yea, for ought I know, though you meet not with God as you desire at that time, yet God may own and crown that undertaking as much as the most heart-melting exercise, because there is most of obedience in that, and conscience of duty is as acceptable a motive to duty as sense of present recompense.

But withal, keep up a course of secret prayer; withdraw yourselves into a corner according to the rule, Matt. vi. 6. God is wont to dispense his choicest blessings to solitary souls. When Jacob was left alone, he wrestled with the angel of the covenant and prevailed.—Gen. xxxii. 24. John and Ezekiel had their visions and revelations, when withdrawn from the world. Solomon saith, " Woe to him that is alone," but blessed is he that being alone hath God to bear him company. Our dear Saviour tells his disciples, " You leave me alone, yet I am not alone, for the Father is with me ;"* and when no creature is with us, we have most converse with God. For observe it, when persons are most secluded from other society, they are aptest to be subject to divine impressions, or to Satanical suggestions. Therefore, Christians, learn to get alone ; improve solitary hours ; pour out your souls in your closets, and God will pour in grace. Think not to seek and find Christ in a crowd. An honest intent for retirement, to enjoy Christ, did occasion a monastic life, but certainly there is much sweetness in secret prayer, when the soul can freely open its bosom to God, and expostulate boldly, yet humbly with him. There the Christian may use such postures, pauses, pleadings, as would not be convenient before others. You may tell him your whole heart, and he will deal with you as with friends, and open his breast to you. Observe it, sirs, a Christian hath some secret errand to God, that the dearest friend and nearest relation must not know of, cases that are not to be entrusted with any but God alone. Here then, comes in the necessity and excellency of secret prayer ; therefore, again, let me earnestly request you to go alone (as you know Christ did often) and tell God your whole heart ; hide nothing from him; plead no excuse from worldly business. Satan and your corrupt hearts will find many occasions for diversion ; but say to them as Abraham to his servants, " Stay you here whilst I go and worship the Lord yonder." Steal time from the world and thy work ; occasional duties are like accidental bargains,

* John xvi. 32.

that make careful tradesmen rich. Bread eaten in secret is sweet, and such morsels make the soul well liking. Consult with such Christians as converse much with God in a corner, and you shall see their faces to shine as Moses's did after his retired conversings with God in the mount. When Elijah hoped to raise the woman's dead son, he took him into the loft, and there prayed.* When thou wouldest quicken up thy dead heart, take it alone, go into a loft, and fall on thy face or knees and pray, and see the blessed effects thereof. Cyprian notably describes his sweet and solitary recesses into a place where no hearer could hinder his discourse, or intemperate noise of the busy family could obstruct. There he experienced and obtained what he enjoyed without learning, not through a long series of study, but by a compendious act of divine grace. †

7. To obtain a treasure, endeavour after intercourse with God in every performance. Rest not satisfied with a bare outside of duties, or a trudging in the common road or round of formality. If you look not beyond ordinances in the use thereof, you will get no more treasure than a merchant whose ship sails to the Downs, and quickly returns again. He that would be rich must use duties as a bridge or boat to bring his soul to God, and as a chariot to bring God to his soul. Every ordinance should be like those merchant ships that

* 1 Kings, xvii. 19, 20.

† Ac ne eloquium nostrum arbiter profanus impediat, aut clamor intemperans familiæ strepentis obtundat, petamus hanc sedem: dant secessum vicina secreta, ubi, dum erratici palmitum lapsus nexibus pendulis per arundines bajulas repunt, viteam porticum frondea tecta fecerunt.—Et paulo post:—Accipe quod sentitur antequam discitur, nec per moras temporum longâ agnitione colligitur, sed compendio gratiæ maturantis hauritur.—*Lege totam Epist. lib.* 2, *cap.* 2, *ad Donat. pag.* (mihi) 105, 106.

bring food or gold from afar.* The Christian must travel far beyond the Indies, even as far as heaven, to fetch a heavenly treasure into his heart, " The soul of the diligent shall be made fat."—Prov. xiii. 4. It is not a shew of eating, nor merely a sitting at the table that filleth. A pretence of trading makes not rich. He that stands upon the bridge and walks not, will never get over the water. It is not the goodness of the boat, but our motion by it that wafts us over. A golden bucket will bring us no water, except it be let down into the well. The choicest ordinances will bring us no spiritual or saving profit, except we have to do with God therein. God's institutions work not by any innate physical virtue that is in them, but morally, that is, by a careful improvement of them, and especially the blessing of God with them. A man is not, therefore, a good scholar because he went so long to school, and for saying so many lessons ; nor is an ignorant Papist a whit the better for dropping so many beads, or pattering over so many pater-nosters. The apostle saith, " Bodily exercise profits little."— 1 Tim. iv. 8. He means not only recreations or superstitious usages, but even God's own ordinances; saith an expositor,† " The mere verbal complimental use thereof will not advantage the soul ; but godliness is profitable to all things." The right spiritual worship of God brings along with it abundant incomes. Some observe, that religious worshippers are said in Latin, *Deum colere*, because thereby they " sow to the Spirit" and are sure to " reap of the Spirit life everlasting ;"‡ besides the inward refreshments they reap in this life, and truly in worshipping God there is great reward ; but it is easier to be much in duties, than to be much with God in duties. If we had been as often with God

* Prov. xxxi. 14. † Vid. Marlorat, in loc. ‡ Gal. vi. 8.

as we have been before God, we had been readier than we are. Job was persuaded that if he could find God, and come near to his seat, he would not plead against him with his great power, but would put strength into him, Job, xxiii. 3, 6; and I dare say, if thou couldest meet God in duty, he would meet thee in mercy, Isa. liv. 7; and if God meet thee he will bless thee,* and fill thy soul with a blessed treasure, a treasure of heavenly blessings. If thou draw nigh to God, he will draw nigh to thee. Let me, therefore, persuade you to make conscience of earnestly seeking communion with God, and influences from him in all ordinances and performances. You are great losers if you miss of God in duties; you take God's name in vain and lose your labour, nay, you lose a blessing, and get the curse of doing the work of the Lord negligently. But, O how blessed a thing it is to say with holy St. Bernard, " I never come to God, but I meet with God; I never go from God, but I carry God with me." Therefore, in all your attendance upon God, carefully prepare before; mind your work, regard the object of your worship, and diligently examine your hearts afterwards, how the Lord hath dealt with your souls; and blessed is he that can say as David in the point of obedience, Psal. cxix. 56, " This I had, because I kept thy precepts." What had he? Why, he had a heart to remember God's name in the night, holy thoughts whereby he might meditate on divine things. So say you, this I got in such a duty or ordinance, and this doth furnish my soul with heavenly conceptions, and new matter of meditation. It is the power of the Spirit that must make ordinances effectual; though the gospel be the ministration of the Spirit, yet the choicest truths, promises, sermons, sacraments, will be but a dead letter,

* Exod. xx. 24.

and law of death* to the soul, without the Spirit: therefore, you are to wait for the Spirit to breathe and blow upon the garden of your souls, that the spices, divine graces, may be nourished, and so may flourish in our hearts and lives. Ordinances are empty cisterns if God be not in them; they are full and filling if the presence of God be in them. O, therefore, look after God in every spiritual performance.

8. Spend time well. Lose not a mite or minute of this precious article. Fill up all your waste time with some profitable work in your general or particular callings. Cast not at your heels the least filings of these golden seasons; you have lost too much time already. Now buy up the remainder; engross this precious commodity; take the fittest opportunities, like good merchants, for a dear time is coming, nay, " The days are evil."—Ephes. v. 16. Imitate such tradesmen as miss no opportunity of getting gain at home or abroad, by night or by day, by planning or by practising; only make use of present moments, and promise not to yourselves to-morrow, as worldly tradesmen are apt to do, and be sure you take God along with you, whom they forget and leave behind. Take time by the forelock, for it is bald behind, and you can get no hold of it.† You little know what one pregnant day may bring forth; it may produce a birth and burden of more duty, difficulty, or misery, than hitherto you have met with. Time-redemption is an act of great discretion, but time-neglect brings thousands of souls to a despairing, Had I wist. The apostle said, above a thousand years ago, " the time is short," much more may we say so, since the ship is drawing so much

---

* Literæ damnatoriæ, aut leges mortis.

† James, iv. 13—15.   Fronte capillatâ, post est occasio calva.

nearer the harbour; the sails are contracted; and the end of all things is at hand.* The world grows old and naught; your own days cannot be long; it may be, " this night thy soul may be required," and leave thy body as a putrid carcass. O, then, a treasure for another world will stand you in infinite stead! O, consider often, that this time, this span-long life is the seminary of eternity, the preludium of an everlasting state; and, therefore, lavish not away your time, cast it not at your heels in a brutish prodigality, you will have time little enough when you come to die. A rich gallant, at death, cried out bitterly, " Call time again! O, call time again!" Another would offer a thousand pounds to purchase a day; but, alas! time cannot be valued with the vastest sums of money. One mispent day cannot be recalled with the gold of Ophir. That is but dross where time comes, and time and chance is upon the whole creation.† You have but your appointed time, and all your times are in the hands of God; if once lost, they are lost for ever. The dead and damned can say, we have only heard the fame thereof with our ears; ‡ but, alas! they are past the hopes of time-enjoyment or improvement. When your glass is once run, and your sun set, there is no more working or gathering time in order to eternity, and therefore, " Whatsoever your hand finds to do, do it with all your might, for there is no work nor device in the grave whither you go."—Eccl. ix. 10. Be not you like those silly fishes that are taken in an evil net, because they " know not their time," ver. 12. but ply the oars while you have time. Let no day pass without drawing some line towards your great centre. ||

* 1 Cor. vii. 29. Συνεστάλμενος, tempus contractum; Met. à velis contractis.

† Eccl. ix. 11.   ‡ Job, xxviii. 22. || Nulla dies sine lineâ.

You that are Christians had need be good time-students, time-merchants. The holiest men have been most careful of time, and they that have been the most fearful to lose an inch of time have been best treasured. Read histories* and observe experiments; in all, you will find men of the choicest spirits have been most diligent time-improvers, and some have accounted that day lost, whereupon they have not done some good with either tongue, or purse, or pen ; yea, heathens have bewailed that day as spent in vain, wherein they have not done some memorable action. How much more ought Christians to lament the loss of time ? I once heard an eminent Minister say, " He could eat the flesh off his arm in indignation against himself for his lost hours," and truly, the most of us are Epimethiuses, after-witted, we lose time and then smart for our loss ; it is to our cost. We are too like the mole, of which naturalists say, " It begins to see at death ;"† we open our eyes when they must be shut. Let us therefore, improve time while we have it, and study profitable things, and lay up every day something ; so shall we find soul-riches increase, according to that proverb, " many littles make a mickle." When God offers grace do not put him off, for delay will be interpreted a denial. An aged Christian, now with God, advised me, " To be either like Christ, or Mary ;" the first was always doing good, the latter still receiving good. Were you and I constantly thus employed, our treasure would soon be raised to a large proportion, and we should be sooner ripe for glory.

9. Gather something out of every thing. That man is likely to be rich that will not let a good bargain pass,

* See Clark's Lives of the Fathers.

† Oculos incipit aperire moriendo quos clausos habuit vivendo. —*Plin.*

but lay hold on it, and lay up any thing that he can get a penny by. A wise tradesman despiseth not little things, for multiplication of small numbers produceth a great sum. They that wilfully contemn the smallest good, will in time look upon the greatest as contemptible:

> Who say, I care not, those I give for lost;
> And to instruct them will not quit the cost.—*Herbert.*

Hence it is, that Christ saith, " Gather up the fragments that nothing be lost." Thus should you make a collection of the least things that others cast away. Get something out of every word, rod, or work of Providence, in a way of favour or displeasure. " Receive not the grace of God in vain." Hinder not your own proficiency by carelessness or inadvertency. Be you diligent, and God will teach you to profit.* See what you can make of every thing you meet with. A wise physician can tell you the virtue of every simple, and can extract some good out of those herbs, that an ignorant person casts away, as useless weeds. Prov. x. 14. it is said, " Wise men lay up knowledge," that is, whatever objects occur they consider how they may hereafter stand them in stead, what use may be made thereof, and so gather from them a profitable inference, and store that up for future times. Thus do you, if you would lay up a treasure; be not unwise, but understand what the will of the Lord is, by all that your eyes behold, or ears hear. Learn to make comments upon all the creatures, suck sweetness out of every flower, not for sensual delight, but spiritual profit. Let not so much as a good or bad report concerning yourselves or others sound in your ears, without special observation and improvement. Whatever your trade or calling be, you may and must spiritualize it

* Isaiah, xlviii. 17.

for your soul's good; there is never a profitable science, saith one, but it leads to the knowledge of God, or of ourselves, so that we need not be at a loss for a treasure, if we have hearts to improve objects of sense. It was a good design in the Rev. Dr. Hall, and discovered an honest fancy to improve vacant hours and visible objects in his occasional meditations: go you and do likewise; by which blessed art of heavenly chemistry, you may both please your fancy and profit your hearts; use your wits and exercise grace, for that is the way to increase it. The truth is, there is nothing but may do us good, if we have good hearts; the sins of others may be of great use to us, that we may consider our standing, and take heed lest we fall; the afflictions of others will work our hearts to sympathy, prayer, and charity; the indignities we suffer will awaken, quicken, and strengthen us, if our hearts be honest in observing and improving them; there is not a minister that we hear preach, but from him we may get good by what he saith. The Rev. Mr. Hildersham[*] often said, he never heard any godly minister preach, though but of weak parts, but he got some benefit by him. Divine Herbert[†] saith—

————Do not grudge
To pick out treasures from an earthen pot;
The worst speak something good; if all want sense,
God takes a text, and preacheth patience.

But above all, get something out of every chapter you read—dig deep into those golden mines, and you shall be rich. Digested Scripture is the matter of regular prayers, holy discourses, and heavenly meditations; only run not cursorily over them, but let your thoughts dwell upon them, and extract some marrow and quintessence out of them. We usually read the Scriptures,

[*] Clark on his Life.   [†] Church-porch, *p.* 15.

travellers go over mountains, that are barren on the surface, but when dug into, afford precious minerals: so the words and the syllables of God's book itself, slightly considered, have no great efficacy, but the sense and purport thereof containeth spirit and life to the intelligent and observant reader.—John, vi. 63. There is such a depth in Scripture,* that if you read the same place a hundred times over, yet still you may get fresh notions and impressions from it. O, therefore learn to read, understand, and improve the word of God, this will help you to a treasure; knowledge is fed by Scripture truth, and holiness is the counterpart of Scripture precepts; graces are the accomplishment of Scripture promises, and if your comforts and experiences be not suitable to the word, it is because " you have no light in you." †

10. Maintain communion of saints. Oh, forsake not the assembling of yourselves together; keep up this sweet good fellowship both in private conferences, and in public ordinances. For the first, you must observe and obey the wise man's counsel, through the book of Proverbs, to converse with the wise. David professeth himself to be a companion of those that fear God, and he, though a great king, esteemed the saints more excellent than all his courageous worthies or grave senators, and therefore professed that all his delight was in them.—Ps. xvi. 3. But it is not enough to be in good company, you must improve it, by hearing and asking questions. That is a notable passage in Prov. xx. 5. " Counsel in the heart of a man is like deep water; but a man of understanding will draw it out." Profound men are apt to be silent, therefore must be excited by profitable questions, and it is an

* Adoro Scripturæ plenitudinem.—*Tertul.*
† Isai. viii. 20.

evidence of knowledge to propound a useful question seasonably, as well as to answer it solidly.

> ——— Doubts well raised do lock,
> The speaker to thee, and preserve thy stock. *

It is our great loss that we can make no better use of one another; unimproved society is the bane of Christian converse, for when we meet one another, and trifle away time without advantage, it increaseth our guilt, and discourageth our hearts, for we are apt to say, we will meet no more, because our coming together is for the worse and not for the better, for many times our spirits are embittered by exasperating contentions. But O sirs, when you meet together purposely, or accidentally, improve your time in some holy discourses. Spend not all your fleeting hours about news or worldly affairs, but set afoot some religious talk. Talk sometimes as Christians, as well as men and chapmen. Let somebody begin and break the ice. Many are apt enough to cast down the bone of contention; do you present the marrow of religion, that you may edify one another. Sit not together as mutes, or as men of the world, discoursing about matters of state or trading, or of the weather, or your ages, which was Pharaoh's question to Jacob, † and that to his sons was of the like import; but if there be ever a wise man among you, fetch some spark from heaven, and throw it amongst your companions, that every one may bring his stick to the fire, and by the bellows of mutual love, it may be raised to a flame, that thereby your hearts may be warmed, and even burn within you, as did the hearts of the two travelling disciples by Christ's opening to them the Scriptures; and then record and lay up what you have got in profitable conversation. Thus was the book of Proverbs collected, and hereby you might fill

---

* Herb. Church-porch, *p.* 11.   † Gen. xlvii.

books and memories with useful observations; yet, take this caution, let not your end be to hear stories and notions, nor yet only polemical discourses, to furnish your heads with arguments for all subjects and companies, but let your principal end be to get your hearts bettered, grace strengthened, lusts weakened, lives reformed, consciences resolved. Oh, the advantage you may have by Christian society! You may get good by others, do good to others; yea, observe it, your profitable discourses with others will reflect upon yourselves with advantage. Scholars find that conference rubs up their memories, revives their reading, and in a sort, gives them the mastery over their notions, and imprints them deeper within them, when almost obliterated. Hence a famous scholar did return many thanks, to one that was many degrees below him, for affording him so fair an opportunity of private discourse; and a Jewish Doctor could say, he had learned much from his masters, more from his equals, but most of all from his scholars, hence their proverb, " I have learned by teaching."* Experience doth tell us that having to do in others' doubts, temptations, desertions, corruptions, directs us how to deal in our own cases; therefore, I advise you, be not shy in helping the weak, because thereby you do a double service to yourselves and to others, by one act or motion of your lips feeding others, and digesting your own food. Besides, this Christian communion being God's institution, is seconded with his benediction, and gracious acceptance. The members of Christ's mystical body, speaking the truth in love, † or truthing it in love, as the word imports, do grow up into him in all things, even Christ the head, and so that which is lacking in one joint, is made

* Docendo didici.
† See Eph. iv. 15, 16. Ἀληθέυοντες δὲ ἐν ἀγάπῃ.

up by the usefulness of another; and for God's acceptance of the saint's holy conference, see the famous text in Mal. iii. 16. But that which I am urging is,—the advantage that your souls will have by it; one live coal laid to a dead one, kindles it; a ripe grape put to a green one, ripens it. Company is of an assimilating nature,—and grace, like fire, will beget its like; and it is an advantage to trade with rich merchants in precious commodities, for then we shall get well-stocked with riches. So it is here, yea observe it, when a company of Christians meet together for spiritual purposes, Jesus Christ makes one more, and he is instead of many more; he walks from person to person, and inquires what they want, and Joseph-like, richly fills their sacks with a transcendant treasure. Where Christ keeps house, there is nothing wanting, he that girded himself to serve his disciples will wait to be gracious, and satisfy hungry souls. Christ walks in the midst of the golden candlesticks, and feeds the lamps of the sanctuary with oil. Go forth, therefore, poor soul, by the footsteps of the flock, " and feed the kids, beside the shepherds' tents;"* be found in the communion of saints,—be not content to have that article in your creed merely, but let it be in your practice. Wait on God in public ordinances; every religious act there will help to fill your souls, prayer, reading, singing psalms, the word preached, the sacraments administered. You may get good by baptism, and the Lord's supper, faithfully used, and believingly improved; and therefore, let every soul, that would have a treasure of grace, be found in the use of these holy ordinances; yet, observe this caution, that though the sacraments be necessary, and the great means of spiritual life, yet not in that manner and respect, as food is to a natural life,

* Cant. i. 8.

because they contain in themselves no vital force or efficacy. "They are" saith a reverend author,* "not physical, but moral instruments of salvation;—all receive not the grace of God, who receive the sacraments of his grace, neither is it ordinarily his will to bestow the grace of sacraments on any, but by the sacraments." A little after, he saith, "they are moral instruments, the use whereof is in our hands, the effect in his; for the use, we have his express commandment; for the effect, his conditional promise; and, we may expect his performance of the promise, upon our obedience to his command." He quoteth Hugo, comparing the sacraments to a vessel, and the grace therein to the medicine therein exhibited, and we should apply the spiritual good therein to our distempered spirits.† But I have been too large on this head. I shall shut up this piece of the directory for obtaining a treasure, with an expression of Cyprian's, "He cannot be fit for martyrdom, who is not armed by the Church for the conflict, and that mind faints, which is not raised and animated by receiving the eucharist,"‡ or Lord's supper. So the communion of saints in that choice ordinance, is a fortifying and furnishing exercise.

* Hooker's Eccles. Polity, Book 5, par. 57, page 229.

† *Hugo, de Sacramentis, lib.* 1, *cap.* 3, 4.—Si ergo vasa sunt spiritualis gratiæ sacramenta, non ex suo sanant, quia vasa, ægrotum non curant, sed medicina.

‡ Primo idoneus esse non potest ad martyrium, qui ab Ecclesia non armatur ad prælium; et mens deficit, quam, non accepta Eucharistia erigit, et accendit.—*Cyp. Epist. ad Cornel, lib.* 1, *Epis.* 2, *page* 41.

CHAP. X.

TRUTHS WHICH A CHRISTIAN SHOULD TREASURE UP.

THE second head of directions, is to descend more particularly to give some instructions respecting what the Christian is to treasure up. In opening the doctrine I told you, he is to treasure up these four rich commodities, wherewith he may furnish his inward man, namely,

Truths, Graces, Experiences and Comforts.

I shall resume my discourse on these, and give you a particular account of something in all of them, wherewith the bosom of a Christian is to be filled and furnished.

For the *first*, a Christian is to store up all truths: the filings of gold are precious, the least star in the firmament hath some influence, so all truths have their peculiar preciousness and efficacy. Truth is a sacred deposit, which God hath committed into the hands of ministers and people,* which must not be lost at any rate, for all the world cannot give a price proportionable to the least truth. To this end was Christ born, yea, and shed his dearest blood, even to bear witness to the truth, and to purchase the publication of it. It is very dangerous to be careless of lesser truths, for there is nothing superfluous in the sacred canon.† Things comparatively little may be great in their sphere, season, and consequences, and it is sad to break the golden chain of truths. Yet we are, especially, to treasure up fundamental and seasonable truths; doctrines that we

* Τὴν καλὴν παρακαταθήκην. 2 Tim. i. 14. 1 Tim. vi. 20.
† Matt. v. 19. Jam. ii. 10.

are to venture our souls upon, and such as we may have a peculiar use for, truths suitable to the day we live in. Hence it is that the apostle would have believers established in the present truth, 2 Pet. i. 12, that is, say some, "The doctrine of the gospel which was at this time newly revealed;" or else, as others interpret it, "Such truths as are most opposed and contradicted;" for we find that every church and age hath its present errors, whereby false teachers seek to undermine the truth, and seduce the professors of it; therefore, should every soul be well stored with such truths as may antidote him against present prevailing corruptions in principle or practice.

There are four sorts of divine truths that I would counsel all Christians to get their heads and hearts well stocked with, which are these, namely,

Doctrinal, disciplinary, practical, and experimental truths.

1. Doctrinal truths. "Hold fast the form of sound words."—2 Tim. i. 13. The word, ὑποτύπωσις, used here, signifies a model or platform, a mould or frame of words, or things, methodically disposed, as printers set and compose their characters in a table. Thus gospel doctrine is the mould, and hearers are as the metal which takes the form and impression of that into which it is cast.* A Christian is to get the body of divinity incorporated within him. It is not below the most able, knowing, and judicious person to read, yea, and commit to memory catechisms, and systems of divinity. I beseech you lay this good doctrinal foundation, and you will find infinite advantage by it through the whole course of your life. This will teach you to discourse distinctly, hear profitably, and read the Scriptures and good books with judgment, being able to try all things, and

* Rom. vi. 17.

reduce every thing to its proper place. Take a taste and sample of this sort of truths in these particulars:—

(1.) That the holy Scriptures are of divine authority.

(2.) That God's word is the sole, complete, supreme judge of all controversies.

(3.) That God is an infinite, simple, and immutable Spirit.

(4.) That there are three glorious persons in the unity of the Godhead.

(5.) That all things depend upon God's eternal decrees.

(6.) That man was created in perfect holiness and happiness.

(7.) That all mankind are polluted and ruined by Adam's apostacy.

(8.) That Christ, God-man, is the only mediator betwixt God and man.

(9.) That Christ, by doing, enduring, and dying, hath satisfied justice, and justified sinners.

(10.) That such as sincerely repent and believe, are justified and accepted.

(11.) That baptism and the Lord's supper, are seals of the covenant of grace.

(12.) That there shall be a general resurrection and day of judgment.

2. Disciplinary Truths. These, in their kind and sphere, are to be stored up and contended for. It is true, these are not so fully laid down in Scripture, nor is there so much stress laid thereupon, as on doctrinal truths, at least as to every punctilio relating to circumstantials, which hath occasioned many hot disputes among the strictest Christians; yet, withal, the essentials of discipline are of great use, and in a sort, neces-

sary, if not to the being, yet to the well-being of the church.* Our Lord Jesus " is faithful in his house," and hath not left every thing to human prudence, though possibly something may be said for a prudential application of general rules to particular cases. It is lost labour to enter into controversies here; much precious time and pains have been wasted herein, yet, Mr. Hooker † acknowledgeth, " That although there be no necessity it should prescribe any one particular form of church government, yet touching the manner of governing in general, the precepts which the Scripture setteth down are not few, and the examples many which it proposeth, for all church governors, even in particularities, to follow; yea, that those things, finally, which are of principal weight in the very particular form of church polity, are in the self-same Scriptures contained." So says he. Neither are these truths to be slighted, but we are to be attentive to them, and observant and retentive of them. Hence, when the gospel church is described, God saith, Ezek. xl. 4. " Behold with thine eyes, and hear with thine ears, and set thine heart upon all that I shew thee." Under correction, I conceive such disciplinary truths as these are not obscurely delivered by God, as,

(1.) That upon Christ's shoulders lies the government of his Church.

(2.) That Scripture precepts and precedents, are the rule of church administrations.

(3.) That church officers are to be duly qualified and called to their work.

* Quamvis enim non sit nota simpliciter essentialis et reciproca, scil. ecclesiæ (sicut neque reliquæ duæ, i. e. verbum et sacramenta) ad completum tamen ecclesiæ statum necessariò debet adesse.—*Ames. Medul. lib.* 1. *cap.* 37.

† Hooker's Eccl. Polit. book 3d. part 4, fol. 69.

(4.) That Christ's own officers have power to dispense the word and censures.

(5.) That holy things are for holy men, and ordinances must be kept from pollution.

(6.) That visible, credible profession is the ground of church communion.

(7.) That admonition must precede rejection and excommunication.

(8.) That heretical persons, and disorderly walkers are to be censured.

(9.) That evidence of repentance pleads for re-admittance.

(10.) That the duty of magistrates is to cherish, defend, and propagate the church, of ministers to oversee, and of members to watch over, and admonish one another.

(11.) That at least there may be associations of churches by their officers, for mutual communion and consultation.

(12.) That synods and councils consulting about church affairs, are but companies of men subject to error, are not to have dominion over men's faith, or lord it over consciences, &c.

3. Another sort of truths to be laid up are practical truths. Fundamental truths of practical concernment, are in a sort the life of religion. Our religion is not a mere notion; christianity lies much in the heart and life. The young candidate's question, in the gospel, had mainly reference to practice, " Good master," saith he, " what shall I do that I may inherit eternal life ?" * Socrates is accounted the wisest man, because he applied his studies and knowledge to the moral part—the squaring and ordering of men's lives. Saith Dr. Hammond, † (and quotes an ancient saying) " The end of

* Mark x. 17. † Practical Catech. p. 2.

Christian Philosophy is to make them better, not more learned; to edify, not to instruct." The truth is, conscientious practice is both the end of knowledge, and the means of further knowledge. If we live up to God's will known, we shall know more of his will that is to be done;* if we give up ourselves to truth, we shall be made free by truth. Truths of a practical import tend to deliver the soul from the bondage of sin, to bring us into the liberty of the sons of God, and to make us account God's service, perfect freedom. Some truths are to be believed, others to be lived upon, others to be lived up to, and so are more practical; such as these:

(1.) That all creatures are made for the glory of God.

(2.) That the covenant of works cannot be kept by any mere man since the fall.

(3.) That true faith closeth wholly with a whole Christ.

(4.) That none can expect pardon without a sincere gospel repentance.

(5.) That good works are the fruits and evidences of a lively faith.

(6.) That those only are good works that have a right source, rule and end.

(7.) That man's best duties are imperfect, and merit no good at God's hands.

(8.) That the moral law is a Christian's rule of obedience.

(9.) That God alone is to be worshipped, and that according to his will.

(10.) That the observation of a Sabbath is a moral and perpetual duty.

(11.) That magistrates are to be honoured, and their lawful commands obeyed.

* John vii. 17.

(12.) That every man is to attend upon and act according to his general or particular calling.

4. We ought to lay up experimental truths, which are vital, and vivifical, that beget and maintain good blood, as it were, in the soul. These are the sweetest solace to a sound believer; these reach and teach the very heart, bow the will, engage the affections, awaken the conscience, and influence the whole conversation; the delightful revolving of these divine truths in the mind, helps the soul to walk in the sweetest paradise of contemplation. These mysterious, marrowy truths are like that song that none could learn but the " hundred and forty and four thousand that are redeemed from the earth," Rev. xiv. 4,; or like that " new name which no man knoweth, saving he that receiveth it."—Rev. ii. 17. Such truths are better felt than spoken, sooner experienced than expressed; indeed, like those [ἄρρητα ῥήματα] unutterable words that Paul heard in paradise.—2 Cor. xii. 4. Such truths as " are hid from the wise and prudent, but revealed unto babes.—Matth. xi. 25. This is a right " knowing of the truth as it is in Jesus," a lying under the power and impression of divine revelation; without this experience, knowledge is a cold, dull, moonlight speculation, without the clear, quickening heat of the sun of righteousness; nay, the choicest truths of the gospel cannot be discerned but by experience. Divinity is not a speculative, but effective or influential knowledge.* Treasure up such truths as these :—

(1.) That by nature we are averse to good, and prone to evil.

(2.) That we have no free will with respect to saving good, but are passive in conversion.

---

* Theologia est scientia effectiva, non speculativa.
Gerson.

(3.) That regeneration is a thorough change of the whole man, in heart and life.

(4.) That faith and repentance are the gifts of God's free grace.

(5.) That a sinner is justified only by Christ's merits imputed, not by works.

(6.) That conformity to God is an inseparable companion of communion with God.

(7.) That every child of God hath the Spirit of adoption, to assist in prayer.

(8.) That the best saints in this life are sanctified but in part.

(9.) That a Christian's best and bravest life is a life of faith.

(10.) That sincere saints may be assured of the truth of grace, and their title to glory.

(11.) That a justified person cannot totally and finally fall away.

(12.) That some spiritual good is exhibited in, and conveyed through the seals of the covenant.

Such precious truths as these, Christians, you are to gather, and seal them up among your treasures, and you will find that such a treasure will furnish your minds with saving knowledge, fortify your hearts against errors and opposition, satisfy your spirits amidst all doubts and objections, teach you to profit by God's verbal and real dispensations, and prepare you for fiery trials, and hottest persecutions. You cannot stand for truths you know not, and you will not stand for those truths that you do not adopt, and look not upon as your treasure; you must hold fast what you have received, and therefore must you receive what you may retain, and lay up what you may live up to, and live upon them in an evil day; as a minister, so a member of the church must hold fast the faithful word, as he hath been taught.—Titus, i. 9. He must maintain truth with all his might, struggle and contend for it, fight and die in the defence of it; truth and our souls must be married, and never divorced. There are truths that we may venture our souls upon, and must venture our lives for. That is an atheistical speech of some, that the martyrs in Queen Mary's days died in the pet, and were too prodigal of their blood; and that God requires no man to be cruel to himself for his sake. But the saints have otherwise learned Christ, than to deny him, or his truths before men, for they would not be denied by him another day; they have not otherwise learned to love him [*] than to lay down their lives for him, if he call them to it; and, thus, by being overcome they do overcome, as their Saviour before them; and as it is on record, Rev. xii. 11, "They overcame by the blood of the Lamb, and by the word of their testimony, and they loved not their lives unto the death." It is the duty of every Christian to lay up such truths in the close cabinet of his heart, as he may live and die by, and adhere closely and constantly unto. We must do by truths, as Cæsar by his books, who having to swim through a river to escape the fury of his enemies, carried his books above water with his hand, but lost his robe; [†] so though we should be put to swim through a sea of trouble in following the Lamb, yet must we keep the Lord's deposit, though we should lose our garments of earthly enjoyments; yea, our lives themselves, rather than part with the sacred and saving truths of God contained in this blessed book of books, the holy Scriptures, which are to be our treasures. Hence, saith the wise man, [‡] "Take fast hold of instruction, let her not go,

[*] Aliter amare non didici.
[†] Major fuit cura libellorum, quam purpuræ.
[‡] Prov. iv. 13.

keep her, for she is thy life." Hence, some good souls have been willing to be burnt themselves, rather than willingly to burn their Bibles; and have been racked in pieces, rather than suffer themselves to be rent from the truth. It is our great duty to hold fast, and hold forth the word of truth; to be witnesses to the truth actively, and for the truth passively, and if we maintain it, it will maintain us. " Because thou hast kept the word of my patience, I also will keep thee from the hour of temptation."—Rev. iii. 10. The word of his patience may be taken either effectively, for such a word as works a quiet, composed, submissive frame of spirit, or eventually, for that word that may put a man upon the exercise of patience, so that he may suffer great hardships for it, and lay down his life, as a sacrifice on the behalf of it, for a Christian must not flinch back, but in the strength of God run the greatest hazard for approved, experienced, sacred truths. " I know," saith a reverend Divine,* " there is a difference in truths, and the value we are to set upon them, as in coins, whereof one piece is a farthing, another no less than a pound." Only take this rule in general,—despise not the meanest truth,—prove all things by Scripture rules,—lay up and hold fast what is consonant thereunto, but above all lay the greatest stress upon fundamental points of religion, and be not beat from your hold, through fear or favour.

So much for treasuring up Scripture truths.

* See Dr. Hall's Peace Maker, sect. 1, p. 1 ; read it through.

CHAP. XI.

THE GRACES WHICH A CHRISTIAN SHOULD TREASURE UP.

THE second class of precious commodities that a Christian's breast is to be stored with, is, divine graces. Every grace is of vast worth, and excellent use; yea, the least degree of sincere grace is worth a mine of gold, or a prince's crown and kingdom. It is said of the grace of faith, that the trial of it (or faith tried in the furnace of affliction) is much more precious than gold, that perisheth.—1 Pet. i. 7. None can set a right and perfect estimate on a grain of true grace, which is no other than the offspring of Heaven, the purchase of Christ's blood, and the blessed fruit of the Spirit of grace. It is part of the divine nature, the image of God, and seed of immortality. Grace is the monument and ornament of the soul; it is the only emolument and accomplishment of a Christian. Let the world be hurried to gather great estates, filling their houses with goods, their barns with grain, and bags with gold. Let the pious soul get filled with the fruits of righteousness, the graces of the Spirit.

There are four sorts of graces, which I shall advise all Christians in a special manner to treasure up in their hearts, which are these,—

Directing, subjecting, profiting, and persevering graces.

1. The believing soul is to lay up, with diligence, directing, conducting, deciding, and satisfying graces, that is, abundance of knowledge, wisdom, prudence, and judgment, that he may have light and discernment about the things of God. Days are coming, when

Christians may need the wisdom of the serpent, as well as the innocence of the dove. A Christian in his journey is often puzzled with various paths, and intricate meanders. O, how much worth is a spirit of understanding, whereby we may choose the good, and refuse the bad, and keep the straight road to heaven? Hence the apostle prays for his Philippians, that their love might abound more and more in knowledge, and in all judgment, that they might approve things that are excellent.—Phil. i. 9, 10. The means to keep us from erring about [ἀδιάφορα] things indifferent, is to have a solid apprehension concerning those [τὰ διαφέροντα] things that are excellent, or differenced from others, as the word imports; that is, those things that tend to sincerity and innocency of life; therefore, he adds, " that ye may be sincere, and without offence till the day of Christ." That is the best policy which helps on piety; a spirit of discerning is useful to exact walking; an enlightened conscience helps the soul to be without offence. No man can walk circumspectly, but " he that hath his eyes in his head."* He that walks in darkness with a blind eye knows not whither he goeth. The eye of the mind is the light and guide of the will and affections, and if that be blind, those blind faculties fall into the ditch of error, terror, apostacy, and misery. The Christian's eyes must be full of light. We cannot have too much knowledge if it be sanctified. In one act of religion, a Christian is to look many ways, inwards, at his principle,—upwards, to the pleasing of God,—forwards, at the reward,—downwards at the profit of men, &c. There are many eyes upon us, and our eyes must be upon many; some long to see our well-doing, others watch for our halting. We had need get wisdom to carry ourselves usefully towards the good, and wisely towards those that are without. There

* Eph. v. 15. Eccl. ii. 14.

is great necessity for true solid knowledge, to discern our own duty and exercise charity, to mind our own business, and yet to do good offices to saints and sinners, and to keep within our place and station. We shall find some difficulty so to carry ourselves as not to give offence carelessly, or to take offence causelessly. We should learn to see with our own eyes, and not be led by multitudes, either wise, or learned, or godly. Oh, what a blessed thing it is to be wise unto that which is good and simple concerning evil!* With how much more ease may a Christian go through his Christian course with, than without, a solid knowledge! for " wisdom is profitable to direct;" † yea, it strengtheneth the wise more than weapons of war; ‡ therefore, it " excelleth folly as far as light excelleth darkness " ‖ Practical wisdom is infinitely beyond speculative; hence, saith Solomon, " the wisdom of the prudent is to understand his way."—Prov. xiv. 8. This treasure of directing graces is practical; it helps the tongue to answer discreetly, the feet to walk properly, the hands to work completely, to spend no time or pains in bye-ways, and it also concerns a man's self; it doth not range abroad, and forget home. The greatest politician is a very fool when he cannot order his own affairs with discretion. He that is not wise for himself is not wise at all. God will accept, and men will praise that man that doth well to himself. Paul prays for the saints at Colosse, " that they might be filled with the knowledge of his will, in all wisdom and spiritual understanding." Col. i. 9. For what end? Why, not to talk, but to walk worthy of the Lord.—Col. i. 10. § That is the only valuable knowledge which ends in holy practice.

* Rom. xvi. 19. † Eccl. x. 10. ‡ Eccl. ix. 18. ‖ Eccl. ii. 13.

§ Quicunque ad hunc scopum non dirigunt studia sua, fieri potest ut multum sudent ac laborent, sed nihil quam vagantur per ambages, nullo profectu.—*Calv. in loc.*

Soul-profiting is the end of spiritual understanding; they that aim not at this end, and by their studies are not furthered in this work, may have the repute of learned men, but will never pass for judicious Christians.

Oh, sirs, take much pains to lay up those graces that may direct you. Certainly there is a vast difference betwixt a Christian of a solid judgment, and another of a weak head, though both sincere; the one knows duty and lawful liberty, the other's conscience is wofully perplexed with nice and needless scruples, which render him a burden to himself, and offence to others, and expose him to a world of temptations. An unsettled soul, that yet is well-meaning, but ignorant, forms a theatre upon which Satan and seducers do act dreadful tragedies. It is unstable souls that wrest and pervert the Scriptures, that are only constant in inconstancy, "and are tossed to and fro with every wind of doctrine."* Alas, these receive a new impression by every sermon or company, and as quickly abandon, as they speedily close with a new notion, so that you cannot tell where to find them; but now, a sober, solid, well-taught Christian hath fixed the staff, and you may know where to find *him*, and he knows where to find his own principles; he moves always upon the solid axle-tree of Scripture truths and duties; by the light of revelation, he can ordinarily find his way through the dark mists of error, and by the hand of the Spirit he is conducted along the often obscure entry and narrow passage of duty, to rest and satisfaction. Hence, it is said, that a "spiritual man judgeth all things,"† that is, which are doubtful, and is by this stock of directing graces assisted to behave himself wisely in a perfect way.— Psalm ci. 2.

2. Treasure up subjecting graces, that may help you

* 2 Pet. iii. 16. Jam. i. 8. Eph. iv. 14.   † 1 Cor. ii. 15.

to bear God's will, and freely to submit to his disposal; such as patience, humility, self-denial, weanedness from the world, heavenly-mindedness, and that rare jewel of Christian contentment in all conditions. Oh, what a happy soul is that to which nothing can come amiss, which is furnished for every storm! Paul was a brave scholar in this suffering school, he had " learned, in all estates to be content."—Phil. iv. 11, 12. It is a hard task, and long trade, but what cannot grace undertake and overcome, through the help of assisting grace? The truth is, a treasured Christian may say, with David, " My foot standeth in an even place." * Come what can come, a good man will light upon his feet, and stand upright, and not wrench his foot by turning aside into crooked ways; as he lies square to every command of God, so he doth righteousness at all times. Wicked men's design is to push away the feet of the godly from their standing in holy paths and outward comforts; † therefore, must they " make strait paths for their feet, lest that which is lame be turned out of the way," Heb. xii. 13. that is, get a principle of health and rectitude in opposition to that wayward and wandering disposition of heart, which is naturally in all men, that you may not turn aside to the right hand nor to the left, but hasten with a right foot in a straight course to the goal of glory. Grace strengthens the nerves of the soul, and helps against halting. With courage and holy resolution the feet of the saints are shod, that they may walk steadily in slippery places. " The whole armour of God," even the precious stock of Christian graces will fortify the believing soul against the sharpest encounters; above all, preparative for sufferings, there is nothing doth so bow the spirit to bear burdens, subject so much the heart to the Lord's plea-

* Psal. xxvi. 12. † Job. xxx. 12.

sure, help the soul to wait his time, and secure from danger, as the heart-quieting grace of faith. This is the way to strength and safety. A believing soul is fit for any condition, and will live by his faith when all things fail; nothing can daunt him, all things are easy.[*] " He is," saith an ancient,[†] " invincible in labours, strong for dangers, rigid against pleasures, hardened against the alluring baits of the world." Oh, the excellency and necessity of faith, courage, and a Christian magnanimity! A believing soul moves in a higher orbit than other saints, as one saith, " and leads up the van of the militia of heaven." Faith sets the soul as an impregnable rock in the midst of the sea, and breaks the waves of men's malicious threats and hot revenge, so that it can say, as David, " in God have I put my trust, I will not fear what flesh, what man can do unto me."—Psalm lvi. 4, 11. Amongst other subjecting graces be sure you lay up a good treasure of that incomparable grace of meekness, which captivates the understanding to the obedience of faith, and moderates the will to a due submission to the Lord's disposal, and silenceth the lips against all murmuring expostulations. This precious grace takes all well that God doth, and doth not rage against the instruments; it yieldeth active or passive obedience to superiors with cheerfulness, though it dares not yield up its judgment to the guidance of any mortal man, or church on earth; yet, it meekly lies under the censures and punishments of men,[‡] " committing all to him that judgeth righteously," as Christ did.—1 Pet. ii. 23. These and such

[*] Psal. cxxv. 1. Prov. xviii. 10.

[†] Invictus ad labores, fortis ad pericula, rigidus adversus voluptates, durus adversus illecebras.—*Ambr.*

[‡] See Meekness largely discussed in Dr. Hammond's Pract. Catech. p. 107—118.

like suffering graces and dispositions, must Christians store up, that they may suffer according to the will of God, both for cause, and call, and carriage, in the sharpest conflicts they may meet with upon earth. The truth is, sirs, you little know what lies betwixt you and the grave ; you have not yet resisted unto blood, but you may ; you little know what religion may cost you ;* you may go through a long " vale of the shadow of death," to death, and " fight with beasts at Ephesus," and then mount up in a fiery chariot to heaven. Sit down then and reckon the charges in building the tower of religion, and whether you have armour of proof to carry you through an army of dangers and difficulties. Stock yourselves for a storm ; frame your backs for a burden ; melt your wills into God's will, as you desire to hold out against fainting and despair, and as you desire to hear that blessed *euge*, and sweet encomium, from Jesus Christ, Revel. ii. 3, 7, " Thou hast born, and hast patience, and for my name's sake hast laboured, and hast not fainted ; to him that overcometh I will give to eat of the tree of life, which is in the midst of the paradise of God."

3. Endeavour to treasure up profiting graces, I mean such as will help you both in doing and receiving good. For the *first*, lay up such graces as will render you serviceable in your places, Rom. xiv. 19, " Let us follow after the things which make for peace, and things wherewith one may edify another," such as brotherly love, or kindness, charity, meekness, forbearance, gentleness, condescension, mutual sympathy, compassion to souls, and zeal for God's glory ; a public spirit and a heart to lament the sins and sufferings of the church. It is a blessed thing to be of public use; it adds lustre to what is truly good, to be diffusive and

* Luke xiv. 26—34.

communicative. Some Christians have those useful gifts and graces, that others, though truly good, may want. The more good you have, the more good you may do. The " manifestation of the Spirit" is given to every man to profit withal.—1 Cor. xii. 7. God lays *in*, that we may lay *out*, and we are to lay up great treasures on purpose that we may do the more good. That is an excellent expression of Luther's, that " all things are made free by faith, and all things are made serviceable by charity or love." * It is the property and pleasure of a good soul to be doing good. Living springs send forth streams of water, dead pits must have all that they afford drawn out with buckets. The fuller a gracious soul is, the more free will be the communication. There is as much comfort in doing, as in receiving good. You must be fitted for both, therefore, pray for, and put on, as the elect of God, bowels of mercy, kindness, humbleness of mind, meekness, long suffering, Col. iii. 12, 13, that you may be disposed to glorify God, edify others, and serve your generation, according to the will of God, and at last give a good account of your talents and stewardship. Blessed is the man that hath his quiver full of these valuable shafts, and his boxes full of cordial receipts, whereby he may both wound sinners by admonition, and heal them with the sweet words of consolation. And then, *secondly*, you had need treasure up profiting graces, that is, such as will help you to get good to your own souls by all God's dealings with you. Mix trials as well as the word with faith, receive all with meekness, bring forth fruit with patience. All that God doth is for our profit, even tokens of his anger are for our advantage; corrections are for our instruction; partaking of his holiness is the peaceable fruit of righte-

* Omnia libera per fidem, omnia serva per charitatem.—*Luth.*

ousness that God aims at in all our troubles.* All things would work together for our good, if we had a receptive principle; to him that hath a treasure shall more be given, according to the proportion of grace received and improved. Ordinances would do us more good if we had grace to get good by them. A heart sanctified and stored with improving graces, is like tinder, which soon takes fire, and is apt to keep it, till it be forced out. Naturalists observe, that transmutation is easy in symbolical elements, such as agree in some prime qualities. Water is more easily turned into air than into fire; even so, a holy and spiritual heart will be easily wrought on by holy and spiritual ordinances; for here is an agreement in qualities. Gracious qualities make the soul both receptive and retentive of heavenly impressions. Grow in grace every day, and then you will get good by all that God doth. There are several graces that dispose the soul to spiritual proficiency, as sensibleness, brokenness, and tenderness of heart, fit to receive divine impressions, which plough up, and prepare the ground for the seed; † and then, apprehensiveness of spiritual wants, being burdened with sin, breathing after God and grace, with longing, hungering desires, which capacitate the soul for both sanctifying and satisfying incomes. Strength of grace is usually seconded with sweet discoveries. "I write unto you, young men, because ye are strong and the word of God abideth in you."—1 John ii. 14. Strong and stored Christians have many precious epistles from heaven.

4. Treasure up persevering, perfecting and crowning graces. Furnish your hearts with such graces as may help you through this world, and through death, and land you safe on the shore of eternity; such as

---

* Heb xii. 6, 10. † Jer. iv. 3.

these, sincerity, humility, faith, hope, love, the fear of God, delight in him, resignation to him, resolution for him, contempt of the world, desire of heaven; if you have these graces you shall never fail or fall. Unsound professors may and will fall away, but such as are thus rooted, shall grow up as high as heaven; hypocrites may ascend many steps towards heaven, but he that hath sincerity at the bottom, and perseverance at the top, of this ladder, shall not miss of glory. O, see to the uprightness of your hearts, and truth of your graces; be not mistaken about your state; build high by laying the foundation low; if the root of the matter be in you, it shall not be eradicated; saving grace will end in eternal glory. "The girdle of truth, the breast-plate of righteousness," the shoes of heroic resolution, " the shield of faith, the helmet of hope,"* the sword of Scripture truths, and constant, fervent prayer, will help the conflicting soul to a glorious conquest, and God will set an imperishable crown upon the conquering head of a persevering saint. If you lay up persevering graces, you will hold on and hold out; "if your love abound in knowledge and in all judgment, your souls shall be without offence till the day of Christ." Phil. i. 9, 10. What would you give, sirs, to come safely to heaven? Why! do but lay up a good foundation for yourselves, against the time to come, and thereby you do, as it were, lay hold upon eternal life, 1 Tim. vi. 19. Press forward, and be aiming at perfection; beware of, so much as, seeming to fall short; heap up such graces, so many, and such degrees and measures of them, that an abundant entrance may be made for " you into the kingdom of Christ, 2 Pet. i. 11; the great direction there prescribed is an addition of one degree of grace to another, or rather of one sort

* Eph. vi. 14—18.

of graces to another, and the word in Greek, which is translated, " add ye," 2 Pet. i. 5, is an elegant allusion to virgins' dances, * who link themselves hand in hand, and observe a decent order in their recreating exercises; and it is observable that the same word † is used in 2 Pet. i. 11, to express the adding or ministering to such a soul the entrance into glory, to note to us, the nearness and propinquity betwixt the highest degrees of grace and the state of glory. The link, or rather chain of divine graces, reacheth from the first uniting grace of faith, to the God-enjoying grace of perfect love, and these virgin-graces going hand in hand in a believing soul, lead it higher and higher, till they bring it into the Prince's presence, and bridegroom's chamber. ‡ Oh, how merrily will you dance to heaven, with these concatenated graces! the Lord still holding the end of this golden chain, and drawing your souls every day nearer to glory; for the same Apostle saith, " We are kept by the power of God, through faith, to salvation, 1 Pet. i. 5; so that the soul is happy, by the Lord's keeping and strengthening the grace of faith; we shall persevere, by the assistance of God, as the efficient cause, and in the exercise and increase of all graces, especially faith, as the means. Thus are Christians to treasure up all persevering graces, that they may not faint by the way, but hold out, and that their last may be more than their first, and this brave fabric of grace may be raised up as high as heaven; only I intreat you, be sure that you lay Christ for a foundation, and dig deep in humiliation. You will never have a perfection of

* Ἐπιχορηγήσατε, proprie significat chorum ducere, ab ἐπὶ, χὸρος et ἄγω, duco.—*Beza.*

† Ἐπιχορηγήθησεται.

‡ Psalm xlv. 14, 15.

degrees, except you have a perfection of parts in integrity of heart; and you will never reach glory, unless Christ draw you with him, in his ascension by his merit, and Spirit; therefore, see to your interest, and then grow in grace, and if you do these things, you shall never fail.

CHAP. XII.

EXPERIENCES WHICH SHOULD BE TREASURED UP.

THE third sort of precious useful things which the Christian is to lay up, are those various experiences, he hath in all passages of his life. Certainly, a Christian may be a great gainer this way; this is a grand duty, a character of solid wisdom, and a means of more. So saith the Psalmist, concerning the various acts of divine Providence, in Psal. cvii. 43, " Whoso is wise, and will observe those things, even they shall understand the loving kindness of the Lord;" as if he had said, such as set their hearts to consider of the Lord's blessed and embroidered workmanship in the world have wise and observant spirits, and shall grow still wiser, and see more of God in his dispensations, than other men.* God opens his secret cabinet to observant Christians, but he is much offended with those that regard not his works, and threatens to destroy them, and not to build them up.—Psal. xxviii. 5. But this is too high a work for brutish, sottish souls; † it is the good soul that lays up experiences. The righteous man, saith Solomon, wisely considereth the house of the wicked, Prov. xxi. 12;

* Psal. xxv. 14. Isai. v. 12. † Psal. xcii. 5—7.

that is, he takes notice what becomes of it, how the Lord deals with wicked men, and their houses; and so in all other affairs, both public and private, he observes, God's carriage to both good and bad, in mercy and judgment, as Scripture testifies. *

But I shall rather keep close to the Christian's personal experience which relates to himself, and desire every child of God to treasure up experiences of these four sorts, namely,

Of the vanity of the world, the treachery of his heart, the bitterness of sin, and heavenly discoveries.

1. Lay up experiences of the world's vanity. Solomon was making such a collection all his life long, and recorded it in his Ecclesiastes, in his declining old age. He had great opportunities, and extraordinary faculties and means that capacitated him for such an experiment; he knew better than any man breathing, what the flattering world could do for her beloved minions, yet, cries out at last, " all is vanity, yea, vexing vanity;" and the whole book is an induction of particulars, to prove this assertion. And, what can the man do that cometh after the king? † Alas, sirs, if you make the like investigation, you must needs make the same conclusion; you cannot search more into, nor make more of the creature than Solomon, yet he found vanity engraven upon the choicest enjoyment; and have not you also found the like in your time and observation? Well then, Christian, rub off the rust and dust of old experiences, read the wise man's last and soundest lectures on the whole creation, and let your dear-bought experience comment thereupon, and lay up both text and comment in your hearts for after-times. Poor soul! consider, didst thou ever trust the world, but it deceived thee? Hath it not failed thee at such a time?

* Jer. ix. 12, 13. Hos. xiv. 9. † Eccl. ii. 12.

and disappointed thee in such a case? O, how didst thou bless thyself in such an expectation? but, alas, thou didst but grasp the sand or smoke. Hast thou not found riches uncertain, friends inconstant, relations vanishing? * Have you not seen the world passing away, † and the treble enjoyments of it, pleasure, profit, and preferment, just like the sliding stream of a swift river, hastening towards their primitive chaos of vanity and confusion? However men may be bewitched with the world's bravery, yet the Spirit of God judgeth of it but as a mere phantasy, or pageant shew, or as a mathematical figure, which is but a notion, an idea in the fancy or imagination; ‡ at the best it is but an accidental figure without substance. What solid content have you ever found in it? When you have sought to the creature, hath it not answered, " It is not in me to fill the soul, or do you good?" or at best, it is but like a dream of the night vision, when the hungry and thirsty think they eat and drink, but are faint when they awake. ‖ Have not your souls found this too true by sad experience? Why now, lay up these things, produce them out of your stock, and learn thereby to trust the world no more. Oh, what good may these do you upon a temptation to carnal confidence! Tremble, Christian, to pierce and prejudice thy soul again, never lean upon this broken reed, that will run into thy hand and heart, and pierce thee with many sorrows here, and be in danger of drowning thee in eternal perdition.—1 Tim. vi. 9, 10. The truth is, there nothing answers our desires and hopes in this world, §

* 1 Tim. vi. 17.   † 1 John, ii. 16, 17.

‡ Acts, xxv. 23. 1 Cor. vii. 31. $\sigma\chi\bar{\eta}\mu a$.

‖ Isai. xxix. 7, 8.

§ Nihil æque adeptis et concupiscentibus gratum.—*Plin.*

nothing pleases us so well in the fruition, as in the expectation, we find the world but a lie, and the sweetest comforts, lying vanities, and, as one saith, our leaning-staff becomes a knocking cudgel. Well then, since you have found it so, look upon it as such, and lay up that experience.

2. Lay up experiences of the treachery of the heart. Read over Mr. Dyke's treatise on the deceitfulness of the heart, and compare your own experience with that book; but especially read and study well this multifarious book of a depraved heart, consider and remember those ways of guile and guilt, that have cost thy soul so dear; as thus, in such a duty my heart gave me the slip—in such a temptation, my heart led away my hand or foot, and caused my flesh to sin—in such an enjoyment my perfidious heart stole away—in such an affliction I had discontented risings of heart, and my tumultuous, quarrelsome spirit made me to speak unadvisedly with my lips; I will never trust this deceitful heart again. Who but a fool will venture his whole estate with a known thief? What wise man will trust a known juggler? Solomon saith, " He that trusteth in his own heart is a fool;"[*] and I shall be the most errant fool that breathes, if after so many cheating tricks, I should confide in this perfidious traitor. Ah, Christian, I appeal to thine own experience, how many a woful instance hast thou had of the heart's deceitfulness! It is apt to deceive, and as easy to be deceived, and self-deceit is the most dangerous. The heart, since the fall, is naturally of a vafrous, subtile, and fickle temper, and is still made worse and worse, by the deceitfulness of sin, Heb. iii. 13, which is, as it were woven and twisted in the frame and constitution thereof, and so those two cheats conspire to undo the poor soul;

[*] Prov. xxviii. 26.

and were not God a more fast friend to the saint, than he is to himself, there were no salvation for a poor sinner; for every man is a Satan to himself,* and the sincere saint will pray most, with divine Austin,† to be delivered from that evil man, himself; and is more afraid of the folly that is bound up in his own heart, than of assaults from without; and, indeed, the reason of a soul's self-confidence, is self-ignorance, or not laying up experiences of the heart's deceitfulness. The truth is, a poor self deceiving sinner dares not look into his heart, lest he find not things there as he fancieth, or would persuade himself, but puts all to the venture, like a desperate bankrupt. A child of God, however, cannot but see this treachery that others hide or counterfeit, and willingly sees it, and as sadly laments it, and as watchfully avoids those deceits. Observe it, though deceivings by the heart be bad, yet observing and laying up such sad experiences, is certainly good, and of singular use to the sincere and serious soul. The Lord help us all so to note, and be afraid of our naughty spirits, that we may trust them less, and God more, while we live.

3. Lay up experiences of sin's bitterness. Consider what have been the insinuating ways of sin and Satan to entangle you, and the sad effects of sin. What tears, and groans, and bitter bickerings it has cost your captivated souls, to extricate yourselves, and regulate your state. Oh, the intricate windings of that crooked serpent! What strange and subtile methods and devices has Satan used, to trap and overtake you with his fresh and furious assaults! How often hath he presented the bait and hid the hook? Hath he not set before your credulous souls the pleasure or profit of a

* Quisque sibi Satan est.
† A malo homine meipso libera me, Domine.

base lust? Hath he not extenuated sin at first to bring you to commit it, and afterwards aggravated it to drive you to despair? Sin doth cheat us with golden mountains, as one saith, but leaves us in the mire at last. Though sin was delightful at the first, yet it always proved bitterness in the end.* Ask your own hearts, what fruit had you of those things whereof you are now ashamed? The awakened conscience will answer the end of those things is death;† deadly pain, or eternal death; repentance, or vengeance. Your wild oats sown in youth with delight, rose up in bitter hemlock and wormwood. Though wickedness was sweet in the mouth, yet it is turned to be as the gall of asps within, yea, the cruel venom of asps, as Moses testifies, that is, capital, deadly, biting poison; so it proves. ‡ Oh, the dreadful stings and pangs that sin leaves behind it! With what fears and tears, terrors and horrors does it fill the poor penitent soul! What broken bones and affrighting cares had the offending prodigal before he was admitted into his father's sweet embraces! How long did the humble suitor lie at the gates of mercy before he could get admission, or see the King's face? or obtain the joy of God's salvation? Not that God is so hard to be entreated, or delights in a poor creature's malady or misery, but that he may affect the heart with the evil of sin, stir up more longings after grace, prize Christ and pardon, and learn to sin no more. Therefore, he keeps the soul long in suspense, even when his bowels yearn upon it, as Joseph's did

* Jam. i. 14, 15.

† See the Slights of Sin opened in Capel on Temp. page 21—36.

‡ Rom. vi. 21. Job. xx. 12, 13, 14. Deut. xxxii. 33. וראש et caput; per metonym. venenum, quod capiti aut dentibus serpentis vel aspidis inest; venenum capitale et mortiferum.

upon his brethren; on the like ground, as he dealt with Miriam, in healing her body of the leprosy. If her father, saith he, had but spit in her face, should she not be ashamed seven days.—Num. xii. 14. Thus God would have us to know the worth of his favour, by the want of it for a season. Surely, sirs, if you would lay such sad experience in store, it would prove a notable antidote against the next assault; the burnt child will dread the fire. Oh, what sin-abhorring resolutions had the penitent soul in its deep humiliations! If you had come to David whilst he was bathing himself in briny tears, and said, what sayest thou now to murder? How dost thou like thy fleshly lusts? Wilt thou buy repentance at so dear a rate, and fall again into uncleanness? Would he not have answered, " Oh, no! God forbid that I should sin again?" I will be racked, or torn in pieces, rather than dishonour my God, grieve his Spirit, and fill my poor soul with such tormenting troubles. Certainly, when poor David was roaring, by reason of the disquietness of his Spirit, when there " was no rest in his bones because of his sin,"* he had other thoughts of his sin than when he was adventuring upon it. There is scarcely any man so brutish, but will abstain from that which experience tells him hath done him hurt. A wise man will forbear stale drink when he knows infallibly it will bring upon him excruciating pain. So the Christian that hath laid up experience of sin having cost him dear, will thus argue, " I remember what an ill condition sin brought me into, I had need to sin no more lest a worse thing come unto me. Sin broke my bones, but now if I sin again, I fear it will break my neck; sin filled my soul with heart-shaking fears, but I may expect it will now fill me with heart-desolating

* Psal. xxxviii. 3, 8.

despair; it brought a hell into my conscience before, but now I fear it will cast my soul into hell." Lay up and make use of such sad experience, and I may then almost say, Sin if you dare.

4. Lay up divine discoveries, which your souls have had sweet and satisfying experience of. If you be Christians, such you have had, I dare say, and you dare not deny. I find very many precious saints that have kept a diary of God's dealings with their souls, as the Rev. Mr. Carter, and many others.* There are two sorts of experiences that I shall recommend to you to treasure up: special providences, and spiritual influences.

(1.) You are to lay up experiences of God's gracious providence about you. The wise God hath so disposed of affairs concerning his people, that one part of our lives may help us in another; the van and former part of our days may contribute to bring up the rear and remainder of them; as thus, the soul argues, the Lord hath helped in such a strait, directed in such a doubt, prevented such a fear, broken such a snare, and he is the same God still, and will help for the future. Let the saints set up some Ebenezer, † as a memorial of former goodness; let them make use of the excellent Scripture logic, Hath delivered, doth and will deliver. Write down signal providences, or lock them up in the safe chest of a sanctified memory, and produce them when you are non-plused, and have your back to the wall. Sweet experiences of bye-past deliverances are not the least part of a Christian's treasure, though I would not have you dote upon them, or imagine that God can go no further than he hath gone, which may more daunt you in new and greater troubles; yet withal, do not despise them, and slight them, but lay

* Clark's Collect. page 21.   † Stone of help.

them up and plead them with the Lord as the church often doth.* One part of Psalm lxxiv. is a sad complaint of God's anger, and the church's affliction; the other part is an encouraging rehearsal of former providences. Thus, the assistance formerly vouchsafed, proves an argument for the saint's future encouragement.

(2.) You must also lay up experiences of soul-enlargement and refreshing comforts, as thus; in such an ordinance I met with God, and beheld his reconciled face; in such a duty, my graces were quickened, exercised, increased; in such a chamber, or closet, my heart was warmed, melted, and satisfied; in such a company, with such a society, was my soul enlarged, resolved, and sweetly transported beyond myself. Oh! what a blessed day or night was that unto me, when I experienced the manifestations of God's favour, enjoyed the smiles of his face, and had a clear acquittance sealed to my conscience, ensuring the remission of my sins! I well remember it, and my heart danceth within me to think of the sweet days of mutual intercourse that God and I have had together! These are not always to be expected, such sweet-meats of divine joy are not a Christian's constant common fare; a pining time may come; I will make much of, and long store up, such sweet and secret hints of love against a time of need. God forbid that I should lose this token for good, this broken ring, this pledge from heaven. This may stand me in stead, in a dark and gloomy day, when the Lord may frown upon me as an enemy, and put me from him as though he would forsake me; then will I say unto God, as Job, " Thou knowest that I am not wicked, †
Lord, dost thou use to deal so with wicked men, or reveal thyself thus to them that know thee not?" Art

---

* Isa. li. 9, 10, chap. lxiv. 1, 2, 3.   † Job, x. 7.

thou wont to stir up in the careless world, such peninent bemoanings, such ardent breathings, and such vehement pantings after thyself? And hast thou ever given such familiar discoveries to unregenerate souls, as my heart hath had experience of many a time, and is this the manner of man, O Lord? Are these thy ways with unsanctified souls? Wilt thou hold communion with those that never were united to thee? Doth not such communion pre-suppose a union? Either this experience is false and counterfeit, or I am thine, for whom thou " lovest once, thou lovest to the end;" though I be fickle and inconstant, yet thou art the same, and unchangeable in thy love. Now I dare not say that all these sweet experiences are mere fictions, dreams, and shadows; no, God forbid. I humbly hope they were genuine evidences of thy special love, arising from and built upon thy word; yea, they carried their evidence along with them, and left such impressions upon my soul as can never be forgotten or worn off. I can appeal to thyself, O Lord, if such passages were not betwixt thyself and my heart, which no creature upon earth hath known, and since thou canst not deny thine own name, engraven on my heart and sealed sweetly to me, I commit the matter wholly to thee, though now thou seemest to carry strangely towards me, as though thou hadst quite cast me off, yet thou art my God still, my loving father, and only friend; I cannot part from thee, I will not let thee go. There was once love betwixt us, and though now in wisdom and faithfulness thou seemest to smother thy bowels of mercy, and restrain the effects of thy love; yet, thou hast the same heart now as thou wast wont to have; I know it by the workings I feel in mine own breast towards thee; and therefore, Lord, I hang upon thee, and plead with David,

" Where are thy former loving-kindnesses which thou shewedst to me?"*

Thus, Christians, thus lay up, and thus draw forth your sweet experiences in such a time of need, in this night of desertion, as Tamar once did produce Judah's staff, signet and bracelets, as her pledge when she was brought out to be burnt. † O, sirs, when God deals graciously with you, cast not these precious love tokens at your heels, as whorish spirits do, but lay up these testimonies of love, sent from your husband, Christ, among your choicest treasures, that you may produce them as occasion serves.

CHAP. XIII.

COMFORTS AS A TREASURE, SHOULD BE LAID UP IN THE HEART.

A FOURTH description of treasure to be hoarded up in the breast of a believer, consists of the sweet and satisfying comforts of the Spirit. It is true, these are the sovereign and immediate effects of the sanctifying and sealing Spirit, yet, ordinarily comfort is dropped from heaven into the believing soul, in a way of duty and holy endeavour. The nearer we approach to the sun, and the more light and heat; now exercises of religion are a soul's approaching to the sun of righteousness, and for this cause, it is good for us to draw near to God, that we may anchor and centre our souls upon him, where only we can have rest. This present reward we may find in keeping God's commandments; grace

---

* Psalm lxxxix. 49. † Gen. xxxviii. 25.

and peace, holiness and comfort go usually hand in hand; "for wisdom's ways are ways of pleasantness and all her paths are peace," Prov. iii. 17. "And great peace have they that love God's law, Psalm cxix. 165. Every gracious act hath some degree of comfort annexed to it; peace is in them, as well as on them, that walk according to rule, * and these good old ways, † bring us to rest in God, and produce a blessed sabbath of rest in our spirits. If you keep God's commands, Christ will " send the comforter to you," nay, " himself will come unto you, and make his abode with you."—John xiv. 15, 16, 23. Be much in the performance of holy duties, and seek the enjoyment of God in ordinances; therein you may behold the light of his countenance, and hear his pleasant voice; there you may suck and be satisfied at those breasts of consolation; through those blessed pipes you may derive solid joy, and experience ravishing sweetness. Improve Scripture truths, act spiritual graces, lay up reviving experiences, and the result of all will be refreshing comforts.

But besides these, I counsel you to hoard up and make much of such thoughts as may be streams to feed and fill the well of solid, settled comforts in your hearts. Take only these four directions.

1. Lay up all your comfort in God alone. God " is the father of mercies, and the God of all consolation." ‡ There is not a beam of light or stream of joy, but what proceeds from this sun and spring of grace and happiness. The great God that made all things with a word, can speak and make peace in the confused heart. It is one of his royal incommunicable prerogatives, Isa. li. 12, " I, even am he that comforteth you." If God comfort, who can sadden? and if God afflict, who else can comfort? ‖ The air lights not without the sun;

* Gal. vi. 16. † Jer. vi. 16. ‡ 2 Cor. i. 3. ‖ Job xxxiv. 29.

the fuel heats not without the fire; neither can any instrument cheer up a drooping heart, where God suspends his influence; but God's children have been encouraged and comforted in him in the absence of other comforts, as David and Habakkuk.* O Christians, learn this divine art of fetching all your comforts from God! Lay up your stock of comfort in the rock of ages; this will be as " honey out of the rock, as water from the fountain," that comes freely, sweetly, purely, and abundantly. If you lay up all your comfort in the streams, what will you do for comfort when the streams are cut off? If you hang your comfort on every hedge, it will be far to seek in a day of need; but if God be your portion, the antidote is at hand, so that you need not fear poisoning or perplexing evils, for his very " rod and staff shall comfort you." Old Chytræus had this only and all-sufficient medicine and remedy in his troubled affairs, to support his fainting heart; the father's heart, the faithful word and powerful hand of Jehovah, and thus he sings,

> Una est in trepidâ mihi re medicina Jehovæ,
> Cor patrium, os verax, omnipotensque manus.

Hence, it was, that holy David disclaims all the world, and saith, " he hath none in heaven, or earth, besides God, Psalm lxxiii. 25, 26, and when all was gone he had still a sufficient portion on the absence or opposition of all the world. Hence it is, that the saints have been like mount Zion, and remained impregnable in the midst of waves, being settled upon the rock of ages. O sirs, could you account God your exceeding joy, how sweetly and cheerfully would you go to his altar upon all occasions! Psalm xliii. 4, and if you lay up your comfort in God, you may know where to find

* 1 Sam. xxx. 6.   Hab. iii. 17, 18.

it when you have need of it, and none can take your joy, because they cannot take your God away from you.

2. Lay the stress of your comfort on free grace in justification. Here, only, is the spring of all your comfort, Rom. v. 1, " being justified by faith, we have peace with God." Yea, peace within, in our own consciences, " for we glory in tribulation."—Rom. v. 3. Gratuitous justification is the ground of all consolation. Christ's righteousness imputed, is the sweetest word in all the Scriptures, which is ten times repeated in Rom. iv. Though Papists make a mock of it, let Protestants make much of it; it is the sweetest flower in our garden, the Jachin and Boaz of our gospel temple, the ladder whereupon souls ascend to heaven. Our only comfort is bound up in the covenant of free grace, not in that of works. Stick to this; contend earnestly for this; let all go, rather than let this go; it is the chief article and principle of our religion, upon which the church stands, without which it falls, as Luther saith. * O, therefore, let no mud defile this blessed stream; study free grace,—ascribe all to free grace,—lay up thoughts of undeserved, distinguishing grace. Remember what our blessed Redeemer hath done and endured; let the dolours of his soul be the solace of your hearts; fetch your only comfort from his bitter cross. Consider, how fully Christ hath satisfied divine justice! how large and liberal the gospel proclamation is! how our dear Redeemer opens his arms and bosom to embrace repenting prodigals! how he bids all welcome, and never yet cast off any that came unto him! how he hath pardoned infamous sinners, and hath received gifts even for the rebellious! Revolve these in thy mind; bring the promises warm to thy heart; let thy hyssop of

* Articulus stantis aut cadentis Ecclesiæ.

faith sprinkle Christ's blood upon thy conscience, for generals afford no comfort. Particular application is the only means of consolation. A hungry man takes little pleasure in gazing upon a feast, while he tastes not of it. David's table spread with dainties in the midst of his enemies, rather vexed than pleased those envious spectators. It is a blessed thing to think of pardon of sin, justifying grace, adoption, reconciliation, but what comfort can we take therein, except we can say, he loved me and gave himself for me; my Lord and my God; my Redeemer liveth; a crown of life is laid up for me?* O, this, this is the life of our lives, the support of our souls! Yet, if you cannot always say, that grace is yours, Christ is yours, and heaven is yours, yet be much in the thoughts of free grace; pore not upon your vileness and unworthiness, but ponder upon that which can answer all in one word. " I will have mercy, because I will have mercy and on whom I will have mercy." Lay up such Scriptures as these, Rom. iii. 24, Isai. liii. 4—6, and xliii. 25, Heb. viii. 12, that by the comfort of these and such like Scriptures you may have hope; they may be worth mines of gold, and all the world, in a day of darkness, to the doubting Christian.

3. Store up your clearest evidences of sincerity. The Spirit ordinarily conveyeth comfort by shining upon his own work, and by helping the soul to make practical syllogisms; as thus, whosoever doth sincerely call on the name of the Lord shall be saved,; † but saith the soul, I do sincerely pray and perform other Christian duties, therefore I shall be saved;—or thus, grace is with them that love our Lord Jesus Christ in sincerity, ‡ but saith the soul, I love the Lord Jesus in sincerity,

* Gal. ii. 20. John xx. 28. Job xix. 25. 2 Tim. iv. 8.
† Rom. x. 13.   ‡ Eph. vi. 24.

therefore, I have the grace or favour of God. The major proposition is a Scripture assertion; the minor, or assumption, is from a soul's inward experience of sincerity, and the Spirit of God witnessing with an upright heart and conscience, helps the soul to this demonstrative inference and conclusion, that he is a child of God, in God's favour, and shall be saved; and thence arises satisfaction aud consolation. The poor soul by a reflex act, doth view the seeds and sproutings of a sincere faith and love, and saith, though these have not purchased my husband's love, yet are they sweet effects thereof. These divine ornaments of saving graces do satisfyingly evidence that my soul is betrothed to Jesus Christ. If your souls be all glorious within in sanctification, it is a good sign that your clothing is of wrought gold in justification. Make sure and clear your effectual vocation, and then you clear up your eternal election.* The sanctifying Spirit witnesseth with the sanctified soul that it is a child of God, † and thus, some understand those three that bear witness in earth, the spirit, water, and blood, to be the cleansing acts of the Spirit, evidencing the soul's interest in our Saviour's efficacious merits; ‡ but this I desire of you, to clear up the truth of grace; fall upon the old trade of inquiring after marks of sincerity, yet do not think the bare hearing of them, or having such notes in your books or memory will be sufficient means of comfort, but lay your hearts by them in a close and convincing application, improve them by a self-imposing examination, and then fetch inferences therefrom in a rational way of argumentation, and lay up those deductions against a time of need; write it down that thou mayest have it to shew under thy hand against the quarrels of an unbelieving heart. Treasure up the means and in-

* 2 Pet. i. 10.   † Rom. viii. 16.   ‡ 1 John v. 8.

struments of your peace and settlement, the time when, and place where, your souls were satisfied; the low and hopeless state your souls were in, before the Lord did visit you from on high. O lay up carefully, the various circumstances about your satisfying comforts, the seasonable incomes thereof, their powerful entrance, and self-discovering, soul-recovering evidence. Lay up the gradual progress, or sudden elapses of comfort into your hearts, with the strong abiding impression they left upon your spirits. Finally, lay up the sweet result and strengthening effects of those your consolations, that so for the future, in the multitude of your disquieting thoughts within you, these comforts may again delight your souls.—Psal. xciv. 19.

4. Lay up tears in God's bottle, prayers in God's book, comforts in others' breasts, and promises in your own. I put all under one head, for brevity sake. (1.) Lay up many tears in God's bottle:—comfort is the portion of mourners,* it is promised by God, purchased by Christ, applied by the Spirit of comfort, and only suitable to weeping, mourning souls. It is the usual, constant design of God to comfort those that are cast down, to heal the broken in heart, to revive drooping souls, and contrite hearts.† Do you mourn for your sins, God will comfort you in yonr mourning. The sorrows of the saints are like the pangs of a travailing woman, that tend to and end in comfort, John xvi. 21. Repentance is the ready road to contentment. The same word in Hebrew, that signifieth first, to repent, ‡ doth also denote comforting or ceasing from sorrow, ||

* Matt. v. 4. Isai. lxi. 2, 3.

† 2 Cor. vii. 6. Psal. cxlvii. 3. Isai. lvii. 15.

‡ נחם Doluit, pœnituit, 1 Sam. xv. 35.

|| Niph. נחם dedoluit, dolore desiit, vel consolationem dat, invenit. Isa. xl. 1.

because true comfort belongs only to the penitent. The Jews fable, that with such as weep in the night, the stars and planets weep, and if they let the tears fall down their cheeks, God is ready with his bottle to receive them, which he pours, say they, upon the enemy's edicts to blot the writings that the Jews shall receive no hurt thereby. But sure I am, God is much affected with his children's tears, and comes, as it were, with a handkerchief to wipe away those tears, or rather, as the Scripture speaks, puts their tears into his bottle,* and reserves them for their future comfort. Shedding penitential tears is a spiritual seed-time, and they that sow in tears shall reap in joy; even sheaves of comfort are the harvest of this precious seed-plot. † This briny water shall be turned into refreshing wine. According to the depth of your sorrow, will be the height of your comfort. Not a tear shall be lost that is of the right sort. Every gracious sigh rises before the Lord as delectable incense, and every drop distilled from a broken heart, shall in time multiply to a flood of joy. Who was more dissolved into tears than holy David? And, who had a heart more full of joy, or a tongue so full of the high praises of God, as that sweet singer of Israel? O sirs, grieve much for sin, and you shall rejoice in, and for your grief. Plenty of tears prepares for, and ushers in plenty of joy. But (2.) Lay up many prayers in God's book, as well as tears in his bottle, be frequently approaching to the throne of grace. The sighs of your spirits will be echoed back with the sweet breezes of God's Spirit. The Spirit of grace will be a spirit of peace; as prayer goeth up, comfort comes down; God makes children joyful in the duty of prayer, as well as in the house of prayer. "For this," saith the Psalmist, "shall every one that is godly

* Psal. lvi. 8. † Psal. cxxvi. 5, 6.

pray unto thee; surely, then, in the floods of great waters they shall not come nigh unto him," Psal. xxxii. 6. Prayer reacheth to heaven, and fetcheth heaven into the heart; prayer seeketh, and the soul by faith in prayer seeth, God's face, which is a heart-rejoicing sight; it scattereth fears, lighteneth the soul, and preventeth shame and sorrow.* "Ask," saith Christ, "and ye shall receive, that your joy may be full," John xvi. 24. Therefore, Christians, pour out your hearts to God, and he will pour in comfort to you. And then, (3) Comfort others, as you are able, empty yourselves of experiences, by communicating them to afflicted souls, and they will return upon you with double advantage. There is much pleasure in opening our hearts to Christian friends. When you say, come, and I will shew you what he hath done for my soul, God will do more for your souls; if you help others, God will help you. You little know how it may comfort you to impart comforts to others. Mr. Knox rose off from his sick and death-bed, and would needs go to the pulpit, that he might impart to others his sweet meditations on Christ's resurrection, and the solacing consolation he felt in his soul. There is no envy in spiritual things; it is the property of a child of God to long, that others may taste of that which his soul feels comfort in; and, indeed, God makes the breasts of some, to be the storehouse of comfort for others. 2 Cor. i. 6, "Whether we be comforted, it is for your consolation and salvation;" not only by way of sympathy and affection, but by way of intercourse and communication. Besides, the more you comfort others, the more you have to pity and comfort you; the law of gratitude will engage them, and the treasure you have laid up in

* See Psal. xxxiv. 4, 5.

them will dispose them to be helps to you in the day of your sadness. (4.) Store up Scripture cordials, covenant promises in your souls. Psal. cxix. 50, " This is my comfort in affliction; thy word hath quickened me." This was David's portion, heritage, and song in the house of his pilgrimage. Especially improve and apply gospel promises. These are, *fasciæ Christi*, the swaddling clothes of Christ; these are like *aqua vitæ* * to the fainting soul. The Scripture is full of them. Some have observed that the covenant of grace is mentioned directly a hundred times, but by clear and necessary consequence, a thousand times in the book of God. God hath laid in all these promises for our comfort, that we through patience and comfort of the Scriptures might have hope. † To this very end is it, that God hath not only spoken but sworn, that we might have strong consolation.—Heb. vi. 18. Promises are the breasts of consolation, at which you may suck and be satisfied; promises are sacred anchors, to keep the soul unmoved amidst the fluctuations of time; white sails for the blessed spirit to waft souls to the haven of rest; they are gospel pails, bowls, and breasts to suckle and feed the lambs of the flock, and rich mines to make the Christian rich in grace, and rich in comfort. ‡ Therefore, let Christians always have these divine antidotes at hand for the help and support of their fainting souls. Only look to your right to, and improvement of, the promises. Divines observe a two-fold right to promises.

First, A hereditary right. As we are co-heirs with

---

* Water of life. † Rom. xv. 4.

‡ Promissiones sunt sacræ anchoræ, vela candida, mulctralia evangelica, cœlestes uteres, spirituales aurifodinæ.—*See Dr. Spurst, on Promises.*

Christ, so an interest in, and union to, Jesus Christ, gives us this right. Secondly, A right of aptitude, fitness, or disposedness, and this is by having holy dispositions, gospel qualifications, and the required conditions of conditional promises. This is necessary, as well as the other,; look you after both, and then you shall have the comfort of the promises, and a sure foundation of lively hope.

Thus I have endeavoured to help you to hoard up these four precious and necessary treasures of truths, graces, experiences and comforts. Let none of your souls be found destitute of these, or of a large share thereof, particularly of this last. O let not the consolations of God be small in your eyes;* set a high price upon them, store them up; they are not the least part of your treasures; these will fit you for God's service, qualify you for enduring afflictions, fortify your spirits against temptations. You that at present are dandled upon the knee of God's fatherly indulgence, satisfied with favour, and sit at the high table eating and drinking in God's presence, feasting your souls with the pleasant repasts of assurance; consider how soon the Lord may turn the tables, give you bare commons and water of gall to drink, and fill your souls with bitterness. Be sure, you shall not always live by this kind of spiritual sense, a time of heaviness may come, when you must cast anchor in the dark, and act a faith of adherence upon an unseen Redeemer. Yea, trust in that God whom your souls do also fear as one that is ready to kill, † and you will find it a hard thing to hang about an angry, chiding, scourging father. Therefore, lay up the comforts your souls do now partake of; give God the glory of them, and recollect them in a time of darkness. Plead them before the Lord,

* Job xv. 11.   † Job xiii. 15.

and upon a due sense of those, though now you see him not, yet love him, and believe in him, and in due time you shall " rejoice with joy unspeakable and full of glory."—1 Pet. i. 8.

CHAP. XIV.

ON THE PRESERVATION AND INCREASE OF A CHRISTIAN'S TREASURE.

THUS I have largely handled directions for obtaining a treasure, and particular instructions relative to different portions of treasure to furnish the soul. Now, it is also necessary to beware of losing or diminishing this treasure. It is a piece of wisdom to keep as well as get, to maintain as well as obtain, a treasure.* A little negligence loseth that suddenly, which had been got with much diligence. Solomon saith, " there is a time to cast away stones, and a time to gather stones together," but there is no time to cast away these precious treasures; you must keep what you have, and still be gathering more. Now to help you herein, take these ten practical directions.

1. Let not Satan rob or circumvent you. He is that evil one that envies a saint's treasure. He steals away the " seed of the word",† lest it become a treasure of divine truths; he it is, that most grudgeth our growth in grace. The better the soul is treasured, the more assaults must he suffer from the evil one. A pirate makes most at a rich laden ship; a thief breaks not into the beggar's cottage; the devil lets his sworn vas-

* Non minor est virtus quàm quærere parta tueri.
† Matth. xiii. 19.

sals live in peace, but raiseth an uproar in the believer's heart. This juggler will "transform himself into an angel of light," that like a familiar he may pick our pockets with more ease and less suspicion. As he foists in dangerous errors under the notion of truth, so he lures to damnable sins under the paintings of virtue. Take heed of both; observe it, new notions may eat out the heart's root of religion, as well as corrupt practices. Satan may rob us of our treasure by subtile insinuations of new light, as well as grosser temptations to apparent works of darkness, for these drink up the marrow of those spirits that should be laid out otherwise. Therefore, take Paul's advice, "refuse profane and old wives' fables, and exercise yourselves rather to godliness."—1 Tim. iv. 7. Strivings, though they should be even about the Scriptures and the law, may come to be "unprofitable and vain."—Tit. iii. 9. Great triflers are no good treasurers, and many great disputers have argued away much of their religion, or at least have filled their heads with notions, rather than their hearts with saving truths or pious affections. Precious saints have complained that even necessary disputes have put their spirits out of tune. You have zeal little enough for the vitals of religion; let none run in by channels. The Lord help you to prize more a fundamental truth, and a degree of saving grace, than a fine notion or victory over an antagonist. Take heed lest Satan dart into you a spark of false zeal and blow it up to an eager dispute for an opinion, to divert or excuse you from occupying your attention with the more weighty matters of Christianity. O Christians, be not ignorant of Satan's various methods to get an advantage against you, that he may rob you of your treasure.* You know, the old serpent, when he was

* 2 Cor. ii. 11. xi. 3, 14.

young, outwitted our first parents in their best estate; now he is grown more cunning by almost six thousand year's experience, and we more foolish in this dotage of the world; we are, therefore, in great danger of being undone. O let us watch and pray that we enter not into temptation; keep out of Satan's road; hold him at a distance, suspect his wiles, and resist his power, that neither his seven heads by plotting, nor his ten horns by pushing, may deprive our souls of our precious treasure.

2. Fill not your hearts with the world. Carnal men have the world set in their hearts, and are therefore called, " the men of this world,"* that have their portion therein, and that is totally inconsistent with this heavenly treasure; for the more you admit the world into your hearts, the more you thrust out divine things. As the shining sun eats out the burning fire, or as the abundance of weeds sucks up the virtue of the earth that should nourish the herbs and fruit trees; just so do riches choke the word by a wicked encroachment which they make upon the heart. The love of the world jostles out the love of God.—1 John ii. 15. Love and royalty can endure no rivals. It is true, " religion begot wealth, but the daughter devours the mother,"† as the Proverb hath it: worldly-mindedness is directly opposite to heavenly treasures. O let not your hearts be in the world, though your heads and hands be in it. The heart is to be reserved for God; if riches be placed in that closet, Christ will be thrust into the stable; if riches increase, set not your hearts thereon. ‡ In the Apostle's times, the saints " cast their money and estates at the Apostle's feet," ‖ thereby signifying,

* Eccl. iii. 11. Psal. xvii. 14.
† Religio peperit divitias sed filia devoravit matrem.
‡ Psal. lxii. 10. ‖ Acts iv. 37.

saith an Ancient, " that they were fitter to be trodden upon, than doted upon, or rather to be a step-stone to divine things, than a burden on our backs;" but the truth is, these outward things are to many, rather a stumbling block to cast them down, than a footstool to lift them up. It is better to be without great estates, than to have them for a snare. Tremble lest you be overcharged with the cares of the world, or be bewitched with the delights here below. Be not like that carnal Cardinal, that preferred his part in Paris to his part in paradise; but say, as that noble commander to a common soldier, " Thou art not Themistocles, take this trash to thee;" for so he called and accounted the Persian spoils, of richest jewels and goodliest ornaments. So do thou scorn to load thy noble soul with such unworthy baggage; cast out those wares that will sink the ship of the soul. One staff will help in your journey, but a bundle will be burdensome carriage; a garment fit for the body is easy and useful, but one that is too wide, or with a long train, is in danger to be troublesome to the party that wears it, and others; not that I would have you to cast away the tender mercies of God, though you must " cast your bread on the waters;" but cast the world out of your hearts. Let not your precious souls, like the serpent, feed on the dust. If you possess much of the world, let it not possess you; fear yourselves in this most. How many Demases are hereby shipwrecked! How many Sampsons have lost their best strength by the embraces of this Delilah! Alas! thousands have been cheated of their spiritual riches by its syren songs, and bewitching charms, and, therefore, let our souls stand at a distance from it, make no friendship with it; let us more suspect its fawnings, than fear its frowns. A false friend will prejudice us more than an open foe.

Let no earthly treasure take off our spirits from one that is heavenly, lest we abate of the divine stock that our precious souls are furnished with.

3. Mortify the corruption of your hearts. Cast out those intestine enemies, carnal affections. Sin and grace are like two scales, as one goeth up, the other goeth down, or like two buckets, as the one mounts up full, so the other falls down empty; the more full the heart is of sin, the more empty it is of goodness. Sin is the thief in the candle that dims our light and comfort; it is as mire in the channel that stops the current of grace. Sin is a great prodigal that wastes a fair revenue. Adam, by one fall, lost every thing. Sin is the canker and moth that mars all our enjoyments; it is a drawback to high attainments; it is the only make-bait betwixt God and the soul, which hinders communion with God and communications from God.* The devil, the world, and the flesh, are the soul's mischievous and mortal enemies, but the flesh is nearest and worst; therefore, these fleshly lusts are said peculiarly to fight against the soul. † Divines distinguish three sorts of temptations, ascendant, objected, and injected. Ascendant temptations are such as spring up from some stirred humour or inferior faculty within us, that borders next upon the sense or affection. Objected, are such as reflect from some outward object, baited and suited to the organ. Injected, are such as the tempter immediately affects the faculty itself with. This last proceeds from Satan, the second from the world, but the first from our own hearts, which is of all others most dangerous. Except the wicked one find something in us he can have no advantage against us. ‡ Our base hearts entertain little thieves within, which open the door to Satan without, who comes to spoil us

---

* Isa. lix. 2.   † 1 Pet. ii. 11.   ‡ John xiv. 30.

of our treasure; therefore, take heed of this wily, beguiling thing, touch not the forbidden fruit, admit no parley with lust, commit no sin, though ever so secretly, a secret way of spending hath exhausted large estates. Heart sins dallied with, and delighted in, will do your souls a deadly mischief. A privy stab may let out your heart's blood; an unsuspected leak may sink a well laden ship, and therefore let a Christian say as good Joseph, who though might have committed lewdness with his mistress secretly and safely as to man, yet cries out, "How shall I do this wickedness and sin against God?" O sirs, consider how unsuitable and incongruous it is for a vessel of mercy to admit iniquity! it is as if a cup of gold were filled with the vilest filth. O let not your precious souls be filled with the loathsome impurities of sin. Remember your dignity and duty, and " keep yourselves from an evil matter;" have not any " fellowship with the unfruitful works of darkness; mortify earthly members; possess your vessel in sanctification and honour; purge out filthiness of flesh and spirit,"* and thereby you will not only maintain, but increase your soul's treasure.

4. Observe the Spirit's impulses. Yield to the genuine motions of God's blessed Spirit; " grieve him not,"† lest he grieve or leave you; he is delicate, and will deal with you as you deal with him. Christ Jesus hath left the Holy Ghost to supply his place, and now the Spirit is God's great factor in the world; if he knock at your doors, he hath a good bargain for you. O slight not such a chapman lest you dally away your market. The Spirit never puts you upon duty, but he calls you to some profit. Now, it is good making hay when the sun shines, and sailing when you have wind

* Eph. v. 11. Col. iii. 5. 1 Thes. iv. 4. 2 Cor. vii. 1.
† Eph. iv. 30.

and tide to help you. Take this advantage, lest if you miss it, you be left to your own strength, and then what can you do? The Spirit is that gentle nurse, and strengthening hand that helps the infirmities of the dead or daunted child of God in prayer.* O refuse not this assistance. The Spirit is that holy fire, that sets the soul in a flame for God. " O do not quench it." † This Holy Spirit is a queen, that comes attended with a goodly train of graces and comforts, called the fruits of the Spirit, and, therefore, labour you to be filled with the Spirit,‡ and then you have this blessed treasure. It is true, you cannot expect it as Christ had it, beyond measure, ‖ yet your portion will be a treasure, and help you to maintain and increase that heavenly treasure in the heart. The incomes of the Spirit promote renewed acts of grace. As the sea ebbs and flows according to the influence of the heavenly bodies, so doth grace in the heart move, according to the operations of the Spirit. The more you yield up yourselves to the guidance of the Spirit, the more you will feel the assistance of the Spirit. § This will be a preservative from sin, a preparative to duty, an evidence of your state, and an entrance into glory; yea, then the peace of God, as well as the God of peace, shall keep your hearts and minds through Christ Jesus, Phil. iv. 7. φρουρήσει, shall keep as with a guard in a garrison, that is, shall stand centinel for you to prevent the furious assaults of your spiritual enemies, and be a safe convoy to the ship of your souls, to preserve you from rocks and sands, storms and pirates, till you come to the port of heaven; therefore, O ye Christians, make much of the Spirit, maintain familiarity with him, and he will

---

* Rom. viii. 26.   συναντιλαμβάνεται.
† 1 Thess. v. 9.   ‡ Gal. v. 22. Eph. v. 18.
‖ John iii. 34.   § See Gal. v. 5, 16, 18.

maintain your treasure, keep up intercourse with him, and he will keep his interest in you. Allies and confederates have the same friends and foes, and if you have the Holy Ghost to take your part, you shall be kept by the power of God, through faith unto salvation. If received faith cannot keep you, yet supporting power is able; never did any fall out of the hands of God; therefore, I beseech you, give up yourselves to the Spirit's guidance, and governance and he will be your guard and defence; that God who preserves his people's bones, will preserve their souls, and he that keepeth the feet of his saints, will also keep the fruits of his love in the souls of his servants, and if you thus do, " he that is able to keep you from falling, will present you faultless before the presence of his glory with exceeding joy."—Jude 24.

5. Carefully watch your hearts ; though God hath undertaken to guard you, yet you are bound to watch your own hearts. That is the command, Prov. iv. 23, " Keep thy heart with all diligence ;" in the Hebrew * it is very full and emphatical, in or above all keeping, take care of thy heart; thou mayest, and must look to other things, but above all, let thy eye be most intent upon, and thy study most about, the frame of thy heart. But why so? What great need of industry about the heart ? Why, he tells us, out of it are the issues of life, that is, all our treasure is there, our greatest stock and store; if that be neglected, our wealth is exposed to apparent hazard, therefore, keep thy heart with all diligence, lock up thy treasure, and set a guard upon it ; admit no strangers into this closet, let not other things make an inroad upon thee, or at least, a thoroughfare of thee. There is no keeping a treasure in a common room. A man that fears his purse in a strange place,

* מכל משמר נצר לבך.

hath always an eye upon it, he dare not let it go out of his sight; in a time of great robbing, a stranger suspects every one, and goeth not forth unarmed. O sirs, consider you are strangers on this earth; many thieves are abroad, they aim at you, they have plundered many of their treasures, and cast down many strong men wounded; therefore, look about you, keep strict watch, be not found asleep on guard, as the ten virgins, or Christ's own disciples, but gird up your loins, watch and be sober, and if drowsiness at any time seize on you, rub your eyes, shake off sloth, and awake out of sleep, and when there is any one knocks at your door, boldly ask, who is there? Whence comest thou? Art thou a messenger sent from God, or from Satan? Art thou for me, or against me? What is thy end or errand? Make your thoughts stand still, and go no further till they have undergone an impartial trial, whether they have a pass and commission under the great seal of heaven, and be warranted by the word, and tend unto the glory of God, and the soul's eternal good; and though vain thoughts may step into thy heart, yet, suffer them not to lodge there, for thy heart is not thine own, thou dost but keep it for thy Lord and Master; there he hath laid up a treasure, and if any thing be wanting through thy fault, thou canst not give a good account, but must be exposed unto shame, and grief, and loss. Principally and particularly watch thy heart when thou art before God in duty; beware of distractions, diversions, and excursions of spirit from God; these will waste and weaken thy treasure, by running out in a wrong channel, and diverting or spoiling the soul's activity; for the narrow, shallow spirit, cannot mind many things at once.* Besides, wandering thoughts are as dead flies in the box of pre-

* Quando animus dividitur ad multa fit minor.

cious ointment;* these vain cogitations obstruct the operations of grace, and insensibly steal away the affections from God; even dust, though small, may hinder the clock from going. Raise up your affections heavenwards, centre and settle your hearts upon God, say to distractions, as Nehemiah to his enemies, I am doing a great work, and I cannot come down, or as it is storied of John Baptist, who being asked of his companions to play with them, when he was a child, yet answered, " I am not born for sport;" thus do you say to your trifling hearts, it is not fit that I should leave the work of God, to attend upon toys; I must mind my business, or I shall go behind in my spiritual trade. That man is in danger to be on the losing hand, that stands gazing at others, or runs playing at foot-ball on the market-day, when others are busy making bargains, and getting money. O Christians, you either gain something, or lose in every performance; if the heart be not fixed on God, you are on the losing hand. Every thing is beautiful in its season, do what you do with all your might, pray when you pray, work when you work, but let not these things interfere. Set not up any idols in your hearts, drive away that which may interpose betwixt God and your souls, as Abraham drove away the fowls that sat upon the carcase. The Jewish Rabbins say, † that if a serpent bite a man by the heel, while he is at his devotions, he must not stop, nor stoop to shake it off, and heathens have recorded instances of some that have rather suffered their arms or legs to be burnt, with a coal from the altar, than move whilst sacrificing; and do not Christians blush, upon consideration of their slight occasions of diversion from God in duty? O learn from hence to be more instant and intent in worshipping

* Eccl. x. 1. † Lightfoot's Miscell. page 26.

God, whereby your treasure will be maintained and promoted.

6. Be most jealous over yourselves after the sweetest enlargements. There is the greatest danger after you have been with God, and loaded your souls with choicest treasures of refreshing incomes. I have observed almost a score of Scripture instances of saints' saddest falls, suddenly after God's doing some signal thing for them, or their doing some notable thing for God; and I appeal to experienced souls, if they have not sustained saddest shakings and losses, after the sweetest gains. Dear, barren years usually succeed great plenty; a great spending follows a time of gaining; a long journey comes after a good bait, and a sharp winter after a pleasant summer. God in his wisdom usually lets Satan loose upon such as he hath armed to the combat. Paul must have Satan's messenger to buffet him after abundant revelations. Peter acts Satan's part in dissuading Christ from suffering, after he had acted an angel's part in acknowledging him for the Messias. The French have often got that again by craft, which the English had obtained by prowess, and we know in all wars, supine negligence hath undone many an army, after famous victories. This *pugna osculana*, as historians call it, is when the conquered gathered strength, and so returned upon the conquerors when they were dividing the spoils. Just thus, doth Satan with God's children, when the soul has been with God, and got its vessel well fraught with spiritual riches, then it is in greatest danger of pirates; then Satan doth bestir himself most, his malice and policy take that as the fittest season to foil and plunder the well-laden soul; and then the soul is most apt to grow secure and carnally confident, and so gives Satan the greatest advantage; as a man that hath run fast, or worked

hard, sits down and cools suddenly after much sweating, doth thereby endanger his health, and life too, by a dangerous surfeit; so when the heart hath been sweetly warmed with the love of God, and is powerfully affected in a holy duty, it is then most in danger of a spiritual ague, a chill fit of deadness, for such a one blesseth himself, and thinks now he may sit still, and take his ease, and then comes a fall. This is the believer's round; this is his wheeling condition in the world. Peter confesseth Christ nobly, then magnifies himself too confidently, then denies his master shamefully, and at last goes out and weeps bitterly, and so was kindly received by his loving Master. This, this is the Christian's round, ebbing and flowing state, up-hill and down-hill condition, in this howling wilderness. But how sad is it, that a Christian should so soon forget his enlargements! and so soon return unto folly, after his heart is broken, and peace is imparted to him!* O, why should the soul so quickly turn out of the way, wherein so lately it had such encouragements? † Why should we give Satan such occasion to represent and insinuate to the God of heaven, that his servants will not be hired to continue with him, for all his present rewards, and promises of future happiness? Ah, sirs, is there not much reward in keeping God's commandments? Is there not more pleasure in holiness, than any sin? Why should you think to eke out your spiritual delights with sensual pleasures? Think seriously of it, be afraid to stain your milk-white souls, that are newly washed in the blood of the Lamb, by wallowing in the mud of sin. Be ashamed to dishonour God, to torment yourselves, to gratify your grand enemy, and lose that in an instant, which was so hardly obtained. Be not high-minded, but fear; be jealous over yourselves,

* Psal. lxxxv. 8. † Exod. xxxii. 8.

with godly jealousy; rejoice with trembling, cast not off fear, nor restrain prayer before God, keep conscience tender, eyes open, and hearts resolved for God. Pray over David's prayer, for the continued settlement of those affectionate impressions upon your own hearts, in 1 Chron. xxix. 18. For, alas, the best man on earth, is no more than the Lord makes him hourly; we are like a staff that must fall, if the hand be removed, or a stone that descends, if not carried or cast upwards; if we were as good as Paul or Peter, we should fall foully, without supporting grace; therefore, be jealous of yourselves after enlargements, and take heed, lest by security, you become a sacrifice to the devil, as Luther speaks. *

7. Another help for continuing and increasing this good treasure of the heart, is, to be frequent and exact in the search of your hearts. Be much in reviewing the frame of your spirits, " commune with your heart," ask what it getteth or loseth every day. Wise tradesmen often cast up accounts, and provident housekeepers look into their provision to see how it holds out, and wherein there is most danger of want. O Christians, be serious in this self-sifting work, and keep a distinct account how things are with you, whether you get or lose ground. Take the advice of a royal, learned writer to his princely son,† " Censure yourself as sharply as if you were your own enemy." A little further, " therefore, I would not have you to pray to be delivered from sudden death, but that God would give

---

* Nos nihil sumus, Christus solus est omnia qui si avertat faciem suam nos perimus et Satanas triumphat, etiamsi aut Petri aut Pauli simus : sicut Deo sacrificium est spiritus contribulatus, ita haud dubiè Diaboli sacrificium spiritus præfractus et securus.— *Luth. Tom.* 1. *Lat. fol.* 522.

† King James, Basil. Doron, page 16, 17.

you grace so to live, as that you may every hour of your life be ready for death." Sirs, study your hearts, try your ways, deal faithfully with your own souls, for you must undergo a critical search at the great day; yea, now in this world, God is about to " search you with candles," * and rouse up secure sinners from off their lees. A trying time may come, search yourselves first, you may by searching come to discern your state, and what degrees of grace you have, your " spirits may know the things of man " that concern yourselves, and may descend into the inward parts of the belly ;† therefore, make use of this reflective faculty of conscience, try your hearts, measure yourselves at this time with what you were formerly, and thereby you will understand how things are, and this will be a singular help against losing ground, will prevent apostacy, prepare you for, and engage you in a work of thankfulness, or repenting, suitable to what you find in your hearts. Only be clear and distinct about your state, that you may deplore, or congratulate yourselves on your condition accordingly. Thereby, God will have great glory, your souls much comfort, and if you find things amiss, that self-trial will be a step to reparation. ‡ O friends, take some time to pose ‖ and search your own hearts, in the multitude of businesses abroad, be not strangers at home, you will find work enough there. I shall conclude all with the words of a contemplative Divine : " The varieties of an ever changing condition whilst in this vale of misery, cannot be without perpetual employment for a busy soul, therefore," saith he, " O God, let me be dumb to all the world, so as I may ever have a

* Zeph. i. 12. † 1 Cor. xxi. 10. Prov. xx. 27.

‡ Dr. Hall's Sol. 13, called Bosom Discourse. For this subject of Self Exam. see Baxt. Saint's Rest, 3rd part. ‖ Examine.

tongue for thee and mine own heart." Take, yet, a verse from divine Herbert :—

> Sum up at night, what thou hast done by day,
> And in the morning, what thou hast to do ;
> Dress and undress thy soul, mark the decay
> And growth of it ; if with thy watch, that too
>   Be down, then wind up both, since we shall be
>   Most surely judged ; make thy accounts agree.

8. Timely make up spiritual decays. This seconds the former. If you find yourselves declining, do not rest satisfied ; let not an ill matter go on, decays and delays therein are dangerous, the further you proceed the worse will things be. A little rent in a a garment, if neglected, grows large and incurable ; a breach of water upon banks is quickly repaired at first, but afterwards in process of time, is widened to unavoidable inundations. Suits in law are easily taken up in the beginning, and fallings out amongst friends may be soon composed at first, but when contentions beget animosity, and then a grudge, the agreement is more unfeasable, and the offended party more unreconcileable. If you miss your way upon the road, how speedily may you, at the first, step back, and rectify your error ! But the further you go in a wrong way, the more is your danger and labour in returning. Many diseases, that have proved mortal in the issue, might have been cured had they been looked to in time ; and, therefore, the rule is, *obsta principiis*,[*] hinder the first beginnings of a disease. We know it is easier to keep off an enemy, than turn him out when once he is entered. The juice of a lemon is soon wiped off a knife when first sprinkled on it, without impression left, but its abiding thereon corrodes the metal, and leaves an indelible character. Even so, guilt is sooner removed immediately after it

[*] Principiis obsta : sera medicina paratur, cum mala per longas invaluere moras.

is contracted, than when it is long delayed; deferring doubles the guilt and makes the wound deeper. David's long absence from God procures to his back a heavier burden and broken bones, but Peter got the breach made up quickly by a speedy repentance; therefore, David learned, by sad experience, to make more haste to God, and not to delay his repentance and course of obedience.—Psal. cxix. 59, 60. O Christians, fall presently about this work. Vow this day unto the mighty God of Jacob, and you will not find rest for yourselves in your houses or beds, " till you have found a place for the Lord" in your hearts. Make not up the day till you have made your peace with God. Give not sleep to your eyes, till you can, through grace, say, your souls rest in the Lord, and God rests in his love to you*; and, if you die in that sleep, you shall sleep in Christ. Go to God, poor sinning, pining soul, and say to him, Lord, I feel my heart growing out of order, thou dost not grant to me thy wonted presence; sin is encroaching upon me, temptations prevailing, grace weakening, my spirit cooling, all things go to wreck within me; but I am not satisfied in this declining state, I cannot live at a distance from thee. I dare not neglect the means of my recovery. O revive thy work, restore thy quickening Spirit, repair and make visible in my precious soul thy glorious image, which consists in " knowledge, righteousness, and true holiness;" renew in my heart former affections, and restore unto my soul thy wonted favour. And thus, sirs, do you betake yourselves, first, to your hearts, and then to God, and use your utmost endeavours to recruit with speed your treasure of truths, graces, comforts, and experiences, and as a candle newly extinguished will quickly catch fire, so the smoking flax of your lan-

* Psal. cxxxii. 2—5.

guishing graces will quickly be restored and revived, and your fainting spirits, if taken timely, will suddenly be recovered. Say, then, with sweet Herbert in his Poems—

>Sin is still hammering my heart,
>   Unto a hardness void of love ;
>Let suppling grace, to cross his art,
>   Drop from above.

9. Be much in layings out. Mental and spiritual treasures have this strange property, that the more you lay out the more you increase therein: here that text is applicable, Luke vi. 38, "Give, and it shall be given unto you; good measure, pressed down and shaken together, and running over, shall be given into your bosom." We see, in other things, use makes prompt and perfect: it is use chiefly that makes the right hand stronger than the left—a key much used is bright, disuse makes it rusty—a pump much used brings forth water easily and abundantly—instruments of iron and steel are brighter with use. Thus it is in human learning, gifts, and graces ; expenditure enricheth the possessor, and Solomon saith, "The liberal soul shall be made fat, and he that watereth shall be watered also himself," Prov. xi. 25. A liberal soul is a soul of blessing, as the Hebrew hath it, because it is a blessing to others, and the more blessed by God; for to him that useth well shall be given more, as that is usually interpreted, Matt. xxv. 29, (though that must be referred to talents of the same kind, for improving common grace doth not necessarily procure special grace ;) God doth not impart these habits to lie dead in you, but you must stir up the gift of God, employ your stock, lay out your money to exchangers; be not either non-residents or non-agents—Christianity requires activity. The truth is, all excellencies in the

world are worthless, if they be useless. There is much good ground in the world that is neither cultivated nor owned—a world of precious metals in the bowels of the earth, which will never be coined; it is the constant use of money whereby it answers all things. " Improvement, (saith a reverend man,) gives a true value to all blessings; a penny in the purse is worth many talents in an unknown mine; that is our good that doeth us good, and that whereby we do good; and the more we do good, the more we are good." * Therefore, sirs, be active for God; read, pray, meditate, confer, and do every thing with your might, as men that are bound straight for heaven, and would do all the good you can upon earth, and draw with you as many as you can to glory. O how this will enrich you, and increase your stock! But this I have enlarged upon before; only observe, that it is the property of true grace to be communicative, and that it is a blessing annexed to its exercise to be aggregative. A Christian gets most by laying out—God helps those that are ready to help the souls of others.

10. Be thankful for treasures received. Give God praise, and God will give you more grace. As our duty ascends, mercy descends. Man's blessing God, brings down more blessings from God. Adore free grace, and you shall have more fruits of free grace. You are bound to bless God for worldly comforts and earthly treasures, much more for heavenly riches. Should we bless him for filling our houses with goods, and satisfying our appetites with victuals, and shall we not bless him for filling our heads with truths, and our hearts with grace? Must we bless him for a crust, and shall we not much more for a Christ? Shall we thank God for earth, and shall we not for heaven? I

* Soliloq. 20. Stock employed, p. 72, 73.

fear Christians are much defective in this angelical and evangelical duty of praise. They are much in complaining of their defects and imperfections, and that is good in its due place, and season, and measure, so as to humble them and promote endeavours; but withal, you ought to be thankful for what you are or have. Self-denial and gratitude are very consistent, and contribute mutually to improve each other. You may and ought to bewail your barrenness, though you must also thank God for degrees of fruitfulness; for what you have attained is the fruit of special grace. From God alone is your fruit found—he alone hath tilled, and sown, and given the increase; let him have all the crop and harvest: to him is this debt of thanks owing. Pay for the old, and fetch new; admire his free grace that you have any divine incomes; though you have not what you desire, yet you have more than you deserve, and so much as deserves your thankfulness. That is a churlish creature that drowns past kindnesses in a sea of desires after more. I do appeal to thine own conscience, hast thou not something in thy soul worth thanks? Hast thou not seen thy sin and misery—laid them more to heart than outward troubles? Dost thou not prize Christ above the world and long after communion with him? You cannot deny but you have received sweet impressions of divine truths, and various experiences; and as for graces and comforts, deal but faithfully with your own hearts, and see what they will say to you. Begin to enumerate your mercies, and you will see further occasion of gratitude; especially recount your spiritual blessings " in heavenly things in Jesus Christ." Thus doth holy David, Psalm ciii. 1—3; he stirs up " all within him to praise God," and reckoneth up spiritual mercies first. And canst not thou say, he hath satisfied thy heart, and replenished thy soul "with good things?" Lay thy hand upon thy heart, and ask it whether thou hast not abundant cause of thankfulness? and give God praise according to thy convictions. This is one great end God hath in bestowing mercy, and returning an answer of prayer, that the soul may praise him, which is the tribute of glory that is due from the creature to our Creator. See Psalm l. 14, 15, 23. Mr. Greenham observes,* "That in our liturgies, among a hundred prayers, scarce one thanksgiving is found; and yet in civil matters, either by a natural logic or cunning rhetoric, we have learned to begin a new suit, with a thankful commemoration of succeeding in the old." But, I beseech you, show not yourselves ungrateful—praise God for what you have received, yea, bless him for your sure grounds of hope—perform your duty, and trust God for the performance of his promise—bless God that he hath laid up so large a treasure in Christ for indigent souls—bless him that he hath laid out so much thereof upon the many thousands that are now filled brimful of grace and glory—and bless him for the sweet overflowings of distinguishing grace to your languishing souls. Sirs, you are often questioning the truth of grace; but exercising yourselves in this duty of thankfulness will evidence sincerity, and preserve your stock, and be a means of further proficiency. Unthankfulness and unholiness are linked together in Scripture; † and the more thankful you are, the more holy you are and will be—God loves cheerful worshippers. The great variety of musical instruments in God's worship of old, should be echoed with cordial praises in gospel times. Praise is comely in God's account, and thankful souls have largest incomes. What saint was ever loaded with such riches of grace as the

* Joel ii. 26. inter opera, fol. 8, 13. † 2 Tim. iii. 2.

chosen vessel, blessed Paul? and who was fuller of thankfulness, or sounded out the praises of God so much as he? He had it much on his lips, who had so much in his heart; and the more he speaks of it, the more he is filled with it. Every breath, let out in praises, draws in new supplies of grace. Do you glorify God, and he will satisfy you; pay this rent, and God will not turn you out of doors—give him this tribute, and you shall have your freehold; praise God for your little here, and you shall have fulness of grace and riches of glory to praise him in and with to all eternity.

I shall close all these directions to maintain a treasure, especially this last of thankfulness, with a sweet poem of divine Herbert's, called Gratefulness.

> Thou that hast given so much to me,
>   Give one thing more—a grateful heart;
> See how thy beggar works on thee,
>   By art.
>
> He makes thy gifts occasion more,
>   And says, If he in this be crost,
> All thou hast given him heretofore
>   Is lost.
>
> But thou didst reckon, when at first
>   Thy word our hands and hearts did crave,
> What it would come to at the worst
>   To save.
>
> Perpetual knockings at thy door,
>   Tears sullying thy transparent rooms,
> Gift upon gift—much would have more,
>   And comes.
>
> This notwithstanding, thou went'st on,
>   And didst allow us all our noise;
> Nay, thou hast made a sigh and groan
>   Thy joys.
>
> Not that thou hast not still above
>   Much better tunes than groans can make;
> But that these country airs, thy love
>   Did take.

Wherefore I cry, and cry again;
  And in no quiet canst thou be,
Till I a thankful heart obtain
                          Of thee.
Not thankful when it pleaseth me,
  As if thy blessings had spare days;
But such a heart whose pulse may be
                          Thy praise.*

CHAP. XV.

DIRECTIONS FOR BRINGING FORTH GOOD THINGS OUT OF THE CHRISTIAN'S GOOD TREASURE.

THERE remains yet another part of this directory, namely, how a good man is to bring forth good things out of the good treasure of the heart. In the explication this hath been largely insisted upon, that a Christian must lay out, and make use of his treasure in the great duties of meditation, religious performances, spiritual conferences, and in doing and enduring much for God. Passing these, I shall only add something on the manner of improving this treasure in the forementioned duties.

A Christian's treasure must be drawn out speedily, seasonably, sincerely, and suitably.

1. The Christian is to bring forth things new, as well as old—lately obtained, as well as long since hoarded. You are to improve truths on the first acquisition. Many good convictions, conceptions, impressions are lost, for want of speedy use; and many souls are undone by neglect and delay. "The slothful man roasteth not that which he took in hunting;" †

* Herb. the Church, p. 116. † Prov. xii. 27.

that is, he lets it lie by and mar upon his hands : he takes pains to hunt for it, but will not take pains to roast it. That meat is best that is fresh and new, and quickly used—it is a folly to keep it till it be old and good for nothing. O how many such sluggards are there in spiritual things! How many have I seen who have travelled far to hear a sermon, and been affected under it, yet lose all before they come home, for want of following it home! Many hunt after the means of grace, and take abundance of pains to run to ordinances, (which is to be commended,) but, alas, make little improvement thereof to their present advantage : their hearts were full of desires before, and of delight under the droppings of the sanctuary; but in a little time, these things grow stale, and by degrees wear out for want of a speedy improvement. The Jews were not to keep any of the manna, till the morrow, if they did, it stank; and God's people must not so lay up the word, as to neglect the present use thereof, for that will hinder the operation thereof; many a choice notion is lost for want of rubbing it up in a speedy recognition; many a powerful conviction of sin and duty dies, for want of speedy observation and application. The preacher lays on the plaster, but the wound is not cured, except it be kept on by the soul's voluntary consideration; when blossoms are knit, though the flourish be gone, yet they are more secured from injury by frosts and winds, than before ; good emotions speedily brought into act, are knit, and have a due consistency and settled continuance. O sirs, your work is not done, when public ordinances are at an end, you must, as the well-bred Bereans, try by Scripture what you hear, and see how it suits your case. A man will try a pair of gloves or shoes, how they fit him, when he first receives them, and use them afterwards, as he hath occasion ; and, will not Christians honour the word so far? David can do nothing with the armour that he had not proved, nor can you manage that word which doth not fit you, therefore, you must first prove, then approve, and then improve truths, as you have occasion; yea, you must take the first season you can for it, as soon as you come home, draw out this treasure, lest a day's neglect wear it out, and so you have heard and believed in vain,* as the apostle's hearers, who were like him that beholds his natural face in a glass, and then quite forgets his own physiognomy,† and hence the word is as water spilt upon the ground. Remembrance hath in it apprehension, deposition, retention, and production; as a man takes a shaft in his hand, puts it in his quiver, retains it there for a season, and when he would recreate himself, draws it out again; just so is treasuring any thing in the memory. The end of laying up is laying out, only let not our hearts be as leaking vessels to let slip what we hear,‡ but let us lay hold on, lay up, and lay out for our own and others' good. The best help to preserve, is to improve truths. Speedy exercise helps to spiritual dexterity. Speculation will never make a man an artist; a few hours of practice will do more than many days of contemplation: set on the work betimes, and the next opportunity make apparent what you received from God the last season of grace: let your deeds speak what David in words professeth, Psalm cxix. 56, "This I had, because I kept thy precepts." So in such a conflict, let your practice and success say, this I got from God in such a duty, this I had in such an ordinance, this is by the sweet help I had in such a performance, methinks I feel the virtue of that repast. O what good will this do you? It will excite thankfulness,

* 1 Cor. xv. 2.   † James i. 23, 24.   ‡ Heb. ii. 1.

engage you to the like performance, accustom you to this divine commerce of fetching from God and acting for God. Make speedy use of spiritual profit, and draw out the treasure speedily.

2. Seasonably. All things are beautiful in their season, though you must draw out of your treasure speedily, yet not unseasonably;* you must not be so hasty as to be premature. Let your summer fruits be also ripe grapes. A Christian must learn to time all his actions and expressions; circumstances much vary cases; that may be a duty at one time, which is not so at another. Divines lay down this rule in expounding the commandments—negatives bind at all times, and in all circumstances; affirmatives are constantly binding, yet not in all circumstances. Brotherly admonition is a christian duty, yet it is not a duty to reprove a man when he is drunk, or in a passion. Here christian prudence interposeth, and is of singular use: though David was full of a treasure of good thoughts, yet he knew there was as well a time to keep silence, as a time to speak, therefore he kept his lips with a bridle, while the wicked were present, Psalm xxxix. 1. David here did not bind himself to perpetual silence, but to a constant watch: so we must consider, when speaking may do good, and when hurt. Our Lord Jesus knew how to speak a word in season,† and though he was always full of a heavenly treasure, yet sometimes he answered not a word, and waved doing a good work, until he saw a fitter season; ‡ that God might be more glorified, souls edified, and his designs furthered. Some companies at some times may not be fit for holy discourses, and we must not cast pearls before swine,

* Sunt aliqui, quorum fructus quia nimis properè minus prosperè oriuntur.—*Bern. de Sanct. Ben. Serm.* 1.

† Isaiah l. 4. ‡ Matt. xxvii. 14. John xi. 6.

lest instead of receiving them, they rend us;* "a wise man's heart discerneth time and judgment," saith Solomon;† and a godly man brings forth fruit in due season, saith David. ‡ "A word fitly spoken, is like apples of gold in pictures of silver," Prov. xxv. 11. in Hebrew, it is a word spoken upon its wheels; fit times are wheels which carry words to greater advantage. There is a nick of time, into which, if a word or work fall, it becomes sweet and successful, and because most men miss of this, their misery is great upon them. Ambrose ‖ observes, that very many by speaking, scarce any by keeping silence, fall into sin,—and quotes the son of Syrach, saying, a wise man will first spy his opportunity before he opens his mouth,—and concludes, let thy words be under the yoke and balance, that is, in humility and measure, and so thy tongue shall be subject to thy mind: so also for self-conference, as well as discourse with others, you should draw out truths, and press them seasonably upon your own consciences; also threatenings and promises, precepts and prophecies. Oh, what stead may these stand you in? to check you for sin, or to cheer your hearts in the ways of God: to curb or conduct you in your progress; they may come in opportunely, as Abigail to David to prevent a rash attempt, to rouse up your drowsy or drooping spirits, to calm your quarrelsome or troubled hearts. Do you awaken your own spirits, call to remembrance your experiences and comforts at a dead lift, as David did in a like case,§ and the Spirit of God will bring truths also to your remembrance, in a fit juncture of time; ¶ and certainly in those dubious workings and ambiguous debates betwixt the carnal

* Matt. vii. 6. † Eccl. viii. 5. ‡ Psalm i. 3.
‖ Amb. Christi Offic. lib. 1. cap. 2—4.
§ Psalm lxxvii. ¶ John xiv. 26.

and spiritual part, seasonable thoughts carry it and cast the scales for God: a small grain may help to preponderate in an equal poise—Christians know what this means. O, what good hath a seasonable thought done many a sinking soul! On the contrary, unseasonable thoughts, though good in their own nature, have much prejudiced and distracted the soul, as when a Christian is at prayer, to have an impulse or inclination to read or meditate, when hearing to converse, &c.—this is to make religious duties to interfere. God's Spirit is a Spirit of order, and this is not a methodical or seasonable bringing forth, or laying out of this treasure. All Divines conclude, that thoughts,* though about good objects, if they be out of place do become vain thoughts, and weaken the worship of God: beware of those, but nourish pertinent thoughts, and make seasonable use of this heart treasure.

3. Sincerely. Be upright in your layings out; my meaning is, make shew of no more than indeed you have, profess not to have that to which you never attained. Beware of hypocrisy; there are many forthputting professors, that talk of many things they understand not; that brag of many truths, graces, comforts, and experiences, which they never felt in their own hearts, like the false prophets, that are said " to steal the word every one from his neighbour." † So, many steal phrases, passages, and observations, which they glean up from other Christians, which they know nothing of, but learn them by rote, and speak

* See Mr. Cobbet on Prayer, part 3, chap. 3. page 416. how to discern them, page 423.

† Jer. xxiii. 30. Arbores autem quæ fructum faciunt sed non suum, hypocritæ sunt, cum Simone Syrenæo crucem portantes non suam: qui religiosa intentione carentes angariantur; et quæ non amant, amore gloriæ quam desiderant, facere compelluntur. —*Bern. Serm. fol.* 120.

them like a parrot: these are just like some scholars that pretend to much learning, and acquaintance with many books which they never saw, and though they talk much, yet if they be well sounded, are found very shallow. Herein appears a great difference betwixt a child of God and a hypocrite: the latter cares not how good he makes men believe he is; the former is jealous lest others should think too well of him, and is afraid he should fail of their expectation; his heart is broken with this one thought, that he is not such a one as Christians account him to be, he hath not such a treasure as men think he hath. O, thinks the poor soul, by my discourses, prayers, and carriage, I have given occasion to my dear friends to imagine that there is more good in me than indeed there is; they see the better side, but God and my conscience know of much rottenness in these garnished tombs: this made Mr. Bradford subscribe his name with the epithet of a very painted hypocrite. Nay, this is it that lays many a good man under a temptation, not to appear well to others, lest his treasure within him should not answer, or bear out his professions; though that may be a temptation, yet it is a good token of sincerity, when a good report even of the truth itself, doth promote self-abasing humility. But that to which I urge, is uprightness in words and works; let your heart and tongue be tied together; rather *be good* than *seem good;* approve your heart to God, that your " praise may not be of men, but of God;" profess to be what you are, and be what you profess; be sure you have that within you, which you pretend unto. Uprightness is a good means to evidence and increase your treasure; " The upright shall have good things in possession."—Prov. xxviii. 10. Alas, sirs, what will fair words and a false heart advantage you? Fine flourishes and a polluted inside will render you odious; groundless brags end in woful disgrace; God knows what you have, and men will know in time, Prov. xxvi. 23, " Burning lips, and a wicked heart, are like a potsherd covered with silver dross." This gilded earth makes a fair shew of seeming zeal, but alas! he shall be detected, " his wickedness shall be shewed before the congregation."—Prov. xxvi. 26. Some men's religion is like pepper, hot in the mouth, but cold in the stomach; or like a man in a fever, whose face and outward parts burn, but his heart shakes and quivers for cold; and oh what zeal have some in external profession! but, alas, are destitute either of any principle at all, or at least, want that treasure or measure of grace they pretend to. Dr. Hall * tells us of one, that said, " It is good to enure the mouth to speak well, for good speech is many times drawn into affection; but," saith he, " I would fear that speaking well without feeling, were the next way to draw a man to habitual hypocrisy." But let me earnestly persuade all to sincerity and simplicity, for as Bernard saith, † " Of two imperfect things, it is better to have a holy rusticity, than an offending eloquence. If our intention be upright to God-wards, our work will not be dark and dangerous in God's account, but they that are not pure by righteousness, cannot be innocent by simplicity."

4. Draw out of your treasure suitably, that is, not only acting answerably to what you have within, that

* Dr. Hall in Medit. et Vows, cent. 1. page 77.

† Ex duobus imperfectis multo est melius habere rusticitatem sanctam, quàm eloquentiam peccatricem; magis veneranda est sancta rusticitas, quàm verbosa loquacitas. Soror in Christo dilecta, si nostra intentio est simplex apud Deum, in judicio ejus nostra operatio tenebrosa non erit; qui casti esse per justitiam nesciunt, nequaquam esse innocentes per simplicitatem possunt.—*Bern. Serm.* 56, *fol.* 1299.

your layings out be not more than your layings up, *
which was the last head ; but you must produce holy
actions and expressions in some degree proportionable
unto God's vouchsafed means and appointed ends.

(1.) Let your treasure within, and performances without, be suitable to your receipts and advantages.
Where God lays out much, he looks for much ; the
more pains he takes, the more fruit he expects. You
must bring " forth good fruit," and " much fruit, that
you may glorify God, and edify others."† Wicked men
manifest a prodigious contrariety to the Lord's tillage,
but godly men should not manifest any disparity betwixt their receipts and returns. Enclosed grounds
must not be like the barren wilderness. God's garden
should be more fruitful than the common field. Trees
of God's planting and watering, are not to be like the
trees of the forest. Well tilled souls should abound in
fruits of righteousness. The Scripture compares the
church to a vineyard, and particular souls to vine-trees,
that must " bring forth grapes ;" and, indeed, a vine
is good for nothing if it be not fruitful, not so much as
to make a pin of, to hang a vessel upon.‡ Now, let us
consider, if God have not done as much for his
vineyard amongst us, as for that in Isa. v. have not
our returns been parallel to theirs ? the most part
have brought forth wild grapes, the best have not
brought forth full grapes, ripe grapes, at least not sweet
grapes, but legal acts of too, too constrained obedience.
Have not God's children often rather acted from a spirit
of bondage, than of liberty ? Well now, God hath a
controversy with his vine, justly may he command the
clouds to rain no more upon it, nay, he will cast the
wild vines into eternal fire, and his own chosen vines
into the fiery furnace of sharp affliction ; therefore,

* Ne promus sit fortior condo. † John xv. 5, 8.
‡ Ezek. xv. 3.

be fruitful, bring forth abundantly, answer God's call and cost, as the heavens hear the earth in sending down fructifying showers, and the earth hears the inhabitants in bringing forth abundant fruits, so " let us bring forth much fruit;" hear we the Lord's summons, and echo back answerable fruitfulness to the droppings of the sanctuary and the sweet showers of divine grace. The fruits you are to bring forth are those " fruits of the Spirit," mentioned in Gal. v. 22, " Love, joy, peace, longsuffering, gentleness, goodness, faith, meekness, temperance;" these fruits are our produce, as Bernard speaks,* and God accounts our produce to be as his own fruits.

(2.) Answer God's designed and appointed ends; that is, God's glory, and the edification of your own and others' souls. Be not self-seeking, but self-denying in all your layings out, else it is a sign you are barren, and you lose your labour. Israel is but an " empty vine, if he bring forth fruit to himself."—Hos. x. 1. The vine of Eshcol will commend the land of Canaan. Clusters of ripe grapes will glorify God, the chief husbandman, and evidence the fatness of the soil, even the courts of our God and gospel ordinances. God takes himself to be glorified " by our bringing forth much fruit,"† and is it not a blessed thing to be an instrument to glorify God? This was the end of our creation, of our redemption, of all the impulses and operations of the sanctifying Spirit; awake, therefore, to much fruit-bearing, and let God's glory be the main thing in your eye and aim. Let the observant Christian that takes care of the vineyard of his own soul, reap some comfort, but let our " Solomon (Jesus Christ, the prince of peace) have the thousand pieces of silver,"‡ all the glory

---

* Fructus isti, profectus nostri, et nostros profectus, suos fructus deputat.—*Bern. Sup. Cant. Serm.* 63.

† John xv. 8. ‡ Cant. viii. 12.

to himself, to whom only it belongs. A Christian must speak the language of the Psalmist, "Not unto us, not unto us, but to thy name be the praise,* for God will not give his glory to another."† Herod was eaten with worms, because he made a fine oration, "and gave not God the glory."‡ It is gross sacrilege to ascribe any thing to ourselves. "Let him that glorieth glory in the Lord." If you be called to make a confession of your faith, and to produce your treasure before courts, and judgment-seats, speak out, be not afraid of men, or ashamed of the gospel, yet take those two rules with you, 1 Pet. iii. 15. In the middle of the verse you have a profession required; in the beginning and the end, there are the dispositions necessary. *First*, "Sanctify the Lord God in your hearts." There you perceive the principle and end. See that you have grace, and act for God's glory. *Secondly*, "Be ready to give an answer with meekness and fear;" there is the manner, with cheerfulness and humility, without vain boasting or ostentation. Some may speak confidently, and carry it highly, even to suffering for a good cause, and yet be the devil's martyrs, by seeking to get a reputation among men, or to bear up an opinion, or please a faction, or gratify a humour, or merit something at the hands of God. The end makes or mars the action. Vain glory spoils great achievements; yet, it is a miserable thing to "bear the cross," and "not to follow Christ." ǁ So I may say of prayer, almsgiving, or mortifying acts, or any other excellent ways of laying out of a treasure, if they be only to be seen of men, the work is as if it were not done, and the doer in danger of being undone. Another subordinate end is, our own soul's good, and the good of others. "I do all things," saith Paul,

* Psal. cxv. 1.   † Isa. xlii. 8.   ‡ Acts xii. 23.
ǁ Væ portantibus crucem et non sequentibus Christum.—*Bern.*

"for your edification," so must we. God hath interwoven his glory and the good of souls, so nearly, that they are both promoted together. You must make God's glory the ultimate end of all your actions and expressions; in all things natural, as eating and drinking; civil, in buying and selling; and spiritual in praying and conversing. Take that notable text in 1 Pet. iv. 10, 11, " As every man hath received the gift, even so minister the same one to another, as good stewards of the manifold grace of God—that God in all things may be glorified through Jesus Christ, to whom be praise and dominion for ever and ever. Amen.

CHAP. XVI.

THE EXCELLENCY AND ADVANTAGE OF HAVING A TREASURE IN THE HEART.

THE last use to be made of this point concerning this heart treasure, is partly of consolation, and partly of exhortation, wherein I shall both encourage those that have it, and provoke to emulation those that have it not, that they may labour to reach it, and obtain it. And for the better urging this, I shall further illustrate the usefulness of this heart treasure in these ten particulars.

1. A treasured soul is of great worth. A gracious Christian is the rarest piece of all God's workmanship, called [ποίημα] Eph. ii. 10. It is a word that is no where else used, it signifieth an artificial work, fabric or structure, that notable operation, wherein the God

of heaven shewed singular care and skill, as well as love and grace. This new creature in one soul is a greater work, and of more worth, than this goodly frame of the world. A renewed soul is the epitome of the creation, the clearest image of divinity upon earth, the true portraiture of God in man, and a blessed treasury of spiritual perfections. The soul of the man is the man, and grace is the ornament of the soul; every man is so far excellent, as he is religious; a Christian's greatest glory is, in what he is God-wards;* gracious souls are truly precious, and such as are precious in God's sight are honourable, and of more worth than the richest princes and largest kingdoms.† Well may they be the Lord's jewels, that have a treasure of jewels locked up in their breasts. These precious sons of Zion are comparable to fine gold, though men esteem them as earthen pitchers.‡ It is true, they seem to be of little worth to the outward view of a carnal eye; like their dear Redeemer, of whom it is said by his despisers, " he hath no form nor comeliness, and when we see him, there is no beauty that we should desire him;"|| so the saints appear mean and sordid, but if you could see all, you would find them all glorious within. The servants of God are like unto the tabernacle under the law, whose outside was rams' skins, goats' hair, and badgers' skins—coarse stuff; but the inside was gold, silver, precious stones, and curious workmanship. Just so are the saints compared therefore to the tents of Kedar, to the curtains of Solomon, Song, i. 5. § The word Kedar doth signify blackness, and Kedar (Ishmael's second son's posterity) dwelt in tents made

* Animus cujusque est quisque: tantus quisque est, quantus est apud Deum.
† Isaiah xliii. 3, 4.   ‡ Lam. iv. 2. || Isaiah liii. 2.
§ See Ainsworth in locum.

of hair-cloth; thus the church and particular souls are dwelling in tents, and through afflictions, persecutions, and many corruptions in this howling wilderness and weary pilgrimage, are black and unlovely to look upon; but if you could open the tent door, and see into the secret cabinet of a believer's heart, you would discover a treasure of the rarest graces, truths, experiences, and comforts, that ever mortal eyes beheld; you should behold them as glorious as the beautiful hangings about Solomon's bed, "as comely (saith the text) as the curtains of Solomon." Take but another familiar resemblance; suppose you see an earthen pot full of gold, let him that only sees the outside and knows not what is within, be asked the price thereof, possibly he will answer, not many pence, but the pot with the treasure in it may be worth many thousand pounds; a sorry canvas purse may contain a vast sum of money, nor must the whole be rated according to the poor facing, but the rich lining. A Christian hath an excellent treasure in an earthen vessel; you must not censure him before you see every part of his character fully disclosed at the great day: his life is hid at present, but when Christ who is his life appears, he shall appear with him in glory. * The saints here are as princes, walking in disguise in a strange country, and it doth not yet appear, who or what they are, but God hath his time to unveil their glory, and reveal their excellency. The pearl cannot be found, till the shell of the fish be broken; and when these vile bodies are turned to dust, then this precious treasure shall be made manifest. O the excellency of a poor child of God; it would make him holily proud to consider what he is, the honour God hath put upon him, and the treasures laid up in him. As a man is a little world,

* Col. iii. 3, 4.

so a Christian is a commonwealth, a church, and a heaven (as it were) within himself; he hath a monopoly of the best commodities, a rich magazine of precious things for the delight of God, profit of men, and comfort of his own soul. Though wicked men do account them not worthy to live in the world, as though this earth were too good for them; yet God saith of the saints, " of whom the world was not worthy," they are too good to breathe in this foul air, and shall be translated to heaven. Here I might far exceed bounds: for a close, take brave Luther's character of a saint:* " He is," saith he, " a child of God, an heir of heaven, the brother of Christ, the companion of angels, the lord of the world, and partaker of a divine nature." Be cheered, therefore, O thou trembling Christian—be provoked, O thou careless soul, to look after a large treasure. Who would not be of this number? methinks it should excite all rational and intelligent creatures to a holy covetousness, and ambition to be filled with these treasures, and to be clothed with all this glory.

2. This treasure makes the soul fit for any condition; nothing can come amiss to the Christian thus furnished, he is prepared for all dispensations, nothing can make him miserable; let Paul and Silas have their treasure with them, and they can sing in the stocks at midnight; let David be in a pilgrimage, his treasure will make him both company and melody; a Christian cannot be banished from his treasure, he may say more truly than the philosopher,† " I carry my all with me." When the proconsul told Cyprian

* Christianus est filius Dei, hæres regni, frater Christi, socius angelorum, dominus mundi, particeps divinæ naturæ.—*Tom.* 1 *Lat.* 106.

† Omnia mea mecum porto.

he would banish him, he answered, "he is no exile that hath God in his mind;" separate God from a child of God, and then you undo him; if you could rob him of his treasure, you might make him miserable, but not otherwise. He that is out of hell, and hath a heaven in his heart, hath no cause of shame or terror; when he is under sharp trials, and others condole with him, he may say, as Christ to the daughters of Jerusalem, "weep not for me, but weep for yourselves;" of himself, he can say as Paul, "I am ready, not to be bound only, but also to die at Jerusalem, for the name of the Lord Jesus."* God hath laid a treasure *in* his heart, and he is willing to lay it *out*, which way soever the Lord shall call for it. By this way of laying out, the treasure is not impaired but increased; by afflictions, truths are improved, graces exercised, experience added, and comforts wonderfully enlarged, and these advantages countervail the smart of affliction. This is a holy " merchandize," saith an ancient, " to lose some things, that we may gain greater."† The believing Hebrews " took joyfully the spoiling of their goods, knowing in themselves that they had in heaven a better, and an enduring substance.—Heb. x. 34. Observe it, they know in themselves, that is, they had experience thereof in their own hearts, and now by this loss of their estates this experience was made more clear, was increased, and confirmed. Oh blessed exchange! to part with earth and get heaven, to get riches off the heart, and to get better riches into the heart. I must tell you, that one grain or degree of grace is more worth than heaps of wordly riches, and happy is that soul that endures the loss of these, to get a good share of the

* Acts xxi. 13.
† Mercatura est quædam amittere, ut majora lucreris.—*Tertul.*

former. Read the eleventh chapter of the Epistle to the Hebrews, and follow that blessed army of martyrs, that long cloud of witnesses, and fear not man, for you shall be gainers in the result of all. A treasured soul is still gathering more to himself in every dispensation from words spoken, from the rod laid on, and from every interposition in his favour. The honest heart makes a good use of, and is prepared for every event, being satisfied as well as edified, whatever the Lord doth with him. But more of this anon, only observe, that a treasured soul can pick out of a sermon worth nothing, or from a providence, that which another cannot. We read of Mr. Ignatius Jurdain,* a zealous magistrate in Exeter, that a formal man having once preached a sermon at the cathedral, about Heaven, the discourse was for the most part frothy, and beneath the dignity of such an argument: after sermon, Mr. Manton having occasion to visit Mr. Jurdain, after many good instructions, he asked Mr. Manton if he had heard the sermon that morning; he answered, yes. "And did you not," said he, " hear those wonderful things which God hath provided for them that love him?" and then readily selected all those passages that were any way subservient to use and profit. " It was wonderful to me," saith Mr. Manton, " to see a holy heart could draw comfort out of any thing: the sermon as repeated to me, was another kind of sermon, and seemed to be savoury and spiritual. I remember with what warmth and vigour he spake of it, even till this day, and hope that I shall never forget it." Such is Mr. Manton's account. O sirs, if you had a treasure, you would hear sermons with profit, and endure troubles after another manner than you ordinarily do.

3. This divine treasure qualifies the saint for noble

* Mr. Clark's Collect. in the Life of Mr. Ign. Jurd. page 481.

enterprises. The people that do know their God, shall be strong and do exploits; whereas unsound persons may be corrupted by flatteries, Dan. xi. 32, or chased away by threats. The greater treasure you have, and the more singular things may you do for God; the Lord will own you to do much for him, and you shall glorify God in suffering much for him. Paul's vessel was well fraught with this treasure (and it may be for this cause he is called a chosen vessel, * and he alone is so called, though doubtless others were so also) and what mere man did more for God than blessed Paul? Who ever travelled over so much of the world to preach the gospel, as this unwearied Apostle? He preached all along from Jerusalem round about to Illyricum, or Sclavonia, in Europe, which is, saith Pareus, in a direct line, 1400 miles; but he went ἐν κύκλῳ in a circuit, visiting circumjacent places to preach the gospel; † yea, a good author reckons up Paul's travels in the Lord's work to be above 10,000 miles, so that he may be called, as George Eagles, that good martyr in Queen Mary's days, "Trudge-over-the-world, for he laboured more abundantly than all the rest." ‡ And whence was it that Paul was in labours more abundant? It was, because he had a large stock to expend, a well furnished head and heart, and the Lord made his labours very successful; and observe it, treasured souls are very instrumental for God. Such he calls out to be as captains in the warfare, and leaders in his field to go before others in the sharpest service and most hazardous undertakings; these he puts to the trial and brings them off victorious. It was a fine speech of Queen Elizabeth's, when she

* Acts ix. 15. σκεῦος ἐκλογῆς, est Hebraismus; a vessel of choice.
† Rom. xv. 19. See Hen. Bunting on the travels of Paul.
‡ 1 Cor. xv. 10. 2 Cor. xi. 23.

was locked up close in the tower, " desiring God not to suffer her to lay her foundation upon the sands, but upon the rock, whereby no blasts of blustering weather might prevail against her." Whereunto she added, " The skill of a pilot is unknown but in a tempest, the valour of a captain is unseen but in a battle, and the worth of a Christian is unknown but in a trial and temptation. This earthly globe, O Lord, is but a theatre on which thou hast placed us, to get some proof from hence of our sufficiency." Thus proceeds that peerless princess, " Oh the advantage of a well-stored Christian! such a little David, thus furnished with a scrip full of smooth stones of the brook, I mean, a head and heart full of Scripture truths and saving graces will be able to vanquish the proud Goliah, or chief spiritual adversary." * How did silly women encounter and conquer the learned Doctors in the Marian days? The subtlest Jesuists have been puzzled and non-plussed with the solid answers of spiritual-minded Christians. That precious promise is sweetly performed to God's children, Matt. x. 19, 20, dictating to them what they must speak; the reason there given is, " the Spirit of your Father speaketh in you;" yea, so full of matter have the treasured saints been, that when bodily organs have ceased, their full hearts have found a miraculous vent. Read the church histories. Take a specimen of wonders. When Romanus,† that noble martyr, had his tongue plucked up by the roots, by the tormentors, he praised God, and said, " He that speaketh of Christ shall never want a tongue." When his cheeks were sore rent with knives, he said, " I thank thee, O captain, that thou hast opened to me many mouths to preach my Lord Christ." So it is recorded of Barlaam,

---

* Mr. Thom. Heywood's Engl. Elizab. p. 105.

† Acts and Mon. fol. 90—92.

a martyr, that having fire and frankincense put into his right hand, wherein yet, he had some strength, his enemies laying him on the altar thinking that he by the heat of the fire, would scatter some incense on the altar, he let the flame eat about his hand, which he kept fast closed, singing, " blessed be the Lord my God which teacheth my hands to war and my fingers to fight." Sirs, if you have a treasure, fear not, though you cannot expect such miracles; yet it will be produced in such a manner, and at such times as may most glorify God, silence the wicked, and comfort your hearts. I know it is the discouraging fear of trembling souls. If God call me to sharp encounters, I shall deny my Lord, betray his truths, bewray my weakness. But, poor Christian, fear not, God's " grace shall be sufficient for thee,"* thy little strength shall do wonders; if thou hast a right treasure within, it will appear to the admiration of others and beyond thine own expectation. Oh for such a treasure as is before described.

4. A treasured soul is God's delight. A full treasure in the heart, of the good things of heaven, is pleasure to the Almighty. God takes delight among the sons of men, and amongst men, the believer's heart is the Lord's highest throne, next to that in the highest heavens; and amongst sincere Christians none can make God so welcome, or give him better entertainment, than he whose heart is beautified with these blessed ornaments. Such a soul makes its Saviour a sumptuous feast, and gives him a cheerful invitation. So in Solomon's Song, ch. iv. 16, saith the church, " Let my beloved come into his garden and eat his pleasant fruits," that is, let him enjoy satisfaction in the fruits of his own free grace. He hath provided himself a sacrifice, a feast; let the graces of the Spirit delight

* See Revel. iii. 8—10.

and solace the heart of the author; no sooner doth she invite him, but he comes, Solomon's Song, ch. v. 1. "and gathers his myrrh with his spices, and eats his honeycomb with his honey;" that is, he reaps the graces and virtues of the sincere soul, with as much delight, as the grape gatherers or husbandmen reap their fruits in the vineyard or field. Oh with what pleasure doth the Lord accept the holy actings of a treasured saint! but he contemneth the costly sacrifices of a graceless soul; he cares not for their "thousands of rams," or "ten thousands of rivers of oil." No, no; a soul stored with graces is better than a house full of sacrifices; the honeycomb of human infirmities is dispensed with, where there is store of honey in gracious acts, and heavenly dispositions. A little honey is better to God than the mere comb of duties, though artificially composed, and exactly performed. Happy is the soul whom the Lord delights thus to visit, that is thus fitted to entertain the "high and lofty One." O that Christians could say, as the church, in Song, vii. 13, " At our gates are all manner of pleasant fruits, new and old, which I have laid up for thee, O my beloved." So the soul should say, this grace or that disposition I will lay up for my spiritual husband, Jesus Christ, and bring it forth to give him content; this smell of sweet perfume shall meet him at his entrance! I will entertain the beloved object of my dearest affections at the doors at home, in the fields abroad; I will bid him welcome upon all occasions; I will walk closely in my family sighing out blessed David's wish, " O when wilt thou come unto me!" * I will get upon my knees in my closet, and there I will seek, and shall find my father, that " seeth in secret;" † I will go unto his table and partake of his holy supper, and " while the King sitteth

* Psal. ci. 2. † Matth. vi. 6.

at his table, my spikenard will send forth the smell thereof;"* my " bruised spices," my exercised graces, shall be as pleasant odours to him; he will " smell a sweet savour" from my sacrifices, and my prayers and praises shall ascend before him as "incense,"† acceptable to God through Jesus Christ. It is not every one's happiness thus to enjoy God, or to be well-pleasing to him. Some may come near with Moses, when others must worship afar off; none so capable of intimate communion with God as the well-furnished Christian. Ordinarily, he that hath the greatest treasure hath the sweetest visits. To such as bring out of their treasure the precious fruits of the Spirit, to such will God open the precious treasures of his love. Observe it, there is much good laid up for them that have grace, but it is brought forth to them that use grace. ‡ Well then, Christians, lay up much grace and draw it out; send your lamb to this ruler of the land; bring your presents to Jesus Christ. The wise men set us an example in that welcome they brought to Jesus in his cradle, Matt. ii. 11, " They opened their treasures, and presented to him gifts, gold, frankincense and myrrh," answerable to his three offices, of King, Priest and Prophet. No man was to come to the Lord empty-handed in the time of the law; and if you come full-hearted with this treasure, and full-handed in drawing it out, be sure the Lord will be open-hearted to admit you, and open-handed to fill your hungry souls with ravishing incomes; you shall have Jesus Christ to lodge with you all the night of affliction. Who would not have this treasure that he may be welcome to heaven?

5. A treasured soul can live well in a time of spiritual dearth. " In the days of famine such shall be

* Cant. i. 12. † Gen. viii. 21. Psal. cxli. 2.
‡ See Psalm xxxi. 19.

satisfied." * When others are hungry and thirsty, and their souls fainting, a treasured Christian hath good commons; for the Christian thus stocked hath laid up that which stands him in stead in an evil day. It is true, a " famine of the word," is an afflictive judgment to a child of God. † Ordinances are to the saints their glory, the excellency of their strength, and the desire of their eyes, ‡ and the want of the word for a season doth more grieve them, than the total loss doth affect the wicked, though it concern them more; for God's children have that to live upon that natural men have not, they have a stock of inward strength that will carry them to the rock of ages, a stream of grace in their hearts that will lead them to the fountain of grace. Real saints are never famished, but always furnished. They can make a better shift to live than others can, they have something within doors: a treasure of truths, graces, comforts, and experiences, makes the saint a rich feast, for God is where these are. The flowing rivers of living water, ‖ that are among true believers, and the hidden manna, § will make a good meal when God himself sits at the table. They that cannot go to public assemblies may find the Lord's presence a little sanctuary; he is every where to be found, and can make amends in private, for want of public liberty. The word opened and applied is convincing, satisfying, and edifying. Well, they have their lesson still before them, the Bible in their hands, and a promise of the Spirit to bring things to their remembrance; and why may not the treasured soul, whose senses are well exercised by a habit of Scripture knowledge and self-conference preach to himself in the want of other preachers? Certainly, an able Christian, at full age

* Psal. xxxvii. 19.   † Amos viii. 11, 12.   ‡ Ezek. xxiv. 21.
‖ John vii. 38.   § Rev. ii. 17.

may digest strong meat,* though he carve for himself. One leaf of the Bible was in Luther's account worth a world, much more all a Christian's treasure whereby he is enabled to improve Scriptures. Histories and tradition tell us of some good Christians, who in dark times having got a few leaves of the Bible, run with them into a corner, and either read themselves or hired others to read, whereby they received incredible comfort and profit, and arrived at a high degree of knowledge and courage. So likewise the souls of God's children may seek and see God's face in private communion of saints, in conference, prayer, and praise; God may make it a happy exchange to them; the private lesser glass of secret duties may represent God as clearly to the eye of their souls, as the broad glass of public ordinances. I speak not this to derogate from public ordinances; they are to be preferred when God grants liberty; and when God withdraws them, the want of open vision is much to be lamented. We are to be sorrowful for the breaking up of solemn assemblies, and mourn sore when the gates of Zion mourn.† But this I mean, when by persecution public teachers are driven into corners, then the Lord may supply that want to his children some other way. Lest, however, this be condemned as novelty, I shall express it in the words of a learned author.‡ Buchanan asks the question, "What shall they do that want the opportunity of frequenting the public ordinances?" He answers, "Such must travel abroad, and seek far and near for them, but if they cannot find them, they must exercise themselves in religious duties at home; because," saith he, "the kingdom of God is within them, and because the word without the sacrament may be the power of

---

* Heb. v. 14. † Zeph. iii. 18. Lam. i. 4.
‡ Institut. Theol. De Sacram. loc. 46, page 601.

God to salvation." And he further adds, " That the faithful can never be without the matter and marrow of a sacrament, though they may be compelled to want the visible sign." * Oh what a blessed thing it is to have a principle of grace, and this blessed treasure! It is surely worth something to have light and plenty, in a time of darkness and scarcity.

6. Consider this benefit of a heavenly treasure in the heart of a Christian, that every thing turns to the increase of his stock. It is the strange, attractive property of this treasure, that it will fetch from all things to fill it up, and make it greater. Like fire, it will turn every thing into its own nature. It is a divine alembic, † that can extract pure spirits out of all things, according to that catholic promise in Rom. viii. 28, " We know that all things work together for good," prosperity and adversity, riches and poverty, renown, and ignominy, thraldom and liberty, sickness and health, success and disappointment, satanical suggestions, violent temptations and victorious conquests, all work for good; yea, some extend this also to corruptions, yet these but accidentally, or being managed by the constant care of a wise, gracious and able physician; as poison may be turned into a remedy, ‡ or, as they say, " the drinking of that wine wherein a viper hath been drowned cureth the leprosy;" even thus, God can so husband even the breakings in of temptation, and breakings out of corruption as to make them turn to good, being an occasion of deeper humiliation; a rope to bring down the topsails of spiritual pride; a spur to promote a holy jealousy and watchfulness, and a means to work in the soul charity and sympathy towards

* Re sacramenti nunquam destituuntur fideles, etiamsi visibilibus signis carere cogantur.

† A Still.   ‡ Venenum aliquando pro remedio fuit.—*Sen.*

others, to alienate our hearts from this sinning, weary world, to endear our hearts to God for pardoning grace, and to make us long for a sinless state in glory. These and such like ends and uses God hath and makes of sin, or else he would not suffer this dead body, or rather " body of death," to haunt the souls of living saints. Our wise God raised a stately structure over the ruins of Adam's fall, or he had never suffered it. God doth his servants good by their sins; this uncouth experiment made good Mr. Fox to say, " That his graces did him most hurt, and his sins most good." A strange paradox, but a gracious soul knows what this means, that hath many a time by divine assistance, fetched heaven out of hell, light out of darkness, sweet advantages from sad miscarriages. Sometimes the Christian can say, I had sinned, except I had sinned, the furthest way about hath proved the nearest way home, God hath suffered me to break my bones by falling, that he might set them more strongly. " We cannot go to heaven," saith an experienced divine,* " by Geometry, we must fetch a compass by the gates of hell, and hear what news with Satan, ere we be duly humbled, or can relish the promises aright." Yet mistake not, no thanks to sin or Satan for this, but to free grace, that orders all things for the best; nor let any adventure upon sin with such a conceit, for this were to "sin that grace may abound;" that is the devil's logic and dangerous presumption. But when the Christian hath fallen thus, the Lord helps him to improve his falls for spiritual good; but much more all dispensations of providence, sweet and severe; if it go well with the treasured soul, it is drawn nearer to God by these cords of love; if ill, it is whipped further from sin and the world by these scourges of anger. He can

* Mr. Capel, on Tempt. page 234.

fetch a good crop of spiritual fruit out of the barren heath of a wilderness condition. If from outward poverty he get this advantage, to be " poor in spirit," it is a rich gain, and worth a mine of gold; and so of other afflictions. The north wind is sharp and piercing, the south wind soft and cherishing, but both blow good to the Christian, and make his spices flow out, or graces break forth into lively exercises.—Cant. iv. 16. Yet further, this treasure doth in a sort consecrate all states, so that let a man have more or less, he hath a sufficient treasure if he have this treasure within; " godliness with contentment" is not only enough, " but gain," yea " great gain;" it seasons all things. That man hath nothing that wants this—that man who hath this wants nothing. Wicked men may have much, but godly men have all things.* When Jacob and Esau complimented each other about the present which Jacob sent to pacify his angry brother, Esau said, " I have enough my brother," Jacob also said, " I have enough;" but in the Hebrew, Esau said, " I have much," † and Jacob saith, " I have all," or " all things are to me," ‡ intimating that Jacob's treasure was far beyond his brother's, even as the whole is more than the part. There is a secret blessing attends this hidden treasure, which gives content with want or abundance, and if God see good he will increase the store. However, a saint's *modicum*, or little, amounts to more than wicked men's *multum*, or large revenues, as the word of truth testifies.—Psalm xxxvii. 16.

7. This treasure is safe, it is well locked up, and cannot be lost, Phil. i. 6, " being confident of this very

* Habet omnia qui habet habentem omnia.

† Gen. xxxiii. 9, 11. יש לי רב multum est mihi.

‡ יש לי כל sunt mihi omnia.

thing, that he which hath begun a good work in you, will perform it until the day of Jesus Christ." It is true, an external profession, and mental accomplishments may be lost, but sincere saving graces shall not be lost. It is also true, a saving treasure may be obscured, but cannot be destroyed; yea, it may be diminished, but is never totally wasted. The infinite Jehovah is the keeper of Israel. He that is the portion of your cup, will maintain your lot.* It is not so much the truth, nor yet the strength of grace that keeps you from falling, but it is God only who alone is able to keep you from falling, and who supports the weak Christian. Received grace will not preserve without assisting grace; faith as a habit, will not carry on the soul to death, or through death, but we are kept by the power of God, through faith unto salvation.—1 Pet. i. 5. The power of God, as the efficient cause,—faith, as the the instrument; God keeps faith, and faith keeps the soul steadfast. They that have Mary's part and Mary's spirit, shall never be poor; God will fulfil the desires of them that fear him, and will likewise fill the hearts of his saints with a rich treasure. " My God," saith Paul, " shall supply all your need according to his riches in glory by Christ Jesus."—Phil. iv. 19. It is a mighty full expression, and refers to all want, spiritual, as well as corporeal. Our heavenly father gives his travelling children a sufficient stock to bear their charges through the world, and discharge every debt of duty to God and man, in some measure of sincerity. This is that twopence with which the good Samaritan furnished the wounded man,† as some allegorize. It is true, some saints live at a high rate, in great expence, in costly duties, but this very chargeable living in high and hard exercises, and efforts of self-denial, do much increase

* Psal. xvi. 5. † Luke x. 35.

the Christian's store. A Christian is no loser, but a gainer, by flesh-displeasing performances; the more strength you lay out for God, the more you fetch in. This is one means to keep a spiritual treasure from being lost. Neither men nor devils can deprive you of it; you may take up blessed Paul's bold and triumphant challenge, Rom. viii. 35, " Who shall separate us from the love of Christ?" All the powers of darkness cannot loose this knot betwixt a precious Saviour and a gracious soul. The covenant is ordered in all things, and sure, it contains the sure mercies of David,* it is a covenant of salt. " The mountains shall depart, and the hills be removed, but my kindness shall not depart from thee, neither shall the covenant of my peace be removed, saith the Lord, that hath mercy on thee." Isaiah liv. 10. Grace is the seed of God that abides for ever; God may repent of bestowing common gifts, but these saving gifts and this holy calling are without repentance. All the motions and commotions in the world cannot rob the believing soul of its treasure. Those flames that shall burn the world cannot dissolve, but will rather cement and solder, the blessed union of a saint to his Saviour; the treasured Christian may stand upon the world's ruins, and say, I have nothing of all this huge heap to lose; I shall not be a mite poorer for the stupendous conflagration of this goodly fabric. Let brutish worldlings weep and wail over their fair houses, large domains and full bags, numerous cattle, and gorgeous attire; I am rich still, as rich as ever I was, and some richer, for what I had in hope and expectation, I have now in full enjoyment and possession. Augustine sweetly discourseth concerning one Paulinus Bishop of Nola, who, having lost a great estate by the invasion of the Barbarians, prayed thus,

* 2 Sam. xxiii. 5. Isaiah lv. 3.

"Lord, I shall not be troubled for silver or gold, for where my all is, thou knowest;" for, saith Austin, *there* he had his all, where he, who had forewarned the world of these approaching evils, had warned him to lay it.* A little after, he saith that some were tortured by the Barbarians to discover their riches, but adds he, "*nec prodere nec perdere potuerunt bonum quo ipsi boni erant;*" they could neither betray nor lose that good by which they themselves were good, namely, their graces and virtues. Oh sirs, what would you give to have your estates secured in a losing, plundering, desolating day. Here is an insuring office, the God of heaven will secure the well-laden ship, that it shall come safe to shore. Certainly this is a rich privilege in a day when we can be sure of nothing, that, *that* only which can make us happy, *that* and nothing else can be made sure.

8. God knows and owns, that treasure which sometimes is hid from the possessor. This is a sweet consideration; Col. iii. 3, "Our life is hid with Christ in God," that is, sometimes it is hid from our own eyes, as well as from the eyes of others, but still it is hid with God, and he that hides can find. Saints are called God's hidden ones, and their life is hidden, alike in respect of safety, secresy, and obscurity. A Christian may have more of God in him than he knows of; it is one thing to have grace, another to know that we have grace. A child of God may have the seed and root of holiness, yet want the bud and blossom of actual comfort. A sincere soul hath always the solid foundation for, yet

---

* Domine, non excrucier propter aurum et argentum, ubi enim sint omnia mea tu scis: ibi enim habebat omnia sua, ubi eum condere et thesaurizare ille monuerat; qui hæc mala mundo ventura prædixerat.—*Vide plura in lib.* 1, *de Civit. Dei cap.* 10, *cui Titulus est*—" Quod sanctis in amissione rerum temporalium nihil pereat."

may, at some time, be without the actual possession of divine consolations. Sometimes God withdraws the light of his countenance, and leaves the soul in darkness and desertion; he often suspends that act of the Spirit, which may evidence the soul's interest and sincerity; sometimes the Christian is lazy, and useth not God's appointed means to beget assurance; or by thinking of more comfort, than God is willing to impart, may deny what he hath; or by entertaining some beloved lust, or by the prevalency of melancholy, or inability of natural parts, this treasure may be hid from the eyes of the believer himself. These, and other reasons, divines * have laid down as causes of a Christian's want of comfort or assurance. Every saint knows this by too sad experience, that he is often at a loss, and cannot tell what to make of his condition; he hath his nights as well as days, a nipping winter as well as a flourishing summer. The sap of grace may retreat into the root—the herbs and flowers, and plants, may shrink and disappear—and this goodly new creation may droop and lose its glorious verdure, yet life may be there. A summer may come at the return of the year, when the glorious sun of righteousness shall reflect beauty upon these hidden graces, and draw them forth into lively fruits of gospel obedience, whereby the saint shall live again, and know that he lives; believe, and know that he believes. In the mean time, while such a soul doth walk in darkness and see no light, let him trust in the name of the Lord, † and stay himself upon his God; let him even cast anchor in the dark, and repose his troubled heart upon the rock of ages; faith is a venture, and you must ven-

* See Dr. Sibb's Soul's Conflict. Symond's Deser. Soul's Case. Baxter's Rest, part 3, p. 156—169.

† Isaiah l. 7.

ture your all on this bottom, use God's appointed means for obtaining comfort, improve free grace, study the promises, awaken your graces, recollect experiences, renew your repentance, walk closely with God, be importunate at the throne of grace, and certainly joy and comfort will spring forth speedily. Peace is the usual result of the exercise of grace, and as the striking of flint and steel together produceth fire, so the lively acting of sincere grace, upon its proper object, begetteth the light and heat of joy and warmth; yea, it is the observation of a good divine,* that the comfort of letting out our hearts to God, is a greater comfort, than any comfort we can have in receiving any thing from God; but this is sure, if you have a treasure of graces, God will, in due time, give you a treasure of comforts; if he do not fill you with joy and peace in believing, yet he will maintain his interest in you, and keep you from fainting; if you have not spiritual suavities, you shall have secret sustentation; if your state be not sweet, yet it shall be sure; his grace shall be sufficient for you, and that is equivalent to the mercy desired, and the less comfort you have in the way, the more you shall have in the end, and it matters not much whether comfort come an hour before death, or an hour after, since it will certainly come, as a man of God once said. In the mean time, approve your hearts to God, he searcheth the hearts, and knoweth what you are and have, though neither yourselves nor others know it; he sees how your principles lie within you, and knows, that is, approves the way of the righteous, † and though your way be troublesome, yet your end shall be peace, ‡ and though you may be ready to misjudge your state and acts in a hurry of temptation, yet your happiness doth

* Mr. Burrough's on Hos. ii. 19, page 606.
† Psal. i. 6. ‡ Psal. xxxvii. 37.

not depend upon your account of yourselves, but upon God's account of you in Christ. A gracious soul may not know the acts of faith, yet may be satisfied respecting the object of faith; he cannot say sometimes, I know that I do sincerely believe, but yet may say, I know in whom I have believed,[*] and desire again to believe. The good soul may say, I know not how things are with me, I have lost myself in a thicket of cares and fears; yet, I put my hand into his, who knows the way, and can lead me out, and let him, who in tender care of my soul shed his precious blood for it, see to the safe conducting of it to a blessed place of rest, and to the lodging of it in the bosom of Abraham.

9. A treasured believer hath a treasure in heaven, and indeed, his best treasure is above; for this treasure in his heart is the counterpart of a treasure in the heavens. These are always conjoined. Never is any soul brought up to heaven, but first God brings down heaven into it. God furnisheth the soul by the operations of his grace, and then takes possession of it by the earnest of his spirit, before he fill it with glory.—2 Cor. v. 5. Hast thou a treasure laid up in thy heart? That is, the first fruits of a larger vintage; light is sown for the righteous, and, I may say, in the hearts of the righteous; if gracious treasures be laid up in the temple of your souls, glorious things are laid up in the new Jerusalem for you, such things as eye hath not seen, nor ear heard, nor heart conceived. Happy art thou, oh poor soul, or rather rich soul, poor in this "world, rich in faith, and heir of a kingdom," yea, " of the kingdom ;"[†] thou mayest both sigh and smile at the mad and frantic world, that weary themselves for very vanity, that torment themselves in caring and toiling for an earthly treasure, which, when obtained, doth rather beget torment than content, and leads at last to final desperation.

[*] 2 Tim. i. 12.   [†] James ii. 5.

It is recorded of Stigandus, archbishop of Canterbury, that he lived very poorly, saying and swearing " that he had nothing, no, not a penny; * yet by a key fastened about his neck, there were found great treasures after his death, which he had hid under the ground ; but, alas, that key would not open heaven's gates, nor would that treasure purchase glory. But the believing soul hath his treasure above, and by faith he hath interest in the Lord Jesus, who hath, indeed, the key of David, and is already entered into the holiest of all, and hath set heaven's gates wide open to his purchased and prepared ones, and who is gone to prepare a place for them. Oh sirs, fear not ; you that have grace shall not miss of glory, as your Head is in heaven, so you shall be called to be with him ; he will open the gates of glory to those that opened their hearts to receive the King of Glory. The treasure of grace raiseth the heart to this treasure above, and lays up provision for an eternal state. This stream runs to that ocean, and shall at last be swallowed up therein, where there " is fulness of joy, where there are pleasures for evermore."† And let this excite all persons to hoard up a treasure in their hearts and in heaven, which " neither moth nor rust can corrupt, nor thief break through and steal." ‡ Alas, poor creatures, if you get a treasure in the world, what will you do for a treasure when you must be gone hence ? Your earthly treasures will not purchase eternal happiness. You cannot always live here, therefore lay up in store for yourselves, a good " foundation against the time to come, that you may lay hold on eternal life."—1 Tim. vi. 19. Make friends of the " mammon of unrighteousness, that when these fail, you may be received into everlasting habitations."—Luke xvi. 9. Like that provident King of the Spartans, who

* Mr. Fox's Acts and Monum. fol. 174.   † Psalm xvi. 11.
‡ Mat. vi. 20.

observing the people to dethrone their kings at the year's end, and thrust them into a foreign isle to live in misery, did not figure away in that prodigality wherein his predecessors lived for one year, but provided a great estate for himself in that country where he was to be banished, that he might live comfortably when he was degraded: just thus must the wise and gracious Christian do; provide amidst the enjoyment of all things, for a day of darkness in the want of all things. As time is the seminary of eternity, so the soul is to lay up here for an eternal state hereafter Blessed is that soul that is found with these treasures in his heart; a crown of righteousness is laid up for those in whose hearts is found the work of righteousness, and upon whom are found the robes of righteousness. Let such bless God for grace, and long for glory.

10. Consider yet further, treasures of glory are proportioned to treasures of grace in the heart. It is true, they that have least glory in heaven shall want none; yet withal, it is very likely there will be degrees of happiness, and they that have had most grace will have most glory. My reason is, because grace doth widen and capacitate the soul for larger revenues of glory. Many vessels of great and small quantity cast into the ocean are all full, but some hold more, and others less; such is the immense and inconceivable happiness of the saints above, that all shall have all, and none shall want any thing to complete their felicity. As it is impossible for a soul to be in heaven and not be happy, so there shall be no nook nor corner of a glorified soul, but it shall be filled with happiness. These clean vessels shall be filled with the new wine of the kingdom; "God shall be all in all," all good to all souls, and in all souls; yea, such is the vast and infinite ocean of glory, that they

shall " enter into their master's joy," not it into them, though they shall be as full of it as their hearts can hold. Oh how will they bathe themselves in those rivers of pleasure! The mind shall be full of light, the will of holiness, and the affections of raptures and satisfaction; " when we awake we shall be satisfied with his image," Psalm xvii. 15, nor shall there be any envyings of one another's happiness, though one star differ from another in glory, but every one shall bear his part in the lower or higher praises of God, as one saith, with a harmonious variety in perfect symphony. Certainly, that unfading crown of glory shall be as weighty upon every saint's head, as he is able to bear, though that weight shall be their joy; nothing is heavy in its proper element, and heaven is the proper element of the " spirits of just men made perfect ;" hence it is said, " the four living creatures," that is, the community of the faithful, " rest not day nor night, praising God," Rev. iv. 8, yet their work is their rest, only some have an instrument of six, some of eight strings, others sing praise to God upon an instrument of ten strings, having more enlarged faculties fitted to that angelical duty. It may seem that as there are degrees of torments in hell, for it will be more tolerable for some than for others,* so there will be degrees of happiness in heaven, by the rule of contrarieties ; " For," saith Beza, † " that Scripture of sowing and reaping sparingly, and liberally," in 2 Cor. ix. 6. refers not only to charity and temporal advantages, but piety and eternal incomes." Thus doth Calvin ‡ interpret it also, and the parable of the talents, whose reward was propor-

* Matthew xi. 22. † Vid. Bez. Quæst. et Resp. p. 98.

‡ Cæterum messis tam de spirituali mercede vitæ æternæ, quam terrenis benedictionibus, quibus Deus prosequitur homines beneficos exponi debet.—*Calv. in loc.*

tionable to the improvement.—Luke xix. 16—19. It is true, parabolical divinity is not argumentative, yet the main scope of a parable hath a demonstration in it, and it may seem probable that those whom God honours with most grace, and that honour God with most service and suffering should be most honoured with glory; but nothing of merit is in all this, for giving heaven as wages for work is an act of commutative justice. But what equality is there betwixt finite services and infinite glory? None at all. No, no; eternal life is the gift of God. Let proud papists say, they will not have heaven gratis; let the real saint look upon gospel blessings as fruits of free grace, and the city above as built all of this free stone, and the way paved thither with the meritorious blood shed by our dear Redeemer; but whether there be degrees of glory or not, be sure the treasured soul shall have its share; we shall however be best able to resolve this question by experience,* vision and fruition will form the best determination. Now these great things are riddles and mysteries to us, because we look but through a glass darkly; we have but faint emblems and poor glimpses of that glory which shall be revealed, but then we shall see God as he is, and know all things fit for creatures to be acquainted with; a thousand of these hard knots shall be untied, and our souls fully irradiated with the beams of divine light.

* See this question answered in Buch. loc. 36. De vitâ æternâ, page 446. Decided that there shall be degrees of glory from 1 Thess. ii. 19 Dan. xii. 3. 1 Cor. xv. 41.

CHAP. XVII.

SOME OBJECTIONS ANSWERED, AND THE EXHORTATION URGED.

BUT here come in many doubting souls, with their several sad complaints and self-puzzling objections.

1. Alas, saith one, I fear I have no such treasure as is here described, for I have a very ignorant head, and therefore an empty heart; these treasures enter in by the door and window of knowledge, but I know nothing yet as I ought to know. I cannot conceive aright of one truth, and how should I then have a treasure of truths?

I answer, it is well thou art complaining; unsanctified knowledge puffeth up with conceits of imaginary attainments, gracious souls are sensible of defects and lament their ignorance. David was a saint well-treasured, yet calls himself a beast; Agur was a wise and holy man, yet professeth that he was more brutish than any man, nay, he saith "he had not the understanding of a man."—Prov. xxx. 2. It is a hopeful sign to hear Christians bewail their ignorance, but it doth not become any man to brag of his knowledge: the lowest humility is the highest attainment: self-denial is a sign of, and means to spiritual riches: it is a sign thou hast profited, when thou discernest and bewailest thy non-proficiency. Besides, you must know, that you are not to determine on your treasure of truths, by the number of truths known, but by the manner of your knowing them, and your estimation of them. Do you value the truth so, as to buy it at any rate, and to sell it at no rate? nay, are you not willing to part with your lives rather than truth? Hath not truth had efficacy in your hearts, authority over your consciences, and prevalency in your conversation? Do you give up yourselves to the truths you do know? and walk with God according to light received? if so, then you have a treasure both of truths and graces. It is a wonder to consider how little light, and how much heat, Christ's own disciples and zealous martyrs have gone straight to heaven with. I speak not this to sooth up any in ignorance, or to patronize negligence, but to quiet the poor doubting, disconsolate conscience, that is affected with a sense of its ignorance.

2. Ah, saith another, is it possible that I should have a treasure of grace that have such a treasure of sin? the Lord knows, my heart is even stuffed full of corruption, there is such a huge load on my back, such a monstrous body of death, that I much fear whether I have any grace at all in my heart, my sin bears me down like a violent torrent, lust is predominant, and —can grace prevail?

I answer, I am glad to hear these complaints from thee; it is no new thing for a Paul to cry out of a " body of death:" living men feel the weight of a burden, but dead men are not hurt. Dost thou really complain of the power of sin? then it is a tyrant, not a king in thy heart. Dost thou sigh and fight against sin? bless God for that light to see it, and life to oppose it: the forced damsel cleared her innocency by crying out,* so doth the vanquished soul evidence integrity by earnest cries to God; it is not a complete conquest, while the soul is struggling with its enemy, and gives not up the fort of the heart. But know this, that a Christian may have a large treasure of grace in his heart, and yet feel violent workings of

* Deut. xxii. 27.

depravity; grace may be strong, yet corruption impetuous; God may give it a commission to make violent incursions upon the well-furnished soul, for wise and gracious ends: only consider whether thy prayers be ardent, contests vehement, and mournings for it bitter and more than ordinary; if it be thus with thee, thou mayest have a treasure for all that, not only a principle of grace, but a large measure thereof; for opposites illustrate one another, and though there be strong lustings of the flesh against the Spirit, yet if there be also proportionable strugglings of the Spirit against the flesh, the soul's condition may be safe, and for aught I know, it may be rich in grace.

3. But, saith the Christian, you talk much of a treasure of comforts, but alas, I know not what that means—alas, comfort is far away; surely if I had any grace, I should have peace, but I have been long under sadness and in many disconsolate fears; I am apprehensive I have no treasure of grace.

Answer. Grace and peace are not inseparable, they may be disjoined, as Scripture and experience testify, many a gracious soul hath been in deep sorrows, a soul may have a hell within it, and yet at last go to heaven; a Christian may sail through a tempestuous sea to a quiet haven. Yea, further observe, that a Christian may have a treasure of grace, yet want a treasure of joy and comfort; the reason is, because comfort is an effect of God's Spirit, who acts as a sovereign, and not by necessity; for if the Spirit shine not upon the graces of the Spirit in the soul, it will have no comfort, though it be full of grace. Now, God doth sometimes suspend the comforting presence of his Spirit from the best of his servants, for righteous and gracious ends: hence we find eminent servants of God, that feared God above many, complaining of the want of comfort, as Job, and David, and Heman; yea, sometimes we find our dear Redeemer, who had a treasure of grace and the Spirit above measure, complaining of God's forsaking him, and consequently of the absence of joy and comfort. Poor soul, do not murmur that God doth not always feed thee with these sweetmeats, which are the fare of the upper table, and are reserved for a heavenly banquet: what though thou hast not always actual possession of comfort, yet thou hast a solid foundation for it: what if thou be not continually dandled on thy Father's knee, and kissed with the kisses of his mouth, yet thou art a child still, and thou canst not deny but sometimes he doth visit thy soul with heart-solacing consolations, and thou mightest have a treasure of them if thou couldest be ready for them, or rightly improve them.

4. Alas, saith the troubled heart, if I knew my state were safe, I could be better satisfied amidst the want of comfort; but I have cause to call every thing into question, I have been so barren and unprofitable under means of grace, ordinances, and providences; I may cry out, My leanness, my leanness, woe unto me! if there had been any real good in my soul, it would have been more increased under my long-enjoyed helps.

I answer, there is never a soul under heaven, but hath sad cause to complain under ordinances and enjoyments; where is the man that can stand forth, and say he hath gathered in harvest as much as he might have done? But there is a profiting for the obtainment of grace, hast thou had any experience of this? hast thou been wafted over by the boat of ordinances, unto a state of grace? I hope thou canst not deny this. Well then, thou hast attained to the main proficiency, bless God for that: and for a progress in grace, examine thyself a little more strictly.—Is not Jesus Christ more endeared to thee? Do not the things of God relish better with thee? Dost thou not more disregard the world, and all preferments that it offers to thee? Is not thy prevailing purpose to cleave to God notwithstanding oppositions, more fixed and settled in thy heart, upon long experience of the ways of God? Dost thou not every day see more demonstrative reasons to confirm thee in thy choice of this better part? And let me ask thee, whether thou hast not grown downwards in humility, self-denial, hatred of sin, love to the saints, though thou canst not say, thou hast grown upwards in joy, faith, heavenly-mindedness, and communion with God? Do not think thou art above complaint and proficiency in this life; none have attained to a perfect treasure in this valley of tears, and shadow of death; you will have cause to complain of defects and imperfections, which with your perfect Saviour's complete righteousness, your God will graciously cover and cure.

5. But, saith the poor soul, methinks I fall very far short, not only of what I might have attained to, but what others, with the same privileges, have arrived at. I am outstripped by such as set out long after me; they that were converted some years after me, have attained to more treasures of gifts, graces, and abilities for edification, and I lag behind, what shall I think of myself?

I answer, thou hast cause to lament thy non-proficiency, and bewail that thou hast not kept pace with others. There should be a holy emulation amongst Christians, and a striving which shall be richest in these good things of heaven; but withal, comparing yourselves with others, is no good rule, except it be to shame your negligent hearts and excite diligent endeavours; because some have better parts, and may sooner attain to higher degrees of knowledge ; and some, God intends to call out to extraordinary service or suffering; others, God designs to snatch away sooner by death, and so lays up much in a shorter time. Besides, though they may seem to have a larger treasure, yet you do not know what they may have to do with it; they may be put to it, and all they have be little enough ; they may have such corruptions, temptations, afflictions, desertions, as may exhaust a great treasure; possibly they put the best side out, and you see the bright side, and not the black side of the cloud ; you hear their prayers, discourses, exercises amongst others, but you know not their dolorous griefs, and bitter complaints, before the Lord in secret. Could you lay your ears to their closets, you would overhear their sad sighs for their fulness of sin, emptiness of grace, and naughty frame of heart. It may be your treasure is more settled, and theirs more floating, and you see it when the tide is high. You should take in all, before you judge yourselves by others, and indeed, no man is a competent judge of another's frame of spirit, you may even fall below hypocrites themselves in seeming enlargements.

6. Yea, saith the soul, but I fall below others in real usefulness. If there were a treasure within, methinks it would appear more to the glory of God and good of others, but I do no good in my place, I cumber the ground, and bring not forth fruit as others do, who do God a great deal more service, than I do.

I answer, the Apostle saith, there are diversities of gifts and operations, so also, all members have not the same office, and consequently not the same usefulness.*
Some move in a higher sphere, and some in a lower, but if thou art placed in the heavenly orbit of the

---

* 1 Cor. xii. 4—6. Rom. xii. 4.

church, thou hast some influence; there is not a finger or toe in the body of Christ, but is of some use, and cannot be spared without making the body lame and defective; not a loop or pin in the tabernacle of the church, but as it fills up some space, so it bears some weight; not the choicest member can say to the meanest in the church, I have no need of thee. Paul, though a great apostle, stood in need of the prayers of the meanest Christian. An iron key may sometimes open that lock, which a silver one cannot. There is never a saint in the world, that knows the good that he doth, nor shall it be known to others the use he is of, till he be taken away, and then the place will feel a loss of him: a city, a country, and kingdom may be spared upon the prayers and uprightness of one righteous person. Let not more worthy members despise the ignoble, since they cannot be without them; and let not inferior members envy the more honourable, because God appointeth every one his station, and accepteth the meanest member's faithful service; a sweeper of chimneys may honour God in his place, as well as a pastor of souls in his; a plain Christian in a leathern coat may, if faithful in his station, do God as much service, as a great Doctor in his purple robes. If thou be serious in the work of God, thou mayest promote the cause of God in thy family, which may reflect a lustre on the whole church.

7. But alas, saith the soul, I am so far from increasing my treasure, that I fear I am on the losing hand. I am spending, wasting, decreasing by sinful practices; what I gain in a duty or ordinance, I lose by an act of sinning, and have much ado to recover myself. Oh this inconstant, unstable spirit! What shall become of me?

I answer, the case is sad, and much to be lamented, but so it is with the best of God's children. David saith, thou hast lifted me up, and cast me down, while we are tossed upon the fluctuating waves of the sea, we must expect a mariner's motion—to mount up to heaven, and go down to the depths,* to have rich enjoyments, and sadder abatements, that we may know both how to want, and how to abound in point of enlargement. Sometimes our hearts are opened, as the heart of Lydia, to receive of that grace which becomes our treasure, then again our hearts are shut up, and we are in danger of shutting out divine incomes. Sometimes the sails of our souls are spread to receive the lively gales of the Holy Spirit, but how often are they contracted, and we then resist the blessed operations thereof? Let us complain of this, as our sin and shame, but thus it must be in this sublunary state, to make a distinction betwixt this vale of mutability and the heavenly mount of unchangeable blessedness; yet, take notice, that the believer's treasure may be maintained, and even increased by this variety of conditions; by standing still, or falling back, he may grow more self-suspicious, penitent, vigilant, and diligent, and make the more haste after his God, to redeem the time that he hath left, and pick up his scattered crumbs. When a covetous man hath wasted any thing, or missed a good bargain, he will seek to make amends, by future diligence. Thus will the gracious soul do: so that God may overrule slips, to make a firmer standing, stumbling to produce a speedy motion forwards, and falls to occasion a greater heedfulness and sensibleness. Hast thou not found it thus believer? Hast thou not been a gainer by thy losses? Have not these spiritual Egyptians of raging corruptions, paid tribute to thy soul, to increase thy spiritual stock? Have not these Gibeonites been hewers of wood and drawers of water, to help thee in the service of the

* Psal. cvii. 26.

sanctuary? I question not, but thou hast found these bitter enemies, as occasions at least, to put thee on to watch thy treasure better. The Canaanites were to be to Israel, as pricks in their eyes, and thorns in their sides ; * just so are sins to the saints—those pricks in their eyes make them weep more for sin, and those thorns in their sides spur them on towards the city of refuge. There are different sorts of Christians, some are solid, sober, and more regular in their movements, that keep forward in a good, even pace in the ways of God ; others are more unstable, sometimes pushing forwards, and then drawing back again, yet these may be God's children, as well as the former. Sometimes it is occasioned by the natural levity and fickleness of their spirits, or other causes, yet still the almighty arm of Jehovah is under them, and all his saints are in his hand, and though these unstable souls may not excel, yet they shall keep their hold, and be still approaching nearer to heaven, to that immutable state, where there is fulness of joy, and rivers of pleasure flow for evermore.

Thus much for answer to some objections ; I shall now conclude all with a brief and serious exhortation, and oh that I could persuade and prevail upon all to look after their share in the treasure, so largely opened to you. Methinks it should be an easy thing to persuade men to embrace a treasure, but oh how hard it is to engage them to look after a treasure for their souls ! I see what a wretched thing a carnal heart is, and poor souls fight against their own interest, and forsake their own mercy.

One would think that they who are poor in the world would be induced to think of some treasure at last. I beseech you, let reason be heard, argue rationally, and

* Num. xxxiii. 55.

let your souls be framing such thoughts as these—God hath cast my lot in a mean estate, and I work hard for a bare living; I toil and travel night and day, and I can scarce get coarse clothes for my back, and food for myself and my family; I would have got something beforehand, but I see it will not do, times are hard, trade is dead, I despair of growing rich; the world is like a shadow, the more I pursue it, the further it flees from me, and have I been pursuing after that which I cannot overtake? and which, if I should overtake, can do me no good, may do me much hurt; and, in the meantime, have I neglected my immortal soul, and the getting of a treasure in it to make it rich and happy? These spiritual goods are the best that can be got, and these may be got, and little else. O my soul, shall I be poor in this world and poor to all eternity? Must I live in misery here, and be in greater torment hereafter? Oh why should I be such a perfect beggar, doubly poor, of a poor estate, and of a poor, low, degenerate spirit? Oh rather let me be poor in spirit that I may be an heir of a kingdom, a better than this dunghill world can afford. If I want bread for my body, Lord, evermore give me the bread of life for my poor soul; the garments of Christ's righteousness to cover my nakedness; fine gold that I may be rich; though I be separated from my neighbour, let me be united to the Lord; though I be despised by men, yet let my soul be owned by the Lord; although I have not a foot of land, or house of mine own in this world, yet, oh that I may have right to mansions above, that I may take possession at death of the inheritance of the saints in light. Thus do you that are poor argue the case, and rest not satisfied without the true riches; if you cannot get earth, make sure of heaven, and then you make no bad bargain. Keep up this trade of religion, when other trades decay; live above the world, learn to act faith, put the bond in suit, make a virtue of necessity, and if you cannot get left-hand mercies, be sure of right-hand mercies, and then you are happy for ever.

Let rich men also look after a treasure above. I know it is a hard thing to persuade such as have treasures on earth, to look after treasures of heaven, and in heaven. It is impossible for them that trust in riches to be saved, and most men do so. Oh how apt are men of great estates to please and applaud themselves on account of their large possessions, especially after the malicious revilings of the poor, or the awakening convictions of God's Spirit by some heart-shaking Boanerges; they go home and thus bespeak themselves—" what need I regard the vain calumnies of the sons of Belial, or the furious invectives of these bawling priests ; I have need of nothing, and I fear no man; I am able to live of myself; let every man look to himself. * It is a hard world, and we must look to ourselves ; God hath blessed me with an estate, and I trust he loves me, and I shall do as well as others." Such workings are in rich men's breasts ! The God of heaven knows your secret, self-flattering thoughts, but they will be found to be vain another day; when you lie upon a death-bed, ready to breathe out your despairing souls, what will money do in the chest without grace in the heart? What art thou better for hundreds or thousands a-year? What art thou the better for the honourable or worshipful titles of lord, knight, esquire, or gentleman ? I have heard of a person of quality that cried out upon his sick-bed, " ten thousand pounds for a good conscience !" but alas, pardon and heaven cannot be bought with

* ——— Populus me sibilat, at mihi plaudo
Ipse domi simul ac nummos contemplor in arcâ.—*Hor.*

money; purity and peace of conscience are valued at a higher rate, they cost the precious blood of Jesus Christ, and are not bought but given in God's way and in God's time. He was a fool that pleased himself with conceits of filling his soul with his full bags and furnished houses, or fruitful fields; what are these to the immortal soul, which is of a spiritual nature? No, no; riches profit not in a day of wrath; you cannot stop the mouth of conscience in the pangs of death with a little worldly trash; try this in lesser things, and see whether "money, which answereth all things," will fill your hungry bellies, cure the head-ache or tooth-ache, or remove fevers;* alas, it cannot, you know it cannot. How then, can riches satisfy, or sanctify, or save the immortal soul? A time is coming when the careless and covetous worldling would be glad to exchange earth for heaven, and would be willing to cast all his rare commodities overboard to save the precious vessel of his never-dying soul; but he that has made the world his god, will have no God to relieve him when he is leaving the world; he that has spent his strength and time to compass his worldly ends, will have nothing but his labour for his pains, in the upshot; what hath he gained, (let him brag of his bargain) "when God taketh away his soul?"† Nay, this very treasure that he hath heaped up, shall rise "up in judgment against him;" so Heinsius reads, ‡ James v. 3, as though their gold and silver would become a treasure of tormenting fire to the rich and wretched misers; and, oh what an astonishing consideration is this, that a covetous man

* Non domus et fundus, non æris acervus et auri,
Ægroto Domini deduxit corpore febres.—*Hor.*

† Job xxvii. 8.

‡ Ὡς πῦρ· ἐθησαυρίσατε ἐν ἐσχάταις ἡμέραις.—Heins. Exercit. page 563.

should gather the fuel to that fire which shall torment him for ever, and that his beloved minion, the world, with which he hath committed adultery, shall be the instrument of his torment; yea, some think further, that this earth, where wicked men have had their heaven, shall be the place of hell-torments after the great day of judgment. Certainly, this world, which hath bewitched sensual souls, shall be burnt with fire; and how just is it, that where men have acted their pleasant comedy, they should suffer this last and everlasting tragedy? Oh sirs, think of this betimes, do but in cold blood consider whether your great estates will form a screen betwixt God's flaming wrath and your sinning souls another day. Bethink yourselves betimes, whether you would have God or the world to stand your friend at death or judgment, whether you would have a heart laden with this heavenly treasure, or a conscience loaded with guilt, and filled with excruciating worms; whether you would hear that sad word, "Woe unto you that are rich, for ye have received your consolation," or "Come, my friends, enter into your master's joy." Remember you were forewarned of those things, look about you betimes.

Here I might admonish all ages and sexes to get their hearts full of this treasure. You young men, begin the world with this stock, this alone will fit you for all callings, places, relations and conditions; you are entering the world, and you know not what you may pass through betwixt this and the grave; without this treasure you are fit for nothing; this will fit you for any thing, this will render you well-accomplished gentlemen, merchants, ministers; this will carry you through all companies with credit and profit; it will be an excellent guide and guard in your journeys; this will season your younger years with gravity, prudence, and humility, and ripen your souls for heaven as your bodies are ripening for the grave.* Oh my brethren, set up with this stock, begin in grace, and you shall end in peace; begin with this treasure, and you shall end in everlasting pleasures.

And you that are aged, look after this treasure; old men are addicted to hoarding; why, here is work for you; be hoarding up in your hearts, divine truths, graces, comforts, and experiences; in " malice be ye children, but in understanding be ye men." Give me leave to admonish old men, and fathers, to labour to " know him that is from the beginning;" † you delight much in antiquity, here is an object for you to contemplate, even " the ancient of days." Oh mind not toys and earthly treasures, even the best of them; let your hoary heads be found in the way of righteousness, and your hearts be filled with the fruits of righteousness. Alas, shall you be full of days and empty of grace? Shall you be drawing to a period of your lives, and be destitute at the end of your lives? Ah sirs, that you should be taking your leave of the world, and yet have laid no foundation, made no preparation for a better life; alas, what shall become of you? the Lord be merciful to you, and lay hands on you and pluck you " as brands out of the fire." It is a monstrous sight to see a wicked old man! how unbecoming is it to hear an old man swear, to see an old man drunk, or unclean! it is, indeed, a shocking sight! such are worse, because they should be better; the grey hair which should be a crown of glory, is a testimony of sloth, and monitor of approaching wrath. Ah sirs, think it not strange, if at the great day you be set on the left hand, that have all

* Read Proverbs i. 4; ii. 1; and iv. 1; or rather, read the first nine Chapters in Proverbs.

† 1 John ii. 14.

your days made choice of left hand blessings. The God of heaven awaken you to provide for eternity, before the flames of hell awaken you when there is no remedy.

Let all, and every one, without fail, without dallying or delay, look after this treasure. Oh let your souls be furnished with a store of holy thoughts, you are always thinking, the mind is active, never idle, always in motion. Oh get it furnished for contemplation! bring some work to this millstone, else as Luther saith, " it will grind itself thinner," or be as a lamp that is soon extinct without a fresh supply of oil. You can neither discourse in company, nor spend your time in solitary retirement profitably, without this treasure. But I have been too tedious. Let not all these words be in vain to you, or rise up in judgment against you.

A few words to those precious souls into whose bosom the Lord hath dropped this heavenly treasure. These, I might urge to bless God for it, live up to it, make much of it, maintain and increase it, and be sure you do not part with it upon any terms. In giving your attention to this treasure, let it not be in the least impaired, wasted or injured. It is, I may assure you, a greater loss to lose one grain of grace, than a mine of gold, or both the Indies. The gaining of the world cannot countervail the loss of a soul, and if your treasure be gone, your souls are gone. Take fast hold of " instruction, let her not go, for she is thy life."—Prov. iv. 13. Let all go rather than part with your treasure. Cæsar, swimming through a river to escape his enemies, carried his books above water with his hand, but lost his robe; so do you. Though you should swim through a sea of sorrows, yet be sure you keep fast the Lord's deposit, make not " shipwreck of faith and a good conscience." Let neither the treasures nor pleasures of the world rob or cozen you of this glorious treasure. Take two famous instances of constancy in the primitive times. * The one is of a soldier, whom the Prætor could not with torments remove from his christian profession, at last he commanded him to be laid in a soft bed, in a pleasant garden among flourishing lilies and red roses, and being left alone, a beautiful harlot came to him, and embracing him wantonly, solicited him to sin; he resolutely opposed; at last, for very vexation, and to prevent by his pain the danger of pleasure, he bit off part of his tongue and spit it in her face, and so bravely overcame. This valiant soldier would not endanger his treasure for sensual enjoyment. The other example is, of one Hormisda, a great nobleman's son, who, for religion was condemned to keep the king of Persia's elephants, and to go naked. One day, the king looking out, and seeing him tanned with the sun, commanded a shirt to be put upon him, and to bring him before him, when the king asked him " if he would now deny Christ." Hormisda tore off his shirt, saying, " if you think I will deny my faith for a shirt have here your gift again." See here, a young man stripped naked, rather than lose his inward treasure. Imitate his resolution. Say as Job did, chap. xxvii. 5, 6, " Till I die, I will not remove my integrity from me, my righteousness I hold fast and will not let it go; my heart shall not reproach me so long as I live." Live upon your stock, make use of it upon all occasions, draw forth the seeds of grace, bring " forth much fruit," improve your treasure for maintaining constant intercourse with God. Josephus tells us, † that there was a tumult raised among the Jews, because their

* Acts and Mon. par. 1, fol. 63, fol. 100.
† Joseph. de Bello Jud. lib. 2, cap. 8.

holy treasure was wasted upon a conduit, reaching the space of 300 furlongs, but if you spend your treasure in maintaining ways of conveyance betwixt God and your hearts, it will produce an increase, and keep up peace with God, and peace of conscience. Communion with God will compose all mutinous insurrections in your own hearts; pay to God the constant tribute of duty and obedience; give him the glory of all, that he hath done for you; sweep the temple of your hearts; free it from all dust and filth; prepare a clean lodging for this blessed guest: the Holy Spirit is compared to a dove, and we know the dove is a delicate creature, and leaves its residence when it is defiled, so will the Spirit. Be holy in all your conceptions, and in all manner of conversation; learn that blessed round that Enoch took of walking with God; solace your souls in him, scorn any thing that the world can offer, as a temptation to divert your hearts into another channel; ask the world what it can give, that may be a valuable consideration for the loss of communion with God; make such a challenge as Saul did in another case,—can the son of Jesse give you fields and vineyards? So ask, can the world give pardon of sin, peace of conscience, grace here, and glory hereafter? If it say it can, believe it not, it is a vain brag and impudent lie, like that of Satan's to Christ. If it cannot, as certainly it cannot, why shouldest thou leave the substance, and embrace the shadow? Oh make not so mad, so bad a bargain! I stand the more upon this, because there is danger, lest you should be cheated out of your treasure by the world, as Delilah beguiled Sampson, or as the maid got the apple out of the giant's hand by fair means, which the champions could not wrest from him. Do not delight in the creature, lest it abate your content in God; be not afraid of afflictions that accompany godliness, you may get a larger increase of your treasure by trouble, than by any other means; as it is storied of Tiberius, that passing by a cross upon a marble stone, and causing the cross to be dug up, he found a large treasure under the cross. So may, and do, gracious souls find treasures under their crosses.

But to draw to an end: the Lord engage all your hearts to make sure of this treasure, and to make much of this treasure. Lock it up in the inmost closet of your hearts, lay it out in ways of holiness as the Lord gives opportunity, raise up your hearts heavenwards, improve solitariness, do all the good you can in your places, sanctify the name of God in all things you do or receive, watch over your own spirits, be faithful unto death and he will give you a crown of life. I shall conclude all with an elegant exhortation of Cyprian: " Thou only, whom the heavenly warfare hath sealed up in these spiritual tents, keep incorrupt, keep sober this blessed discipline of religious virtues; be thou diligent either in praying or reading, sometimes speak thou to God, sometimes hear God speak to thee, let him instruct thee by his precepts and dispose of thee; whom he hath made rich, no man shall make poor; thou canst not now be subject to any penury, when thy breast is satiated with variety of all heavenly delicacies;"* thus he, " Blessed is the soul that hath this blessed treasure, and is mounting upwards to everlasting pleasures.

* Tu tantum quem jam spiritualibus castris cœlestis militia signavit, tene incorruptam, tene sobriam religiosis virtutibus disciplinam, sit tibi vel oratio assidua vel lectio; nunc cum Deo loquere, nunc Deus tecum; ille te præceptis suis instruat, ille disponat; quem ille divitem fecerit, nemo pauperem faciet; penuria esse nulla jam poterit, cum semel pectus cœlestis sagina saturaverit.— *Videas plura in Cyp. Epist. lib.* 2, *Ep.* 2, *ad Donatum.*

AN

APPENDIX,

CONCERNING MEDITATION, WITH SOME HELPS TO FURNISH THE THOUGHTS WITH SUITABLE AND PROFITABLE SUBJECTS.

THAT the vacant pages may be supplied, it will not be out of place here, to annex a specimen or example, to help the active thoughts in the great duty of meditation; yet, here I shall not undertake to handle the common-place of meditation, which you may find insisted upon, purposely, by Mr. Fenner, Mr. Ball, Mr. Baxter in his "Saints' Rest," and many others—and abundant examples thereof, in those incomparable works of that reverend, contemplative divine, Dr. Hall; but what I shall do on this behalf, is only to pursue the design of the foregoing treatise, in presenting some considerations to help the Christian to a treasure of good thoughts, that he may not want a subject of meditation, wherever he is. Before I proceed to the examples, I shall speak a few words concerning thoughts and good thoughts, and deliberate good thoughts in the duty of meditation.

Thoughts in general, according to Scripture, are the internal acts of the soul, of what faculty soever, mind, will, memory, affections; to remember, is to *think*[*] on a person or thing; to take care is to *take thought*;[†]

[*] Gen. xl. 14.   [†] 1 Sam. ix. 5.

to be troubled, is expressed by *thoughts* of heart;* and so thoughts denote any internal operations, consisting of reasonings, motives, desires, designs, and resolutions, as opposed to external words or works; so Isaiah lxvi. 18, " I know their works and their thoughts." But thoughts are also taken more strictly, as being the proper products of the understanding faculty, the immediate musings of the speculative power, and so not only opposed to words and works, but also to the acts of the soul of another nature, and thus critics distinguish (as the word itself acts the critic, betwixt the thoughts of the heart, and the intents of the heart, in Heb. iv. 15. ‡ The thoughts then are the soul's self-conferences, discourses, parleys, interviews; hence there is mention in Scripture of speaking in the heart, Deut. ix. 4, communing with our own hearts, Psal. iv. 4, applied both to the godly and the wicked; the subjects of these discourses within, are either from without, or from within, ‖ sometimes the subjects are fetched from abroad; as if good, the thoughts are furnished from the word of God, or otherwise, Prov. vi. 22, " When thou awakest, it shall talk with thee," that is, thou shalt find the word as a sweet companion, affording thee matter of self-conference; so also, the matter of thoughts may arise from within, but they are ordinarily evil, and so every imagination of the thoughts of man's heart is evil; the word signifies every figment, § creature, or workmanship, that the mind hammers within itself, as in a forge, mint, or on an anvil; for thoughts are, as it were, spun out of ourselves, they are webs of our own weav-

* Judg. v. 15.

‡ Καὶ κριτικὸς ἐνθυμήσεων καὶ ἐννοιῶν καρδίας.

‖ Psal. lxxvii. 6. Psal. xiv. 1.

§ Gen. vi. 5. וכל יצר omne figmentum.

ing, for thoughts can work of themselves, when there are no outward objects presented. Now my design is to furnish and rectify these internal operations of the heart, and to help the soul with such subjects and objects as may find it profitable work when it hath no creature to converse with, that the thoughts may be holy, sweet, spiritual, and heavenly. Now there are four qualifications essentially requisite to the constitution of good thoughts. 1. They must be materially good, not employed about sinful or trifling things, that do either prejudice, or not at all profit the soul; but exercised in some spiritual, suitable meditations about God, Christ, the word, or what may tend to edification. 2. They must be formally good, that is, regulated by the word of God, as the rule thereof, to square and order the thoughts, both for principle, manner, and end. 3. They must be seasonably good, every thing is beautiful in its season; a thing may be good in its own nature, yet not good as to those circumstances of time and other respects wherewith it may be clothed. 4. They must be eventually good, as to the fruit, effect, and impression of these thoughts; he that thinks, should aim at God's glory and his own soul's good; and the fruit of the thoughts must be good, tending to quicken or strengthen some grace, kill or crucify some lust, enlarge or encourage the straitened or saddened heart. Now, this is not a mere exercise of the mind and memory about good things, but a working them upon the heart, the impressing of these things on the will and affections; it is not merely speculative, but practical and experimental, it must be a set and solemn acting of all the powers of the soul upon divine things, in order to spiritual advantage, or raising the heart heaven-wards.

And now I shall present to your thoughts twenty useful subjects to meditate upon, which may by the

Lord's assistance, become in your souls a sacred treasure of heavenly thoughts.

1. Let your thoughts be exercised upon the the infinite, eternal and incomprehensible majesty of God. Here you may soon lose yourselves in the vast ocean of his blessed essence, yet launch not too far, but bound your thoughts by the sure compass of Scripture discovery. Thus think: Oh what a holy, omniscient, omnipresent Spirit is the almighty maker and possessor of heaven and earth! What transcendent mysteries are locked up in the trinity of persons, in the unity of essence! How impossible is it for a mortal eye to approach that inaccessible light! " none can see God and live," yet have poor sinners a glorious reflection of the Godhead in the person of our dear Redeemer, and in his sweetly proclaiming his blessed name, and displaying his glorious attributes of wisdom, power, holiness, justice, goodness and truth to the sons of men. By these, we taste and see what a Being the Lord is. Oh how great is this Jehovah whom we worship! " the heaven of heavens cannot contain him," he is the King of kings and Lord of lords; he sitteth upon the circle of the earth, and the inhabitants thereof are as grasshoppers; he is clothed with honour and majesty, thousand thousands minister unto him, ten thousand times ten thousand stand before him; he is the God in whose hands my breath is, the searcher of hearts, the hearer of prayer, the Lord of hosts, and King of saints. O my soul admire him for his greatness, fear him for his justice, love him for his goodness, trust him for his faithfulness, worship him in the beauty of holiness, and delight thyself in his transcendent perfections.

2. Fix your thoughts upon the works of creation, study this large, voluminous book, every page thereof will find you fresh matter of meditation and admira-

tion; every creature hath a tongue to tell us of the power and wisdom of its Maker; and thus let your thoughts be working: Surely, this goodly fabric of heaven and earth speaks aloud the glory of the great Creator. If this vast globe of the earth be above twenty thousand miles in compass, then of what a vast extent are the heavens, which are stretched out as a curtain! How admirably hath God laid the beams of his chambers in the waters, and suspended the earth upon nothing! How firmly hath he built his stories in the heavens, and fixed the glorious constellations as fountains of light! Oh what beauty there must be in the "Father of lights," that hath set up the resplendent luminaries! These great bodies were created of nothing by the word of God's power, while there are deep mysteries in the least and lowest creature; every herb, flower, plant, spire of grass, twig or leaf, worm or fly, scale or feather, billow or meteor, hath enough in it to puzzle the most profound philosopher, and speaks the power and wisdom of our great Creator; how much more the curious piece of man's body! "I am fearfully and wonderfully made," but much more may I stand admiring the strange nature of my immortal soul, and still reflect with thankfulness and admiration upon the power and goodness of my omnipotent Creator.

3. Think on the capacity, excellency, and immortality of the precious soul; you cannot think without it, and should you not spend some thoughts upon it. This distinguisheth you from beasts. Thus, then, meditate: What divine spark is this that God hath breathed into this lump of clay? this immortal soul which God immediately created, is greater and better than the world, and cannot be satisfied with the world; it is a spiritual being, and of the same

nature with the angels; it is of an active nature, and can make quick excursions to the creatures, and sallies through this vast universe, and must return like Noah's dove, because there is no place to rest the weary foot of her affections upon. God alone is the anchor and centre of this tossed wanderer. This soul is capable of communion with God in spiritual ordinances and eternal happiness; it must return at last to God, that gave it, to receive from him a sentence of absolution or condemnation. Oh my soul, thou art in constant motion, whither art thou moving? what art thou doing? what condition art thou in? and what must become of thee when thy body shall be left a putrefying carcase? Soar aloft my soul, and mind things above; debase not thy noble nature with the pursuit of things that are below thyself. Get well adorned with the graces of the Spirit, and enriched with an interest in Jesus Christ, make God thy portion, lay up lasting treasures in heaven, and then return unto thy rest, and God will deal bountifully with thee.

4. Think much upon the sacred word of God, " meditate on it day and night,—let the word of God dwell richly in you," and let your thoughts be furnished with, and dwell much upon it; what is in your Bibles is God's, but what is in your hearts is your own. Thus then, let your thoughts be working: Oh the infinite condescension of the great Jehovah! What is worthless man that God himself should write so large an epistle from heaven to him with the hand of his blessed Spirit? What care hath God taken to direct, move, incite, and encourage fallen and sinning man to attain eternal happiness! What precepts, promises, threatenings, examples, are sprinkled up and down in this blessed book! Oh the antiquity and authority, excellency and efficacy, power and purity, perfection and suffi-

ciency, verity and perpetuity of the sacred Bible! Methinks when I take up this Holy Book, I take wonders into my hand, and when I look within it, I meet with mysteries, that the wisdom of the greatest clerks can never reach, and yet the meanest capacity, by the help of that Spirit who indited them, may wade this deep ford of divine secrets. How plainly held forth therein are necessary truths and duties that lead the soul to God and eternal happiness! How familiarly and affectionately doth God converse with man therein! How pat and proper to my state are the precious promises in these blessed pages! every word hath its weight, and comes as pertinently as if the Lord had named me. Methinks, there is no such virtue or savour in any other writings. What reviving doth it bring to my heart. O blessed be God for the holy Scriptures.

5. Let your thoughts be employed about the glorious works of providence. Oh how sweet are they! Whoso is wise will consider them. Pause after this manner: O my soul, take a view of this beautiful checker-work of divine providence; consider the days of old, and the years of many generations; recollect what the Scripture records of drying up the "sea, driving back Jordan," the "standing still" and "going back of the sun in the firmament;" reflect upon the miracles of mercy for the church, and of judgment upon her enemies; nay, consider, O my soul, what wonders God hath wrought in thy days, in thine eyes. Oh what national, domestic, personal deliverances hast thou seen! even such as may astonish the atheist, and silence unbelief for ever. Thou needest not want matter of holy musing, if thou take a strict survey of the course of thy life, and particular providences about thy soul, body, estate, name, relations, and all thy concernments, which may afford a vast field of devout meditation. Those ways

of providence that seemed uncouth and unlovely whilst seen but in their birth and parts, how comely now are they in their mature product and perfection! I saw not then, but I have fully seen since what the Lord aimed at in his strange dispensations. Oh the happy connection, symmetry, and contexture of all things, combining together by the concurrence of providence to accomplish, and to centre in the grand end of all things, namely "the glory of God." How wonderful are his "judgments, and his ways past finding out!"

6. Think humbly upon man's apostacy. Let your thoughts be sometimes taking a view of the origin of all our present sinfulness and wretchedness in such thoughts as these. Woe is me, whence and whither are we fallen? God made man "upright, but he sought out many inventions;" once man was "created after the image of God," now is he defaced after the image of the devil; once was man entire and straight, now he is deformed and crooked in all his faculties; once holy and happy, now filthy and subject to all sin and misery; once he was the darling of God, lord of the world, and a fit companion for the blessed angels, now he is God's enemy, the devil's slave, and the basest part of the whole creation. Oh mutable free-will that chose to fall, that might have chosen to stand! surely man, in his best estate was subject to vanity. Oh, how little was the pleasure, and how lasting is the pain! But, O my soul, find not fault with Adam,—if thou hadst been in his stead thou wouldest have done as he did, yea, thou dost the same every day, too, too voluntarily, and of choice: sin is a "transgression of the law," and this holy law thou breakest every moment. Oh my soul, what a miserable case art thou in? what enmity to God, antipathy to good, and constant tendency to all evil is in thy depraved nature! Woe is me,

where is the light in my understanding, the rectitude of my will, the regularity of my affections? Where is the tenderness of my conscience, the tenacity of my memory, and the victory over my inferior unruly passions? Lord, where am I, and what will become of me, except free grace interpose for my deliverance?

7. Think, oh think much upon the stupendous work of man's redemption. Here the ransomed of the Lord may and must expatiate in heart-melting meditations on the way of their recovery, thus: Here stand and ruminate, my soul, upon the sweet, transcendent contrivance to save lost man. Oh why, wherefore was it, that the heart of God was working for men, and not for devils? they were as near and dear to God, when standing, and as perfect in their natures. Was it because man had a tempter, and they had none? No, certainly; though that may be a truth, yet no reason for chusing man, and leaving devils to be reserved in chains of darkness to the judgment of the great day. No, no; free grace alone made the difference; but, what was the way of man's redemption? Why, truly, the Son of God, the second Person of the glorious trinity must become man, and put himself into the sinners' stead, to do and endure, be and bear what man must have gone through and undergone. Oh stupendous mystery! oh transcendent mercy! who could have devised such a way? who durst have desired such a thing, that God should part with his only begotten Son for such an end? Oh the manifold wisdom of God! Oh the inconceivable love of the Father, to send his Son, and of his Son to come on such an errand! Great is the mercy of God, " great is the mystery of godliness, God manifest in the flesh." O the wonders in his strange hypostatical union, the completeness of his person, the usefulness of his offices! Oh the bitterness of his

temptations, travels, trials, reproaches, agonies, desertions and death, sharp to him, sweet to us. These will be the subject of saints' thoughts, and praises in heaven, to all eternity.

8. Think upon the terms and tenor of the gospel, how, and upon what conditions, Christ and all his benefits may be made over to you; and that is, on a cordial accepting of Christ in his mediatorial offices, as he is tendered in the gospel, to justify, sanctify, and save. Thus then, conceive thereof: Oh strange mercy, boundless love; God might have appointed the conditions of salvation to have been travelling tedious journeys, conquering kingdoms, or lying so many years in misery. He might have said, thou must either keep the moral law exactly or die eternally; but he saith believe in the Lord Jesus, and thou shalt be saved, nor hath he left thee, O my soul, to do this by thine own strength, which had been as impossible as the former, but he that requires faith of thee, promiseth to give faith to thee. Faith is in the covenant as well as forgiveness; Jesus Christ hath purchased strength to believe, as well as salvation for believers. Oh blessed contrivance, all is laid upon our gracious and all-sufficient surety; he is exalted to be a Prince and a Saviour, he is the way, the truth, and the life, the author and finisher of our faith, he saves to the uttermost, all the elect who have faith, and none of them shall miscarry. This, this is the kernel and marrow of the gospel, that Christ is the surety for all believers and hath undertaken to bear them all to heaven by the power of his Spirit, and by virtue of his atonement, and he wants neither ability nor fidelity to bring about this glorious enterprise for poor souls.

9. Think, and think again, what interest you have in this Redeemer and redemption, for all are not sharers

in it, all will not be saved by it, nay, but few of those that hear the tidings of it. Think thus, oh my soul: What is thy state? where is thy standing? what interest hast thou in Christ? what title to the promises of the covenant? hast thou a sound and saving faith, a thorough heart-shaking, heart-breaking repentance? I hear in the word that Christ becomes the author of eternal salvation to all them that obey him. Oh my soul! hast thou given up thyself to him in the obedience of faith? What operations of the Spirit hast thou felt for thy effectual vocation? what regenerating work hath passed upon thee? art thou translated from death to life, from darkness to light? art thou, indeed, transplanted out of the old stock into the new and living vine? what particular application hast thou made of this general redemption? hast thou viewed a bleeding Christ with a bleeding heart? and looked on him whom thy sins have pierced with a repenting, believing frame of spirit? hast thou accepted of Jesus Christ in his mediatorial latitude, as Prophet, Priest, and King, to subdue thy lusts, to guide thee by his sceptre, and save thee in his own way? Oh my soul, be serious in this inquiry, it is no trifling matter—it is as much as thy soul is worth—it is of great concernment to all eternity! The way is strait and narrow—thousands are deceived and spend no thoughts upon it, till they be past hope or remedy. The stroke of death will suddenly determine the business. Oh look to it, before that blow be given, lest it be too late.

10. When thou hast cleared thy state, then think with comfort on the rich privileges of believers. Here thou mayest have a spacious field of contemplation; God allows thee to solace thy soul in such thoughts as these: O the inestimable, incomparable, invaluable advantages of the saints! What sayest thou, oh my guilty,

weary soul, is it nothing to have sin pardoned, thy debts paid, the bond cancelled? Certainly, to a soul heavy laden, under a sense of guilt, an assurance of pardon is the most joyful tidings in the world, and shall my filthy, naked soul be clothed with this blessed robe of Christ's perfect righteousness? Oh the riches of free grace! Shall such a base and bankrupt beggar become the beautiful spouse of the King of heaven? It was infinite mercy that kept me thus long out of hell, but will the Lord also make this polluted soul an heir of heaven? shall Jesus Christ be my elder brother, the Spirit my comforter, and God himself my Father? Oh boundless and bottomless riches of free grace! moreover, O my soul, thou hast interest in all the promises, the assistance of the Spirit in prayer, and free access to the throne of grace. The providences of God are working for thy good, the protection of heaven shall be over thy person, and the blessing of the Almighty shall be upon thy undertakings. Thou hast, O my soul, sweet fellowship with God, the benefit of communion of saints, and the presence and service of the holy angels; he will guide thee with his counsel, and at last receive thee to glory. And is not this a *ne plus ultra* of preferment? Can thy covetous or ambitious thoughts reach any further? No, no, my soul, God hath done for thee beyond thy expectation, even to admiration.

11. Now then, my soul, let thy thoughts be working upon some returns. What doth God require of thee in lieu of all these rich and royal favours? Oh set thy heart to study duty, lie under a sense of the law of thankfulness, desire the Lord to write that blessed law upon the table of thy heart, consider what thou hast to do, but here my soul is non-plussed. Alas, what returns can I make unto my God for all these benefits? what can a poor, worthless worm do, in requiting infi-

nite kindness? Myself, and all I am, or can do, are the Lord's due, and here I offer up all to thee, O Lord, as a whole burnt sacrifice, which is most reasonable. Oh that it may be acceptable through Jesus Christ! my heart, my lips, my life shall praise thee,—bless the Lord, O my soul, and all that is within me bless his holy name! Oh that my heart were well-tuned to sing the song of Moses, and of the Lamb! alas, my soul, how low and dull art thou! how short and shallow in thy poor returns for these rich receipts! surely my soul will sing a new, and another kind of song amongst the heavenly choir of blessed saints and angels in eternal mansions. In the mean time, O my soul, be winding up thy heart, screwing up thy faint affections; be much in the work of thankfulness, lay out thyself for the glory of thy Redeemer, sin no more, serve him better; walk with God, wait upon him, worship him with all thy heart; do all the good thou canst in thy place, hie apace towards heaven, and lift up thy head with expectation, desire, and exultation, for the day of redemption draweth near.

12. Think much, and seriously on the evil of sin, how offensive it is to God! how destructive to the soul! that so you may eschew and abhor the very risings and appearance thereof. Thus let your thoughts be employed: What a monstrous, shocking, venemous thing is sin! it is the very epitome of all evil, worse than the devil himself, the most loathsome creature that crawls is very good if compared with sin. It is a heart-plague, more evil than all the plagues and diseases that are incident to the body of man,—it is worse than hell itself. O sin, what hast thou done? was it not sin that cast the angels out of heaven, Adam out of paradise, and thousands, yea, tens of thousands of souls headlong into hell? was it not sin

that drowned the old world, burnt Sodom, and will set the whole world in a flame at the last day? is it not sin only that provoketh the eyes of God's glory, grieveth his Spirit, breaketh his laws, and bringeth swift destruction on impenitent sinners? Nay, O my soul, consider, was it not sin that betrayed, arraigned, accused, condemned, crucified and buried the Lord of life and glory? Oh then, who would have any thing to do with unprofitable, pernicious works of darkness? what fruit hast thou, poor soul, from sin, but shame, and grief, and death? Oh what hurt hath it done thee! what grief, and tears, and sorrows, and pangs hath it cost thee! and all these better than the proper product of it, even eternal damnation. O my soul, God hates nothing but sin! hate sin, then, with a perfect hatred, or with respect unto it, sin no more, lest thou offend a good God, gratify Satan, and damn thy soul for ever.

13. Think much on the vanity of the world, and the uncertainty of all things here below; read to yourselves sometimes, lectures on the instability of all worldly excellencies, and take off your own fingers from playing with them, lest God use some severer course to loosen your hearts from things below. Thus think, O my grovelling soul: What is it that thou seest in this garish strumpet to allure and entangle thy affection? how comest thou to dote upon her painted beauty? what real good, what solid comfort hast thou ever found therein? what are the profits of it, but a little white and yellow earth, of the same nature and origin with thy vile and perishing body, and far inferior to thy noble soul? what are the sorry honours of the world but bubbles, dependent on the slippery tongues and ears of mutable men, that can kiss and kill with a breath or beck? and,

what are the sordid pleasures here below, but swinish epicurism, that debase the best part of human nature, transform men into beasts, and leave a stinging guilt behind them? Alas, my soul, why wilt thou set thine eyes upon that which is not? what will riches avail thee in the day of wrath? where is the hope of the hypocrite, though he hath gained the whole world, when God taketh away his soul? what was Cain better for all his fair cities, or Nimrod for his large dominions, or Absalom for his beauty, or Ahithophel for his policy, or Judas for his bags, or Dives for his delicate fare? Hell-fire burns up all these, and heaven cannot be purchased with them. Alas, the fashion of the world passeth away, and when it is gone, what is a man better for being a gentleman, knight, lord, or prince? *Mors sceptra ligonibus æquat.**

14. Let your thoughts be exercised about the the present, and final state of all the children of men, the vast difference betwixt the good and bad, the godly and the wicked, in this world and the world to come, and thus let your hearts be musing: Admitting that the wicked flourish like a green bay-tree, and do enjoy the world at will, that they are not in trouble as other men, but eat and drink, and laugh and play, and change their sports for more delight, and wash their steps with butter, and have more than heart can wish. In the mean time, the godly are daily afflicted by God, tempted by Satan, persecuted by the world, they are chastened every morning, and lie down with sorrow every evening, they eat their bread, and water their beds, with tears. Oh the bitter, heart-breaking griefs, by reason of the withdrawings of God, the unkindness of men, but especially from corruptions within! Well now,

* Death levels sceptres and ploughshares.

my soul, wilt thou call this the only wretched man and the former the only happy person? God forbid, so shouldest thou offend against the generation of God's children; thou must not acquit the wicked nor condemn the righteous. No, my soul, look not with carnal but with spiritual eyes, " judge righteous judgment," he is not happy that hath the world at will, but he only is happy " whose God is the Lord." Search the Scriptures, and see there who is called, and who is accounted happy. " Mark the perfect man, the end of that man is peace," whatever be his trouble in the way; observe the wicked, it " cannot be well with him" in the end; Crœsus, at last, found Solon's words true, " There is no man happy before death." O my soul, wisely consider the state of the godly and the wicked, and it will beget strange effects upon thee for thy encouragement and wonder.

15. Sometimes let your thoughts run out upon the state of the church and people of God, that you may joy or sorrow, pray or praise God, with, or for Zion, and the saints. Upon blessed Paul's heart lay the care of all the churches, and shall we cast away the thoughts thereof? Well, then, my soul, art thou a member of the church, and wilt thou not spend some thoughts on it, and for it? Let me feel the pulse of Christ's mystical body, how fares it with her? is she in health, or is she sick? what diseases is she labouring under? do her sacred lungs move fast in prayer to God? doth she flourish in her pure and powerful administration of divine institutions? is she fair as the moon in the holiness of her members? clear as the sun in the soundness of her doctrine, especially in that fundamental point of justification by Christ's righteousness imputed? (hence, the woman, the church, is to be " clothed with the sun,") and is she terrible as an army

with banners, in the due administration of wholesome discipline, and execution of censures? do the lights shine clear in the candlesticks? are ministers in their places burning and shining lights, and do the faithful " walk in the light of the Lord?" have the saints communion in all ordinances, walking together in mutual edification? or, are they broken in pieces by persecutions or separations? How is it with this militant church? O my soul, take a full view thereof, that thou mayest rejoice with her, or mourn for her.

16. Think, O think often upon death, your own death; O that you were wise to consider your latter end; amongst all your thoughts, spend some upon your dying day, set a death's head before your eyes, and think to this purpose: Oh what a dying, fading creature am I! I dwell in a tottering tabernacle, in a house of clay, that is ready to be crushed every moment like a moth; this vile body of mine is made of perishing ingredients, and my life is like a vapour. O my soul, thou lodgest in a brittle case, how certainly shall, how suddenly may it be broken! and then thou launchest forth into the vast ocean of eternity; death will shortly loose the knot betwixt these old companions, soul and body—nature abhors a dissolution, but what saith grace? is the sting of death plucked out by the death of Christ? hath the Lord of life warmed and perfumed the grave for thee? Canst thou, O my soul, look beyond death at glory, and own it as thy Father's porter, or attendant, that takes thee by the hand to lead thee into his palace and presence-chamber? Surely, if thou have a grounded sense of God's love, thou wilt, with the wearied traveller, long to be at home, and go to bed to take thy thy rest, thou wilt desire to depart and to be with Christ, which is best of all? Only be sure, poor soul, that thy work be not to do when thy time is done. Get

ready for that fatal stroke, it is a solemn business to die, it is but once to be done, and it must be well done, or thou art undone for ever. Look upon every day as the last day, defer not another day to repent and make thy peace with God, that thou mayest be found of him in peace.

17. Pass on a little further in thy meditations, and let thy thoughts thus be exercised about the great things of the resurrection of the dead, and the solemn day of judgment: O my soul, consider what an illustrious day that will be, when the great trumpet shall sound, the graves shall be opened, the dead shall be raised, and the living shall be changed,—the holy angels shall gather from the ends of the earth, the scattered bodies and bones of all the saints, from righteous Abel, to the last convert on earth, and again marry the blessed pair of soul and body together, and convoy them up to meet their " blessed Saviour in the air," that they may with him judge the world of ungodly sinners. Methinks I hear on the contrary, the wretched howlings of despairing souls, whose bodies, will they, nill they, are dragged out of their cursed holes, and are forced to come trembling before the just Judge; fain would they skulk in darkness, and not appear, being convicted in their consciences, and not able to stand in judgment, but appear they must, and yet they dare not. Methinks I see the Judge set, the books opened, and myriads of rational creatures attending the righteous Judge to receive their final sentence. On the right hand stand, the blessed saints in white raiment, lifting up their heads before their beloved husband, who absolves them, saying, "Come ye blessed of my Father, inherit the kingdom prepared for you," welcome home from a weary world—here are mansions

ready for you—sit down upon these thrones—take these palms of victory into your hands, I set these crowns upon your heads, and you shall be with me for ever. On the left hand, the filthy goats, despairing, wicked wretches, expecting the dreadful sentence, " go ye cursed," wishing they had never been, or that now they might not be, calling to the senseless rocks to fall upon them, but all in vain ; the despised Saviour is their angry Judge, devils are attendant on the pronouncing of the sentence, ready to hurry them to its execution.

18. Let this, then, carry thy thoughts, O my soul, a little further to a serious meditation on the intolerable torments of hell: as soon as that sentence is out, then issues the order, take them, devil; surely the punishment of loss is inconceivable. Oh how bitter it is to a poor child of God in this world, to endure the short withdrawings of God's pleasant face from their souls. What bitter lamentations and expostulations hath it wrung from them! and yet, what is that in comparison of being banished from the presence of the Lord, and from the glory of his power? Cain's mark of trembling proceeded from the dreadful sense of this formidable expulsion. Though wicked men care not for God's presence here, yet they shall feel to their cost what it is to want his presence hereafter. Together with God they lose all that is comfortable, they shall never have a good day afterwards, they lose ordinances, mercies, hopes of heaven—they shall never hear a sermon more, nor enjoy a day of grace again. Above them is the wrath of the Lamb, whose melting bowels are turned into a consuming fire to them—under them is the devouring lake of fire and brimstone gaping to receive them ; on their right hand are the blessed saints whom they despised, triumphing in the execution of justice

on them, and entering into their Master's joy. On the left hand stands that cursed fiend who drew them into sin, now as ready to draw them into hell, to be tormented with himself for ever; behind them are their short and sorry pleasures in this world, and multitudes of abominations in a wicked life—before them is a sad eternity of never-ceasing torments—within them is a gnawing conscience—without them the saddest objects that ever eyes beheld; old companions in sin roaring under wrath, legions of devils blaspheming God, and scourging their fellow prisoners, their beloved minion the world, all in a flame, and themselves fire-brands there for ever. O my soul, think on these dismal subjects sometimes, and let it work kindly on thy heart, to make thee avoid the way to hell, and walk in the way to heaven.

19. On the contrary, O my soul, mount up to heaven in thy contemplations, soar above the clouds, and take a view of paradise, as soon as the bridegroom of his church hath admitted his beloved spouse into his presence-chamber. O the rapturous joys, and transporting emotions at this blessed meeting! Heaven echoes again at the triumphant hallelujahs of all the redeemed ones. How shall sorrow and sighing flee away! Sin and sickness shall be known no more—Satan with his fiery darts, and wicked men with their drawn swords, cannot reach thither. There shall be no more complaints of ignorant and erroneous heads, of dead and hard, unbelieving and distracted hearts, or of lame decrepit feet, there shall not be a tear upon a saint's cheek, for God will wipe away tears from all faces, not one complaint heard, nothing but joy and triumph, solace and satisfaction; the blessed presence of the eternal God shall be all in all to those happy souls. Oh what is a sight of God worth? but what will it be above, where it is immediate, constant and uninterrupted? No need there

of ordinances, God himself will be instead of all, it will be another kind of enjoying of God than poor souls felt in this world, though that was sweet, yet this shall be infinitely sweeter; now, at the best, we see but through a glass darkly, then face to face; communion with God is the heaven of that heaven, yet shall there be every thing beautiful and desirable—there my soul shall be filled with all perfections, and grace shall be complete, the mind shall in an instant have as large a comprehension, as Solomon, or Adam in innocency; my will shall be conformed to the divine will, in perfect rectitude and integrity; my affections shall be spiritually and regularly fixed on the Lord my God, with fulness of delight and joy; my body shall shine as the brightness of the firmament, yea, it shall be made like unto the glorious body of Jesus Christ; my whole man shall be fit for the high employments of heaven, and the enjoyment of God—there shall I meet with Abraham, and all the patriarchs, prophets, apostles, and martyrs, and all my christian friends that have died in the faith; and oh the animating joys that will arise from such a blessed sight!—there we shall meet and part no more, agree and fall out no more, rejoice together and be sad no more. O blessed day! my soul, be thou cheered in the forethoughts and foretastes thereof.

20. Once more, then, O my soul, and but this once, fix thy thoughts upon eternity! How canst thou forget it? What is this sorry point of time in comparison of the vast ocean of eternity? Alas, poor mortals, act a part on this stage awhile, and then are gone into another world, which must endure for ever! This little inch of time is a seed-plot for eternity; upon the well or ill improving of this time depends an everlasting state in weal or woe. Oh what wretched folly is it to lose eternal happiness for a transient draught of sensual delights! Oh what should not any endure

here a short moment, to escape eternal terments! Methinks nothing hath weight in it, but as it relates to eternity. Eternity is the only accent and emphasis of joy and sorrow. This is that which makes the joys of heaven joys indeed, and the torments of hell torments with a witness. Oh for a poor, damned soul that hath been a thousand years, or a thousand thousands of ages roaring in hell, to think that it is not one moment nearer an end than at the first instant when it was cast into that devouring fire. This cuts to the heart, this adds new terrors to the despairing soul— here must I abide for ever. Oh that I might be consumed so as not to be! cannot, may not I, poor wretch, be once at last annihilated, and be as if I never had been? No, no; once in hell and for ever in hell; the great gulf of God's decree once crossed, is impassable again; so, on the contrary, eternity increaseth every moment the joy of the glorified—here I am, and here I shall be for ever, saith the happy soul, my state is better than Adam's in the earthly, or the fallen angels when in the heavenly paradise; I shall never lose these joys. Oh what a durable reward have I for a little temporary service; my sorrow is past, my joy remains. How comes it to pass, that those light afflictions that were but for a moment have wrought out for me this exceeding and eternal weight of glory? Surely, because it was my Father's good pleasure to give me this kingdom; this eternal life is the gift of God. Oh, who would not do or endure any thing for this eternity of joys? Thus the soul will bathe itself in these rivers of pleasures at " God's right hand for evermore.

I have now dispatched these set and solemn subjects for your thoughts to work upon; I shall but briefly add some occasional grounds for holy thoughts, which, if you have a right frame of spirit, you may gather much from, to be a sufficient treasure for heavenly meditations. Take some instances in such as these.

1. When you awake in the morning, think thus: The great Jehovah can, and will as easily raise our mortal bodies at the general resurrection, as my frail body now; this sleep is the image of death—death is but a sleep, the grave my bed, the resurrection the morning. Oh that when I awake, I may be still with God, and then at my last awaking, I " shall be satisfied with his likeness," and the upright shall have dominion in that blessed morning.

2. When you have had a good night, think: Blessed be the keeper of " Israel, that neither slumbers, nor sleeps," the " Lord only makes me dwell in safety," even " thus he gives his beloved sleep," and if natural sleep be so refreshing, oh, what is it to be received to the arms of my best beloved Christ? what enjoyments have those souls that walk all the day in the light of his countenance! and sleep all the night of affliction upon the lap of his love!

3. When you are putting on your apparel, think: How came I to the necessity of covering my nakedness? By Adam's fall, sin ushered in shame, and these garments hide our shame; shall I, then, glory in my shame, or be proud of that for which I should be humbled? O rather let me be truly sensible of my spiritual nakedness, and look after the robes of Christ's righteousness to cover my soul's deformity, that the shame thereof may not appear.

4. When you see the morning sky, or rising sun, then think: Truly light is sweet, and it is a pleasant thing for the eyes to behold this sun. Blessed be God that hath set up this candle, by which poor mortals may see to walk or work; what a dark dungeon, and confused chaos would this world be without it! but oh

the blessed mercy we have in the light of the glorious gospel! without which we should be in the darkness of ignorance, and go into utter darkness.

5. When you pray in your chambers, think: Now my Father in heaven sees me in secret, darkness or closeness hides not from him—my God sees the movements of my body, and imaginations of my heart. Oh for an upright frame of spirit! oh that my heart were now seasoned for God all this day! The searcher of hearts will have his eye upon me whither soever I go. Oh that I could set the Lord in my sight in all places, companies and occasions.

6. When your families are together, think: How sadly and suddenly might a breach have been made! Oh that God should make this image of death, a means of life! We are alive, that is rich mercy; we are in health, that is more; we are called together, so will God gather his saints together. How many of this family shall be of that number! Lord, grant that none under my charge may be an Ismael, or an Esau. Oh that we may all meet in heaven.

7. When you are to read the word, or go to prayer in your families, think: Oh what mercy it is, that I may read this blessed book! Lord open mine eyes that I may understand the wonders of thy word. What an infinite, glorious, gracious God is this, to whom I am to pray. Oh for a suitable frame of heart! Oh the mercy of a throne of grace, of a blessed advocate! Who knows but some soul may be touched now, if I pray aright?

8. When you go out of your houses to work or travel, think: The world is full of snares and temptations and my heart as full of sin and treachery. Little, ah, little do I know what corruptions may break out, or afflictions break in upon me before my return; the

least occasion of sin may seduce me, the least accident may overthrow me—the Lord bless and preserve my going out, and my coming in, from this time forth and for evermore.

9. When you are travelling by the way, think: My life is a journey, I am in constant motion towards eternity. Every action is another step; heaven is my home. I cannot get thither without diligent exertion; Lord let me not miss my way, or miscarry in the end; take me by the hand, support me by thy Spirit, keep me from fainting, give me some good baits, and bring me to the end of my faith at last, even the salvation of my soul.

10. When you see various objects before your eyes, deduct some holy matter therefrom, as thus: What a vast world is this! and yet, what is this to the heavens? and what are both earth and heavens to the immense and infinite God? what multitudes of people are there in this city? but, oh what an assembly shall meet at the great day! O my soul, art not thou too like yonder hard rock, or fruitless tree, or barren mountain? Look about thee, make something of these objects.

11. When you are discoursing with others think: Of every idle word I must give an account, and in a multitude of words there wanteth not sin. O my soul, think twice before thou speak once. Will this be to the glory of God and others' edification? Let no corrupt communication proceed from thee; say what thou wouldst say if Jesus Christ stood by thee in his human nature; speak here as thou must speak in heaven, or wouldst be found speaking at death.

12. When you are alone, oh think: I am now in the presence of the omnipresent God; these are precious hours that go over my head. Why should I squander

away my time and thoughts about trifles? O my soul thou hast a noble faculty of reflection! find work at home, busy thyself about thy soul, thou mayest find work enough. Oh that I might be never less alone than when alone! When thou hast no creature to converse with, my soul, converse with God.

13. When you eat, think: O how beneficial are the creatures to us living, and how serviceable, being dead! they accomplish the end of their creation and appointment. O my soul, sit thou as queen-regent, over thy sensual appetite! take heed of excess, put a knife to the throat of intemperate desires, be not brutish in a sinful abuse, be saint-like in a sanctified use of creatures; look up to God for a blessing, else these dead things cannot preserve life.

14. When you rise up well refreshed, think: If the creatures be so nourishing and supporting, what is the Creator! oh the sweetness of the blessed feast of fat things in the gospel? oh the delicacy of the wine in my Father's kingdom? why should I abuse the gifts, forget the donor, eat and drink, and rise up to play? many better than I want these refreshments. Oh for a thankful heart! what a bountiful master do I serve! what a great housekeeper is the Lord! that provides for so great a family in heaven and earth.

15. When you go to public ordinances, think: O how glad am I when people say, Come, let us go up to the house of the Lord! what a mercy is the Sabbath, this sweet day of rest? what a blessed thing to have the benefit of these public places, and solemn assemblies! it is a comely sight to see people flock to ordinances, as doves to their windows. Lord, grant that some soul may be caught this day in the net of the gospel. Oh for a prepared, and profiting heart! this may be the last day of grace.

16. When you are to hear a sermon, think: The preacher comes as an ambassador, from God to me; it is God that speaks, the great Jehovah, that can command audience and attendance, and with a word can command us into hell-torments. The truths, O my soul, thou art to hear, are words of eternal life, and do nearly concern thy everlasting peace; prepare thyself for the receipt of them, slight them not; for ought thou knowest, life or death may depend upon this sermon: heaven or hell is now before thee.

17. When you are to partake of the Lord's supper, think: I am this day to sup with Christ, and have I on my soul a wedding garment? have I an interest in Christ, the maker and substance of this blessed feast? where is thy appetite, O my soul? dost thou rightly discern the Lord's body? rouse up thy faith and love, thy hope and desire; his flesh is meat indeed, his blood is drink indeed, his love is better than wine. Lord, fill and satisfy my famishing soul with spiritual repasts.

18. When you depart from public worship, think thus: O my soul, thy work is not done when public work is over, when that is ended, thou must now begin; ruminate upon the word, what hast thou got? what light to thy understanding? what conviction to thy will, what direction to thy affections? O my soul, look to it, thou art this night either a step nearer to heaven or to hell, for this day; get good, be good, do good, or all these helps will render thee inexcusable.

19. When you meet with, or part from your acquaintance, think: If it be so sweet a thing to meet with my dear, and long-tried friends, how much better is it to meet with God, my best beloved, most loving friend; God is a friend that is nearer than any brother or neighbour: I meet now with friends, oh that I knew how to improve their friendship, to get good by them,

or do good to them; we must part once for all, oh that we may meet in heaven at the resurrection of the just!

20. When you are busy in your particular callings, think: Who sets me a work? is it not God? whom do I work for? is it not for God? do I seek myself, or strive to grow rich? then I am carnal; oh my soul, be moderate in the pursuit of the world, let not the cares of the world overwhelm thee: drive on evenly, both thy general and particular calling; let nothing interpose betwixt thy God and thee, or hinder thee in spiritual worship; abide with God in thy calling.

21. When you reflect upon the nature of your callings, gather something in your meditations therefrom, as thus: Am I a magistrate? I judge not for man but for God, who will judge the unrighteous judge, and now sits among the gods: am I a minister? upon me, rests the charge of souls that cry out, we are perishing, study, labour, pray for us: oh what account shall I give? If I be a merchant, tradesman, husbandman, weaver, lawyer, soldier, scholar, oh the spiritual improvement I may make of all these!

22. When you consider your relative connections, think: Am I a husband? I must dwell with my wife, as a man of knowledge: am I a wife? I must be a help to my husband in all things: am I a parent? I must not provoke, but profit my child, and train it up for God: am I a child? I must yield all reverence and obedience to my parents, as unto God, in whose stead they are: am I a master or superior? my master in heaven, sees how I carry myself, and is no respecter of persons: am I a servant? oh for a submissive spirit.

23. When you hear any news, good or bad, think too of the blessed tidings in the gospel: good news from heaven, glory to God in the highest, on the earth peace, good-will towards men, the best message that

ever angel brought, or man received. Let God say, that he is my salvation, I am fortified against bad news, the righteous is not afraid of evil tidings, his heart is fixed, trusting in God. Let Christ be advanced, Antichrist destroyed, and I am satisfied.

24. When you see or hear of any prodigies, think: Who knoweth the power of God's anger? Oh the dreadful majesty of the Lord of hosts, who made the sea and dry land, who commands all the elements, and works his wonders in the fire, water, earth, and air—they that dwell in the uttermost parts of the earth are afraid at his tokens; Lord, what mean these things? what wilt thou do with us? our sins cry for vengeance, prevent it, or hide thy saints till thy wrath be past.

25. When you hear or see the sinful acts of men, think: Oh, what are the best of us by nature? Who makes me to differ? Free grace stops my course, else I had been reeling with the drunkard, blaspheming with the swearer, revelling with the wanton; Lord, let me not bless myself in morality, but let me arrive at sincerity of disposition; never leave me to ways of mine own heart. Ah how is God dishonoured! What long suffering doth he exercise! but justice will awake.

26. When your own corruptions break out, think: Oh the vileness of this naughty heart! oh wretched creature that I am, "who shall deliver me from this body of death?" Little did I think to have been thus beguiled and surprised; God is just and I am vile; I have grown secure and God hath left me. Oh how justly might he have taken me in the act of sin and cast me headlong into hell! My soul, defer not to humble thyself, and make thy peace with God.

27. When any sad crosses befal you in body, estate, name, relations, think: Oh what sin is it that God now chastens me for? Lord, bore mine ears, to hear the voice

of the rod,—bow my heart in obedience to thy will. Oh that instruction may come along with correction; my soul, search thy heart and ways, this stroke of God is either a token of his love, or the beginning of his wrath. Oh that I may see a Father's heart, and feel a Father's hand, and attain my Father's end therein.

28. When you are delivered out of apparent danger of death by sickness or sad accidents, consider: Oh my soul, what if thou hadst now been snatched away, and thy body left a mass of corruption! where hadst thou been? wast thou ready for glory? what assurance hadst thou of a better state? didst thou not then wish thy soul had been in a better posture? Mend the matter now, give God the glory of thy deliverance, serve him better, be more prepared against another time.

29. When night approacheth, candles are brought in, and the spacious sky is full of stars, think: There is one day more of my life now past and gone, I am thus far, nearer eternity. Lord, set up the candle of thy grace in my soul in this night of darkness, error, and dismay; shew me the light of life—let the blessed day-star arise in my heart. Oh when shall my soul be translated above yonder twinkling stars to shine as a star in the firmament of glory!

30. When you put off your clothes, and go to bed, think: Thus, even thus must thou, my soul, put off thy body at death; thou must be unclothed, that thou mayest " be clothed upon with a house from heaven. O my soul, be daily undressing thee of the body of sin, and lay thyself in the grave of Christ, " be buried with him in spiritual baptism," give up thyself into his hands, and lay thyself to sleep as thou wouldest be found at death, or when raised at the great day of resurrection.

These, and such like occurrences, must put you in

mind of such meditations, and thus your thoughts may become a blessed treasure.

I shall now conclude the whole with a few considerations to move us all, thus to employ our thoughts upon profitable subjects.

1. Consider the strictness of God's command, Josh. i. 8. "Thou shalt meditate therein," that is, in the Book of the Law, "day and night." "Set your affections on things above."—Col. iii. 2. How dare you neglect a positive duty? The same God who commands thee to pray and believe, who forbids thee to steal and murder, doth enjoin thee to meditate. It is not a thing indifferent.

2. Remember God's omniscience and omnipresence; when David had duly considered that God did search and know him, when sitting down and when rising up, did understand his thoughts afar off, and was acquainted with all his ways, he tells God that his thoughts were precious, Psalm, cxxxix. 17, and in the following verse he says, " When I awake I am still with thee." Let God's omnipresence produce in you the like meditations.

3. The saints of God have thus employed their thoughts, and the better the saints, the more holy have been their thoughts. Isaac went into the fields to meditate.—Gen. xxiv. 63. David meditated in the night watches, Psalm lxiii. 6, on the word, and on the works of God.—Psalm cxliii. 5.* Oh be not unlike the saints, resemble your brethren, follow them to heaven.

4. This is a true character of a child of God; † all saints are described to be such as have thought upon his name, Mal. iii. 17, for, indeed, they that are of the Spirit, " do mind the things of the Spirit."—Rom. viii. 5. Holy thoughts are proper fruits of a sanctified mind.

---

* Psalm cxix. 15, 23, 48, 78, 97, 99, 148. † Matt. vi. 21.

None sees the thoughts but God; a good heart approves itself to the searcher of hearts.

5. Holy thoughts help against Satan's temptations; these are as cold water to quench Satan's fiery darts; these are a precious antidote against the poisonous allurements of the world, for these find the soul something else to do than to mind toys; the best way to silence scolding women, and barking dogs, is to mind our work and way, and let them alone.* Will a judge go off the bench to play with boys? Give them Nehemiah's answer, ch. vi. 3.

6. This exercise of the thoughts will help against corruptions,† thereby you will see more of the evil of sin, " and in vain is the net spread before any bird," Prov. i. 17. Also it lifts the soul heavenwards; a bird in the air is not taken by a net on the ground,—yea, when the heart is taken up with divine enjoyments, it cannot relish the husks of sin; the child will not part with the apple, while the taste of it is in his mouth.

7. This is the highest excellency and improvement of our spirits—it is the noblest employment of the soul, and advancement of its faculties. The soul is of a high birth—it is a debasing of it to mind low things—the saints being of an elevated and noble extraction by their second birth, must and will mind the things of heaven, in all things besides, excelling others, in this, excelling themselves, as it is said of Bucholzen.

8. This is best way for the improvement and increase of grace; gifts are promoted by verbal, but grace by mental exercises. If the thoughts feed on Christ, the soul becomes spiritual, like its food; the air, food, and climate have great influence upon bodies; conversing with wise and learned men makes persons

---

* Non vacat exiguis rebus adesse mihi. † See Psal. cxix. 11.

such, exercise increaseth habits, holy thoughts increase faith, love, joy, sorrow for sin, &c.

9. Holy thoughts excite heavenly affections. "While I was musing, the fire burned."—Psalm xxxix. 3. Thoughts are the bellows of the soul, and stir up suitable emotions in the heart. Would a Christian have a humble, tender, melting heart? let his thoughts be employed upon the law and love of God, or on such subjects as are proper to produce such affections, and try what impression they will make.

10. Holy thoughts are a good preparative to holy duties, and help in performances.[*] David joins prayer and meditation together. " Give ear to my words, consider my meditation," Psalm v. 1; when " the heart is meditating a good matter, the tongue is as the pen of a ready writer."—Psalm xlv. 1. Meditation fixeth the heart, and tuneth the instrument for prayer, hearing, reading: oh how it composeth the spirit!

11. Yea, holy thoughts form a great part of a Christian's devotion, and such a portion of it, that when public ordinances are obstructed, or private societies interrupted, yet the holy soul may sally out to its God, upon the wings of holy thoughts, in the presence of the most malicious adversaries; thoughts are free from men, no bolts can hinder this access to God.

12. This is an excellent part of time-redemption, when we are walking or riding by the way, working in our callings, shut up in prison, deprived of pen, ink and paper, still our thoughts may be busy, we may have good thoughts wherever we are; though we can do nothing else, yet we may think of God and good subjects: and that is the way to obey that excellent precept, Redeem the time.

[*] Psalm. xix. 14. Psalm xlix. 3.

13. This exercise of the thoughts is indeed a Christian's walking with God, as Enoch and Noah are said to do: it is the way to have our conversation in heaven: it is a communion with God, a walking in paradise, an enjoying of God: it is indeed an angelical life, the life of heaven, an anticipation of glory, and a taking possession of heaven in our thoughts. Oh blessed frame!

14. This helps the Christian in sad pressures and soul-conflicts; good thoughts counterwork bad. David could out-argue his disquieting thoughts, Psal. xlii. 5. so may the Christian. Thoughts fed and furnished from the word, will encounter and conquer the severest trials. " Unless thy law had been my delight, I should have perished in mine affliction."—Psal. cxix. 92. These thoughts are an antidote which keeps sufferings from the vital spirits.

15. Holy thoughts help the Christian to rivet and retain divine truths in the memory; ruminating on truths, turns them into blood and spirits, juice and nourishment: our heads and hearts are like riven vessels, all runs out, unless the vessels be well moistened with heavenly meditation. Oh what a tenacious memory, large understanding, and vast abilities have some attained to by this means!

16. Holy thoughts prepare the tongue for profitable discourse, and render Christians useful. He that hath his thoughts best employed when alone, will have his tongue best exercised in company: if you converse with such a one in your houses, in trading, on a journey, upon any occasion, still his thoughts will prompt his tongue to profitable conference; and oh the good that such a one may do!

17. Holy thoughts answer God's thoughts. " I know the thoughts, saith God, that I think towards

you, thoughts of peace, and not of evil," Jer. xxix. 11; and if we can make such an appeal as this to God, that he knows the thoughts we have towards him, to be not evil but good—how acceptable will it be to God! On the contrary, what gross ingratitude will it be, if our thoughts be not God-wards!

18. Divine things are only worth thinking of; other matters are not worth a glance of our eye, or a thought of our mind, whatever relates not to the soul and to eternity is not worth minding. "We look not," saith the apostle, "at things that are seen, but at things which are not seen."—2 Cor. iv. 18. These latter are things of great moment, and of nearest concernment to our immortal souls.

19. Thinking upon these heavenly subjects helps the soul to attain the end of its creation and redemption. The supreme and ultimate end is God's glory, the subordinate end, yet involved in the former, the soul's salvation; the God of heaven takes himself to be highly honoured by the heavenly-minded Christian, this is a sanctifying, and so a glorifying, God in our thoughts or hearts.—1 Pet. iii. 15.

20. Lastly, This is an actual preparing of the soul for heaven, the heart is there already, and this is part of a meetness " to be partakers of the inheritance of the saints in light."—Col. i. 12. " Blessed is the soul, whom its Lord, when he comes shall find thus," thinking and doing well. Oh the blessed change they shall make! They may say, as sweet Dr. Sibbs, " Going to die, I shall change my place, but not my company;" and when the poor soul arrives at glory, the thoughts shall be fixed, grace completed, and the soul transported with everlasting joys.

I have been the shorter in hinting only these motives, because Mr. Baxter hath fully driven this nail to the head in such like arguments to "heavenly mindedness," in his book entitled "Saint's Rest," part 4, p. 51—96. Read them seriously.

I have done with this subject also. Oh that God would undertake to write all these things with power upon the tables of your hearts, and elevate your thoughts to heavenly subjects, and bring suitable things to your minds to meditate upon. Oh that he would deeply impress them upon your souls, and keep alive those impressions upon your hearts, that you may not lose the divine savour of the things of God, after your serious and awakening meditations, but pray with holy David, 1 Chron. xxix. 18. "O Lord God of Abraham, Isaac, and Israel, our fathers, keep this for ever in the imagination of the thoughts of the heart of thy people, and prepare their heart unto thee."

I shall conclude all with a Poem of divine Herbert's in his Temple, called, "The Temper."

> How should I praise thee, Lord! how should my rhymes
>   Gladly engrave thy love in steel,
> If what my soul doth feel sometimes,
>   My soul might ever feel!
>
> Although there were some forty heavens, or more,
>   Sometimes I peer above them all,
> Sometimes I hardly reach a score,
>   Sometimes to hell I fall.
>
> O rack me not to such a vast extent,
>   Those distances belong to thee,—
> The world's too little for thy tent,
>   A grave too big for me.
>
> Wilt thou mete arms with man, that thou dost stretch,
>   A crumb of dust from heaven to hell?
> Will great God measure with a wretch?
>   Shall he thy stature spell?
>
> O let me, when thy roof my soul hath hid,
>   O let me roost and nestle there!
> Then of a sinner thou art rid,
>   And I of hope and fear.

Yet take thy way, for sure thy way is best,
   Stretch or contract me, thy poor debtor,
This is but tuning of my breast,
   To make the music better.

Whether I fly with angels, fall with dust,
   Thy hands made both, and I am there,
Thy power and love, my love and trust,
   Make one place every where.

THE

SURE MERCIES OF DAVID;

OR,

SECOND PART

OF

Heart Treasure.

PREFACE

TO " THE SURE MERCIES OF DAVID."

TO ALL THE HEIRS OF PROMISE, THE SAINTS OF THE MOST HIGH GOD, THE SONS AND DAUGHTERS OF ABRAHAM, WHOM GOD HATH BETROTHED TO HIMSELF IN THE SWEET GOSPEL COVENANT, AND WHO LIVE IN HOPES OF THEIR NUPTIAL DAY, PREPARING IN GRACE TO ENTER INTO THE CHAMBERS OF GLORY AT DEATH AND THE GENERAL RESURRECTION, GRACE, MERCY AND PEACE.

TWO things, my dearly beloved in the Lord, are absolutely necessary to make souls happy; first, that the thing possessed be fully adequate to the nature of the soul; and secondly, that it be made over to it legally and everlastingly: for if either any thing be defective at present required to give content, or there be danger of losing it, it is not commensurate to the soul's state or need; for as this immortal spark infused into man, whereby he has become a rational creature, is vast and capacious in its desires and dimensions; so it is very lasting, yea, everlasting in its continuance and duration; therefore the riches necessary to make it happy must be both suitable and durable. But all the creatures fall short in both. The soul of man travelling through this spacious universe in its contemplations, and following the guidance of the intellectual faculties, the soul's ear and eye,—can get no satisfying sight or report in answer to that curious inquiry, who will shew me any good? To fix upon the creature, is to set our eyes upon that which is not, for it is vanity; yea, to place our hopes on that which hath a lie in its right hand, and so becomes vexation of spirit in an overwhelming disappointment. Woe to man, if there were no hopes for him but in this life, and great would be his infelicity, if it were true that there is no God, as atheists say and think. How poorly should this princely thing in man be served with the sordid husks of creature enjoyments! How base and brutish would its life be! How well becoming man would that epitaph of the Epicure be, which, Cicero saith, " was fitter to be written on an ox's grave than a man's?—*Hæc habeo quæ edi, quæque exsaturata libido hausit*; " the things my greedy appetite hath devoured are mine." Let such brutified sots, that understand nothing of the worth or proper food of immortal souls, feed on husks, but let the heaven-born saints aspire to other nourishment; if the mixed multitude of common professors linger after the Egyptian food of cucumbers, melons, leeks, onions, and garlic,* real saints fare better—they feed on heavenly manna. The flesh and blood of Christ is the proper *pabulum animæ*, or nourishment of the soul. The soul hath a more delicate appetite, which requires answerable food; it cannot feed on such coarse stuff as worldly delights. Hear David begging as for an alms—but what alms begs he? " mercies;" and what mercies? " tender mercies." Psal. xl. 11, " Withhold not thy tender mercies from me, O Lord;" as if he said, there are common mercies, that gratify the appetites, and clothe the bodies of good or bad, but these will not serve my turn, nor save my soul; the mercies that will do me good for ever, are tender things of another stamp, that come streaming through the blood of a Mediator, that spring from covenant love, and such as can fill, and feed, and feast my soul for ever.

These are the mercies that God hath dropt into your bosoms, heirs of promise, and these are the mercies described and deciphered in this Treatise; I have gone out to measure the Land of Promise, and according to grace received, I have

---

* Num. xi. 4, 5. Ὁι δὲ ἄλλοι, περιπεφυκότες τῷ κόσμῳ, οἷα φυκία τινα ἐνάλοις πέτραις, ἀθανασίας ὀλιγωροῦσιν· καθάπερ ὁ Ἰθακήσιος γέρων, οὐ τῆς ἀληθείας, καὶ τῆς ἐν οὐρανῷ πατρίδος, πρὸς δὲ, καὶ τοῦ ὄντως ὄντος ἱμειρόμενος φωτὸς, ἀλλὰ τοῦ καπνοῦ.—Qui mundo adhæserunt ut marinis petris alga, contemnunt immortalitatem sicut senex Ithacensis, qui non veritatem et cœlestem patriam, eamque lucem quæ vere est, sed fumum optabat.—*Clem. Alexand. Adm. ad Gen.*

viewed it in the length and breadth thereof, and I have no reason to bring up an evil report on it; it is a land flowing with milk and honey, a blessed and beautiful land, which God careth for, and if the Lord delight in you, he will bring you into it. What though there be giants and Anakim of opposition in heaven's way, fear them not, for they are bread for us, they shall contribute to the saint's nourishment, and their defence is departed from them*; the Lord is with us, let not our hearts faint—God will carry us as upon eagles' wings, he will give us a pillar of cloud by day, and a pillar of fire by night; sure mercies in the way, and everlasting mercies at the end. This is the true Arabia Felix, yet far beyond that, which though it abounded with spices and gold, profits and pleasures, yet stupified the senses of the inhabitants with its palling sweetness: but there is no nauseous feeling occasioned by a participation of heavenly delights; the longer you enjoy them, the more you long after them, and the fuller draught you take, the sweeter relish they have. Oh the pleasure a soul may have in divine things! other things will disgust in comparison of these rapturous delights: no pleasures like those that come from above. But that which adds an emphasis to these is, that they are sure as well as sweet, abiding as well as abounding pleasures: God the author and object of them is immutable—the spring of them is the love of God—the meritorious cause, Christ's blood—the way of conveyance, precious promises; all these are settled and invariably the same; as long as the soul needs mercies it enjoys them, for we have grace to help in time of need. God will not, men cannot tear away these mercies from you, when you have a well-grounded title thereunto: God will not; for the gifts and callings of God are without repentance, and whom he loves once he loves to the end: men cannot, for they are above and beyond their reach. These mercies are made sure to you by a " covenant of salt,"† which is a symbol of incorruption: they wear not away with length of time, nor are they snatched away by human violence: the tyrant's rage cannot wrest sure mercies out of your hearts and hands. This consideration is of singular use in a losing time;

* Num. xiv. 7—9. † Sole et sale omnia conservantur.

men may take away our estates, liberties, and privileges, but they cannot take away our mercies : they may degrade us and remove us from our functions and offices, but cannot so dissettle our souls as to separate them from their relation to Christ, or a state of grace, or the blessed influences of grace. When Popish bishops took from John Huss the chalice, saying, " O cursed Judas, we take away from thee this chalice of thy salvation ;" he answered, " but I trust unto God the Father omnipotent, and my Lord Jesus Christ, for whose sake I suffer these things, that he will not take away the chalice of his redemption, but I have a steadfast and firm hope, that this day I shall drink thereof in his kingdom."* Yea, men may take away the members of the body, but not the graces and comforts of the soul. Notable is the story of Agatha a primitive martyr. When Quintilian had commanded her breasts to be cut off, she said, " Art thou not ashamed, O tyrant, to dismember me of what in thy mother was the original source of thy own nourishment? But go to, rage as much as thou canst, yet two breasts are left, which thou canst not touch, the one of faith, the other of hope ; they supply me with comfort and safety in the midst of torments, and abundant strength to sustain these, is repaired in me by the nourishment I derive from them." † Alas, it were a sad state of an immortal soul to have nothing but what supplies corporeal wants. How soon may worm, or moth, or fire, or thieves, or tyrants, make a prey of visible riches ! The good things of saints are invisible : happy are you whose mercies are divine, you need not fear plundering or spoiling of your best goods ; these are the true riches ; though you be poor in this world, yet if you be rich in faith, you are heirs of a kingdom ; you live as strangers and pilgrims, for your estates lie in another country : and indeed, a Christian is a paradox in this,

---

* Fox's Mart. vol. i. p. 823.

† Quintiliano dixisse ferunt ex cujus jussu præcisæ sunt ipsi mammillæ, annon te pudet, tyranne, membrum illud in me amputare, quod in matre suxisti ? verum, age sævi quantum poteris : duæ tamen supersunt mammillæ, quas nequis attingere, fidei una, spei altera, hæ mihi vel in mediis tormentis solamen et tutamen suppeditant et earum alimento sustinendi virtus in me reparatur.—*Dr. Arrows. Tact. Sac. p.* 195.

as Justin Martyr observes of the ancient Christians,[‡] that they inhabit their own country but as strangers; " they have all things common with others as citizens, yet suffer all things as pilgrims; every strange region is their country, and every country a strange region. A Christian's politics are seemingly contradictory, and truly mysterious: they make a common table, yet are not polluted: they are in the flesh, but live not after the flesh: they live on earth, but have their conversation in heaven: they obey laws established, yet by their way of living go beyond laws: they love all and are persecuted by all: they are not known, yet condemned: they are killed, yet made alive: they are poor, yet enrich many: they want all things, yet abound in all things: they are disgraced, yet thereby honoured," &c. Thus he proceeds, shewing the state of Christians; which is the same now. Oh what a mystery, yet felicity, is it to be a saint! all things are yours, though nothing were yours; a saint by covenant hath right to all, and shall have actual possession of what is for his good: the saints rule the earth, themselves being trampled on by all: they pass through the world as conquerors, and carry the spoils as trophies, along with them till death, and when death is swallowed up in victory, these blessed champions arise triumphant in glory. O Christians, study your state, know your privileges, be always triumphing in Christ: live at the rate of those mercies, make no reckoning of the world but as a footstool to raise you higher God-wards, or as a stepping-stone to pass forwards thereby, through this polluted and polluting world, heaven-wards: bless God for the least outward mercy, but be not put off with the greatest; a little with God is enough, all things without God are nothing. Suppose you be below the higher parts of the dust of the earth in riches, power, and glory, yet you are above them in grace, true riches, and favour with the God of heaven; therein he makes amends: as the Jews have a fable that the waters terrestrial, in the beginning, took it ill to be divided from the celestial by the firmament; the Creator to pacify them promised a sacred use of

[‡] *Omnia cum aliis communia habent tanquam cives, omnia patiuntur tanquam peregrini: omnis peregrina regio patria est eorum, et omnis patria est peregrina.—Just. Mart. Ep. ad Diog. vid. plura.*

them below, in the tabernacle of the covenant; so although you are set below many in other things, yet in this you have preeminence above them, that you are interested in, and employed about these covenant mercies: this is abundant compensation. Be not discouraged, whatever you suffer here, it is not hell; whatever you lose for God, heaven will make amends; faithful is he that hath promised, who also will do it; God is yet able to pay his debts, as able and willing as to the first man that ever sought the performance of a promise: never any went away grumbling or charging God, (as some men are too justly charged) that he minds not what he saith. When David through weakness of faith began to stagger, and expostulate, saying, " Doth his promise fail for evermore?" he quickly checks himself with that reflection, " But I said, this is my infirmity."—Psal. lxxvii. 8, 10.

It would be a blessed thing (which Luther wished for *) " that our faith were as certain and firm as the thing itself believed; but, alas, sin in the flesh doth resist the spirit, so that we cannot so firmly believe;" as he complains. The way to stability is the acting of faith—believe, and ye shall be established. As long as we consult with reason, we shall still be fluctuating. An individual's expedient for establishment, after many temptations of doubt concerning a main article of faith was, a hearty humiliation and subjection of his understanding to the obedience of faith, which brought such clear light of truth and certitude into his soul, that there remained no relics at all of dubitation. We may all cry out with the disciples, " Lord, increase our faith." Alas, the want of faith is the root of all actual sins and insensibleness; yea, the want of a thorough persuasion of the reality of divine things surpasses the world. Most men do but read the gospel as a fine fiction, or a well-composed romance, but work not their hearts to credit these things; a may be, or may not be, in a conjectural uncertainty, is all they arrive at: however, they do not follow home the light and persuasions they have. Alas, did persons seriously think of this, that as sure as they are men or women, as cer-

---

* Optarim fidem tam certam et firmam esse quam et res ipsa, verum peccatum in carne resistit spiritui ut non possim firmiter credere.—*Luth.*

tainly as they eat and drink, work and sleep, so certainly there is a God—a Christ—grace—pardon—guilt—heaven—hell, of which they must very shortly have a full conviction. This could not but have a wonderful influence upon their hearts and lives—their affections and conversation. O what persons should saints be, if they lived under the thorough impressions and convictions of the certainty of divine revelation!

It were a blessed effect, if all the Treatises that have of late been written might convince this profane and atheistical world of the certainty of Christianity. Many have laboured much in this with great success; several ancient writers, as Clemens, Polycarp, Justin Martyr, Tatian, Iræneus, Athenagoras, and Tertullian, have proved by demonstrative arguments the truth of the Christian religion, against Jews, Heathens, &c.;* lately, Grotius, Mornay du Plessis, and at the present day, Baxter, Stillingfleet, and others, have put their sickle into this harvest, through whom the church hath reaped precious fruit. I pretend neither to the learning or authority of those famous worthies, but insist only on the sure mercies of the covenant to raise a poor superstructure upon those solid foundations. It was the design of Luke the Evangelist, in writing his Gospel to the noble and excellent Theophilus, that "he might be assured of the certainty of those things wherein he had been instructed."—Luke i. 4. Such a design have I in this small piece. O that some might stand up and address the Saviour as the disciples did, "Now we are sure that thou knowest all things; by this we believe that thou camest forth from God."—John xvi. 30. O sirs, be not satisfied with uncertain conjectures—endeavour to arrive at a "full assurance of understanding to the acknowledging of the mystery of God," Col. ii. 2.—pray for the spirit of revelation, that you may both know the certainty of gospel mysteries and mercies and your own interest therein, that you may both be strong in faith and full of comfort—advance higher daily in embracing unseen things—rest not in a sceptical ἐποχὴ, or philosophical state of doubt, but strive to arrive at an ἐλεγχὸς, or firm demonstration—rest your souls upon the testimony of God, as to the object of faith, and commit

* Vide Scult. Med. Patrum.

your souls to him in believing and well-doing for evidence of your state—remember that choice word, Hosea vi. 3, " Then shall we know, if we follow on to know the Lord; his going forth is prepared as the morning, and he shall come unto us as the rain, as the latter and former rain unto the earth." That this and all other soul-helps may accomplish this great end of your edification, consolation, and salvation, shall be the earnest prayer of

Your soul's friend, and servant in Christ,

O. H.

June 3, 1670.

THE
SURE MERCIES OF DAVID.

ISAIAH LV. 3. *55:3*

—— *Even the sure Mercies of David.*

CHAP. I.

INTRODUCTORY REMARKS.

THIS evangelical prophet acts the part of an apostolical preacher, pourtraying our dear Saviour in as lively a manner as if he wrote a history, not a prophecy; as if he saw him in the flesh and not in the type only. This chapter contains a sweet relation or revelation of the mysteries of gospel grace, a high sounding proclamation, and pathetical exhortation to the sons of men to embrace the saving benefits purchased by our Lord Jesus Christ.

This exhortation is pressed upon the consciences of men with four arguments, which are, as it were, a satisfying answer to as many tacit objections which may be made by unbelieving souls; these arguments are in the first, second, third, and fifth verses drawn from the —Freeness, fulness, security and abundance of gospel grace.

1. A person may say, alas, I am an unworthy wretch, I have nothing that can commend me to God, I have

neither penny nor pennyworth, money nor price to give, neither grace nor good works to bring to God. May I have a share in it? Yes, it is free, come buy, for just nothing, ver. 1.

2. But he may say, if it be so cheap, it may be it is of as little worth, too dear to take gratis; things of light price are often of as light use, and answer their rate, by being unprofitable—will it do me any good? O yes, it is of vast advantage; if you take pains for any thing else, you do but spend money for that which is no bread, but if you obtain gospel grace, " you eat that which is good, and your soul shall delight itself in fatness," ver. 2.

3. But again it may be said, may I have a share in these mercies? shall I not miss of them? and when I once have them, shall I not lose them again? I am but tantalized if I see such sweet morsels and cannot reach them, and I shall be more miserable if I taste such pleasant things, and have them snatched away. He answers to the first, " all shall be made over to you by a covenant," and to the second, " they are the sure mercies of David," ver. 3.

4. But, alas, may a poor soul say, this is children's meat, what have dogs to do with these sure mercies? I am a sinner of the Gentiles, salvation is of the Jews, and for the Jews; is there any hope for such strangers to the commonwealth of Israel? Yes, Jesus Christ is given for a witness to the people, to all people, that is, Gentiles;* " a nation that thou knowest not, and nations that knew not thee, shall run unto thee," ver. 4, 5.

The text falls under the third argument, and contains,

1. A double duty—hear, and come, that is, believe and obey.

* Isaiah xlix. 6.

INTRODUCTORY REMARKS.

2. A double promise, of life, and a covenant.

(1.) " Your soul shall live." Life is the flower and essence of all outward mercies, but spiritual life transcends a corporeal, temporal life, which is but a dying life, or living death; " Grace is the life of the soul." Spiritual life is the seed-plot of eternal life in glory. Mankind lost life by hearing the alluring temptations of the subtle serpent. Life is recovered by hearing the gracious words of life from Jesus Christ, " Hear, and your souls shall live.

(2.) " I will make an everlasting covenant with you." The words are in Hebrew, " I will cut a covenant with you." * The expression hath allusion to the ancient practice of entering into covenants, which was by cutting a beast into two parts, and the parties covenanting going betwixt those parts, to denote that after that manner should that man's limbs be divided who should violate that solemn covenant.†

Now, the great contents of this covenant are expressed in these words which I have selected and pitched upon to speak fully to, " even the sure mercies of David," which contain,

1. The sum of the covenant, that is, " mercies."
2. The nature of those mercies, that is, " sure."
3. The subject of the mercies, " David."

There is not much difficulty in the words, only it is disputed what is meant by David here. Now in Scripture, David is taken, first, in a literal sense, for David the son of Jesse; and, secondly, in a mystical sense, for Jesus Christ. It way be applicable very properly both ways here.

* ואכרתה לכם ברית Percutiam vobiscum fœdus, q. d. dividantur ejus membra qui juramentum violaverit.

† See the Practice, in Gen. xv. 9, 10, 17, 18. Jer. xxxiv. 18.

(1.) It may be taken for the person of David, the son of Jesse, king of Israel; and then, the mercies of David are the choice promises that God made to his servant David, described in 2 Sam. vii. 13—17, and in Psalm lxxxix. Some make the first words of that Psalm to be the title of it, and render it thus, " I will sing of the mercies of David," because God's covenant with David is abundantly held forth in that Psalm. But this phrase doth rather allude to 2 Chron. vi. 42, where Solomon thus prays, " Remember the mercies of David, thy servant."

(2.) By David, is meant Jesus Christ, who is of the seed of David according to the flesh,* Rom. i. 3, and called by this name of David frequently in the Old Testament, as in Ezek. xxxiv. 23, 24, xxxvii. 24, 25, Hos. iii. 5, and I conceive this to be the meaning of the words, rather than the former, for these two reasons:

[i.] Because in the New Testament, where these words are quoted, the Holy Ghost applies them to Jesus Christ, Acts xiii. 34, " I will give you the sure mercies of David." Indeed, the Greek renders it differently from the original of the Old Testament, for thus it stands in the Septuagint, τὰ ὅσια Δαβὶδ τὰ πιστά; in English, " the faithful, holy things of David," but all comes to the same point, for the mercies of the covenant are holy things. But observe the scope of that quotation in the Acts, which is to prove Christ's resurrection, " for if Christ had not risen from the dead, the promises had not been made good," so that still it relates to Christ.

[ii.] Another consideration that moves me to conceive that by David here is meant Jesus Christ, is what follows in the fourth verse, " I have given him," that

* Acts xiii. 23.

is, David, before-mentioned, or Christ, " for a witness to the people," that is, a witness to testify God's veracity in performing all his promises ; so, then, the words may be thus read, I will make an everlasting covenant with you, according to the sure mercies of David, that is, the Messiah, who is to come—the mercies before promised, and to be exhibited in and by him in the fulness of time. The words are but few, being but three, * yet, they are full of sense and significancy, and are pregnant, travailing with the precious mysteries of gospel grace.

I shall only name some doctrinal observations by the way from the text, with the intention of reducing them to a single point.

Doct. 1. The covenant of grace is made up of mercies, it is a compound of mercies, the root, the branches, the top, the bottom of this chariot is love, grace, grace, all free grace.

2. Covenant mercies are sure mercies, they are not like the uncertain riches of this world, the true treasure is a sure treasure, the better part that cannot be taken away.

3. The sure mercies of the covenant are David's portion : taking David here, literally, and the saints with him, so it signifies beloved ; all God's Davids, or beloved ones have a right to covenant mercies.

4. Jesus Christ alone doth make sure all the mercies of the covenant ; so taking it in the latter acceptation, that David imports the Messiah.

The substance of the text and the fore-mentioned doctrines may be given in this one proposition.

Doct. That covenant mercies granted in Christ are made sure by Christ, to all the heirs of promise.

* חַסְדֵי דוד הנאמנים

The mercies which the Messiah procureth and applieth are sure mercies.

That the covenant of grace is made in Christ, see, Isa. xlix. 8, " I will preserve thee, and give thee for a covenant of the people," that is, " the mediator of the covenant," so the apostle expounds it, calling Jesus Christ a " surety of a better testament," or covenant; and again, he calls him the mediator of the New Testament;* and as the promises are made good in Christ, so they are made good by Christ, 2 Cor. i. 20, " for all the promises of God in him are yea, and in him, Amen, unto the glory of God, by us," that is, they are ratified, confirmed, and applied, by virtue of Christ's own meritorious undertaking. A text full to our purpose we have in Rom. xv. 8. " Now I say, that Jesus Christ was a minister of the circumcision for the truth of God, to confirm the promises made unto the fathers;" hence it is, that he hath sealed the covenant, by his person, obedience, and sufferings, (as afterwards I shall particularly demonstrate) so that the mercies must needs be sure. David, the subject of these mercies doth acknowledge the sureness of them, even in the Old Testament, in that famous text, 2 Sam. xxiii. 5, " Although my house be not so with God," that is, for outward splendour, according to the description of a magnificent family, " yet he hath made with me an everlasting covenant, ordered in all things and sure," as if he should say, it is true indeed, God hath performed his good word to me in making me king, but alas, still my heart is full of corruptions, and my house of distractions; though the sun be risen upon me, yet I cannot say it is a morning without clouds; it is sadly eclipsed and overcast with the obscuring clouds of temptations as-

* Heb. vii. 22. Heb. viii. 6. Heb. ix. 15.

saulting me; I have committed grievous sins which darken my glory, and damp my comfort; Amnon commits incest with his sister; Absalom rebels against his father; I am driven from my throne and city; my whole family is wofully broken, discomposed, and shattered: well, but I have a well-ordered covenant in the midst of all disorders. When I am driven from mine own house, I am not sure that ever I shall return to it, but this covenant is sure; my outward condition is uncertain, but the best mercies of this blessed covenant are so solid and substantial, that I am satisfied therewith; if God deny me the temporal mercies therein contained, yet if I have the spiritual mercies thereof, that is enough for me, " for it is all my salvation and all my desire, although he make it not to grow;" that is, though his blessing upon my house be not as the tender grass springing out of the earth by clear shining after the rain, to multiply my family, making it either numerous or wealthy, potent or magnificent; yet I have all that I look for, and that which gives me content, I have these sweet and sure mercies of this blessed covenant.

For the more distinct and profitable handling of this important subject, I shall, in the doctrinal part, discuss these four particulars, or principle points, and endeavour to shew,

1. What are the mercies of the covenant?
2. In what respects they are said to be made sure?
3. By what ways and means they are ensured to us?
4. How they are said to be made sure in Christ.

CHAP. II.

MERCIES OF THE COVENANT.

I. I MIGHT prepare the way for a consideration of covenant mercies, by declaring what a covenant is, and give some description of this new covenant, and distinctions about it; but I shall rather wave this, because it has been done so extensively already by so many able hands. Only for our present purpose, take notice, that in all contracts or covenants, even in any ordinary conveyance, there are four things very considerable, and indeed, essentially requisite. *

1. There are the parties covenanting.
2. The consideration paid or laid down.
3. The conditions required and performed.
4. The grant made, or the privilege to be enjoyed, upon the conditions, and consideration, called in our writings, the *habendum*, or the thing that we must have and hold.

Now all these are either expressly or implicitly held forth in one Scripture, which is, Heb. viii. 10.

(1.) There are the parties covenanting, God, and the house of Israel: " This is the covenant that I will make with the house of Israel." †

(2.) Here is a consideration evidently implied in these words, " after those days," that is, after those days of types, shadows, and prophecies, " in the fulness of time, the Messiah shall come, who is the substance, who will satisfy divine justice, and make an atonement."

(3.) Here is the condition of the covenant, plainly

* Mr. Herle's Christian Wisdom, chap. 4, page 227.
† Heb. viii. 10.

expressed in these words, " I will put my laws into their mind, and write them in their hearts," that is, I will give that which I require, I will put within them a principle of grace that they may love me, believe in me, repent of sin, and obey the gospel.

(4.) Here is the grant, or good, to be enjoyed, which is the end and result of all the former, namely, "I will be to them a God, and they shall be to me a people," that is, whatsoever I am, or have, or can do, who am omnipotent, shall be employed for their good ; or whatsoever they would choose a God for, or desire to be in a God, that will I be to them with whom I contract this covenant, and I will own them as my peculiar people.

Now the mercies of the covenant consist in these four particulars, epecially in the last.

I shall a little open these, that we may the better find out the mercies wrapt up in the covenant of grace.

1. The parties that enter into this covenant, are God and man. Oh the infinite distance and vast disproportion! *quantus quantillo?* Heaven makes a match with earth, the great Creator with a mortal creature, the glorious King with a silly beggar! Is not this a rich mercy? Shall the cedar in Lebanon contract a league not only with the contemptible shrub, but with the pricking, worthless thistle? shall the sun of righteousness convey beams of love to such poor worms, yea, to such offensive dunghills? shall the beauty of holiness be confederate with sorry man, who is but a lump of vanity or mass of impurity? Yet, thus it is, and this is transcendent mercy ; there is mercy in a covenant : God might have dealt with man in a way of absolute sovereignty, and done with him even as he pleased, without giving us any account of his matters ;

but he treats with man in a rational way, as above the level of other creatures. God takes man up to parley and treat with him, as though he were his equal, " what is man that thou art thus mindful of him? or the son of man that thou visitest him?"* This mutual stipulation is infinite condescension on God's part, and advancement on man's. Man, only man, of all the creatures, is the subject of this covenant; angels had no need of it—devils had no hope from it—brute creatures were not capable of it—only man, and fallen man, hath an interest in it, and benefit by it. Oh the mercy there is in a covenant of reconciliation! Even after man had become bankrupt, spent a fair estate, broken his engagements, and brought himself into a desperate case, that still God should forget what was past, enter into a new and better covenant, entrust him with a new stock, and also lay help, not upon foolish man's weak shoulders, but upon one that is mighty to save! Oh rich, O transcendent love! this leads us to the second thing in this covenant.

2. The consideration interposed; that is, Jesus Christ, and he is eminently the gift of God,† such a gift as never came out of the hands of God, and was never received by the hands of mortal man, a rich and enriching gift, a gift proceeding from love; " God so loved the world, that he gave his son," John iii. 16. Christ is several ways a gift.

(1.) *Nobis*, to us, 1 Cor. i. 30, " who of God is made unto us wisdom."

(2.) *Pro nobis*, for us, Gal. ii. 20, " who loved me, and gave himself for me."

(3.) *Præ nobis*, before us, as an example, copy and pattern, as he suffered for us, so he left us an example, 1 Pet. ii. 21.

* Psal. viii. 4. † John iv. 10

(4.) *In nobis*, in us, " so Christ is said to dwell in our hearts by faith," Eph. iii. 17. Thus Christ is given to believers by sanctification, and inhabitation of his Spirit.

Now, it is in the second way principally wherein Christ was the consideration interposed, or his blood the price paid in this new covenant, namely, as he is given for us, a valuable consideration to pacify wrath and satisfy justice. Thus is Jesus Christ the *lutron*, or price of our redemption; " we are bought with a price," 1 Cor. vi. 20, such a price as never was paid. Men pay money to purchase great possessions, " but we were not redeemed with corruptible things as silver and gold," but with blood, yea, "with the precious blood of Christ," 1 Pet. i. 18, 19. Without shedding of blood there could be no remission, yet the blood of bulls or goats could never take away sin; * nay, the blood of all the men upon earth could never wash away the guilt of the least sin; no, no, it must be the blood of the immaculate Lamb, the blood of God, Acts xx. 28, so called from the union of the two natures, and communication of idioms or properties: and this is the price paid; the Father found out a ransom, and our dear Saviour gave himself a ransom:† certainly this is a transcendent mercy of the new covenant. I agitate not those nice controversies, whether God could not have pardoned and saved man without the consideration of Christ's undertaking? or how God in justice can charge guilt and inflict punishment upon an innocent person? this I am sure, is God's way of saving souls, and we must not dispute, but believe, that Jesus Christ is the mediator of the covenant, and the price of our redemption, as God-man; and this is the marrow of the rich mercy and deep mystery contained in the gospel.

* Heb. ix. 22, 12. † 1 Tim. ii. 6.

3. In a covenant are contained its conditions; what God requires of us, without which we can have no benefit by the covenant. These also are to be reckoned as mercies of the covenant on God's part as well as duties on ours, for they are secured and effected in us, as well as commanded and required by God. Luther makes this to be the main difference betwixt the two covenants; the covenant of works requires obedience, but gives no strength; but the covenant of grace engageth the grace of God for the performance of the conditions; hence it is, that what the law commandeth, the gospel promiseth; * what God requireth, Christ procureth; what justice demandeth, our dear Saviour purchaseth and worketh by his Spirit in the heart. Faith is the great gospel condition, whereby Christ with all his benefits becomes ours, but faith is the gift of God, and " none can come to Christ, except the Father draw him."—John vi. 44. Alas, it is as impossible to believe in Christ as to keep the moral law, from principles of corrupted nature; our state had been sad, and forlorn still, if God had not undertaken to work the faith which he requireth; † it is only the arm of omnipotence that can draw the soul to Christ; Jesus is the only author and finisher of our faith; ‡ there is an exceeding greatness of his power with respect to all them that believe, put forth to create an act of saving faith, ‖ all they that have felt it, can testify that this is a rich mercy; and this is one of the mercies of the covenant.

More particularly there are four important things promised in the covenant of grace, which are covenant mercies.

* Quod lex imperat, gratia impetrat. Evangelium dat quod lex exigit.—*Aug. de Spir. et Litera.*

† Duce Deo venitur ad Deum. ‡ Heb. xii. 2.
‖ Eph. i. 19.

(1.) Saving illumination. Jer. xxxi. 34, " They shall all know me, saith the Lord." By nature we are blind and blockish creatures, but the new covenant brings light and sight to the ignorant and erring sinner, and O what a mercy it is to know God and Christ, sin and misery, duty and felicity—to know Scripture truths and gospel mysteries, our own hearts and the sweetness of grace, heaven and the way thither! Certainly, such saving knowledge is worth a world; truly, such light is sweet, and a pleasant thing it is for the eye of the soul to behold the sun of righteousness, and the beauty of heaven; what blind Bartimeus would not own it as a rich mercy to have his eyes opened? and is it not a blessed thing to be translated out of Egyptian darkness into this marvellous light? O happy are the eyes that are anointed with the new covenant eye-salve, that behold celestial objects through this divine glass of faith, and become faithful guides in the progress of a holy life!

(2.) Genuine humiliation. This is another covenant mercy, Ezek. xi. 19, " I will take the stony heart out of their flesh, and will give them a heart of flesh." A broken heart is instead of many sacrifices; a hard heart is the greatest judgment, and a soft heart the greatest mercy; repentance is God's gift bound up in the covenant of grace. Our dear and blessed Redeemer is exalted as well to be a Prince that he may give repentance, as to be a Saviour to give unto us remission of sins. O what a mercy is the spirit of repentance! they that have this godly sorrow shall never need to sorrow for it—such a repentance needs not to be repented of; " Blessed are they that mourn for sin, for they shall be comforted; happy such as sow in tears, for they shall reap in joy!" Certainly a converted sinner looks on a penitent disposition as a rich mercy; one penitent tear is an orient pearl, of more worth than the whole creation; a bleeding heart is a blessed sight in the eyes of God and man—it lays the Christian under the promise of the covenant, and prepares him for remission of sins and the sweetest consolation.

(3.) Another covenant mercy which respects the condition is sanctification of heart; Ezek. xxxvi. 25, " I will sprinkle clean water upon you and you shall be clean." This is the mercy that David is so importunate for, " create in me a clean heart," no less than creation will effect it; putting off the old man, and putting on the new in a sound regeneration, is a miraculous mercy. O what would a poor soul give for dominion over some particular corruptions, and power to resist temptations! why here it is, this mercy of mortification, which is also a Christian's duty, is unfolded in this blessed gospel covenant, so that sin shall not have dominion over them that are under this covenant of grace. A Christian can do more to mortify sin, and crucify the flesh than another man. Every word of God hath a cleansing virtue; " now you are clean," saith Christ, " through the word that I have spoken to you;" but the promises of the covenant have a direct and immediate tendency to cleansing, 2 Cor. vii. 1, " having these promises," that is, of the forementioned covenant, " let us cleanse ourselves from all filthiness, both of flesh and spirit." It is only gospel grace that can make us evangelically holy; and holiness is the image of God, the beauty of the soul, the duty of a Christian, and the mercy of the covenant.

(4.) A spiritual conversation. This is also included in the covenant, Ezek. xxxvi. 27, " I will put my spirit within you, and cause you to walk in my statutes, and ye shall keep my commandments and do them." O what a blessed thing it is to have a heart to love, and fear, and serve the Lord! O what a mercy to be enabled to perform holy duties, to walk with God in all ways of well-pleasing, to have the law of God written on the heart, and transcribed in the life!* yea, to keep God's commands with ease, alacrity, and complacency, not to have them grievous but pleasant to the soul! and thus it is when the Christian acts from an innate principle of grace and holiness. Well, this is the promised and purchased condition of the new covenant; God undertakes to put a new habit into the soul, his fear which is the beginning of wisdom, and principle of obedience. God gives the spirit of prayer, the spirit of power, love, and of a sound mind; † he promiseth to give them one heart and one way, that they may fear him for ever. ‡ O what rich mercies are these!

4. Yet the great mercies of the covenant are behind, under another division, for a covenant, contract, or conveyance contains the *habendum*, or grant, ensuring advantage to the party covenanting, and that in these words, " I will be thy God," this is repeated fifteen or sixteen times in the Scriptures; this, this is the mercy of the new covenant, the mercy of mercies, the flower, cream and quintessence of all mercies; God gives himself to the soul by covenant, and what greater or better gift can he bestow? if he should give us all the world and deny himself, we are miserable beggars; if he give himself and nothing of the world, we are truly rich; if we have God we have all things, if we want God we want all things. My God is my all, saith the assured believer. It is recorded of Thomas Aquinas, || the great schoolman, that a voice from heaven spake thus to him: " Thou hast well written Thomas,

---

* Jer. xxxi. 33. † 2 Tim. i. 7. ‡ Jer. xxxii. 39.

|| Deus meus est omnia. Bene scripsisti, Thoma, quid petis? Resp. nil nisi teipsum, Domine.

what desirest thou?" and that he answered thus: "Nothing, O Lord, but thyself." This, certainly, is the language of a gracious soul, Lord put me not off with any thing below or besides thyself. What mortal creature durst have presumed to beg of God such a boon, if God had not graciously promised himself in the new covenant? What can the creature desire more? What can it now want when it hath an infinite God? All that God is, hath, or doth, is now employed for the advantage of believers; all his attributes and the good of them, are laid out for the covenanted soul. These words, " my Lord and my God," echoing to their correlatives " I will be thy God," are wonderfully sweet, as they use to say of the pronoun, *mine*, that though it be of the least entity, yet it is of the greatest efficacy;* suppose a man could with one cast of his eye take a view of the perfections of the whole creation, what were all these things to him if he have no interest in them? A clear title to a good thing completes the comfort we have therein. If God were not our God we could have no comfort from thoughts of him. What is God, saith one, if he be not my God? † if he be not our friend, he will be our enemy, and we had better have the whole creation against us, than God against us; but " if God be for us, who can be against us?" Now in the covenant of grace God undertakes to be our God, and this is properly that which this text intends, by " the sure mercies of David:" not in the singular but the plural number, as I conceive, for these two reasons: First, because God is the fountain, spring, and origin of all mercies; " all my springs are in thee," saith David. ‡ Hence God is said to be plenteous in mercy, and he is the Father of mercies. All mercies are vir-

---

* Relativa sunt minimæ entitatis, maximæ verò efficaciæ.
† Quid est Deus, si non sit meus? ‡ Psal. lxxxvii. 7.

tually, eminently, and transcendently in God, and he that hath him that hath all things, hath all things himself.* Secondly, because the covenant contains all mercies in itself; when any one enters into this covenant, behold a gad, a troop, a train of mercies attend upon him; the covenant is a blessed constellation, and all the stars of gospel promises do lend their aid to beautify the covenanted soul.

Take a sample of the mercies of the covenant in both these respects, as

1. What God is to the soul, and so what mercies are bound up in the covenant; in this respect,

(1.) God stands in every endearing relation to those who are interested in his mercy, he is a father to them, 2 Cor. vi. 18; † a husband, " thy maker is thine husband," Isa. liv. 5; " a near and bosom friend," Jam. ii. 23. Abraham was called the friend of God, so consequently God was his friend; for this covenant begets and contracts the most endearing bond of intimate friendship betwixt God and the soul, and if there can be any other relation, that holdeth forth still more tenderness of affection; that and much more is God to the gracious soul, ‡ " as one whom his mother comforteth, so," saith God, " will I comfort you," Isa. lxvi. 13, nay, the Scripture doth testify more affectionate workings in God's heart towards his people than can be found in the most indulgent parents to their natural offspring; sweetness of all relations proceeds from God, and therefore to be found in God; our relative affection is but a drop to this fountain, and our content in relations is no otherwise sweet than as flowing from him, or with relation to him.

* Habet omnia qui habet habentem omnia.
† Psalm x. Matt. iii. 17.
‡ Consult Isaiah xlix. 15, 16. Jer. xxxi. 20.

(2.) God is all that is pleasant, desirable and honourable; hence, we are bidden to taste and see how good the Lord is, and to delight ourselves in the Lord, and are informed that at his right hand there are everlasting pleasures;* he, he alone, is the object and centre of our desires—he alone, is the rock and rest of the fluctuating soul; therefore, David doth charge his soul to return to God as his rest.† God only is the sabbath and solace of the Christian's soul. Communion with God is heaven in the heaven of heavens. No desires so insatiable but may be satisfied with an infinite God, if regularly carried out towards him. O what a blessed thing it is to have God to be the object of our delight! the God of heaven is the King of glory, and he alone is the glory of a people or an individual, ‡ the best ornament is to have a God in covenant, Isa. xxviii. 5, " when the glorious beauty shall be as a fading flower——— then shall the Lord of hosts be for a crown of glory," instead of their crown of pride, " and for a diadem of beauty to the residue of his people." O blessed and beautiful ornament!

(3.) God is all that is required for safety and defence to his covenanted people. He is a sun and a shield; ‖ a sun to direct in times of darkness, a shield to protect in times of danger. There are seven words, Ps. xviii. 2, that set forth this self-same thing: what a protection God is to a believer—a rock, a fortress, a deliverer, a strength, a buckler, the horn of his salvation, and his high tower. Every one of these hath its peculiar emphasis and significancy; I cannot take notice of them all, only hint at the first and last: a rock, you know, is a natural defence, a tower is an artificial defence;

* Psal. xxxiv. 8.   Psal. xxxvii. 4.   Psal. xvi. 11.
† Psal. cxvi. 7. ‡ Psal. iii. 3.   Psal. xxiv. 10.
‖ Psal. lxxxiv. 9—11.

God is both, in a sort, by way of covenant, in the first respect as our God and Creator, in the second as God-man, Mediator, appointed to be the only succour and shelter of fallen mankind; here we may be safe and free from the roaring lion, the raving bear and uncircumcised Philistine; he alone is a hiding-place from the wind, a covert from the tempest, —— " and as the shadow of a great rock in a weary land," Isa. xxxii. 2. An admirable place you have Jer. xvii. 12, " a throne, a glorious throne, and a glorious high throne;" and this, "from the beginning is the place," not only of our defence, but "of our sanctuary." Every word hath its peculiar weight; who dare presume to meddle with a throne or to surprise a sanctuary? The glory whereof will affright and appal them; it is a high throne, how can they reach it? It is from the beginning, and to everlasting, and what mortal man can lay siege to this impregnable tower? The eternal God is the saints' refuge, and underneath them are everlasting arms;[*] therefore, are they safe from total falling, and fear of desperate evils.

(4.) God is all that is necessary for profit, advantage, and usefulness to the saints. It is said, " money answers all things," but God is better, and more truly answers all things; as a precious saint used to say, God is good, when gold is gone; no gain in the world like that which God is to the soul—God is our riches, treasure, portion, inheritance, and our all in all. David saith, Psal. lxxiii. 25, 26, " whom have I in heaven but thee?" and then adds, " my flesh and my heart faileth, but God is the strength of my heart, and my portion for ever." God is fitly called the saints' portion, for he is so one saint's portion, as if he were no one's else, and yet entirely every one's, as if wholly theirs, as

[*] Deut. xxxiii. 27.

indeed he is, yet without division, partition, or diminution. That is a notable passage in the gospel covenant, at least one part of it, the mercy in it we are speaking of, Gen. xv. 1, " Fear not Abraham, I am thy shield, and thy exceeding great reward." First, thy *reward*, as if it were, as indeed it is, reward enough to have God, if we have nothing else. Secondly, a *great* reward worth speaking of, not an inconsiderable trifle, but a great reward. Thirdly, an *exceeding* great reward, no hyperbole can reach its import,* much less exceed it; none can express the goodness of God, but those that experience it, nor can they sufficiently declare it; but is he mine? Yes, Fourthly, by this covenant he is *thy* exceeding great reward. " Blessed are they that are in such a case—Happy is that people whose God is the Lord. †

Thus I have shewed what God is.

2. I shall briefly particularize what God gives and grants to those who are in covenant with him; there are many benefits, and advantages, which are, indeed, rich covenant mercies.

(1.) Pardon of sin, Jer. xxxi. 34, —— " for I will forgive their iniquity, and I will remember their sin no more;" and, O what a mercy is pardon of sin? ask David when he is roaring under his broken bones and disquiet spirit, whether pardon of sin be a mercy?—he will answer yes; O yes, I know it, and could even envy the happiness of a pardoned sinner. " Blessed is he whose transgression is forgiven, yea, many times blessed is he to whom the Lord imputeth not iniquity."‡ This is a mercy that cost a great price, even the blood of the immaculate Lamb of God; it is a mercy that God shews for his own sake; a mercy that easeth the

---

* Christus et cœlum non patiuntur hyperbolen.
† Psal. cxliv. 15. ‡ Psal. xxxii. 1, 2,

guilty soul of a heavy burden; a mercy that hath sweet and satisfying concomitants. O the riches of this mercy!

(2.) God's favour, love, and tender compassion, Jer. xxxii. 40, 41, " I will make an everlasting covenant with them, that I will not turn away from them to do them good—— Yea, I will rejoice over them to do them good," as if he had said, now I am in covenant with them, I will seek and study in every way to promote their spiritual and eternal advantage; yea, and their temporal good also; I will be a fast and faithful friend to them; all my attributes shall contribute their assistance to forward the designs of mercy towards them, and what God doth for them is with his whole heart and with his whole soul—he will, in the relation of a father, take care of his children, and, is not that a mercy?

(3.) Gospel ordinances, Ezek. xxxvii. 26, 27, " I will make a covenant of peace with them—— and will set my sanctuary in the midst of them for evermore—— my tabernacle, also, shall be with them," that is, they shall have the means of grace, the visible tokens of God's presence, and ways of communion with God; and is not this a rich mercy? David looked upon it as such in his banishment from God's house, and every child of God prizeth it at a very high rate: this is one of the mercies of the covenant.

(4.) Seasonable afflictions, with a sanctified use of them, Psal. lxxxix. 30, 32, 33, " if his children forsake my law—— then will I visit their transgressions with the rod." It is infinite mercy that God will take the pains to chasten his offending children; it is faithfulness to the great object of the covenant that God will fetch in his wandering sheep by the sharpest means; it is, as it were, a cruel mercy to let men alone in sin, that they may hasten their ruin; it is the father's care and kindness to chide and correct his son, and it is as needful as food and raiment. A child of God would rather be scourged to God, than allured from him in the paths most agreeable to human nature. This covenant mercy doth change the nature of affliction, and make every thing to work for the soul's greatest advantage; this bitter potion is a useful, healing medicine; this stinging serpent is turned into a harmless, nay, helpful rod, with which the Lord works wonders of mercy upon and for his covenanted people.

But time would fail me to enumerate the large catalogue of covenant mercies. From this fountain, stream to believers those choice mercies of reconciliation with God, filiation, the spirit of adoption, free admission to the throne of grace, acceptance of their persons, hearing of their prayers, assurance of God's love, peace of conscience, communion of saints, the benefits of Christ's passion, resurrection, ascension, intercession, an interest in all the promises, Christ's purchase, the Spirit's aid and comforts, freedom from the wrath of God, the curse of the law and eternal death, and lastly, an interest in, and at death a full possession of, the inheritance of the saints in light. These and such like are the mercies of the covenant; in a word, all the goodness that is in God, and all that can be considered as real blessings in the world, are to be accounted as the "sure mercies of David.

CHAP. III.

THE MANNER IN WHICH COVENANT MERCIES ARE MADE SURE.

II. It may be observed that there are some things absolutely and unchangeably sure, as to their own nature by an intrinsecal necessity; thus God's essence is immutable; with him there is no variableness nor shadow of change: though the heavens perish yet he endures, "he is still the same and his years have no end," Psal. cii. 24—27. thus God alone is the certain and unmoveable centre of the whole creation; he is the rock of ages, originally, infinitely, and independently sure, and so is nothing besides; other things are sure *jure positivo*, not of themselves, but by the virtue of God's appointment and designation, invariable, irrevocable, so as shall not be altered, or otherways ordered; for instance there is no new way contrived to save lost man; thus the scriptures are sure for ever, "O Lord thy word is settled in heaven,"* and our Saviour saith, "till heaven and earth pass, one jot or one tittle shall in no wise pass from the law, till all be fulfilled;"† and in this way is the covenant of grace sure, not because of any intrinsecal necessity, resulting from its nature, but free to be or not to be as the infinite God sees good; as a covenant it depends merely on God's free-grace for making it, he might have forborne entering into this new covenant, and have dealt with man as with the lapsed angels; or he might have reserved to himself a power of revocation, to have called in his patent, and shut up his office of mercy, but now God hath fixed this as the only and everlasting way of

* Psalm cxix. 89. † Matt. v. 18.

salvation: thus this covenant is as sure as that the world shall no more be totally drowned with water; yea, as sure as the standing of the lasting mountains and hills: yet further, as sure as the ordinances of the sun by day, and the moon and stars by night; nay, once more it is as possible that the heavens should be measured by the short span of a mortal, or the foundations of the earth searched out, as for the great and unchangeable God to violate this gospel covenant with his dear Israel. Read this fully in Isa. liv. 6—10. Jer. xxxi. 35—37.

But yet more particularly, this covenant and these mercies of it, may be made sure two ways to believers; namely,

1. Infallibly, so as not to miss of them, and
2. Immutably, so as never to lose them.

1. These mercies of the covenant are sure infallibly, that is, the number of elect souls set apart by the sovereign Lord of heaven and earth to eternal happiness through our Lord Jesus Christ, shall have interest in and possession of the fore-mentioned mercies of David. That God hath chosen some to life as the end, and through Christ as the way of attaining that end is clear in Scripture; Ephes. i. 4. "According as he hath chosen us in him—and ver. 5. having predestinated us unto the adoption of children by Jesus Christ to himself;" and 1 Thess. v. 9. "for God hath not appointed us unto wrath, but to obtain salvation by our Lord Jesus Christ:" electing and redeeming love are of the same latitude and extent; whom God the Father in his counsels regarded, God the Son atoned for upon the bitter cross; "and those that are ordained to eternal life believe," Acts xiii. 48, which text, saith Calvin, teacheth that saving faith depends upon God's eternal election; hence also faith is called "the faith

of God's elect," Tit. i, 1. because it peculiarly distinguisheth them, for all men have not faith. Besides, God hath placed man's salvation upon the sure foundation of his own free grace, on purpose to make these things firm and sure to believers, so that their unworthiness shall not hinder the certain execution of his eternal decrees, Rom iv. 16, "therefore it is of faith that it might be by grace, to the end the promise might be sure to all the seed," that is, that the covenant with all the mercies of it might be made good to all the heirs of promise; "the election, hath obtained it, but the rest are blinded," Rom. xi. 7; hence, saith the apostle, 2 Tim. ii. 19, " The foundation of God standeth sure, the Lord knoweth them that are his: he knows his sheep even before they know themselves, according to his purpose of grace before the foundation of the world.* Hence also, God would not have the enjoyment of these mercies to depend upon man's sorry, mutable, and inconstant will, nor upon any works wrought by man, as the whole strain and tenor of the gospel holds forth : and indeed, if the whole stress lay on man's free will, it would bring us back to a covenant of works ; and if it were possible for any man to attain such mercies, he would be the determining cause of his own salvation,—and then what need of any Redeemer ? Besides, it might so fall out, that these mercies might be applied to none; for, *conditio nihil ponit in esse*, that which is not effectual without a contingent condition upon which it depends, that is to say, the particular movement of this man's will, and so of another's towards God, being in his own choice, is doubtful and uncertain, and so must needs

* Dico, novit Dominus qui sunt ejus, ipsæ oves aliquando seipsas nesciunt, sed pastor novit eas, secundum electionem ovium ante constitutionem mundi.—*Aug. in Joh. x.*

be the privileges which depend upon that condition: therefore, they that make these mercies possibly every one's, make them certainly no one's. The truth is, God hath not left the enjoyment of these covenant mercies to the choice or refusal of the fickle or inconstant will of the creature at his pleasure; but though he doth not violence to this faculty, but from its being unwilling makes it willing, God himself by his Holy Spirit hath engaged to bring souls home by converting grace certainly and infallibly, though sweetly and suitably to the nature of a rational creature. Hence effectual calling, which is introductory to these mercies, is not left at rovers, may-bes, or hap-hazard, but it is put beyond all peradventure; so that there is a *must* and *shall* annexed to it. " Other sheep I have—them also I must bring, and they shall hear my voice."—John x. 16. " All that the Father giveth me, shall come to me."—John vi. 37. The God of heaven hath engaged himself for it, and he is a God of truth to make good his word; he also possesses infinite power, he works and who can let it: " He worketh all things according to the counsel of his own will."—Eph. i. 11. All that God the Father hath given to Christ, the Son hath undertaken to bring to glory by his mediatorial administration: these mercies, then, are sure infallibly, the heir of glory shall partake of them.

2. They are sure immutably; not any that do partake of these mercies shall ever lose them—they shall never be deprived of them. There are indeed some common gifts of the Spirit that God may revoke and take away, as the gifts that Saul had; but these gifts of grace and this effectual calling are without repentance, Rom. xi. 29: he will never repent of, nor retract these

* Vide sis Ames. Coron. ad Coll. Hag. adversus Remons. Artic. prim. de Electione, cap. 4. p. 15. &c.

precious donations—Mary's better part shall never be taken from her; worldly riches may be lost, but spiritual mercies are durable riches. God, the Author of these mercies, is immutable, with him there is no variableness nor shadow of change; he is subject to no variation from the contingent events of second causes. "The Lord will not forsake his people for his great name's sake, because it hath pleased the Lord to make them his people," 1 Sam. xii. 22: he hateth putting away, he will not disinherit his children for misdemeanours, he knows their frame, sees and pities their weaknesses, raiseth them out of falls, and heals their backslidings. Christ Jesus, the purchaser of these mercies, is "the Amen, the faithful and true witness;" "the same yesterday, to-day, and for ever;" "mighty to save, a merciful and faithful high-priest;" "none can pluck them out of his hands; he will lose none of those that his Father hath given him;" "he will save to the uttermost."* This our Joshua will bring his people to the Canaan of eternal rest. The principle of grace, and these mercies themselves, are of a durable nature; grace is an immortal seed, a never-dying root —*principium continuativum.* "He that believeth in me," as the Scripture hath said, "out of his belly shall flow rivers of living water."—John vii. 38. Though grace is loseable in its own nature, yet not in the issue, because God upholds it. "The house built on the rock shall stand immoveable; the righteous is an everlasting foundation: he that doth the will of God abides for ever;† yea, he hath eternal life abiding in him." But may not they depart from God? no, not totally and finally, "for God hath put his fear in their hearts that they shall not depart from him."—Jer. xxxii. 40.

* Rev. iii. 14. Heb. xiii. 8. Isa. lxiii. 1. John x. 28, 29. xvii.
† Prov. x. 25. 1 John ii. 17.

They may sin and provoke God to withdraw the sense of his love, they may lose their standing, comforts, and some degrees of grace, but never be stripped naked wholly of these sure mercies of David; God hath secret hold of them, and they have more hold of him than others have; they are restless and dissatisfied till they enjoy God, and till these mercies be clear to them. This golden chain stretcheth itself from everlasting, it begins in a purpose of grace, and ends in final salvation; " whom he predestinates them he calls, justifies, glorifies," &c.—Rom. viii. 29, 30. It is sacrilege to pluck one link from this golden chain; God is the finisher as well as the author of faith. It is not within the compass of any finite being to rob a gracious soul of the love of God, or stop the course of his free grace to those in covenant with him. Paul can make a bold challenge, Rom. viii. 35, 38, 39, "Who shall separate us from the love of God? and he makes a sufficient enumeration of all things that were likely to conquer the believing soul, and yet concludes, that in in all these things " we are more than conquerors through Christ; there are in the word sweet promises that may answer all cavils and unbelieving fears concerning perseverance, which many able champions have produced and managed with dexterity and success. *

* See Mr. Prins on Perseverance; Dr. Prid. Lect. 7. De Persev. Sanct.; Dr. Ames Coron. Artic. 5. De Perseverantiâ.

CHAP. IV.

THE MANNER IN WHICH COVENANT MERCIES ARE CONFIRMED.

III. THE next thing intended is more particularly to shew in what way these covenant mercies are confirmed or made sure. Now there are several steps of making a thing sure amongst men, and God hath used the same means, (and even done more) to make these mercies sure to the children of men.

1. Men are wont to pass their word. When they promise any thing upon the word of an honest man, they expect credit; and among men this is current, and the God of heaven is worthy to be believed upon his bare word, (if I may so speak) for he is a God that cannot lie nor deny himself: " yea, let God be true and every man a liar:" even a Balaam is convinced of it, and must profess it, Numb. xxiii. 19. " God is not a man that he should lie—hath he said, and shall he not do it? or hath he spoken, and shall he not make it good?" The unchangeable God hath engaged his word in the new covenant: the patriarchs of old gave credit to all that God spake by dreams, visions and revelations, as in the instances of Abraham, Isaac, and Jacob.

2. Men use to give stronger evidence by subscribing their names, and putting their mind and promise into writing;* hence the expression and practice of giving letters of credence, and we use to say " men are mortal, give it me under your hand, that will abide." † Well, our gracious God hath condescended to subscribe his promises under his own hand, the hand of his blessed

---

* Hence Neh. ix. 38. " We make a sure covenant, and write it."
† Litera scripta manet.

Spirit; the word of God is upon record, " therefore whatsoever was written, it is for our learning, (I may add satisfaction) that we through patience and comfort of the Scriptures might have hope," Rom. xv. 4: he hath given assurance to us of these things in the word of truth—" for this cause was the gospel written, that we may know the certainty of these things," Luke i. 4. " and that we may believe," John xx. 31. Who dare now dispute or doubt of the truth and sureness of gospel promises? since "heaven and earth may pass away, but one jot or one tittle shall in no wise pass from the law till all be fulfilled."—Matt. v. 18.

3. Men use to call in witnesses for further confirmation. Some important business requires several witnesses; it is a standing rule, " at the mouth of two or three witnesses shall the matter be established." * Well, the God of heaven hath confirmed the gospel to us by twice three witnesses; there are three in heaven, the glorious persons of the blessed Trinity, the Father, the Word, and the Holy Ghost, and these three are one, one in essence, though three persons, 1 John v. 7, these bear record of Christ's Godhead; and there are three that bear witness on earth, verse 8. these testify of Christ's manhood—the *Spirit*, that is, say some, his breathing out his soul and spirit in his giving up the ghost, and *water*, and *blood*, that came out of his side when it was pierced with a spear, which shew he was real man, and that he did really die; Aretius † interprets these three latter of the Spirit in the ministry of the word, the water of baptism, and the blood signified by the wine of the Lord's supper in which Christ's meritorious sacrifice is represented, and

* Deut. xix. 15.
† Hanc sequor sententiam hoc loco, nec puto aliam posse adduci veriorem.—*Aretius in loc.* See Marlorate in loc.

still this interpretation further confirms the gospel covenant, and consequently the mercies of it.

4. Men use to give assurance to others by affixing their seal; hence the practice amongst us of setting a seal to bills, bonds, leases, purchases, letters patent, and this seal hath usually a person's cognizance or coat of arms, or some impression upon it, and leaves the impression upon the wax. The God of heaven adds his seal; there is the broad seal of the new covenant, baptism and the Lord's supper are given and appointed purposely for the confirmation of our faith, and assuring our hearts of the truth of the promises, as circumcision is called the seal of the righteousness of faith, Rom. iv. 11; for by these seals both the grace of God is confirmed to us, and holy impressions made on the hearts of believers. There is also a privy seal, the seal of the blessed Spirit in our hearts;* Eph. i. 13, "——sealed with that holy Spirit of promise:" hereby God's children are distinguished from wicked men, and confirmed in the truth of the gospel; yea, it beareth witness with their spirits that they are the children of God, Rom. viii. 16. This is an elegant similitude, for all civil charters and testaments become valid by the addition of a seal, and the seal in former times was the note in letters by which the author was known, and a seal is the mark whereby genuine things are discerned from counterfeit: all these are the uses of the Spirit's sealing, to confirm our hearts in the truth of God in his promises, against all the temptations of Satan; this blessed sealing is more prevalent for our confirmation, than all philosophical reasons or demonstrations.

5. Another way to create assurance among men is a solemn oath; "and we know an oath for confirmation

* Eph. iv. 30. 2 Cor. i. 22.

is to them an end for all strife," Heb. vi. 16 ; and thus God willing more abundantly to shew unto the heirs of promise the immutability of his counsel, confirmed it by an oath, or interposed himself by an oath.* It is very important to consider the form of the oath; God swears by himself, who is the living and true God, he could swear by no greater : and it may be observed, that two considerations make a thing more credible—1. The quality of the person speaking; 2. The manner of the speech. Now, the form of the oath to Abraham is exceedingly emphatical; † partly because of the asseveration, " surely ;" partly because of the reduplication, " in blessing I will bless thee," if I speak it, it shall be done. Moreover, the form of the expression in Genesis is strange, ‡ for it is thus—" If I bless thee, thou shalt be blessed," or because I bless thee; or if I do not bless thee, (which is the form of an oath, Heb. iv. 3.) as if he should say, then let me not be true or just, yea, let me not be God. God pledges his faithfulness upon it, and may he not then be believed ? But for what end is this ? it is to confirm his promises, and assure the hearts of all the heirs of promise that he intends to do, and will accomplish what he hath spoken, that they may have strong consolation, and that he may take away all doubts and hesitation ; and all this he doth for the heirs of promise; he would

* Ἐμεσίτευσεν. Invitat præmio salutem ; jurans etiam, vivo dicens : cupit credi sibi. O beatos nos quorum causâ Deus jurat ! O miserrimos si nec juranti Domino credimus.—*Tertul. de Pœn.*

† Gen. xxii. 16, 17. כי־ברך אברכך. כי est particula causalis et conditionalis.

‡ Quid tibi prodest si Deus se juramento constringit, si tu hæc quasi communem audiens fabulam transeas?—Jurare dicitur Deus, ut tu audiens paveas et intremiscas et metu consternatus inquiras quid illud tantum est, pro quo Deus jurare dicitur.—*Orig. Homil.* 9. *super Gen. xxii.*

not have done thus for others, but he doth this and much more to satisfy his doubting children.

6. Yet further, men use to give an earnest or a pledge to assure others of their real purpose to make good the bargain, and this is part of the payment. This also doth our gracious God, Eph. i. 14; his Spirit is the "earnest of our inheritance,* until the redemption of the purchased possession." An earnest is used in purchasing land, in hiring of servants, and in contracting marriage, and whenever the Lord puts his Holy Spirit into the heart, it is as a pledge of all the mercies of the covenant and of our eternal inheritance. And though some men may be unfaithful, so far as rather to lose their earnest, than make good their bargain, yet we may be assured God will not do so, for it is as impossible that any saving grace of the Spirit should be cast into hell, as it is for any sin to enter into heaven. God will not lose his pledge, but fetch the soul to heaven when he hath fetcht the heart to himself; grace is the prologue and prelude to glory, the first resurrection leads the van to the second; a gracious change prepares for a glorious change. "If the Spirit of him that raised up Jesus from the dead dwell in you, he that raised up Christ from the dead shall also quicken your mortal bodies by his Spirit that dwelleth in you."—Rom. viii. 11. The Spirit confirms the promises, and we need not fear any danger of retractation; not but that the promises are firm enough of themselves, but he would establish our hearts in the faith thereof and acquiescence therein, lest there should be any question.

7. Another way whereby men testify their cordial resolution to make their promises good, is, by doing a great part of the work, which gives real evidence that

* 2 Cor. i. 22. and v. 5.

they will do the rest; he that promiseth to give another a thousand pounds, and hath already given him nine hundred, may he not rationally trust him for the rest? or suppose there were but one pound, or a penny behind, there is great reason to confide in him for what is wanting.* Why, truly the Lord hath performed the greatest part of the promises of the covenant; the great promise of the covenant was, " that the seed of the woman should bruise the serpent's head;" that the Son of God should be incarnate, be in man's stead in life and death to satisfy justice, fulfil the law, and by his death bring in everlasting righteousness, and he hath already done it. Now, saith the apostle, Rom. viii. 32, " He that spared not his own Son, but delivered him up for us all, how shall he not with him also freely give us all things?" † God is beforehand with us; yea, if we be indeed heirs of promise, he hath made good another grand branch of the new covenant, in giving the conditions of the covenant, faith repentance, and new obedience; so that the main business is already done, the writings are made, sealed, signed, and delivered, there wants nothing but actual possession; nay, there is a seisin and delivery of part of the inheritance,—and dare we not trust God for the remainder? certainly we have good reason so to do; the contrary is unreasonable.

8. God hath gone further, namely, to work many miracles for the confirmation of these sure mercies;

---

* Should a king promise to erect some college, and give liberal maintenance to students in it, we are certain by a human faith, that he will do such a thing though it be not begun; but if the foundations be in laying, we see its execution in part, and are assured it will be finished.—*Bains on Eph.* i. 17, *p.* 144.

† See Rom. iv. 8—10. Qui misit unigenitum, immisit Spiritum, promisit vultum; quid tandem tibi negaturus est?—*Bern.*

this is a degree beyond what man can reach to make any thing sure. Hence, saith our dear Saviour, John v. 36, " I have greater witness than that of John, for the works which the Father hath given me to finish, the same works that I do, bear witness of me, that the Father hath sent me." This text shews the true and proper end and efficacy of Christ's miracles ; they are not dumb shows, but have a voice, and cry aloud for faith in the intelligent observer ; * yea, and they were wont to beget faith in the spectators, as Nathaniel believed, upon Christ's telling him of his conference at a distance, John i. 48, 49. " The beginning of his miracles manifested his glory, and his disciples believed on him," John ii. 11 ; and others comparing the doctrine of John with Christ's miracles believed on him, John x. 41 ; and indeed the argument of miracles is a cogent, convincing argument, " for no man can do those real miracles except God be with him,"—John iii. 2. Certainly, the wonderful things wrought by Christ ought to assure our hearts of the truth of the gospel, and consequently of the sureness of these covenant mercies. But upon this subject you have evident and abundant demonstrations from the pen of the Rev. Mr. Baxter, in his Saints' Rest, Part 2, in the Preface, and in page 215—234, to which I refer you. The truth is, God hath graciously condescended to confirm the gospel by many infallible miracles which none can question, and all this to make sure to believers these covenant mercies, therefore they are inexcusable that slight this way of the gospel's confirmation.†

9. Another step that God hath taken is the adoption of various means to make known to us these

* Igitur non sunt muta sed vocalissima ; ideo non simpliciter intuenda, sed et intelligenter audienda.—*Marl. in loc.*

† See Heb. ii. 3, 4.

sure mercies, and thereby to give us assurance of them, as,

(1.) An audible, intelligible voice from heaven, at Christ's baptism, and his transfiguration, " This is my beloved son, in whom I am well-pleased,"* and this voice, the Apostle Peter saith, he heard in the holy mount, 2 Pet. i. 17, 18, so that these gospel mercies are not cunningly devised fables, but divine oracles of undoubted truth.

(2.) The constant preaching of honest and unbiassed men, that were eye-witnesses of his glory. They give clear evidence of their hatred of evil, love of truth and goodness, and they could not be perverted by any selfish ends of profit, pleasure, or honour, for these were not proposed, promised or attained; nay, affliction and persecution was their known portion, and, therefore, they certainly could not, would not cozen the world with lies to get what was not attainable in that way.

(3.) God hath qualified men with admirable gifts to enable them to demonstrate the certainty and excellency of these covenant mercies; in the apostles' days, extraordinary gifts, as extemporary prophecying, healing diseases, working miracles, discerning spirits, divers kinds of tongues, † so that all nations might hear these *magnalia Dei*, great things of God in their own dialects, ‡ and now they are translated into all laguages; and God hath continued to distribute ministerial gifts for the church's satisfaction and edification. ||

(4.) He sent even his own Son to be the preacher as well as purchaser of these sure mercies. " He spake at sundry times, and in divers manners in times past by the prophets, but in these last days he hath spoken to us by his Son," Heb. i. 1, 2, the more to conciliate in

* Mat. iii. 17. Mat. xvii. 5.   † 1 Cor. xii. 8—10.
‡ Acts ii. 11. || Eph. iv. 8—12.

us reverence and credence, for he saith, " surely they will reverence my Son;" certainly, he declares to us the whole counsel of God, " for he was in the bosom of the Father, and came from thence for this very end to declare his Father's will."—John i. 18.

(5.) Yea, he hath raised Jesus Christ from the dead, so that we have a preacher sent from the grave to assure us of the truth of these high mysteries and sweet mercies; so the rich man could say in hell, if one went to them from the dead, they would repent and believe, Luke xvi. 30. Now our dear Saviour himself was dead and is alive, and as he is declared to be the Son of God by his resurrection from the dead,[*] so after his resurrection he declared the great things of God, confirming his disciples in the truth of things formerly delivered, and giving further testimonies and instructions, Luke xxiv. 44—49.

(6.) Still other means of manifestation are clear and crystal ordinances, in which, as in a fair glass, we may behold both the face of God, and the choicest mercies of the covenant; here you may not only hear the voice of God, but see Jesus Christ evidently set forth, crucified before your eyes.—Gal. iii. 1. In the sacrament of his holy supper, are exhibited God's grace in giving Christ, Christ's love in giving himself, his body broken for our food, his blood shed for the remission of our sins, and all the benefits of this new covenant.

(7.) Another way of the Lord's manifesting these mercies, and so making them sure is through the sanctifying and satisfying illumination of souls by his holy Spirit—by his holy unction they know all things, 1 John ii. 20, " God hath revealed them unto us by his Spirit," 1 Cor. ii. 10, 12. Now the Spirit comes with conviction and demonstration, answers all the

[*] Rom. i. 4.

soul's doubts and cavils, and leaves it without dispute and hesitation; so that the believer cannot but say, they are sure mercies. He dares not deny this for a world.

(10.) There is yet one other way whereby God doth make sure these mercies of the covenant, and that is by a marriage contract, a mutual and matrimonial engagement in the perpetual and inviolable bond of the covenant, whereby Christ and the soul are inseparably linked together, and this relates to the particular application of these covenant mercies, and completes all the former; for, saith the poor soul, I do not question but these mercies are sure in themselves, in their own nature, and sure to some—but are they so to me? What way may I be assured of my title thereunto and interest therein? Now this, the Lord doth make good by entering into the sweet and familiar relation of marriage with his people; " thy Maker is thy husband, and I am married to you," saith the Lord. * A believing soul is dead to the law, that he may be married to Christ, † and our heavenly husband " hateth putting away," ‡ once married to Christ and for ever married to him, death itself breaks not this marriage contract, nay, it fastens and makes it indissoluble; here Christ and the soul are but as it were engaged, then the marriage is solemnized with the acclamations of glorious angels, and glorified saints, for, saith the apostle, 2 Cor. xi. 2, " I have espoused you to one husband that I may present you as a chaste virgin to Christ." Now souls are fitting for that great solemnity, " when the marriage of the Lamb shall come that the bride may be ready." ‖ She is making herself ready in this world, she is married at the illustrious day of Christ's second appearing;

---

* Isaiah liv. 5. Jer. iii. 14. † Rom. vii. 4.
‡ Mal. ii. 16. ‖ Rev. xix. 7.

so then this marriage contract cannot be broken since it is completed in glory. But yet more particularly consider that remarkable text in Hosea ii. 19, 20, wherein the mercies of the covenant are made over in a way of matrimonial relation, and " I will betroth thee unto me for ever," &c. in which Scripture there are four things that may assure the heart of the security of these covenant mercies.

[i.] The author and husband I, the great Jehovah, the infinite God, the creator of heaven and earth, who speaks and it is done, who works, and none can let it. It is he that saith, " I will betroth thee," and who can forbid the banns of matrimony ? who is able to hinder this conjunction ?

[ii.] Here is the doubling of the phrase for greater certainty and security, " I will betroth thee, yea, I will betroth thee ;" fear not it shall be done ; nay, the third time it is repeated, v. 20. " I will even betroth thee," what can any say more to assure a suspicious bride of a firm contract and marriage, as if he had said, do not distrust me, a marriage shall most undoubtedly take place. All this God saith to meet the incredulity of a guilty soul, that through fear desponds, and dares scarcely look upon it as possible or credible ; yet,

[iii.] Here is the term and date of the marriage, it is not for a week, month, year, seven years, no nor a hundred years only, nay, it is not only during life, as other marriages are made, but it is for ever, unto " all eternity," it never fails, it lasts as long as the soul lasts, that is a long day ; other marriages are temporary, terminable, failable, and " death looseth a woman from the law of her husband ;"* but this is a marriage confirmed, and completed at death, and endures for evermore ; and then,

* Rom. vii. 2.

[iv.] The terms, the conditions, and the manner of marriage speak the sureness of this covenant, and the mercies thereof, observe it : Loving kindness is the motive to it, and mercies are the soul's jointure—righteousness, judgment, and faithfulness, are the writings, as it were, and evidences, to assure these forementioned conditions. Individuals sometimes marry such persons as they ought not to marry, as such as are too near of kin, and contrary to consent of friends, &c. and so are divorced, " but my marrying thee shall be in righteousness." Many marry in a sudden gust of affection, and repent when they have done, but " I will marry thee in judgment." Many marry fraudulently, cheat the persons whom they marry, lead them into a snare, and then leave them, but " I will marry thee in faithfulness, integrity and fidelity ;" we shall never part, and though thou be unworthy now, and mayest transgress, yet, I will fetch thee home, pardon thee, and maintain this marriage relation with invariable constancy and fidelity. What more can be said to assure the believing soul of the sureness of covenant mercies ? Besides, consider, loving kindness is the beginning middle and end of the engagement ; he fetcheth arguments out of his own bosom to enter into this parley, and after he hath contracted this friendship, and intimate relation, the same loving kindness will influence him to maintain it; nay, now his truth and faithfulness are engaged, and he will be faithful in performing all his promises. Consider that notable text, Mic. vii. 20, " Thou wilt perform the truth to Jacob, and the mercy to Abraham, which thou hast sworn unto our fathers from the days of old." Mark, it is mercy to Abraham because promised to him, but it is truth to Jacob, and now is a kind of debt, and must be paid, and made good. God is a " free agent," yet he binds himself by promise, and so becomes a debtor to his creature, or rather to himself on the behalf of his creature.* Thus doth God assure to his saints and spouse the dowry and jointure of mercies that he promiseth to them, in this contract of marriage, betwixt himself and souls. †

Thus I have considered the ways which God takes to make these mercies of the covenant sure to all the heirs of promise.

CHAP. V.

THE MEDIUM THROUGH WHICH THE SURE MERCIES OF DAVID ARE CONVEYED.

IV. THE last thing in the doctrinal part by way of illustration is, to shew how these covenant mercies are made sure, in or by or through Jesus Christ.

Now for clearing of this: observe these four things with reference to Jesus Christ, whereby these mercies are made sure: first, his hypostatical union; secondly, his spiritual unction; thirdly, the covenant of redemption; and fourthly, the execution of Christ's office in the work of man's redemption.

1. Consider the mysterious and astonishing union of the two natures in Jesus Christ, whereby he is both God and man united together in one person; by the former, he hath ability—by the latter, a capacity to make the covenant sure to his people; so that now it is impossible the work should miscarry; as God he is omnipotent and cannot fail or fall short of his end—as

* Reddis debita nulli debens. † See Zach. viii. 8.

man he is adapted to his work, and fitted with a body both for active and passive obedience; so that there is nothing required of man's nature, but Christ, being in our stead, did effectually perform it, for the apostle saith, Col. ii. 9, " that in him dwelleth all the fulness of the Godhead bodily, σωματικῶς, that is, naturally, personally, in such a way as he is in no other, " in him we live, move, and have our being," as creatures. God is said to dwell in the saints in a superior manner, as his children; but the Godhead is not said to dwell in any man except Jesus Christ, God and man. God dwells in the saints by his Spirit as in a temple effectively, and operatively; in Christ essentially, and substantially :* " the word was made flesh," and sometimes there were sparklings forth of his glory and majesty, so that the disciples " beheld his glory as that of the only begotten of the Father."—John i. 14. Well then, since this is an undeniable mystery, that God was manifested in the flesh, and hath undertaken to manage the work of our redemption in both natures, certainly he will make sure work in what concerns him, for so saith the prophet, Isa. xlii. 4, " he shall not fail nor be discouraged, till he have set judgment in the earth ;" he hath the powerful hand of an infinite God, therefore, he is mighty " to save," and he hath the innocent nature of a finite man, therefore he was fit " to suffer."

2. Consider the complete and abundant unction of Jesus Christ, whereby he hath both sufficiency and efficiency to go through his work, and authority for it also; the Scripture tells us that " Jesus Christ was anointed with oil, and that above his fellows."—Heb. i. 9. Christ was not only qualified with gifts fit for office, but also to furnish the souls of all be-

* In aliis sanctis habitat Deus ut in templo et organo, effectivè, operativè, in Christo substantialiter.—*Aret. in loc.*

lievers with supplies both for sanctification and edification. Jesus Christ hath the Spirit but not as others have it, for the saints have only a scantling and small measure thereof, but God giveth not the Spirit by measure unto him, John iii. 34. " To every one of us is given grace according to the measure of the gift of Christ ;" * but Christ hath it above all measure, for he hath the whole Spirit substantially, he is and hath the treasury of grace, a storehouse of riches to supply indigent creatures, " in him are hid all the treasures of wisdom and knowledge," Col. ii. 3, " therefore of his fulness do we receive grace for grace," John i. 16 ; " it pleased the Father that in him should all fulness dwell," Col. i. 19, and this is laid up on purpose for the supply of his members, that from the head may be conveyed influences through the whole body, Ephes. iv. 13—16 ; besides, he is invested with authority for granting these supplies, Ephes. i. 22, 23, " He hath put all things under his feet, and gave him to be the head over all things to the church, which is his body, the fulness of him that filleth all in all." Hence, he tells his disciples, " that all power is given to him in heaven and earth," Matt. xxviii. 18; add to all this, his fidelity, that as Moses was faithful as a steward, much more is Christ as a Son faithful to him that appointed him, Heb. iii. 2—6. Well now, lay all these together, and surely we need not question the certainty of covenant mercies. Since Christ hath sufficiency, authority and fidelity, and is thus abundantly qualified for carrying on this gospel design, he both can and will make good the mercies of the covenant to the heirs of promise ; especially considering,

3. The covenant of redemption, which is an admirable, insuring act of free grace, engaging all the per-

* Eph iv. 7.

sons of the sacred Trinity to carry on this work, especially God the Son of whom we are now speaking. This covenant of redemption is that mutual compact betwixt God the Father and the Son concerning the saving of lost man, wherein each did undertake to act his part in this great affair, as thus: God the Father, hath chosen sinners, and given the objects of his choice into the hands of Christ to redeem, John xvii. 9, he was to part with his beloved Son out of his bosom whilst he came to the earth to do this great work, he was to uphold him, encourage him, put his Spirit upon him, call him in righteousness, hold his hand, keep him, and give him for a covenant of the people, and give him to see his seed;* and though they be but few in comparison of the world, yet he will make him glorious, † and in time he will satisfy him by giving him " the heathen for his inheritance, and the uttermost parts of the earth for his possession." ‡ This is the engagement on the Father's part, and then the Lord Jesus, the Son of God promised the Father that he would assume the human nature, and so become man, putting himself into the sinner's stead and becoming his surety, fulfil all righteousness by obeying the moral law and suffering for our breach of it, be betrayed, accused, condemned, crucified, and buried; that he should rise from the dead, ascend into heaven, sit at God's right hand, intercede for the saints, &c. This part which Christ performed is fully laid down in Isa. liii. throughout. This was the great transaction betwixt the Father and the Son from all eternity. That there was such a mutual agreement, see Titus i. 2, " in hope of eternal life which God, that cannot lie, promised before the world began." To whom did God promise any thing before

* Isaiah xlii. 1, 4, 6. Isaiah liii. 10, 11. † Isaiah xlix. 5.
‡ Psalm ii. 8.

man was created? Certainly, he promised something to Jesus Christ concerning man's redemption as before-mentioned; such a gracious plan was laid, and compact made betwixt the Father and the Son, and he cannot lie nor deny himself.* So 2 Tim. i. 9, "who hath saved us ―― according to his own purpose and grace which was given us in Christ Jesus, before the world began," that is, as Christ was a public person, as head, instead of the elect, so we were given to him by this covenant, and that from all eternity, but how come we to know this, that are but of yesterday, and so dim sighted that we cannot see afar off? Why, verse 10, we read "it is now made manifest by the appearing of our Saviour Jesus Christ, who hath abolished death, and hath brought life and immortality to light through the gospel," for Christ revealeth all the secrets that were locked up in the bosom of the Father. Well then, if this was the mutual stipulation betwixt the Father and the Son, there is no question but they will be faithful to each other. In the Old Testament God the Father trusted God the Son upon his promise to lay down his life, and so brought thousands of souls to heaven before ever Christ was incarnate or suffered; and now when Christ hath gone through the greatest part of his task, he trusteth God the Father to make good his part, that " he may fully see his seed, prolong his days, and that the pleasure of the Lord may prosper in his hand;" and, certainly there cannot be any failing on either part. Now this covenant of redemption is the platform and foundation of the covenant of grace betwixt God and believers; there are the same persons, and the like

* That this is no singular doctrine, but opened before, see Mr. Bulkly's Gospel Covenant, part 1, chap. 4, page 31—46, where it is fully opened. Also, Mr. David Dickson in his Therapeutica sac. book 4, chap. 4, page 23—71.

terms, proportionably, in both; hence, it is, that although a believer find an unfaithful, treacherous, and unbelieving heart in himself, daily departing from the living God, yet this covenant is built upon a higher and firmer covenant betwixt God the Father and God the Son, which cannot be broken and disannulled ; the Father and Son cannot deceive or be unfaithful to each other ; hence, then, it cometh to pass that the covenant and the mercies thereof, are so sure. I shall conclude this head with that notable passage of Christ's to his Father upon this very account, John xvii. 4, " I have finished the work which thou gavest me to do," that is, I have hitherto made good and performed the conditions of the agreement on my part, verse 5, " and now, O Father, glorify me with thine own self," that is, make good thy engagement, in my exaltation. So much with reference to Christ's person ; then for his seed and members, he tells the Father that he had performed his part with respect to them, in manifesting his name to them, praying for them, preserving of them, and now when he was to leave them, he desires the Father to do his part of the work " in keeping those whom he had given him," verse 11 ; " in sanctifying and saving them," verse 24 ; and can we imagine but that God will be faithful to his Son on the behalf of his saints? Certainly he will, for as they were redeemed by the Son, so they were chosen by the Father, and as God the Father gave them to Jesus Christ, verse 6, and Jesus Christ died for them, and thus redeemed them, so God the Son resigns them up again to the Father, who will certainly keep them by his power through faith unto salvation.

IV. Another thing of importance concerning the ensuring of covenant mercies by and through Jesus Christ is, that these are most fully made sure to us by the execution of Christ's mediatorial offices, both in his state of humiliation and exaltation. Let us here consider, first, Christ's offices; secondly, his states.

First, Christ's offices are of three sorts, sacerdotal, prophetical, and regal.

1. As Priest, Christ ensures to us many covenant mercies, for he hath put himself in our stead and offered himself as a propitiatory sacrifice to satisfy divine justice, which is " a sweet smelling savour,"* and of infinite value; hence it is, that Christ is called " a merciful and faithful high priest in things pertaining to God, to make reconciliation for the sins of the people."—Heb. ii. 17. Certainly, remission of sins is one of the grand mercies of the new covenant, and this Christ assureth as Priest.

2. As Prophet he reveals to us the will of his Father, opens to us the sealed book, and anoints our eyes by his blessed Spirit. The Spirit of Christ inspired the prophets of the Old Testament, and the apostles of the New, in writing the Scripture, and ministers in preaching the gospel, and believers in discerning the meaning of the word, and beauty of Christ. † It is Christ as Prophet, that writes his law in believer's hearts which is one of the great mercies of the new covenant, that enlightens dark minds, and unlocks to us divine mysteries, and bringeth us from darkness to light.

3. As King. Christ Jesus doth what he pleaseth for the good of his church, converting and subduing souls to himself, granting to them the spirit of power, love, and of a sound mind, softening their hard and stony hearts, mastering their high and sturdy wills, awing, ordering, and centring their unruly, roving, and raging affections, subduing their strong corruptions, regulating their conversations, begetting and in-

* Eph. v. 2.   † 1 Pet. i. 10, 11.

creasing their graces, supporting them under and sanctifying their afflictions—all which Jesus Christ, as King, works for his covenanted ones.

Yet more particularly, in the second place, let us consider how our covenant mercies are assured to us by Jesus Christ, with reference to his *two estates* of humiliation and exaltation.

1. In his estate of *exinanition* and *humiliation*. Here I might run through the instances of his humble birth, his despicable life, that is, to a carnal eye, his being in the form of a servant, having no form nor comeliness; his hunger, thirst, wanderings, revilings of men, wrath of God and rage of devils—all these confirm the covenant, if we believe the history of the gospel. But there is one thing more that puts all out of doubt, which is, his real, ready, and voluntary death, for as he had a power, so he had a will, to lay down his life, and he died for the confirmation of this covenant, and all the mercies thereof. A pregnant proof of this you have in Heb. ix. 15; the sum of which text is, that Jesus Christ, the great Mediator of this new covenant, hath suffered death for the sins of his people, that were committed against the first covenant, whereby all true believers might have the benefits of the new covenant more surely and immutably made over to them; and this he further confirms by the parallel case of a testament and the testator even amongst men, ver. 16, 17, " where a testament is, there must also of necessity be the death of the testator."* No man can challenge a legacy till he prove the death of him that left it, for while he is alive he may alter his will at his pleasure, or as reason requireth; but when the

* Thus the apostle argues, Gal. iii. 15, " Brethren, I speak after the manner of men: though it be but a man's covenant, yet if it be confirmed, no man disannulleth or addeth thereto."

testator is dead the heirs may look after their legacies. —Jesus Christ is the testator, saints are the heirs, the legacies are these mercies of the covenant. Now the *Testator* is dead the *legacies* come clear, and the *heirs* of promise may claim their interest therein; there is no alteration of the will when the testator is dead, there is no reversing, true Christians now come to enjoy their estates; Christ emptied himself that we might be filled—he lost his life that we might live—" he became poor that we through his poverty might be rich." 2 Cor. viii. 9.

2. Christ's *exaltation* doth much more assure to us covenant mercies; and this exaltation consists in his resurrection and his ascension, both of which tend to their confirmation.

(1.) Christ's " rising again from the grave," assures us of the certainty of these mercies; for though he was dead, yet he is alive, and so lives to be his own executor: if Christ had been detained prisoner by the king of terrors, we might warrantably have suspected that justice was not satisfied, nor mercies fully purchased; but " he was delivered for our offences, and raised again for our justification," Rom. iv. 25, and now he hath conquered death, and " through death hath destroyed him that had the power of death, that is, the devil," and so hath delivered the heirs of promise from the fear of death, Heb. ii. 14, 15; nay, and by his resurrection he raiseth us to a new life of holiness here, and a blessed life of happiness hereafter:* compare Rom. vi. 4. with chap. viii. 11. Christ's resurrection abundantly clears the saints from all accusations and condemnation, Rom. viii. 33, 34; in this, therefore, we may rejoice and triumph as the source of our consolation. See Acts ii. 24—26.

* 2 Cor. iv. 14.

(2.) Christ's "ascension into heaven" ensures and secures covenant mercies to us, both as it sets him in the holy of holies, far above the reach of men and devils, and as he went before "to prepare a place for us."* He bids Mary, John xx. 17, to go to his brethren the disciples, and say unto them, "I ascend to my Father and your Father, to my God and your God;" as if he had said, now you may be assured of your interest in God in a covenant way, for I have on earth completely removed what obstructed your fellowship and obscured your interest; so that now you may call him your God, and come unto him as your Father, without misgivings within or challenges from without.

There are two things in Christ's ascension that assure these mercies to us; first, his session at God's right hand, and secondly, his intercession.

First, Jesus Christ is set at God's right hand in heavenly places, Ephes. i. 20, and the two following verses afford us two choice considerations that tend further to assure us,

1. That "he is far above all principality and power, might, dominion, and every name in this world and that to come," Ephes. i. 21; that is, Christ as man is advanced not only above all states and potentates on earth, but above all angels and archangels in heaven, therefore far above the devils; none can hinder, all are his servants to help forward his design for the good of souls. O what a sweet consideration is this, that our nature is advanced thus high! yea, in the person of the Redeemer there are alike sympathy, ability, and authority; and, therefore, he will effectually manage his glorious undertaking. Yet, that is not all, for

2. In the 22nd verse, it is said, that he "gave him

* John xiv. 2.

to be the head over all things to the church," that is, not only to be the head of the church, but to be head and governor over all things for the good of the church, so that now the whole world is subordinate to him for the advantage of his people, and now every thing shall help them forward towards heaven; yet, further there is something more in the phrase, and that is, that as the head is gone before to heaven, so the members shall undoubtedly follow after, and so salvation shall be sure, and this is very clear in that admirable text, Ephes. ii. 6, " and hath raised us up together, and made us sit together in heavenly places in Christ Jesus." Thus, it is as sure as if we were there already, for we are set there in our representative Jesus Christ, or the holy places and privileges on earth are an earnest of glory, but indeed the saints are already saved,* so saith Paul, verse 5, " by grace ye are saved," and elsewhere, " we are saved by hope,"* so that we have, as it were, taken up our rooms, as one saith, in heaven aforehand, whereunto, we have a just right upon earth by virtue of a union, which is the ground of communion, for " he that hath the Son hath life," † that is, he hath possession of it as by turf or twig, he hath, in a sort, seisin and delivery. Our head is in heaven, and although these things yet appear not in the members, yet because of the hidden union betwixt the head and members, that which is peculiar to the one is appropriated to the other. Hence, saith the apostle again, Col. iii. 3, 4, " Your life is hid with Christ in God,—— when Christ, who is our life, shall appear, then shall ye also appear with him in glory,"—— when the opaque shell of our

---

* Rom. viii. 24.

† Quia nondum hæc, quæ commemorat, in membris apparent—propter arcanam tamen unitatem ad membra certò pertinent.—*Calvin in loc.*

mortal bodies shall be broken, then shall the pearl of grace shine forth in its lustre and glory; yea, " he will also change our vile body, that it may be fashioned like unto the glorious body of Jesus Christ.—Phil. iii. 21.

Yet further, in the second place, Christ's intercession, now that he is in heaven, assures us of the certainty of covenant mercies, for he is Mediator, * a middle person, and so fit to negociate the business with God, for poor man, and he intercedes effectually for guilty souls, by virtue of the worthiness of his own person and merits; and as an advocate in a legal and judicial way he solicits for them and pleads their cause, and he appears in heaven for them, vindicating them from all accusations; and will not all this satisfy? Further, Christ's intercession is of large extent, and of as powerful efficacy, for as he can refuse no cause committed to him, but must and will intercede, when employed, so he cannot but be heard always; and his promise is as full, " whatsoever ye ask in my name, it shall be done unto you," John xiv. 13, 14; nay, " I will do it;" the intercessor is the executor. † But I shall not be large on this interesting subject of Christ's intercession, because many have written much about it; only take notice of that well-known text in Heb. vii. 25, for closing this head, " wherefore he is able also to save them to the uttermost that come unto God by him, seeing he ever liveth to make intercession for them." This text is a notable demonstration of the excellency of Christ's priestly office, tending to the confirmation of this point and the consolation of believers, wherein are these seven things.

* 1 Tim. ii. 5.

† See this Doctrine of Christ's intercession pithily and profitably opened, in Mr. Durham's Expos. of Revel. viii, 1, Lect. 1, page 407—414.

1. The end of it, and that is to *save souls*, and the infinite God will certainly accomplish his end; men may fall short, but God cannot miscarry, " I work," saith he, " and who shall let it.

2. The universality of it, " he saves all," that is, all believers, rich and poor, whether they have more or less worthiness, for they are not saved for their own, but for Christ's merits.

3. The efficacy thereof, " he saves to the uttermost, [εἰς τὸ παντελὲς] that is, to the uttermost point or term of life, even to death and beyond it, or so as none can mend his work, for as he is " the author," so he is " the finisher of our faith and hope," consolation and salvation, none can come after him to finish what he hath begun; and he saves to the uttermost from all classes of enemies; none can challenge an interest in souls after he hath done his work, and he saves to the uttermost, that is, he leaves them not till he have brought them into the highest happiness that creatures are capable of enjoying; there is all manner of perfection in this salvation.

4. Here are the subjects or persons saved, " those that come to God," or the condition, " coming to God by Christ;" now this is such a disposition as he himself doth work, for the power of his Spirit doth effectually draw souls to God, John vi. 44, 45; the condition is believing, and he works the condition. Christ is that sure ladder of Jacob by which souls may ascend to God, and into heaven; never any fell off this ladder, or miscarried that came to God by Christ.

5. Christ's ability to carry on that work, in the first words, " he is able;" this we cleared in the first head concerning the union of the two natures. " He is omnipotent," therefore he is said to be mighty to save, and

if he can do any thing in this soul-saving work, he will not fail those that lay the whole stress of their souls upon him.

6. Here is his capacity to save, for the text saith, " he ever lives;" a living Saviour can revive dying, dead souls. If Christ were not alive, there would be no hope of life by him, in vain should we seek for living enjoyments among the dead; but our Saviour is revived and lives for ever, " he is the living bread that came down from heaven," John vi. 51; " and is again risen and ascended up into heaven, and because he lives, we live also."

7. There is his complete execution of his present office, " he ever liveth to make intercession for them," saith the text, therefore, he must needs complete the work he hath begun on earth; like the high priest under the law, our Mediator sprinkles the blood of his meritorious offering here on earth, upon the mercy-seat now in heaven,[*] and continually bears the names of his saints upon his breast, and appears in the presence of God for us, Heb. ix. 24, so that we have a friend in our nature to own us in open court; yea, God the Father bade him welcome into heaven, and as a token thereof, sets him upon his right hand, which is an evidence of honour, (as Solomon dealt with his mother) and then bids him ask, promising that he will give him all that is in his heart. Certainly, then, the mercies of the covenant must needs be sure, and that through Christ, the Mediator, since his intercession is so prevailing, that he said in the days of his flesh, when praying over Lazarus's grave, " Father, I knew that thou hearest me always.—John xi. 42.

Thus I have dispatched the doctrinal part of this

[*] Levit. xvi. 14. Heb. ix. 11, 12.

subject, wherein I have endeavoured to shew what the mercies of the covenant are; in what respects they are said to be sure, by what means and ways they are made sure, and how they are made sure in and by Jesus Christ, the great Mediator of the covenant.

CHAP. VI.

THE SURE MERCIES OF DAVID FURNISHING A CONFUTATION OF ERRORS.

Now for the application of this point, I shall make use of it several ways. In the first place, for the confutation of Atheists, Papists, Arminians, and Socinians.

1. It confutes the vain conceits of Atheists who call in question the great things of religion; they are first sceptics and disputants, then by degrees they grow Atheists and deny God—as one saith, in the academy of Atheism, a sinning soul takes these sad degrees. He proceeds,

(1.) To doubting whether there be a God or not.
(2.) To living as though there were indeed no God.
(3.) To wishing that there were none: and
(4.) To disputing against a Deity, and then he commenceth doctor in positive conclusions, asserting with the fool that " there is no God," * Psalm xiv. 1.

Many are ready to say, that religion in the power of it is but a fiery meteor, which the influence of those hot dog-stars of the times, ministers, have drawn up and kindled in the grosser region of some sick and melancholy brains, and so like fire is apt to catch in thatched and low built houses, not palaces, and castles, that is,

* Mr. Herle on Policy, page 52.

large and high-built souls. But the truth is, some Atheists do find, even in this life, the certainty of our religion, all shall find it to the their cost hereafter by an irretrievable loss of these sure mercies, and by the intolerable sustaining of everlasting miseries. As Atheism hath been much propagated in these latter days, so God hath afforded instances of remarkable convictions by several modern examples. Cardinal Richlieu, who after he had given law to all Europe many years, confessed to P. Du Moulin, that being forced to many irregularities in his life time, by what they call reasons of state, and not being able to satisfy his conscience, thence had temptations to disbelieve in a God, another world, and the immortality of the soul, and by that distrust to relieve his aching heart, but could not; so strong, as he said, was the notion of God on his soul, so clear the impression of him upon the frame of the world, so unanimous the consent of mankind—that he could not but taste the powers of the world to come, and so live as one that must die, and so die as one that must live for ever; and being asked one day why he was so sad, he answered, " Monsieur, Monsieur, the soul is a serious thing, it must be either sad here for a moment, or sad for ever;" and though Cardinal Mazarin was an Atheist the greatest part of his time, yet he hath left behind him evidence of clear convictions of the immortality of the soul, and certainty of another state after this life, professing that if he were to live again, he would be a Capuchin rather than a courtier, that is, of a Popish religious order, to serve God in their way, rather than choose worldly preferments. It is recorded of Sir John Mason, counsellor to Henry the Eighth and Edward the Sixth, that he called his clerk and steward to him, and said, " I have seen five princes, been privy counsellor to four, seen the things most worthy of observation in foreign parts, been at most state transactions for thirty years, and have learned, that 'seriousness is the greatest wisdom, temperance the best physic, and a good conscience the fairest estate,' and were I to live again I would change the court life for a cloister, my privy counsellor's bustles for a hermit's retirement, and my whole life in the palace for one hour's enjoyment of God, in the chapel; all things else forsake me, besides my God, my duty, and prayer." Thus he expressed himself. It is also recorded of Charles the Fifth, emperor of Germany, king of Spain, and lord of the Netherlands, that after twenty-three pitched battles, six triumphs, eight kingdoms won—after all this success, he resigned all these, retired to his devotion, had his funeral celebrated before his face, left this testimony behind him, that the sincere profession of religion hath its sweets and joys that courts were strangers to; and we know from holy writ that Solomon, after his vast experiments and exact dis-disquisitions left this maxim as the total sum of his large accounts, Eccles. xii. 13, "Fear God and keep his commandments, for this is the whole duty of man." Atheists never yet tasted the sweetness of religion, they never fully studied the word or works of God, both which would satisfy them. It is recorded of Francis Junius, that reading Tully de Legibus, he fell into a violent persuasion that God cared for nothing, neither for his own nor others' affairs,[*] but in a tumult at Lyons, the Lord convinced him of a divine providence by delivering him strangely from imminent death, and also being put by his father upon reading the first chapter of John's gospel, he was abundantly convinced by the force of the argument, and by the majesty and authority

[*] Nihil curare Deum, nec sui nec alieni.

of the style, in such a manner that his body trembled, his mind was astonished, and his soul savingly converted; yea, the works of God are sufficient to leave upon conscience, a conviction of a Deity. Lord Bacon used to say, that "a little smattering in philosophy might tempt a man to be an Atheist, but a thorough study of it would bring him back to be religious, for it would reduce him to a first cause and a last end." But I must not enlarge on these Atheists, see them described and confuted in Weems's Treatise on four degenerate Sons of Adam. I shall only add now the words of Lord Chancellor Egerton. "To be prophane is the simplest thing in the world, for the Atheist lays a wager against the serious man, that there is no God, but upon woful odds; he ventures his everlasting state, the other only hazards the loss of his sensual gratifications. If there were no God, yet the latter doth as well as the Atheist at last, and lives better at present, but if there be a God, as undoubtedly there is, O the vast disproportion at the great day! if the arguments for and against the verity of the gospel were equal, yet the gain or hazard is infinitely unequal; therefore, every wise man will take the safest side. Lord, what an age do we live in! when the choicest truths, duties, and mercies, from a principle of opinionativeness or licentiousness, are questioned or denied. Well, God hath his way and time to convince these wretched Atheists by real and unanswerable demonstrations, so that all men shall say, "Verily, there is a reward for the righteous; verily, there is a God that judgeth in the earth."—Psal. lviii. 11.

2. What has been stated, notably confutes the Papists, because, in the first place, all these good things of the covenant are mercy, not merit; we are under a

covenant of grace, not of works; " the mercies of God are our merits.* We have cause to renounce our own righteousness; alas, what are our best works to obtain favour at the hands of God! Those before conversion, which they call meritorious, *de congruo*, are not truly good works, wanting a principle; and those after conversion, which they call works of condignity, are not exactly good, not being without the stain of imperfection; and, therefore, cannot merit. They hold two justifications according to these preparatories, the first is, when a sinner, of an evil man is made a good man, which is done by pardon of sin, and infusion of inward righteousness, that is, the habit of hope and charity; the second is, when a man, of a good man is made better, and this, say they, may proceed from works of grace, because he who is righteous by the first justification can bring forth good works, by merit whereof he is able to make himself more just and righteous; but we assert that the very thing by which we are justified and accepted is only the mercy of God, and the merits of Christ's active and passive obedience, which are imputed to us and received by faith alone, and our obedience or performances cannot be satisfaction to God's justice, because they are imperfect and defective, " filthy rags," ‡ a rag, and cannot cover us, and filthy, therefore, will rather defile than justify us. At the great day, we must have some thing that can counter-

* Dei misericordia, merita nostra.

† They acknowledged Christ's righteousness to be the only meritorious cause of this first justification, i. e. he procureth the infusion of this grace. All papists assert, roundly, that man is justified, per solam gratiam inhærentem, tanquam per formam integram sine imputatione externæ justitiæ Christi.—*Suarez, Lect.* 7, *chap.* 7, *page* 83.

‡ Isaiah lxiv. 6.

vail the justice of God ; Paul durst not appear in his own righteousness, but in Christ's, Phil. iii. 9, and how dare we? Certainly, Paul's doctrine is an infallible truth of God, Rom. iii. 20, " —— by the deeds of the law there shall no flesh be justified in his sight;" and verse 24, " being justified freely by his grace through the redemption that is in Christ Jesus," and though Papists deride imputed righteousness ; yet it is mentioned ten times in Rom. iv. and frequently asserted and proved through Paul's epistles. So 2 Cor. v. 21, " as Christ was made sin for us, so are we made the righteousness of God in him." Now Christ was made sin for us no otherwise than by God's imputing our sins to him, for it is blasphemy to say Christ was sin by infusion of sin into him, or inherency of sin in him. Besides, our justification comes to us as our condemnation, which was not only by propagation, but by the imputation of Adam's disobedience.—Rom. v. 19. All the mercies of the covenant are to believers made over by a deed of gift, indeed " the wages of sin is death, but eternal life is only the gift of God," with all that leads thereunto, Rom. vi. 23. But, however, Papists may dispute in the schools, yet when they come to lie upon sick and death-beds, they are glad to come off with Bellarmine's, *tutissimum est,* " it is safest to rely only on the mercy of God and merits of Christ for justification." Let us still hold the safe way and leave them to their uncertain, imperfect righteousness ; but it is easily discernible what is the reason of the Papist's opposing free justification by grace only ;* because it would demolish their purgatory, masses for quick and dead, invocation of saints, worshipping of images, indulgences, and their treasures of merits ; hence, a modern Divine hath laid down the grounds that render

* Dr. Prideaux, Lect. 5. De just. fol. 64.

the salvation of a Papist in a sort impossible, and proves undeniably, that their contrivance for justification doth overturn most, if not all, the truths of the gospel, and is utterly inconsistent with God's way of saving sinners;* for it is the same for matter and form with the covenant of works, for the keeping of which, in the same circumstances as Adam in innocence, they say that Christ merited new strength, and now sinners are to stand or fall in the obtainment of life promised, according to their own performing of the condition of works, in the use of that first grace, and by this they merit perseverance and heaven; and lest indwelling corruptions and defects in duties mar this, they say concupiscence is not a sin against the moral law, and that there are many sins venial and not mortal, which therefore do not hinder merit and acceptance. Alas, what a new and anti-evangelical way is this, which confounds justification and sanctification, derogates from the nature of grace, enervateth the merit of Christ, altereth the nature of the gospel covenant, &c. But I must not enlarge, let us study this important subject, and beware of corrupting this fountain, or building on any other foundation than Christ's righteousness alone.

Secondly, the following is also an uncomfortable doctrine of the Papists, namely, " that a Christian cannot be assured of his interest in the covenant of grace, or of his eternal salvation." We hold that a Christian may attain to assurance of faith, without extraordinary revelation. They say a man may indeed attain to a conjectural certainty which only ariseth from hope, in regard of God who promiseth, but in regard of ourselves and our indisposition, we are to be at uncertain-

* See this doctrine stated and cleared in Durham on Rev. fol. 585, &c. vid. fol. 590—594.

ties. Certainly, a child of God may not only be assured of God's fidelity but his own sincerity. These mercies are sure in respect of the subject as well as the object, for the promises run in general and indefinite terms, " whosoever believeth shall be saved;" but I, saith the soul, truly believe, therefore I shall be saved, and this particular application and reflection is as much as if it were said, if thou John, Thomas, Peter, do believe, thou shalt be saved ; now though the heart be deceitful, yet the Scripture hath laid down such characters by which a man may try and discern the sincerity of his own act in closing with Christ, for true believing is a receiving of him as he is offered to us in the gospel.—John i. 12. Besides, the saints " receive the spirit of adoption, which beareth witness with their spirits, that they are the children of God, Rom. viii. 15, 16, and this is " an earnest of their inheritance,"* which assures them of the whole possession ; it is a seal, and takes away all occasion of doubting. † Paul saith of all believers, 1 Cor. ii. 12, " we have not received the spirit of the world, but the spirit which is of God, that we might know the things that are given us of God," that is, these mercies of the covenant, adoption, pardon, sanctification, salvation. God hath laid it upon us as a duty " to make our calling and election sure," ‡ not in itself, but to ourselves, therefore, it is attainable, for God doth not command us impossibilities; he that bids us " try ourselves whether we be in the faith," ‖ supposeth we may come to know upon an exact trial; besides, many of the saints have been assured of their sincerity and salvation by ordinary ways, which all the saints may use, and have a like success in a like full assurance of faith ; and God

* Ephes. i. 14 † Ephes. iv. 30.
‡ 2 Pet. i. 10. ‖ 2 Cor. xiii. 5.

hath bid us " ask that we may receive, that our joy may be full."* Now, we are to " ask in faith," believing that he will grant what we ask, and we have a promise to be heard, yea, he sets us on asking that he may give. But I need not stand long to prove the possibility of a child of God's attaining assurance, for experience doth abundantly confirm it, and blessed be God that in this we can groundedly say the Papists are mistaken.

3. Another class whom this doctrine confutes are the Arminians, and that in two respects: first, on the subject of universal redemption; secondly, on falling away from grace.

(1.) The text saith these are " the sure mercies of David;" God's Davids or beloved ones only have an interest in them, not all men : and in the *Doctrine*, I say, that covenant mercies promised in Christ are purchased and ensured by Christ to all the heirs of promise, and I must add—only to these, and to none besides; and therefore Christ died not for all. Here I shall only use these two arguments, which immediately relate to the present subject :—

First, Christ's mediatorial undertaking is not intended as a price for any but such as were proposed by God to the mediator in the covenant of redemption, to be redeemed by him; but all and every one were not so proposed, therefore not redeemed. I have before considered that great transaction betwixt the Father and the Son: now, it is most certain that the mediator's death and sufferings are to be looked upon as regulated and qualified in respect of their effects, according to what was proposed by the Father, and consented to by the Son. Hence Christ saith, that " he came not to do his own will, but the will of him that sent him,

* John xvi. 24. Mark xi. 24. 1 John v. 14, 15.

and to finish his work, and to give eternal life to as many as God hath given to him :" therefore Christ must by his undertaking ensure those mercies to all those, and none but those that the Father proposed to him in this everlasting engagement. As for that conditional giving of some to Christ, which some speak of, *that* would derogate from his glory, for he must needs know the event, and that such a conditional giving would not effect it; and to say he willed what should not come to pass, or applied such means as he knew would not be effectual to the end, cannot be imagined. Besides, those that are given to Christ are contradistinguished from others that are not given to him; therefore, those only are assigned peculiarly to be redeemed and not others.

Secondly, All those and only those whom Christ redeemed, have all the mercies of the covenant ensured to them, but all have not all covenant mercies ensured to them and conferred on them, therefore all are not redeemed by Christ. Christ is the surety and mediator of the new covenant; and he gives faith, repentance, pardon, heaven to them for whom he is engaged as a surety, they shall not fail of any covenant mercies, that are absolutely necessary to salvation, for he is faithful in the execution of all his offices. Now, we know all men have not saving faith nor repentance; while it cannot be conceived but that his satisfaction must be equally effectual for the procuring of these saving mercies to those whose place he occupied as surety; and indeed God promiseth as a recompence to him, that " he shall see of the travail of his soul and be satisfied ;" yea, " he shall justify many," that is, as many as he undertook for, Isa. liii. 11. If Christ hath borne their iniquites, they must be justified, else he missed of his object; there is an inseparable connexion betwixt Christ's undertaking for them, and his bestowing covenant mercies on them. All that are redeemed by Christ's blood are made "kings and priests to God," Rev. v. 9, 10. They are purchased to be "a peculiar people to God;" they are "washed from their sins in his blood, redeemed from their vain conversation, delivered from spiritual enemies to serve God in holiness all their days," and to be received to heaven when they die. These are the mercies of the covenant which the mediator purchaseth, and applieth to all his people; therefore none else are redeemed: for the proper and native fruits of Christ's death are not divided, therefore he prays for them that were given to him, and for whose sake he did sanctify himself, and passes by others.—John xvii.

(2.) This statement confutes Arminians in their discouraging opinion of the saints' apostacy. Some hold that there may be a total apostacy of saints, as the Lutherans; some that it may be final, as Arminius; others maintain that it may be total and final. We hold that believing, regenerate, justified persons, who are endowed with the divine nature and a lively hope, shall not lose that principle and fall from that state of grace, and be utterly deprived of the favour of God: indeed, we need no argument but this, that these mercies of the covenant are sure mercies, which they would not be if they might be lost. There is the immutability of God's promise in the new covenant, the intercession of Jesus Christ for believers, the omnipotency of the Shepherd of Israel who will not lose one of his sheep, the efficacy of the Spirit, supporting and renewing the seed of God, and life of grace in believers, and this seed of God keeps a believer from sinning in two respects:* first, he hates and nills in part the evil

* 1 John iii. 9.

which he wills and works;* secondly, if by human frailty he fall, he makes not a trade of sin, nor keeps a course in it, but the seed of grace makes him restless till he return to God, and be admitted into favour and fellowship with him. Thus, though good David sometimes " goes astray like a lost sheep," yet since he cannot forget God or his commandments, Ps. cxix. 176. his heart was dissatisfied till his God and his soul were at peace again. This gracious principle inclines a Christian God-wards and heaven-wards; " it is a well of water springing up into an everlasting life," John iv. 14; it is " an increasing grain of mustard-seed;" it is " an incorruptible seed that liveth and abideth for ever, an abiding unction, an engrafted word, an indwelling Spirit," &c.† therefore cannot be lost. Blessed be God for this comfortable assurance, which doth not beget licentiousness as our adversaries reproach it, but diligence in the ways of God for the genuine product of it, as the experience of the saints testifies. But I shall say the less on this, because I have hinted at it before in the doctrinal part, and others have said so much on this subject.

4. The last class that are confuted by this doctrine of " the sure mercies of David," are such as maintain the Socinian error, that Christ's death is not a satisfaction for sin; the Socinians hold that Christ's sufferings were only for the confirmation of his doctrine, or for the imitation of the saints, or at most, only to purchase to himself the prerogative to forgive sins freely. These ends are framed mainly as an engine to destroy Christ's Godhead and personality in the glorious Trinity; and it is recorded of Socinus the patron of this blasphemy, that he held that " the world was not

* Rom. vii. 19.
† Matt. xiii. 31. 1 Pet. i. 23. 1 John ii. 27. James i. 21.

made of nothing," lest he should be forced to acknowledge the infiniteness of God's power, which he denied, and of Christ's divine nature, by whom he made the worlds. * But we, on the contrary, do confidently believe, that when the majesty of God was wronged by the sin of man, and when it behoved man to make satisfaction to justice, or never be freed from the sentence of condemnation, or obtain reconciliation; this being beyond the power of a finite creature—Christ, God-man did interpose himself in our stead to be a sacrifice for us to satisfy justice, and bring in everlasting righteousness, which satisfaction is accepted of God the Father, and imputed to the sincere believer. This is the sum of the gospel, and clearly held forth therein to all that are not wilfully blind. In Isa. liii. 6, it is said, "the Lord laid on him the iniquity of us all," and saith the apostle, "he became sin for us," † that is, in our room or stead; hence he is called "a surety" on paying our debt, and "a ransom," and his death is called "a propitiation, an expiatory sacrifice, by enduring the curse for us, and washing us from our sins in his own blood, and purchasing his church with his own blood," that is, the blood of God-man. ‡ But the Scripture is full of testimonies, and the subject I have been so largely insisting upon in the doctrinal part abundantly evinces, that Jesus Christ as mediator of the new covenant doth ensure the mercies of it to all the heirs of promise by his meritorious undertaking, which I have abundantly proved; and the Socinians denying this, do also deny the merit and excellency of Christ's obedience and death, and his divine nature, and so deserve not to be ranked among the number

* Heb. i. 2. † 2 Cor. v. 21.
‡ Heb. vii. 22. Job xxxiii. 24. Gal. iii. 13, 14. Rev. i. 5. Acts xx. 28.

of Christians. The Lord preserve us from those black and destructive ways of error and heresy, and imbue our hearts with a thorough sense and experience of these " sure mercies of David ;" for all Dagons will fall before this ark of the covenant, and the clear understanding of this doctrine will rectify many mistakes; the right conceiving, and unfeigned embracing of these new covenant mercies, is the greatest help to a sound mind, and sincere heart which are great preservatives against error and apostacy.

CHAP. VII.

THE SURE MERCIES OF DAVID CONSIDERED AS CONTRIBUTING INSTRUCTION.

II. THIS subject may be regarded as contributing instruction, since we may be informed relative to sundry very necessary truths, and directed in several duties from the consideration of these " sure mercies of David," and the previously described way of making them sure.

1. It instructs concerning the great difference betwixt the covenant of works and the covenant of grace. Divines use to make several distinctions betwixt them. But indeed this is the main, that the former was dependent on an inherent righteousness, the other on one imputed ; in the first, man was to perform personal, perfect, and perpetual righteousness—in this second, our surety and great mediator undertakes it for us, and it is applied to us by faith, which is now become the evangelical condition, in the room of the legal condition of complete obedience; so that was settled be-

twixt God and man immediately, this through an interposing mediator, Gal. iii. 19 ; the former was soon broken, because though man was upright, yet he was mutable, and that we feel to our cost; but Jesus Christ the great mediator of this new covenant is " the Lord Jehovah, the mighty God, the everlasting Father, the Prince of peace, able to save to the uttermost; he is God and changeth not, therefore we are not consumed, and therefore are souls saved." Hence saith the apostle, Heb. viii. 6, " He (that is, Jesus Christ) hath obtained a more excellent ministry, by how much also he is the mediator of a better covenant which was established upon better promises." Indeed the excellency of the covenant doth chiefly arise from the excellency of the mediator of it, and the manner of its confirmation, which is Christ, God-man by his active and passive obedience, who is frequently called our mediator.* Although that place in the Hebrews doth rather respect the form of administering the covenant than the matter, and it is a comparison betwixt the dispensation to the fathers under the law, and the dispensation in gospel times ; for they had the same covenant of grace, though under shadows and types, that we enjoy in substance and performance, yet by consequence it holds forth the precedency of our gospel covenant above, and beyond the legal covenant which was made with Adam.

That I may a little further unfold this, there are two things illustriously shining in this gospel covenant : first, the grace and love of God ; secondly, the wisdom of God.

(1.) Consider the infinite mercy, favour and compas-

* Heb. vii. 22. ix. 15. xii. 24. 1 Tim. ii. 8. Verum hæc Apostoli comparatio ad formam potius quam ad materiam referenda.—*Calv. in loc.*

sion, the tenderness, love and condescension of the great God in renewing the covenant which man had broken. I confess there are many curious questions asked concerning these two covenants, such as these: Could not God as well have secured the conditions of the first covenant, by assisting Adam with grace to perform them, and persevere therein? and again, Why might not the first covenant have been spared, and this second have answered the purpose of both? But what is man that he should find fault with God's pleasure? Yet we might answer all these with the assertion and admiration of God's infinite wisdom and mercy. His glorious attributes all aid one another—mercy employs power, power supports truth, truth seconds justice, and they do all employ wisdom, and wisdom doth order all to his glory. If there had not been a first covenant, there had not been a trial of man's obedience; if it had been kept, God's wisdom had not appeared in repairing the breach, nor his love in sending his Son, nor his justice and power in triumphing over Satan's malice, and gaining advantage thereby. Besides, if there had been no first covenant violated, there could not have been such a glorious display of free grace in the reconciliation betwixt God and man, which implies both a covenant and a breach. O the mercy of God in Christ! it is wonderful, stupendous mercy that God was willing to hold any correspondence with man in a covenant way, who had broken with him before. Yet free grace would not any more trust sorry man that had been a bankrupt, with a stock in his own hands: yea, God staid not till man sought out for this surety, but prevented him with free grace. We read that when Augustus made a proclamation, that whoever would bring him the head of Carocotta the Spanish pirate, should have a rich reward; Carocotta hearing of it came and presented his head to the emperor, and challenged the reward: but when man had fallen he runs away, endeavours to hide himself, yet love pursues and overtakes him, and contracts with guilty Adam, a better, and unthought of, unsought for covenant. Parmenio's large letter to Alexander against Olympias, was all answered with one tear of a mother: but where is there any one tear to bewail or make amends for man's horrid crime? no, not a word to procure favour; free grace did all to bring traitors into a league. God's heart was full; he could not hold but call he must, and seek and run to fetch home apostate man, that profligate rebel, who durst not shew his face, or ask forgiveness: but the Lord of life and glory, the King of heaven is ready to forgive, and to give the glorious things of heaven to them that inquired not after them.

(2.) Here behold such a display of wisdom, as "never eye beheld, ear heard, or heart conceived;" the apostle calls it "the manifold wisdom of God." I cannot here stand to open all the parts thereof that fall within the reach of a finite view; I shall only endeavour to unfold one of its branches, by explaining this strange paradox, namely, how it could be possible, since God himself is immutable—since the moral law, which is an obligation of the creature to obedience, is irrevocable—and since man hath now broken it, and death and wrath have been threatened thereupon. I ask, whence does it come to pass that the malediction and condemnation are not executed? no, nor perfect obedience exacted, as the nature of the law requires? The direct and proper force of the law is obedience, the secondary and conditional effect of it, is a binding over to the curse upon supposition of disobedience; but we see the law doth neither, and yet the Scripture testifies of the word of God, that it is " settled for ever in heaven, that his commandments are sure and stand fast for ever, that one tittle of the law cannot fail." * How comes it to pass then, that the law is neither thoroughly obeyed nor executed? obeyed it is not, for " all have sinned, and by the deeds of the law is no flesh justified :" executed it is not, for " there is no condemnation to them that are in Christ, and they are delivered from the curse of the law :" † abrogated or extinguished it is not, for then there would be no sin nor duty, reward nor punishment : no, nor is it moderated or favourably interpreted, by rules of equity to abate the rigour of it, for it is inflexible, and the text saith, " Cursed is every one that continueth not in all things which are written, in the book of the law to do them." ‡ Therefore there is no way but one, that is, that the law should so far be dispensed with, as that a surety be accepted instead of the malefactor, this is the blessed design of the gospel. God is willing to allow and accept a surety, Jesus Christ is willing to undertake and perform this office, and the believer is willing to embrace this blessed mediator, and thus the agreement is made, the covenant is renewed, and the law is established. Yea, by this gospel way of saving souls, he doth magnify the law, and make it honourable; the obligations of the law are discharged in Christ by the second covenant, our surety hath fulfilled its duties by his active obedience, and undergone its curses in his sufferings and death, and both better by Christ than ever it was possible for man to satisfy. Adam in innocency and the angelical nature could not have obeyed the law so perfectly, (at least so meritoriously)

* Psalm cxix. 89.   Psalm cxi. 7, 8.   Luke xvi. 17.
† Rom. iii. 20, 23.   Rom. viii. 1.   Gal. iii. 13.
‡ Gal. iii. 10.

as our surety hath done, and if we had lain for ever in hell, we could not have satisfied justice so as our Saviour did by his short, yet infinite sufferings satisfy for our woful breach of divine commands. Thus, it is often said, is the law established,* Christ was delivered to the law, and we are delivered from it, and now believing souls are married to Christ, and are no more under the malediction of it.† God's grace numbereth the saints as Christ's seed, bindeth all in the same contract, and accepteth man and wife as one in a law sense, so that the wife shines in the rays of her husband's beauty.‡ Divines illustrate it by the similitude of a wall that is green either by the colour inherent, or else by the same colour in some diaphanous transparent body, as glass, through which the sun shining doth affect it with that colour; thus, in the latter sense, Christ's righteousness presents us in his own colour to the Father: so that word is to be understood, Matt. iii. 17, " This is my beloved Son, in whom," not in whom as *with his person only*, but " in whom I am well pleased;" that is, through his merits and mediation I accept of and delight in all that believe, and come unto me by him. O astonishing contrivance of free grace! we cannot well conceive, nor sufficiently admire the wisdom of God in laying this blessed plan and platform for our redemption; rich grace and profound wisdom seem to vie with each other in this glorious fabric. If every man, saith one, were as wise as an angel, and every angel a seraph, (a flame burning with the fervour of divine love, and reflecting the celestial light of knowledge) they could never have found out such an expedient to reconcile God and man; the very angels themselves admire it, and would willingly be-

---

* Rom. iii. 31. viii. 2—4.   † Rom. vii. 4, 6.
‡ Uxor fulget radiis mariti.

come scholars to the church, to understand more of the height and depth of this glorious mystery;* but this shall never be rightly understood till believers, face to face, see him who devised and effected this work, and their faculties be enlarged to take in more of God's grace and wisdom.

2. Another consequence is this, if the mercies of the covenant be made sure in Christ, it lets us see the great difference betwixt covenant mercies and common mercies, temporal and spiritual mercies. Saul's mercies that God took away, and the sure mercies of David founded upon the covenant of grace, 1 Chron. xvii. 13, discover their difference principally in these four particulars.

(1.) They differ in the fountain, origin, and rise thereof, or in the affection of the giver. Outward mercies proceed from common bounty, these gospel mercies from special grace; the former from general munificence, the other from peculiar benevolence; the former are but crumbs for dogs, these are bread for babes, all things come alike to all, so that none can know love or or hatred by the want or abundance of creature comforts, but the mercies of the covenant are always tokens of special affection.† Luther calls the whole Turkish empire but " a morsel cast to dogs," but a portion of grace is a child's patrimony. God hates the wicked though he give them the world; he loves the godly, though he deny them worldly enjoyments; ‡ he may give that to his enemies in anger which he denies his children in love; he gives to many wicked, giftless gifts, as some call them; but he gives his grace, his heart, himself, to his saints with covenant mercies. These are always clear evidences of special

* 1 Pet. i. 12. Eph. iii. 10. † See Eccles. ix. 1—3.
‡ Deus sæpe dat iratus quod negat propitius.

love; they are bracelets and jewels that are sent as love tokens to the espoused saint from the celestial husband.

(2.) They differ in the dimensions of the gifts, their nature, properties and adaptedness to the precious and immortal soul. Temporal mercies may, indeed, supply the outward man, the clothes cover nakedness, fire may warm, meat may fill, and drink may quench thirst, but all these serve but to supply corporeal necessities; they do not reach the soul—he was a fool that said, " soul, thou hast much goods laid up for many years, take thine ease, eat, drink and be merry;"* and well might he be called a fool, for alas, what were those goods to the soul? it was a sensual, brutish soul that could be satisfied with these things; they bear no proportion to the nature of the immortal, heaven-born soul, it is above them, and when it comes to itself, scorns to feed on such refuse or wind. It is recorded of Pasotes, that he called his friends to a banquet, where they should see a table furnished with variety and plenty, but that when the guests went to eat, it vanished away into nothing, and truly so will worldly enjoyments, they promise fair and perform nothing; not but that these are useful mercies in their kind, and do attain their end, which was to accommodate the outward man, though they were never designed to satisfy souls, but covenant mercies fill and feast the soul; pardon of sin, sense of God's love, Jesus Christ, and the benefits flowing from him, these are adequate to the nature and faculties of precious souls. " These satiate the souls both of priests and people with fatness and goodness;† yea, they are abundantly satisfied with the fatness of his house," ‡ this living bread and water nourisheth immortal souls to eternal life; hence it is, that holy

* Luke xii. 19, 20. † Jer. xxxi. 14. ‡ Psalm xxxvi. 8.

David prays, Psalm xl. 11, " —— withhold not thy tender mercies from me, O Lord;" as if he had said, Lord, my soul is a fine delicate thing, it cannot do with the coarse fare of common mercies ; these husks are for the swine of the world, I must have bread at " my Father's table," my soul must have " angels' food," or it will not like nor live: Lord, let me have tender mercies, for my tender soul: otherwise I shall famish and die, therefore he prays again, " Let thy tender mercies come unto me that I may live," Psalm cxix. 77, and again, verse 132, " Look upon me and be merciful, as thou used to do to those that love thy name." David will not be content with any mercies but saints' peculiar privileges, and such as accompany salvation. These, these only fit and fill, suit and satisfy the ardent desires of the immortal soul, but other things cannot; for you may as soon fill a sack with wit, as a soul with wealth. Covenant mercies are only proper for immortal souls.

(3.) They differ in their efficacy and operation, in the effects and impressions they leave upon the heart; common mercies never make any better, but many worse. Covenant mercies always improve the subject with whom they lodge abundance ; common mercies can no more sanctify, than they can satisfy; a large share of the things of the world hath been a snare to many souls; these things are apt to puff up with pride, to steal the heart from God, to beget carnal confidence and security, which prove the bane of grace, and a bait to sin. They that have tried it, find that it is hard to have worldly honour without vain glory,* to have great estates without a covetous desire, and to swim in worldly pleasures without too much sensual delight. Oh the sad demonstrations we have

* Difficile est esse in honore sine tumore.—*Bern.*

had of the truth of this! How may the souls of thousands sadly say, the world hath undone them! Its syren songs have bewitched the credulous, and unwary; the world oftentimes proves a stumbling-block of iniquity that obstructs men in their journey to heaven, and blinds their eyes that they cannot make divine discoveries; even believers have found, by sad experiment, that outward enjoyments have had a malignant influence upon their spirits; they were in a better frame when they were poor, than they have been since raised in the world—according to that distich,

> Pellitus nunc es, fueras sine veste retentus,
> Nudus eras purus, crimen amictus habes.

Well, this is the too, too common effect of common mercies, but covenant mercies always make the soul better. Certainly, sanctifying knowledge, softening grace, the spirit of faith and holiness leave the soul in a gracious frame; and the privileges of the covenant, reconciliation with God, adoption, justification, assurance, communion with God, always work kindly and evangelically upon the heart; these are so many silver and silken cords of love to draw and join the soul to God. These mercies are as coals of fire to melt the heart, and make the conscience supple and pliable to the will of God; he cannot be a wicked man who hath these mercies, and he that hath most of these mercies, is the best; our perfection consists in the possession and participation of these sure mercies of David.* Outward mercies are occasions of ripening the sins of the wicked and fitting them for hell; but covenant mercies ripen saints for glory, by filling their souls with

* Dives qui multa possidet, auro onustus ut sordidum marsupium, at qui justus est, bene compositus est et decorus.—*Clem. Alex. Pædag.*

grace, and filling them for God's use both here and hereafter.

(4.) Common mercies and covenant mercies differ in their duration and continuance; and this is that which is discriminating in this passage—they are called sure mercies, in opposition to those uncertain riches, " that take to themselves wings and fly away; alas the fashion of the world passeth away!" * Earthly enjoyments are but of a short continuance—at death they and we must part, but many times they leave us before we leave them, the dreadful example of many thousands in London, in the late astonishing burning, confirms this— they were very rich, and very poor, in a few hours; many worth thousands in the morning, but before night had not a house to put their heads in. Our eyes have seen and ears have heard how suddenly vast estates have been plucked out of the hands of the securest possessors; a night may put an end to the rich fool's confident boasting. No man is rich who cannot carry away with him that which he hath. † What we must leave behind us is not ours, but some others; and this is the certain end of these uncertain enjoyments—that lose them we must, and we know not when nor how; and what a condition will a poor worldling be in, when his god and he must be parted! But now these mercies of the covenant are lasting, yea, everlasting mercies—they continue even beyond this transitory life, and run parallel with the life of God, and the line of eternity—eternal life is in the rear of spiritual life; grace ends in glory; yea, an immortal crown is one of the mercies of this sure covenant. These form a treasure that is neither subject to inward decays nor out-

* 1 Tim. vi. 7. 1 Cor. vii. 31.

† Nemo dives est, qui, quod habet, secum hinc auferre non potest.—*Ambros.*

ward violence, "no moth can corrupt it, nor thief steal it."—Matt. vi. 19, 20.

Well, then, since this is the vast difference betwixt common and covenant mercies, why should we make so great account of the former, and so little of the latter? What need have we to advance our hearts and eyes to things that are not seen with bodily eyes, and not dote upon things that are seen?* Our souls should decide with brave Luther,† who said, "I earnestly protested I would not be put off with these things." Alas, what poor things are outward enjoyments! Consider the differences mentioned. God may hate you though you abound with worldly comforts, but covenant mercies are infallible tokens of God's love. The former gifts are not suitable and satisfying to the soul, the latter are; outward mercies will make you no better in the eyes of God or good men, but spiritual will render you truly good. The world will take its sudden farewell of you and fail you at your greatest need; covenant mercies will stand by you while you live, and bring you blameless before the divine throne in eternal glory; here will come in that usual distinction of *bona throni* and *bona scabelli*. It is these covenant mercies that are the good things of the throne; outward mercies are but the good things of the footstool. Let heaven-born souls mount up to the mercies of the throne, but let the moon and all sublunary enjoyments be under their feet;; the whole world is too little for the godly man—not but that we should be thankful for the least common mercy: but we should not be put off with the greatest—a little of the world should content a Christian with God—all the world should not content him without God. O how sweet are common

* 2 Cor. iv. 18.
† Valde protestatus sum me istis non satiari.

mercies when they come to us in a covenant way! a morsel coming from the hands of Christ as our mediator, hath a delicate relish; his mediation only takes away the poison, venom, and malignity, that guilt hath brought upon the creature, and reduceth all things to their pristine usefulness, and primitive perfection. O the happiness of the saints! they have all they do enjoy as so many tokens of love; as it is said of the kiss of Cyrus, given to Chrysantas, that it was better than the costly cup of gold which he gave to Artabarus. So common mercies perfumed with covenant love, are transcendently better than the richest treasures of wretched worldlings.

3. Another inference is this, if covenant mercies be thus sure, then it instructs us in the precedency of grace above gifts.* There are gifts of illumination, conviction, interpretation, elocution, prayer, prophecy, which are given for the church's edification; the main difference betwixt gifts and grace is that the former may languish, vanish and utterly perish, but grace never totally and finally decays. God may give Saul a spirit of government, Judas a gift of preaching and miracles, Simon Magus a temporary faith, and yet repent him of these and pluck them quite away. He may, and often doth, dry up the right arm of an idol, idle shepherd, and darken his right eye of knowledge, Zech. xi. 17, so that he who improves not talents or gifts, " from him shall be taken away that which he hath," even real gifts and appearances of grace: per-

---

* Gifts come upon other terms than grace, God gives grace as a freehold, it hath the promise of this and another world, but gifts come upon liking, though a father will not cast off his child, yet he may take away his fine coat, and ornaments, if he be proud of them.—*Mr. Gurnal. Christ. Armour.* Matt. xxv. 29. Luke viii. 18.

sons eminently gifted, may be fire-brands of hell. Men may fall from the brightest intellectual attainments, to brutish sensuality; but the gifts and callings of saving grace are without repentance; " God loveth his own to the end," gracious habits shall not be lost. The apostle elegantly expresseth the difference to my hand, 1 Cor. xiii. 8. " Charity," that is, saving grace, " never faileth, but whether there be prophecies, they shall fail; whether there be tongues, they shall cease ; whether there be knowledge, it shall vanish away." I know the main intent of the place is to commend love above other saving graces, from the duration and perpetuity of it, that it shall continue and be of use in heaven; yet here it is opposed to such gifts as may also be lost in this life—and, therefore, by consequence it will follow, that the one is separable from its subject, the other not. Natural men may make a fair show and flourish with fine gifts, which are, as it were, the trimming and ornament of grace; which, yet may, through negligence or old age decay and wither, true grace may be accompanied with the gildings and varnish of gifts, which may, in time, wear off, whilst a sound principle continues fresh and lively. Besides this, give me leave to add other four differences betwixt common gifts and saving graces.

(1.) They differ in respect of their fountain and spring, the origin from whence they flow. " Gifts," as one saith, " come from God's treasury of bounty, grace proceeds from the choice cabinet of his love." Grace flows to believers through the blood of Christ from God's bowels of tender love, gifts proceed from the hand of God as an act of munificence, upon his Son's glorious ascension and complete inauguration.* It is one thing to eat meat at the king's table, and another

* Ephes. iv. 7.

thing to gather the fruits of royal grace upon some solemn day, as that was of David's, 2 Sam. vi. 19. Saints only have the covenant graces, hypocrites may have a large share in these gifts, nay a larger portion than some saints themselves. Saul, Balaam, Caiphas, may have the gift of prophecy; Judas may preach, but only Thomas and those who are under the influence of grace, can believe, and it is a greater work, saith Luther, to believe, than to work miracles.*

(2.) They differ in their nature and manner of operation. Covenant grace stamps on the soul the image of our heavenly Father, it is the divine nature, God's most curious workmanship, the form and portraiture, the representation and exemplar of God blessed for ever; grace is God's picture, if I may so speak, drawn to the life; it is a forming of Christ in the soul. Now gifts are no such thing—the devil himself hath great gifts, yet hath razed out the image of God; gifts are but the works of God's power and wisdom, such as the sun and stars; yea, even flies and atoms, they are in a sort dead, and we may call them God's lumber; some have noted that gifts are only the effects, but graces are called the fruits of the Spirit; † the one is husk of a common profession, at least, the shell of some rare endowments, but the other is the kernel of sincerity, and fruit of a gospel conversion.

(3.) They differ in their train and retinue, as to gifts none have all, either of all sorts, or any great eminency in all; hence it is said, 1 Cor. xii. 8, 9. " —— to one is given the word of wisdom, to another, knowledge," &c. Moses had a gift of government, not of eloquence; Paul had a gift of planting, Apollos of watering; some of the apostles were sons of thunder, others of consola-

* Præstat credere quàm miracula edere.
† 1 Cor. xii. 11. Gal. v. 22.

tion; some ministers are fitter for opening Scriptures and clearing controversies—others are more for exhortation and conviction of the conscience; some think that pastors and teachers differ with respect to their gifts. But these covenant graces and mercies are linked together, they dance their round in the believing soul, hand in hand, as the word signifies,* 2 Peter i. 5. One grace strengthens another, as stones do in an arch; yea, all graces are radically in faith—some, indeed, have said, that every grace is but faith exercised; however, all graces are infused at once into the soul, though some get the lead as to exercise—the new man is perfect with a perfection of parts, though not of degrees, as it is with a new-born child.

(4.) Gifts and grace differ in their several designs, ends, and effects. Gifts, offices and privileges, are but for others' advantage, and edification; they are given to profit withal.—1 Cor. xii. 7. When Christ ascended, he gave gifts to men—for what end? The apostle tells us " for the perfecting of the saints, for the work of the ministry, for the edifying of the body of Christ, Ephes. iv. 8—12. But now the end of grace is the soul's spiritual advantage, that by it Christ may take possession of the heart, that the soul may have some life and principle of opposition to beloved corruptions, and thereby be better helped to perform religious duties, walk with God, improve privileges, and be made meet for heaven. These, and such as these, are the ends of the graces of the covenant. A man may have rare gifts, yet have a base heart; he may have singular endowments, and yet not be helped thereby, to mortify one lust, perform one duty spiritually, or get one step nearer God: but covenant grace is profitable for those great ends and uses; gifts and grace may be said to differ as the sun and moon; the moon casts a light,

* Ἐπιχορηγήσατε.

indeed, but no heat—but the sun sheds his quickening rays into this lower world—he quickens many things, and maketh all things verdant and fruitful. So doth covenant mercy bring forth many precious things, and divine graces have a lively influence, whereby a man shall both save himself and others, 1 Tim. iv. 16; but a man may have gifts like an angel, and be never the nearer to heaven; he may direct others in the way to heaven, and yet not walk a step therein; he may teach others what he hath not learned himself; he may preach to others and be a castaway. * It is one thing to have the form of knowledge, another to have the power of grace; it is one thing to have angelical gifts, and another thing to have evangelical graces. All gifted persons are not gracious persons; never was any man saved by his gifts, and rarely have they, who have only gifts, been instruments to save others. I dare not say, that it is impossible that a graceless, yet gifted minister, should be a mean of conversion, for God is not to be limited, but it is not ordinary, as common experience testifies.

4. An additional inference is, if covenant mercies be thus sure, then it lets us see the truth of our religion. If the mercies thereof be thus sure, as I have demonstrated, then let us be established in our persuasion of the verity, certainty and infallibility of Christianity; if these be sure mercies, who can doubt of the reality thereof? Every thing in the gospel is made sure, and you may venture your souls upon it; since God hath confirmed these things as a sacred oracle from heaven, who dare dispute them? The God of truth cannot lie nor deny himself; he is so good that he cannot deceive, and so wise that he cannot be deceived. † There is in

* See fully in Rom. ii. 17—24. 1 Cor. ix. 27.

† Divino præcepto intonante obediendum est non disputandum. *Aug.*

him neither imprudence in promising, nor inability in performing. " Heaven and earth may pass away, but not one iota of his word shall fail." You are to believe these things without hesitation, and give your full assent to them ; as the mystery of godliness is great, so it is without controversy. Grotius * observes that our Christian religion doth transcend all the religions in the world in three things. First, " in the certainty of its maxims ;" secondly, " in the spirituality of its precepts ;" thirdly, " in the transcendency of its rewards." We have the unerring testimony of heaven for what we believe; which is surer than any logical conclusions, philosophical speculations, yea, or mathematical demonstrations, and I may add, than Old Testament dreams and visions ; so the apostle seems to extol God's speaking to us by his Son above the divers manners of his speaking to the Fathers, Heb. i. 1, 2 ; nay, the apostle Peter asserts that we have in the Scriptures a more sure word of prophecy, than that voice which came to Christ in the holy mount, from the excellent glory, 2 Pet. i. 18, 19 ; not that any thing can be more sure than the very undoubted words of Jehovah, who is truth itself; but a more sure, that is, most sure, a comparative for a superlative, for the former visions being from God, as well as the prophecies, were themselves as sure as they ; but the meaning is, that the Scripture testimony is more sure than that vision, employed as an argument to convince others, or *secundum nos*, for the authority of the Scriptures is beyond the testimony of angels ; nay, above the credit that

* Aut hæc admittenda religio, non tantum ob factorum testimonia, de quibus jam egimus, verum etiam ob ea, quæ religioni sunt intrinseca: cum nulla ex omnibus sæculis ac nationibus proferri potest ; aut præmio excellentior, præceptis perfectior, aut modo quo propagari jussa est admirabilior.—*Hug. Grot. de Veritat. Relig. Christ. lib.* 2, *cap.* 8, *p.* 52. John ix. 32. Acts xxvi. 22, 23. Acts xvii. 11.

might be given to men, for men might suspect Peter and the other apostles, as though this apparition were but a fiction of their own brains—therefore, he appeals to the undoubted prophecies in the Old Testament, which were by long use settled in the hearts of the godly Jews, who believed all that the prophets spake as coming from God; therefore our Saviour declares that they that believe not Moses's writings, will not believe his words, John v. 45—47, and hence it was that they examined doctrines by the prophets; nay our Saviour himself, affirms, " that if they will not hear Moses and the prophets, neither will they be persuaded though one rise from the dead, Luke xvi. 31, therefore, the apostles had the prophets as patrons of their doctrine, and thence did the faithful fetch a confirmation of the gospel.* The sum of this text is, then, to demonstrate the verity and certainty of the gospel by evidencing the consent of prophetical and apostolical testimony for its fuller confirmation; as if he had said, if you distrust me in commending the evangelical doctrine, I send you back to the prophets, whom, without any exception, you account holy and faithful. These testify of the truth of the gospel, therefore this consent should be evincing and satisfying. Hence it is, that the disciples of Christ have professed such a plerophory, † and abundant acquiescence in their persuasion of Christ's being the Messiah and Saviour of mankind; so John vi. 69, " We believe and are sure that thou art that Christ, the Son of the living God;" and Simon Peter acknowledged it, Matt. xvi. 16; yea, unbelieving Thomas at last cried out " My Lord, and my God," John xx. 28, as being overcome with the

* Habebant apostoli prōphetas tanquam patronos doctrinæ suæ; fideles quoque inde petebant evangelii confirmationem.—*Calv. in loc. Vide sis Mart. Arct. et cætera in Locum.*

† Full assurance.

clearness of that stupendous, condescending demonstration; the apostle John testifies, 1 Epist. i. 1, concerning Christ, saying, "We have heard, seen with our eyes, looked upon, yea, our hands have handled of the word of life;" and this doth he declare to us from experience of several senses. O what a blessed thing were it to have an undoubted assurance of the certainty of divine things! O what life would it put into our graces, duties and comforts! what an antidote would it be against temptations, corruptions and persecutions! Could we as truly believe the reality of the things of God as corporeal objects, what beauty should we discern therein! what comfort should we receive therefrom! what should we not do and endure for them! Did we see the reality, necessity, and excellency of covenant mercies as we do of common mercies, how should our hearts be enamoured therewith? They that have the most prevailing persuasion of the certainty and transcendency of heavenly mercies, are the most exact and eminent Christians; but a faint belief of these things is the cause of sloth; all irreligion and prophaneness proceeds from a want of an effectual assent to gospel revelations. Alas, there is more atheism and infidelity in the world than we are aware of. Did men as certainly believe there is a heaven and a hell, as they see and know there are stones and trees, earth and water, would not this have a wonderful influence upon their practice? would they not be other manner of persons than they are? especially if they did faithfully work upon their hearts the reality of the things of God. Paul and the saints in his days looked not on the things seen, but on things not seen, that is, eternal things, 2 Cor. iv. 18. Moses saw him that was invisible, which made him to endure any thing.—Heb. xi. 27. O Christians, rest not satisfied with a bare conjecture, but press forward till you arrive at a full assurance, you cannot be too sure in these cases. The apostle hath a mighty full expression, Col. ii. 2, to this purpose; verse 1, he tells of " a conflict that he had for them, and the Laodiceans," that is, a care, fear, and desire; good man, he was in a heart-rending conflict, an agony. Why, what is the matter? well, " it is that their hearts might be comforted, being knit together in love, and to all riches of the full assurance of understanding, to the acknowledgment of the mystery of God, and of the Father, and of Christ." Observe the climax, here is,

(1.) Assurance he desires for them; then,

(2.) Full assurance; further,

(3.) Riches of full assurance; yet again,

(4.) All riches of full assurance; yea, not a rash and ignorant assurance, but an assurance,

(5.) Of understanding, that is, with a settled judgment, and not only to have such assurance, and keep it to themselves, but all this

(6.) To the acknowledgment of the mystery of God, that they may make an open profession of it.

But why was he so earnest for all this, verse 4, " This I say, or pray for you, lest any man beguile you with enticing words," as if he had said, you will find all this little enough when a subtle disputer shall set upon you with cunning artifice to draw you from the truth; you will perhaps feel that you have need of the fullest persuasion that creatures can arrive at, that you may keep your hold, and not be driven away from the hope of the gospel. You little know what storms may assault your faith in the truth of the gospel. Peter made a glorious profession, yet his faith was staggered by a temptation; and Satan is a cunning sophister—he desires to have you that he may sift you, and toss you so as to shake away the purest grain of gospel truth ; he will do what he can to cheat you of your religion ; hence it is, that " Paul was so jealous over the Corinthians with godly jealousy,—— lest by any means, (and he hath store of devices) that as the serpent beguiled Eve through his subtilty ; so their minds should be corrupted from the simplicity that is in Christ."—2 Cor. xi. 1—3. Hence it is, that teachers have always been so careful to settle and ground their hearers in the certainty of things they taught, as Luke his Theophilus, and Paul his Timothy.* O sirs, get well assured of these things ! Let your faith and persuasion have its full dimensions ; let it be deeply rooted, and high built ; take not things upon trust— let every truth have its complete emphasis and efficacy upon your hearts and consciences, especially the main momentous gospel truths, which you must venture your souls upon, and live and die by. You had need consider what ground you stand upon, and be fully persuaded in your own minds.

CHAP. VIII.

THE SURE MERCIES OF DAVID FURNISH MATERIALS FOR SELF-EXAMINATION.

III. A further use may be suggested, namely, to try us whether we have a real interest in these sure mercies of the covenant ; it is one of the most important questions that we can be asked, whether we have a right title to covenant mercies ? Alas, we have for-

* Luke i. 3, 4. 2 Tim. iii. 14.

feited our title to God, or to any good thing from him, by our breach of the old covenant, and now we have nothing to do with God, except only to endure the severe strokes of his sin-revenging justice. O what need have we to try ourselves by an impartial scrutiny! For our better assistance in this great and weighty business, I shall a little explain what it is to enter into covenant in general, next inquire what conditions of the new covenant we can find in our hearts, and then shew a little of the nature and effects of these covenant mercies where they exist.

For the first, to enter into covenant with God is to own God as our God, and to give up ourselves wholly to him as his; expressed in these words in Scripture, " I will be thy God and thou shalt be my people"— this, this is the marrow of the covenant, for God to be our God—it is a comprehensive word; it is *substantia fœderis*, as Funius calls it; *anima fœderis*, as Pareus calls it; *caput fœderis*, as Musail—the substance, soul, and head of the covenant; the life of religion is in this: as one saith sweetly, the goodness of duties lies in adverbs, and the sweetness of the covenant lies in possessives.

Well then, the contracting of this covenant betwixt God and a soul consists chiefly in a mutual surrender, or giving up of themselves to each other, expressed in Scripture by a matrimonial contract, when God gives up himself to the believer, and accepts of him, and the believer accepts of God as his God, and gives up himself to him. Now, we are not left to inquire after the act of God, for it is fully expressed in the Scriptures, and it is certainly supposed God accepts the sinner, when the sinner accepts of God, for these are correlatives, nor is there any change in God, the change is only in the sinner, who is now put into a new state and relation. It is certain by the free offers of the gospel, that God doth consent, and the main thing to be inquired into is, whether the soul do consent or not? for if it cordially do, the agreement is made, God and the soul are united, which is a thing of the greatest importance in the whole world. I shall purposely wave controversies in this business wherein this consent lies, whether it be only an assent as an act of the understanding, or be a choice as an act of the will, &c. I conceive it is an act of the whole soul, whereby a poor troubled sinner discovering its forlorn estate by its breach of the old covenant, and sad consequences thereof, and discerning a possibility of a recovery and the way of reconciliation by a new covenant formed and contracted betwixt God and fallen man, sealed and confirmed by the blood of the Mediator, God-man, doth freely, cordially, and decidedly accept of God as his chief good and ultimate end, and give up himself to him resolvedly, unreservedly, and universally, to be the Lord's; to be and do what the Lord pleaseth, to obey divine commands, be at God's disposal in life and death, and thus to continue even to the end of his days.

This is for a soul to enter into covenant with the Lord. The trial will lie in these two things: first, whether we have accepted of God as our God? secondly, whether we have given up ourselves to him, to be at his disposal, yea or no? a little on both these.

1. Whether have you taken the Lord to be yours, or not? We are all naturally idolaters and have our hearts glued to the creature, or something else besides God; we are of those many, who cry out, " who will shew us any good?" who trace the whole creation to find satisfaction, till they are weary, and sit down in despair of obtaining what they seek, for all the crea-

* See Mr. Baxt. Saints' Rest, part 1. p. 177, 178.

tures are forced to echo this unanimous confession, Happiness is not in me. Thus, like Hagar,* we wander in this howling wilderness, till the water of hope be spent in the bottle, and our souls, like Ishmael, be ready to perish under the shrubs of guilt and wrath, and then we sit down in sorrow, ready to pine away in our iniquities, loth to see or think of our own damnation, lifting up our voice with bitter weeping and despair. God hears and asks the troubled soul what it ails, and amidst these confusions he creates a blessed spring of hope in this desert state; opens the eyes, enraptures the heart with the glory of gospel grace, draws water of life out of the wells of salvation, and satisfieth the hungry soul with good things; the ransomed sinner is made to own that God thus owns him in a time of need, and to cry out with repenting Israel, " Once, O Lord our God, other lords besides thee have had dominion over us, but by thee only will we make mention of thy name," Isa. xxvi. 13 ; or with David, " Whom have I in heaven but thee? and there is none upon earth that I desire besides thee. My flesh and my heart faileth, but God is the strength of my heart and my portion for ever," Psalm lxxiii. 25, 26 ; as if the poor soul should say, I have been long seeking contentment here below, but I see by sad experience, all things fail, there is vanity and vexation written upon the sweetest comforts under the moon; I have laid out much labour for that which profits not; I am weary with my disappointments, I will return to my first husband; return unto thy rest, O my soul! God alone is the most, yea, the only, suitable satisfying rest of my wandering and bewildered soul. Let others go a whoring from God to creature dependencies —it is good for me to draw nigh to God ; I am undone

* Gen. xxi. 15—19.

without him; I am sick of love for him. Woe is me, what shall I do? If my soul get not an interest in God I faint, I die, I perish. Lord, put me not off without thyself, let nothing take up my heart besides thee;" let all the pleasures, profits and honours of the world go whither they will, so only I may have my God, I can set God against them all, if God be the portion of mine inheritance, I can say truly, " the lines are fallen to me in pleasant places, I have a goodly heritage,"* I can bid defiance to all the world to make me miserable; when all the world looks black about me, and all my comforts forsake me, when seeming friends scorn me, and open enemies pursue me with cruel hatred; I can then encourage myself in the Lord my God; yea, rejoice in the Lord; should even the whole creation crack about my ears, the earth tremble, and the heavens be rolled together as a scroll; I know that my Redeemer lives and I shall live with him in joy and blessedness for ever. These, or the like, are the musings of the humble, sensible sinner, and though he cannot say the Lord is his, yet, he can say through grace, that it is the desire of his soul to have the Lord for his God, he looks upon that as the happiest estate that a creature is capable of, and if God should say this house or land, and these goods, or this kingdom, or this world, are thine, except he say withal, I am thine, the soul goes away disconsolate, and looks on all those things as nothing worth.

Christians, try yourselves, hath it been thus with you, or hath it not? What settled, prevailing esteem hath the God of heaven in your hearts? Do you look upon all the bravery and delights of the world but as straw and mire under your feet in comparison of your God? Do your hearts pant after the living God? Do

* Psalm xvi. 5, 6.

your souls desire him in the night? Can you boast of your God, and challenge all the world, and say, there is none like unto our God? Can you depend upon him, and cast all your care on him? Do you, in all things, give him the preeminence? Are your hearts endeared to, and enamoured with this glorious, gracious God? But,

I proceed to ask, have you given yourselves up to him? for if you be the Lord's you are not your own, you have wholly resigned up yourselves to him;* you have given him the keys of your hearts, and delivered him possession of your souls, as the only rightful owner thereof; just as the wife gives up her all to her husband, so that " she hath not power of her own body, but her husband;"† so do believers surrender themselves unto the spiritual husband of the church, so that now they have nothing to dispose of without leave; house, land, money, estates, relations, name, time, gifts of mind, members of the body, faculties of soul, life itself, and all they have and do are at God's disposal, and they lay them all at his feet, and dare not dispose of one penny in their purse, or minute of time, or cast of the eye, or thought of the heart, with their good will, but by his permission. Hence, you will hear a believer inquiring with respect to sin and duty, and making conscience of compliance with the Lord's will and pleasure. The Scripture calls this a giving ourselves to the Lord, 2 Cor. viii. 5; yea, there are several outward symbols to evidence it, Isa. xliv. 5, " One shall say I am the Lord's, and another shall call himself by the name of Jacob, and another shall subscribe with his hand to the Lord, and surname himself by the name of Israel." Profession, subscription, denomination, nay, though it be to endure the scorn of

* 1 Cor. vi. 19. † 1 Cor. vii. 4.

a reproachful name, any thing would he do, or undergo, so he might be ranked amongst real saints, and be indeed the Lord's.

And there are four properties of the soul's self-surrender to God. A covenanting soul gives up itself to God these four ways, that is to say,

Really, readily, resolvedly and unreservedly.

(1.) Really, truly, sincerely, without the ordinary, counterfeiting and complimenting expressions common in the world. It is easy, as it is customary, for men to court others with that empty ceremony, Your servant, sir, when they never think as they speak. This, by the way, is to be ranked, at least, among idle words, of which, I fear, many have a sad account to give. Let professors learn better manners and language than to conform herein to the world; well, but a saint's giving up himself to the Lord, is not complimental, but real. Hear holy David, you shall find him in good earnest, Psal. cxvi. 16, " O Lord, truly I am thy servant; I am thy servant, and the son of thine handmaid, thou hast loosed my bonds." Here is,

[i.] An asseveration, " truly."

[ii.] An affirmation, " I am thine."

[iii.] A reduplication, " I am thy servant, I am thy servant."

[iv.] A confirmation by two arguments.

First, " He was his servant by his birth, being born in his house," for if a woman was servant in a house, all the children she bore there were servants to the master of that house. Hence, saith David, " the son of thine handmaid.

Secondly, David was God's by redemption, " thou hast loosed my bonds," for such as delivered any from captivity, had them to be their servants for ever. Thus every genuine believer really professeth himself to be the

Lord's, he is God's bought and devoted servant, he doth, as the servant of old, plainly say, " I love my master, I will not go out," and so is brought to the door-post, and hath his ear bored through with an awl, he receives an ear mark, being subjected to the operation of the blessed Spirit of God, and so made willing and obedient to the Lord's calls.* This engageth him to be much in desiring to know the Lord's will with a resolution to do it; he stops not his ear, he hides not his eyes from his master's commands, but prays as David, Psalm cxix. 125, " I am thy servant, give me understanding, that I may know thy testimonies;" a good man would not be ignorant of any part of his work, because he is a real servant, and makes conscience of upright obedience. Ah sirs, what say your hearts to this? are you in good earnest? do you, indeed, speak as you think, and will you do accordingly? It is no jesting, trifling matter. Israel gave God good words; so that God saith, they have well spoken, when they promised to he the Lord's and to obey him, but God adds, " O that there were such a heart in them that they would fear me," &c.—Deut. v. 28, 29. Alas, persons may say fair, in a glow of affection, but inquire you into the frame of your spirits and actions whether they be of a genuine description.

(2.) This self-surrender to God is ready, free, willing, and cheerful, not with grumbling, and by compulsion. When persons do it because they cannot help it, when they see they must die, and can serve the devil no longer, or when they are under the rod, they will assume the appearance of being religious; but it is full sore against their wills, for they would rather choose to be slaves to their passions. They are, however, forced on by violence or constraint, or else they lie under such

* See Exod. xxi. 5—6.

terrors and convictions, that for the present they are overawed, and dare not but profess to be the Lord's. It is strangers that yield feigned or forced obedience to our David. * But the Lord's true hearted subjects shall be a willing people in the day of his power, Psalm cx. 3, voluntariness or liberalities, so the word signifies: they are all volunteers, and look upon it as their privilege, honour and happiness to be the Lord's servants, as the good emperor Theodosius, who accounted it a greater honour to be the subject of Christ, than to be emperor of the world. Real Christians are like the governors of Israel, † that offered themselves willingly among the people; these have God's heart, since the Lord hath their heart. Those in Acts ii. 41, gladly received the word, and so were baptized; every child of God is a free-will offering, and presents his soul and body as a living sacrifice, ‡ or *holocaust*, and this is acceptable to God. O the account that God makes of these! they are called princes of the people. In Psalm xlvii. 9, the margin hath it, the voluntary of the people; ǁ the volunteers are princes, as indeed all God's saints are kings, and the church hath her princes in all the earth, § because they have power over their base stubborn wills, which is more than to rule over millions of men; they are persons of most noble, generous, and ingenuous spirits—others, are of a low, base, sordid, degenerate disposition, that have not subjected themselves to God, but are slaves to their lusts. Well, sirs, how is it with you? do you voluntarily, and cheerfully surrender yourselves to the Lord, as the bride doth in marriage? Are your hearts so gone after the Lord, as to look upon it as your greatest

---

* Psalm xviii. 44. See Marg.   † Judg. v. 9.   ‡ Rom. xii. 1.

ǁ נדיבי עמים ǁ   § Psal. xlv. 16.

preferment, to give yourselves up to him as the husband of the church? Have you seriously deliberated on things in your breasts; and upon mature thoughts concluded that this is the best engagement you can make? Doth your soul make you like " the chariots of Amminadib," * or a willing people? and the longer you serve this master, the better do you like this service? You do not repent that you gave up your names to him; if it were to do again, would you not do it, though you knew of ten thousand times more troubles in your way than yet you have met with? nay, do you not thank God heartily, that he will accept of your persons and services, and look upon his service as perfect freedom? Is it thus with you? Bless God that he hath shown you distinguishing favour.

(3.) The believer delivers up himself to God resolvedly. There are some that halt between two opinions, that are off and on; one while they will be for God, another while they are staggering like the Samaritans; when the Jews were in prosperity, they would profess to be of their stock—when in adversity, they disowned relation to them. These are a cake not turned, the one side baked for God, the other side dough, † so that one cannot tell what to make of them. God likes not these unfixed, unresolved spirits; but a real saint will attach himself to God whatever it cost him. Carnal friends, that go about to hinder him, say nothing effectual, he will make this agreement in spite of all opposition, they may set their hearts at rest; there is no dissuading him, for his affections are placed; no bonds can hold him, he cleaves to the Lord with full purpose of heart, he hath devoted himself to God's fear—there is no revocation; ‡ all the devils in hell, and men on

---

* Cant. vi. 12. † Hos. vii. 8.
‡ Acts xi. 23. Psalm cxix.

earth, shall not obstruct him in his course and progress to the Lord, " if my father hung about my neck," saith an ancient, " my wife and children stood in my way, to my dearly beloved, I would cast off my father, and push away my wife and my children that I may enjoy my Lord God." Offer a resolved soul, house, lands, pleasures, treasures, they all signify nothing if they be to hire him from Christ. " Let their money perish with them," said a noble Marquis, " that esteem all the money in the world worth one hour's communion with Jesus Christ." Consider Moses and Paul, the first forsook the pleasures of Pharaoh's court for Christ; the latter accounted not his life dear in the cause of Christ;* and, indeed, this is the great condition upon which only we can have an interest in him, Luke xiv. 26, " If any man come to me, and hate not his father, mother, wife, children, brethren, sisters, yea, and his own life also, he cannot be my disciple;" that is, when these stand in competition with Christ, or when he cannot keep both, " if he be not willing to part with these rather than want Christ, he is not worthy of him," as another evangelist hath it.† Ah sirs, how is it with you? are you at a point? do you hang no longer in suspense? will you receive Christ upon his own proposed terms? and will you receive him now, and not delay a moment longer? do you say that upon due considering your ways, " you make haste and will not delay, to give up yourselves to the Lord? are your feet shod with the preparation of the gospel of peace," that is, with a holy resolution to go through the sharpest paths to the beloved of your souls? You care not what befals you, so that this dreadful evil do not befal you to be without God in the world, and many waters of

* Heb. xi. 24, 25. Acts xx. 24. † Matt. x. 37.
‡ Psal. cxix. 59, 60. Eph. vi. 15.

opposition cannot quench this flame of love to your dearest Lord. Try yourselves by this criterion.

(4.) A gracious soul delivers up itself to God, unreservedly, entirely, and universally, and that both with reference to the subject, and the season; the whole soul, and that for ever, wholly and finally.

[i.] The whole soul is given up to God in this covenant agreement; here do hypocrites dodge, and article, and make reserves, and come not off fair, but leave some fort of the heart for an appetite or passion, and are not willing to give up themselves entirely; now God will have all the heart, or none at all—he will not brook a rival or competitor, " my son give me thy heart," and, indeed, the whole soul is a present little enough for the God of heaven; it is a whorish heart that is for dividing. A gracious soul saith, let him have all, as it cannot be content with half a Saviour, so it knows, God will not be content with half a heart, and therefore, cries out, Lord, here I am a poor worm, I have polluted myself with sin, and deserve not that ever thou shouldest own such a wretch as I am; yet, such as I am, I here offer myself wholly to thee. Alas, I am but a poor and sorry offering for so great a king, yet I freely give myself to thee, entreating thee to make me better; I cannot bestow myself on one that either hath more right to me, or can do more for me; here I am, Lord, I am only thine and wholly thine; take me as thine, and make me less mine own, and that will be my happiness, and I shall be fitter for thy service; I dare not part stakes betwixt thyself and any other, for I see, I cannot serve two contrary masters; I will not give my faculties or members any more as instruments of unrighteousness. Chain my soul to thee, unite my heart to fear thy name. This, or such like, is the language of a believing soul, and there can be no covenant without this entireness and complete resignation. Hence are those multitudes of expressions that call for " seeking God with the whole heart, and loving God with all the heart, soul, &c. and serving God with all the heart, * yea, this is the sum of all that God requires of us.—Deut. x. 12. O examine, then, hath the Spirit of God beat down every strong hold and vain imagination; and brought over your hearts wholly to the Lord? What say you, is every nook and creek of your hearts delivered up to this great and mighty conqueror? Is there no creature comfort, or sensual pleasure that hath stolen away your hearts from your divine Lord? Deal faithfully with your souls on this behalf, there is no dallying with the searcher of your hearts.

[ii.] Have you given up your hearts and selves irrevocably, irreversibly, finally? There is no playing fast and loose with the great God; you must not give and take again, that is fool's play; but you must be for ever the Lord's, all your days devote yourselves to keep his commandments unto the end, not like some servants that will keep to their masters as long as they like, or while they please them; but this is a boring through the ear to be the Lord's servants for ever; it is a marriage that lasts for the term of life, " I will call upon him," saith David, " as long as I live."—Psalm cxvi. 2. It is the hollow-hearted hypocrite that ends his religion before he have ended his days, that puts his hand to the plough and looks back, that falls off when tribulation comes; but a covenanting spirit is a constant spirit. " Whose house are we," saith the apostle, " if we hold fast the confidence, and the rejoicing of the hope firmly unto the end," Heb. iii. 6; it is the end that crowns the action. Solomon saith, " the end of a thing is better than the beginning." Christ saith,

* Deut. iv. 29, and vi. 5.

"if ye continue in my word, then are ye my disciples indeed," John viii. 31, and many Scriptures * make this a condition, without which, there can be no salvation; and though the end is not yet come, yet is it the desire and design of your souls to pray, and read, and serve God all your days? You do not, you dare not set bounds or limits to your obedience; but say as David, Psalm lxxi. 14, " I will hope continually, and will yet praise thee more and more," as if he had said, I am so far from casting away my hope and faith that I will continue, yea, and increase in the exercises of religion. Do you resolve with David, to " keep God's law continually, yea, for ever and ever," Psalm cxix. 44, and pray still for supporting grace, verse 117, using all the rest of God's appointed means for your perseverance to the end?

Thus I have dispatched this part of the examination, which is general, to try whether we be entered into covenant with God by reciprocal acts of giving and receiving; whether you have taken God for your God, and given up yourselves to him, as believers are wont to do.

More particularly, I entreat you to inquire into the conditions of the new covenant, or the graces and dispositions promised therein, and lay your hand on your heart, and inquire, whether they be really in you? such as these,

1. I told you saving illumination is one important covenant condition. † Hath the Lord discovered to you the great and good things of his gospel? opened to you his blessed treasury, and anointed your eyes to behold all things in their lively colours? Have you got a clear discovery of the nature of sin and duty, misery and mercy, the creatures' vanity and Christ's

* Col. i. 23. 1 Tim. iv. 16. Jam. i. 25. † Jer. xxxi. 34.

beauty and excellency? Have you with an eagle eye pierced into deep gospel mysteries? This is not a brain knowledge, consisting in notions, but an experimental spiritual acquaintance with the things of God, impressing the soul with the sense thereof, and leading it into the life and spirit of Scripture truths; so that a Christian now sees divine things after another manner than he ever did before, and is led into all truth by the blessed Spirit. God promiseth that "all the children of the church shall be taught of God," Isa. liv. 13, which Scripture our Saviour doth cite and interpret, John vi. 45, of believing or coming to God, "every one, therefore, that hath heard and learned of the Father, cometh unto me." Ah Christians, have you learned this choice gospel lesson of going out of yourselves, and closing with Christ, unconditionally, upon pure gospel terms? This is the great lesson of the gospel, have you learned it? You are dunces, and deserve to be kicked out of Christ's school, unless yeu have learned this great and important lesson; besides, God teacheth many other lessons, as to hate sin, love God, and holiness, and to love God's children. Hence saith blessed Paul, 1 Thess. iv. 9, " as touching brotherly love; ye need not that I write unto you, for ye yourselves are taught of God to love one another." This divine nature prompteth believers to this; they cannot do otherwise except they put off their very nature, for a Christian may find his heart secretly and sensibly carried out to all things and persons that have the impress and image of God, as the very name and the common nature of a brother is potent and prevalent to attract the affections: the truth is, he hath his chair in heaven who thus teacheth hearts—and if God be the teacher, he makes apt and able, active and notable scholars.* O Christians, see and try your learning, ascertain who is your master.

2. Another disposition like this, or indeed, a fruit of the former, is God's writing his law in the hearts of men, " he promiseth to put his law into their inward parts, and write it in their hearts," † so that as tally answers to tally, indenture to indenture, face to face, so the heart of the Christian will echo and answer to the word of God; and he will feel something within his own bosom, that joins issue with the word without; so that he can now say with Paul, I consent to the law that it is good; ‡ whatever I be, the commandment is holy, just, and good. A carnal heart riseth up in rebellion against the word, and secretly loathes a spiritual command, and could wish it even razed out of the Bible, that it might sin more freely; but a gracious soul loves that word best, which restrains corruption most, and binds it closest in new obedience; hence saith David, " thy word is very pure, therefore, thy servant loves it," Psalm cxix. 140; the stricter the word is, the better I love it; I would have the law of God restrain the exorbitancies of my heart and life, it doth me good to be kept in, for I have a wild and wayward heart. ‖ O how glad am I of a word that searcheth, curbeth, and cutteth off my exuberant branches, I willingly fall under it and bless God for it, as one of the greatest mercies of my life. Can you say thus? When

* Cathedram habet in cœlis qui corda docet; quando Deus est magister quàm cito docetur, quod docetur.—*Aug.*

† Jer. xxxi. 33. Heb. viii. 10. x. 16.

‡ Rom. vii. 12—16.

‖ Præsta ei cor tuum molle et tractabile et custodi figuram quâ te figuravit artifex, habens in temetipso humorem, ne induratus—amittas vestigia digitorum ejus.—*Iræn. advers. Hær. lib.* 4, *prop. fin.*

there is a controversy betwixt a pinching word and a repining lust, whether of them do you vote for? which do you give your voice for, and plead on the behalf of? Can you not take God's part, and his word's part, against a naughty, deceitful heart? or do you pick quarrels with the statutes of heaven when you should obey them? Ah sirs, try yourselves in this, and if you find that you have a counterpart of God's word within you, a transcript of this blessed copy in your hearts, then are you within the covenant.

3. God promiseth to give his people in covenant with him, " one heart and one way," Jer. xxxii. 39; this imports both a oneness of heart within itself, and also, a oneness of heart with other saints; before conversion the heart was divided and distracted betwixt various objects; God must have part, Satan part, sin part, and the world another part of the heart; but now the soul gives itself wholly to God, as I have explained; hence David prays, " unite my heart to fear thy name,"* or make my heart one; a real saint is fully, entirely, universally given up to God; but of this, I have spoken before: likewise the covenant of grace makes Christians unanimous; hence it is, that as soon as souls have given themselves to God, they essay to join themselves to their fraternity, and unite with the society of sincere believers; † hence the primitive saints " were together with one accord ;" ‡ yea, they were " of one heart, and of one soul ;" ‖ as the curtains of the tabernacle were coupled with loops, so were Christians with love; hence you hear so often mention made of fellowship in the gospel, and God's children are compared to a building fitly framed together, by

* Psalm lxxxvi. 11.   † Acts ix. 26.
‡ Acts ii. 46.   ‖ Acts iv. 32.

the cement of the Spirit;* yea, to members of the body, with relation to the head, † from whom, that is, Christ, the whole body is fitly joined together, and compacted.—Ephes. iv. 16. Well then, sirs, are you united and become one with the rest of the saints, though you cannot attain to a oneness in judgment in every lesser truth about discipline, &c. yet, are you one with them in heart and affection? yea, of one judgment and way with them, in main, material points of doctrine and practice, having " one Lord, one faith, one baptism, endeavouring to keep the unity of the Spirit in the bond of peace?" ‡ cannot you say to others, " come, let us join ourselves to the Lord in a perpetual covenant, that shall not be forgotten?" ǁ Are not your hearts glad when you see any come in, and worship the Lord? How stand your hearts affected towards such as fear God? Are you of one heart with them? can you cheerfully walk in one way with them as your dearest companions? is your chief content in these truly excellent ones? Then you are among the covenant people of God.

4. The fear of God, is a gracious disposition promised to new covenant converts, Jer. xxxii. 40, " I will," saith God," " put my fear in their hearts that they shall not depart from me." This fear of the Lord is the beginning of wisdom, § and it is often put for all religion: it is a holy, reverential awfulness wrought in a believer's heart, whereby through a serious sense of his glorious majesty, and tender mercy, the soul is afraid to offend God, and careful to please him, as a child is his father, by a conscientious obedience to all God's commands. I cannot stand to enlarge on this fully, but

* Phil. i. 5. Eph. ii. 21. † Col. ii. 19.
‡ Eph. iv. 3—5. ǁ Jer. l. 4, 5. § Job xxviii. 28.

will bring you to the test. Christians, doth the fear of God possess and seize upon your spirits? doth it make you "men of truth, hating covetousness?" doth it engage your souls to serve him "with reverence and godly fear?" doth it make you afraid of his threatenings, fearful to offend him, careful to please him? do you worship him "in his fear?" doth it make you run to him "as your hope and confidence?" are your souls in the fear of the Lord "all the day long?" doth the fear of God cast out the slavish fear of men? doth it make you work out your salvation with fear and trembling? doth it make you tremble at his word, and willing to obey the voice of his servants? doth it keep you humble and self-denying, instead of being proud and high-minded? do you fear God and give glory to him on seeing his works? in a word, do you fear God and work righteousness, fear God and hate wickedness? * Is it thus with your souls. Lay your hand upon your heart, and seriously answer these questions. I know you will all say you have the fear of God; but whether hath it these evidences? and, one word more, whence springs this fear of God? doth it flow not only from the apprehension of God's majesty and strict justice, but from the sense of his free grace and goodness? so God saith, in Hos. iii. 5, "they shall fear the Lord and his goodness;" so saith David, Psalm cxxx. 4, there is mercy with thee that thou mayest be feared." O this is a kindly operation, when the sense of God's love awes the soul to obedience, and works upon it tenderness of conscience, that it can say, I dare not grieve so good a God, or offend so loving a father, who never

---

* Exod. xviii. 21. Heb. xii. 28. Prov. iii. 7. Psalm v. 7. Prov. xiv. 26. Prov. xxiii. 17. Matt. x. 28. Phil. ii. 12. Isaiah lxvi. 2. Isaiah l. 11. Rom. xi. 20. Rev. xiv. 7. Acts x. 35. Prov. xiv. 16.

did me hurt, who is always doing me good—shall I render evil for good? God forbid. This is child-like and ingenuous, and doth demonstrate a covenant relation.

5. Sanctification is another covenant promise, Ezek. xxxvi. 25, " then will I sprinkle clean water upon you, and ye shall be clean from all your filthiness, and from all your idols will I cleanse you." This is a gracious disposition, what can you say to it? not that the soul in this life can be free from the remainders of corruption; for " what is man, that he should be clean? but the power, strength and dominion of sin is crushed in a covenanted soul; so that it may be truly said of the regenerate, that he hath " a clean heart, and clean hands;" and Christ said, " his disciples were clean, all except Judas." Well, then, hath the good word of God made you holy, and cleansed your hearts? do you desire to make clean " the inside of the cup, as well as outside?" I mean, do you cleanse yourselves from all filthiness of flesh and spirit, resolving " to perfect holiness in the fear of God?" are you growing stronger and stronger? He that hath clean hands doth renew his strength. Are you washed from your idols, that is, the sins to which you are most addicted, and keep yourselves from your own iniquity? can you say you hate every false way? can you cut off a right-hand sin, pluck out a right-eye sin, though never so dear and useful, pleasant and profitable? do you resist and conquer, in some measure, your master lusts? so that you can say, that through grace, sin hath not dominion over you, though you feel to your cost it hath possession in you. Can you say you are prepared for duties and ordinances, though you be not cleansed according to the purification of the sanctuary? doth faith in God's promises purify your hearts? do you cleanse your ways by

observing Scripture precepts? do you pray hard, for a clean heart as well as a clear state?* O sirs, try yourselves in these things, unless you be sanctified you are not justified, many are undone through self-deceit—in this case, Solomon saith, there is a generation that are pure in their own eyes, yet are not cleansed from their filthiness, Prov. xxx. 12. Take heed of this, and labour to evidence your justification by your sanctification.

6. Another gracious effect of the new covenant is, " a new heart, and a new spirit," Ezek. xxxvi. 26. This is a holy disposition, a habit of grace, the image of God, the divine nature strangely changing, altering, metamorphosing the soul, casting it into a new mould, and turning the stream and current of the soul's emotions and affections into another channel, to a compliance with God's will, and a tendency towards heaven, and the things of heaven. This is a wonderful act and fruit of God's " free grace," and " sanctifying Spirit ;" and O what a change doth it produce in the heart and life! not only a mental change, to have the mind furnished with some general truths in a notional way ; so that whereas previously a man was sunk in ignorance, now he is grown a knowing person, and learned discourser or disputant ; nor is it only a moral change, whereby a man, formerly a notorious offender, is grown a respectable member of society ; nor yet a formal change, by which a careless neglecter is become a constant performer of religious duties, which is good so far, yet no more than a hypocrite may do, Simon Magus believes, Herod doth many things, Ahab fasts, Judas can pray and preach; but the new creature goes beyond them all, for it

---

* Job xv. 14. Psalm xxiv. 4. John xiii. 10. John xv. 3. 2 Cor. vii. 1. Job xvii. 9. Psalm xviii. 23. Rom. vi. 14. 2 Chron. xxx. 19. Acts. xv. 9. Psalm cxix. 9. Psalm li. 10,

is a cordial, spiritual, evangelical change of the whole man to what is good; so that now the soul hath new emotions, actions, and conversation, a new rule, a new principle, a new end, new affections and delights, a new light and life, new heat and strength, new companions and acquaintance, new griefs, fears, burdens, hopes, hatred, desires, and expectations, " old things are past away, and behold, all things are become new;" so that it may well be called a new creation, 2 Cor. v. 17. Christians, try yourselves in this—what work of God hath passed upon your souls? have you a new heart? are you made holy as God is holy? doth this new heart hate and expel sin? doth it close with real saints as saints? doth it breathe after grace in the souls of relations and neighbours? doth it make you sensible of the smilings and hidings of God's face? doth it raise your hearts to heavenly objects and delights? doth grace in some measure grow, thrive, increase, and come on in your souls? do you worship God in a spiritual manner, and long for communion with him here, and in heaven?

7. A soft heart is promised in the new covenant, Ezek. xxxvi. 26, " I will take away the stony heart out of your flesh, and give you a heart of flesh," that is, a soft, broken and tender heart, a flexible, pliant, and melting disposition; not so much the eyes pouring floods of tears, for that may proceed from a natural constitution, but a soul grieved for sin, as offence against God, which, in the sinner's account and estimation, he looks upon as the greatest evil, and worse than the worst affliction; and, if it were to do again, he would rather be torn to pieces, than willingly commit such sin—he would give all the world, if in his power, that it were undone again ; and, therefore, it is that the Scripture rather expresseth it by mourning than by weeping, for weeping is a passionate act of the outward

senses and excitable faculties, and it may be desirable to give vent to inward sorrow by outward tears, but mourning is a contrition and compunction of heart for sin, as dishonouring God, grieving his Spirit, crucifying his Son, and violating his holy and righteous law. Well, then, have you soft and tender hearts? that is, can you lay to heart your sins as the greatest evils that ever befel you? can you justify God if he should condemn you? can you condemn yourselves as worthy to be condemned to hell for ever? do you loathe yourselves for all your abominations? can you wish you had been upon the rack when you committed such sins? are you weary and heavy laden with the intolerable burden of guilt? and what would you give or lose to have it taken off? is your heart sensible of the absolute need you have of Jesus Christ? are you soft and pliable to God's holy will, attentive to divine suggestions, retentive of divine impressions? doth the least hint of God's mind find in you an observant spirit? when God saith, "seek my face," doth your heart readily echo, "thy face, Lord, will I seek?" do your souls tremble under a sense of threatenings and judgments? does a consideration of God's loving kindness melt and attract your heart? doth this strongly lead and draw you to repentance? Ask your own souls such questions as these, whereby you may know whether you have this condition and disposition of the gospel covenant.

8. The last disposition that is promised in the new covenant, as a singular mercy, is holy practice, or spiritual obedience; so Ezek. xxxvi. 27, "I will put my Spirit within you, and cause you to walk in my statutes, and ye shall keep my judgments and do them." This is a holy, watchful, cheerful, faithful, fruitful

obedience to divine precepts and commands.* So, then, let me question you thus: do you run the ways of God's commandments with enlarged hearts? do you follow God fully, and walk with him uprightly? do you delight to do God's will, and in all things mind your rule? doth the mind of God move you more than the customs and traditions of men? though you cannot say you do exactly keep, yet cannot you say you have respect to, all God's commandments? are you like the centurion's servants, ready to go or come at God's bidding? doth the authority of a divine command more awe your conscience to obedience, than the examples of the most or the best of men? do you with Zechariah and Elizabeth walk in all the ways of God's commandments blameless? do you take heed to your ways that you offend not with tongue or hand or foot? do you worship God in the beauty of holiness? do you make it your business to engage your hearts in your approaches to God? do you lift up your hearts in God's ways, that he and you may meet? do you worship God in the spirit, rejoice in Christ Jesus, not having any confidence in the flesh? Let me ask further, do you gladly follow Christ's example, study conformity to him, and communion with him? is faith working by love? and doth that love engage you to keep God's commands, and render them not grievous but pleasant? do you account Christ's yoke easy, his burden light, and his service perfect freedom? and are you constant and permanent in holy walking every day? and though you may stumble and fall, or turn aside, or stand still, or turn back, yet you

---

* Si ergo talis fuerit vita nostra, ita omnibus membris quadrata et composita ut universi motus nostri secundum Dei leges agantur, vere testamentum Dei erit super carnem nostram.—*Orig. Hom.* 3. *in cap.* 17.

dare not quit and forsake God's ways or choose the ways of sin, to go aside with the workers of iniquity; but you lament your miscarriages, are restless till you get into God's ways again, plead hard for pardon, are more jealous over your hearts, make more haste God-wards, and so through grace keep faithful, that at death you may receive a crown of life.

Thus I have gleaned up the conditions or dispositions of God's children which are promised by God, merited by Christ, and effectually wrought in their hearts by the blessed Spirit, and these are the mercies of the covenant, by which you may try whether you be interested in it; for if you find these new covenant mercies in you, you may conclude you have an interest in new covenant privileges.

Another way of trial, which I shall but briefly hint at, is to discover the influence and effects of new covenant mercies, upon the souls of such as partake of them; that is, such benefits and privileges of the covenant, as reconciliation, adoption, remission of sin, imputation of Christ's righteousness, and others beforementioned. These have a gracious influence upon the heart. Take a specimen:

1. They are transforming and conforming mercies; they change heart and life, as I have said before; they make a person argue from mercy to duty; he that partakes of these mercies, dares not sin that grace may abound, nor argue from mercy to sinful liberty, much less make christian liberty a cloak of lasciviousness; oh no, that is the devil's logic—a child of God thinks and thus reasons: did Christ die for me, and shall not I die unto sin, and live unto him that died for me? shall my dear Saviour shed his blood for me, and shall I think any thing too dear for him? shall he forgive

much to me, and shall I not give all I have to him? shall not I love him much? pray much? obey much? O my soul, how canst thou choose but live in new obedience? doth not the love of Christ constrain thee? hath he reconciled thee to God, and God to thee, and wilt not thou be reconciled to thy offending brother? hath he forgiven thee ten thousand talents, gratis, and wilt not thou forgive such as offend thee a few farthings, for Christ's sake? hath God given thee himself, and dost thou withhold any part of thy poor, silly, sorry self from him? nay, here I am, let him work in me, and do with me as seems good in his eyes.

2. They are cheering, comforting and refreshing mercies; these mercies of the covenant will answer all objections, clear all scores, and put the soul out of doubt concerning its state. Let the devil and an unbelieving heart conspire together to torment the conscience, yet one word of the blessed covenant will baffle all their arguings, and stop their mouths, and still the soul; let God speak out and say, I am thy God in covenant, who then can cause trouble? this was all David's salvation, desire, and consolation. One drop of this holy oil of the covenant will sweeten a whole fountain and sea of the bitter waters of the sharpest afflictions; a taste of the covenant will turn water into wine; this is the tree cast into the bitter waters of Marah, that makes them sweet; sense of pardon takes away the sense of pain;[*] if a particular promise can so comfort the soul, that it may be called a cordial, O what comfort will the covenant afford, which is a cluster and constellation of evangelical promises! the good things of the new covenant keep the head above water, and the heart above terror in all

[*] Isaiah xxxiii. 24.

conditions: these steel the soul with courage in difficulties, comfort in adversity, and are an antidote in prosperity.

3. These mercies of the covenant are reviving and elevating mercies. They lift the heart above the world, and advance it to divine celestial objects and conceptions: a Christian thus clothed with the sun, hath the moon under his feet, and all sublunary enjoyments at his heels; * Christ and things above lie next his heart; † other things are dross and dung in comparison thereof; ‡ a covenanted Christian's treasure is in heaven, and his heart is there; he prefers a grain of grace to all the comforts of the world; common mercies will not content his heart, nor quiet his conscience; he opens his heaven-born soul to heavenly influences; he can easily wink all the bravery of this lower world into blackness and deformity, and pity the sottish senseless sons of men that take up their rest below, and neglect the main concernments of eternity. Ah, thinks the gracious soul, what fools are these that chase these gilded vanities, and pant after the dust of the earth! would to God that they did but see with such enlightened eyes as God's Spirit hath given me. O that they did but taste the sweetness of that grace which my soul is enamoured with, they would thirst after the world no more, but long for God, yea this living, loving God, and never be content till they come to appear before him. How blessed are they that have their sins pardoned, their hearts purged, their souls reconciled! that have God for their portion, and heaven for their inheritance and eternal home!

4. The mercies of the covenant are growing and increasing mercies; the Christian that hath them is like the house of David, that " waxed stronger and

* Rev. xii. 1.   † Col. iii. 1.   ‡ Phil. iii. 8, 9.

stronger ;" they are tending to perfection, and make the soul strive and thrive in holiness ; * " going from step to step, from strength to strength, pressing towards the mark," rising as the sun unto noon-day, or as the water to the spring; yea, " this water shall still be springing up to eternal life."—John iv. 14. Grace makes the soul long after means of growth, and so to " increase with the increase of God, till it be a perfect man in Christ;" the soul is insatiable and never saith it hath enough, " till it have arrived at the measure of the stature of the fulness of Christ," Eph. iv. 13; yea, " till it have attained to the resurrection of the dead," Phil. iii. 11. O sirs, examine your hearts herein—how do you come on and increase in religion? do you grow in grace, in knowledge, faith, love, humility, repentance, self-denial, and heavenly-mindedness? where is your proficiency? have you found grace like a grain of mustard-seed? have these mercies ripened into the blade and full ear of deliberate and proportionable fruit-bearing? A right Christian will never say he is good enough while he sojourns in this lower region, nor yet happy enough till he be with God in heaven.

CHAP. IX.

THE SURE MERCIES OF DAVID TEND TO PRODUCE CONVICTION.

IV. This subject may be considered as an occasion of conviction or reprehension, which may seriously affect sinners and saints.

* Prov. iv. 18.

1. If the mercies of the covenant be sure mercies, (as we have proved fully,) O what folly are those souls guilty of that are Christless, graceless, and careless, that have no interest in these mercies, and never trouble themselves about ensuring these covenant mercies to themselves. How many in the world are destitute of these mercies! There is a generation of men and women that live within the pale of the visible church, that may be called *lo-ruhamah*, for they have not yet obtained mercy; nay, in the state they are in, there is no mercy for them, because they are not yet in Christ, through whom these covenant mercies flow: unconverted souls are unconcerned persons in these mercies; those dogs have nothing to do with this children's bread; and yet who so apt to catch and snatch these precious dainties? they love to hear the glorious privileges laid open—such as, justification, reconciliation, adoption, and eternal life; and yet we must say with sorrow, they have nothing to do with them: if they hear discourses of God's mercy, how are they pleased, tickled, and even enraptured! they make no question but they shall be saved, as well as others; and they think, surely God that made them will not damn them. But ask these poor souls whether they be savingly converted, renewed, or engrafted into Christ by faith? alas, they know not what this means; they never asked their own souls the question; nay, they are ready to think that it is a very needless inquiry, or impossible to know; however this never lay upon their hearts and consciences, as necessary in order to clear up this important case—whether they have obtained mercy? But let all who are thus ignorant know, that " he that made them will not have mercy on them," Isa. xxvii. 11; let all profane rebels against the King of heaven know, that " God will not be merciful to any

wicked transgressor," Psalm lix. 5. God's attributes are all analogical and correspondent; he will not cease to be just and holy that he may be merciful, he will be merciful in his own way; mercy and justice shall go hand in hand. It is a ridiculous folly for men to conceit, they shall have the mercies of the covenant that are not within the covenant; this is that fallacy that logicians call *fallacia dividendi conjungenda*, the fallacy of dividing things to be conjoined; it is most dangerous and damnable in divinity, when souls dream of having peace without grace, or happiness without holiness; but let men know there is no mercy but in the covenant—where no ark of the covenant, no seat of mercy; where there is no work of grace, there is no covenant of grace; where Christ is a Saviour he will be a Sovereign, where he gives remission of sins he will give repentance; his way of blessing is by turning persons from their iniquities;* God will not shew mercy to any but in his own way; such as obtain mercy in the enjoyment of pardoning grace, must obtain mercy in converting grace; sanctification goeth along with justification; Paul obtained mercy by forsaking his old courses; † God saveth us according to his mercy— how? why, " by the washing of regeneration, and renewing of the Holy Ghost," Titus iii. 5; they are saved from sin, that are saved from wrath and hell. It is a self-deceiving, soul-destructive contradiction to dream of pardoning, without sanctifying grace. Thousands in the world fancy a God to themselves made up all of mercy, and let them do what they please, they can bolster up themselves with this conceit, " God is merciful;" and so, as God himself saith, Psalm l. 21. " These things hast thou done and I kept silence: thou thoughtest that I was altogether such a one as

* Acts v. 31. iii. 26. † 1 Tim. i. 13.

thyself, but I will reprove thee, and set thy sins in order before thee;" as if he had said, think not to make me a patron of thy wickedness; it is true, I spare thee and suffer thee to live quietly, but forbearance is no acquittance; think not I love thee because I afford thee outward mercies, which thou abusest to licentiousness, but I am resolved to take vengeance on thee; there is justice with me, as well as mercy, and there is a season wherein I shall pour out the vials of my wrath upon vessels of wrath that are fitted to destruction; a time is coming when I shall tear you in pieces, and there shall be none to deliver. O sirs, the condition of graceless, unconverted souls is sad; for,

(1.) They are under a sure and dreadful sentence of condemnation; for as the mercies of the new covenant are sure to believers, so the curses of the old covenant are as sure to all unbelievers; as the second Adam conveys certain life, so the first Adam conveys certain death to his seed; as " he that believeth on the Son hath everlasting life," so " he that believeth not shall not see life, but the wrath of God abideth on him," John iii. 36; as " he that believeth is acquitted," so " he that believeth not is condemned already," ver. 18; all his other sins are bound upon him by this of unbelief—this is the condemnation. It is as impossible that the devils in hell shall be saved, as that unconverted sinners, while such, shall be saved; for Christ saith again and again, " except a man be converted, except he be born again, he cannot see, he cannot enter into the kingdom of God,"* and binds it with strong asseverations, and dare any one that pretends to believe God's promise question the verity of his positions or comminations? yea, God hath bound himself by oath in this case as well as in the other,

* Matt. xviii. 3. John iii. 5.

Heb. iii. 11. it is spoken there concerning the rebellious murmuring Israelites; "I sware in my wrath," saith God, " they shall not enter into my rest;" or if they shall enter, then, as if he had said, never trust me more; nay, let me not be God—but what is this to us? Yes, the apostle applies it to unbelievers in gospel times, Heb. iv. 1—5, &c. hence he repeats the oath again referring to unbelieving gospellers, that they shall never enter into the heavenly Canaan. And surely unconverted sinners are in a woful plight, of whom it may be truly said, that God himself cannot save them while they continue in that state; for there is no way but one of entering heaven, that is Jesus Christ—and how shall we escape if we neglect so great salvation?* there is no other way revealed, and do we think God will forsake his ordinary road, and quit his glorious design, to gratify a generation of wilful neglecters and rejecters of this blessed contrivance of saving sinners by interest in Jesus Christ? It cannot be, you must either go to heaven this way, or down to hell by your own way.

(2.) Their souls are not sure to be another moment out of hell-torments; poor graceless sinners cannot secure themselves upon any real Scripture grounds, that they shall another hour enjoy that bastard peace of conscience, in which they flatter themselves; for ought they know, their case may be like Belshazzar's, Dan v. 5, while they are drinking, carousing, ranting, revelling, some dreadful hand-writing or testimony of God's indignation may break forth against them which may mar all their mirth, appal their spirits, trouble their thoughts, loose the joints of their loins, and make their knees smite one against another. Oh what terror and horror will the dreadful summons of death

* Acts iv. 12. Heb. ii. 3.

strike into them! How will these fool-hardy warriors against an infinite God, call to the rocks and mountains to cover them! Oh what a sudden change, what a sad catastrophe will the cold hand of death make with them! What a fall will these secure and senseless sinners have from the height of worldly preferment to the depth of eternal torments! Stand a little and look at that rich and wretched miser in the gospel, that had no room for his fruits and goods, that sung a requiem to his soul for many years; yet alas, had not one night to take his ease in. " Thou fool," saith God, "this night shall thy soul be required of thee,"* or they shall require thy soul; that is, the devils who are waiting for a commission from God to catch hold of graceless souls, to hale them to torments as soon as they have forsaken their wretched bodies—so some interpret it. However, the rich man's soul was suddenly snatched from a full table and dainty fare into eternal misery, without a drop of water or hopes of mercy; for let him tear his heart with bitter outcries—" Father Abraham, have mercy on me," neither his father Abraham, nor the God of Abraham will have any mercy for him: † former offers of mercy are now turned into flames of fury; they have wilfully forsaken their own mercy, and now are wofully forsaken by the God of mercy. O consider this you that are yet in your sins, dancing about the pit, and are ready every instant to drop into eternal woe.

(3.) Their present mistake will aggravate their woful state. Oh what a dreadful disappointment will this be, for persons that lived demurely in the world, and passed for very civil neighbours, even for choice saints, yet now to be set on the left hand amongst the goats at the great day; yea, persons that thought

* See Luke xii. 17—20. † See Luke xvi. 24—26.

themselves to be in the ready road to heaven, and to be, as they imagined, about to step into glory to miss their footing, and fall into eternal torments! It is a dreadful sight to see soul and hopes giving up the ghost together, and swept away as the spider's web into the fire of hell.* Alas, for a man that hath all his days been building castles in the air, and erecting the house of his fair profession upon the sliding sand of fancy and imagination! to have all come tottering down with one puff of death, will be a dreadful sight! Ministers told them of this, but they would not believe, nor suspect their state, nor spend one hour in searching whether they were right or not; many a time were they warned of the danger, but they pleased themselves in wilful self-delusion, and now they are past recovery; they would not be brought to a holy despair of themselves, that they might have sure footing in these sure mercies, and now they shall and must despair of ever having part or portion in these desirable and permanent mercies; they would not be beaten from their carnal shifts and senseless pleas, and now they must and shall be for ever banished from them, and feel the bitterness of them. Ministers could not deal with them, but God can; and it will be a heart-confounding day, when the varnish shall be washed off, and all rotten props that kept the soul from awful apprehensions shall be torn up, and they shall see themselves deceived by Satan, the world, and their own self-flattering hearts into eternal misery.

(4.) But once more; many things in and about these sure mercies will augment their eternal misery. Alas, sirs, here there is no speaking to wicked men, they will not abide a sober conference about their souls, they have not leisure nor patience to yield an attentive ear

* Job xi. 20. and viii. 14.

to discourses about these sure mercies; but a time is coming wherein they shall be forced to think of them as lost mercies to their cost: now they have other things to mind, the world doth so fill their ears and hearts, that they thrust these things from them, and judge themselves unworthy of them. They are just like Jeremiah's wild ass used to the wilderness, " that snuffeth up the wind at her pleasure, in her occasion who can turn her away?——but in her month they shall find her."* So there is no dealing with wicked men in their jollity and frolic fits, but their month of sorrow is approaching either here or hereafter; and oh the bitter pangs and travail that shall then possess them! in this world they would not consider, but hereafter they shall have an eternity to consider of these covenant mercies, though in a hopeless way: as

[i.] They will think of the nature of these mercies they have lost. O how free, how sweet, how suitable, how satisfying were they! how sure would God have made them to them! and the better these mercies, the bitterer their sorrow on the loss of them.

[ii.] They will think that once they might have enjoyed them, and been happy in that enjoyment; once they had a day of grace, means of grace, ministers persuaded, the Spirit moved, mercies, afflictions, word, and rod—every thing spoke this language: O embrace these mercies; but I refused, and now they are out of my reach.

[iii.] They will think, and think again, how near they were to the embracing of these mercies; O what convictions, individually they will say, did God fasten on my heart by such and such a sermon! I was once half-persuaded to embrace religion, how near was I to

* Jer. ii. 24.

a full closure! I went home with strong resolutions to be another man; but this deceitful heart beguiled me, and so I put off repentance till now it is too late.

[iv.] They will think what these mercies would have done for them; these mercies would have folded their souls within the arms of God's love; these would have filled their souls with grace, fitted them for God's service, and furnished them for glory; these mercies would have rendered them profitable in life, comfortable in death, and happy for ever: the possessors of these mercies are gracious saints. Yet again,

[v.] They will think with sadness what they have exchanged these mercies for; they have passed off these precious and sure mercies for trash and trifles, for dung and dirt, for a little paltry pleasure or conscience-wounding profit, which now they have left behind them in the world, and only carry the guilt and shame along with them, which must abide by them, when sensual delights are vanished away. Oh what gnashing of teeth and indignation at themselves will this beget for their former madness!

[vi.] They must think how many thousands of souls were made happy by a gracious reception and full enjoyment of these mercies; persons whom they despised in the world, and thought not worthy to come into their company, shall sit down with the patriarchs, prophets, and apostles in heaven; but these wretched souls are thrust out. Oh, says the wretched subject of damnation, I might have been happy as well as yonder shining saint; he was a suffering creature, I was a rejoicing miscreant; now he is comforted, and I am tormented. Yet, once more,

[vii.] The damned in hell will bethink themselves who was in the fault, and whence it comes to pass that these mercies were not made sure to their souls; and they can charge none herewith but themselves: they will then see that none was to be blamed but their own wilful hearts, whatever they may object here, or boast of their willingness, yet God lays the blame there, and so shall they, will they, nill they, they must be speechless, and charge themselves only as making faggots to burn themselves with for ever. Oh, will the soul think, I may thank myself for this ; I wilfully forsook my own mercies to observe lying vanities ; this is the fruit of my own doings, I would needs be damned; ministers and godly friends persuaded, God stopt my way by his providences and ordinances, but I would run into the pit, and here I am shut up in eternal darkness ; woe is me that ever I was born ! O that I had either never heard of or else embraced those mercies, that I have rejected, and that will follow my soul with horror for ever !

Ah sirs, I beseech you consider, such a day will come, and then you will remember these things, and they will lie heavy upon you, then you will feel what an evil and bitter thing it is that you have forsaken God: then you will vomit up your sweet morsels, and remember those sweet words that here you despised ;* then you will remember the possibility and probability you once had, of obtaining these sweet mercies; now they are attainable, but if once you have taken a step upon the shore of eternity, you are past hopes and remedy, for the dead and damned do only hear the sound of wisdom with their ears, but are never likely to enjoy the benefit thereof. † O put not off these things with some slight and transient thoughts, but shame yourselves to a holy diligence.

2. Another sort to be reproved, are God's own children that are guilty of four lamentable faults :—

* Psalm cxli. 6. † Job xxviii. 22.

(1.) They are apt to bargain.
(2.) To compound about these mercies.
(3.) They do not live upon these mercies ; nor,
(4.) Up to them.

(1.) God's children would have the mercies of the covenant; but then they have a mind to indent * with God, to be secured from the crosses attending these mercies; the flesh shrinks and is loth to suffer; we are like Orpah, we would follow Christ a little way, but fain would we make our bargain so, as not to follow him in a rough way. But, sirs, consider would you have the sweets and not the bitters of godliness? Did you not take Christ (in a marriage covenant) for better and worse? will you pick and choose with him? do not right virgin-souls follow the Lamb whithersoever he goeth? Ah sirs, this covenant relation is an express, voluntary, universal, unreserved self-resignation. The bearing of the cross was always supposed and implied; † and if you will not have him with it, you are to be without, for the cross is *evangelii genius*, the very inseparable property, complexion, and companion of the gospel: and Christ would not have any cheated with imaginary hopes of immunity from sufferings, but tells them the worst, and bids them sit down and count the cost;‡ and if you did not so at first, you have not been sincere, and if you did, and still would have Christ—why do you now grumble at bearing that which you freely chose? Besides, know this, crosses for Christ are special gospel mercies, for afflictions are adapted to become real mercies of the covenant, and therefore they are promised as well as any other mercies, Psalm lxxxix. 31, 32, and David acknowledges affliction to be an act and fruit of covenant faithfulness, because it fetched him from his wander-

* To bargain.   † Matt. x. 37, 38. Mark x. 30.   ‡ Luke xiv. 28.

ings, instructed him in God's statutes, and therefore was good for him.* Crosses for Christ never did any hurt, but have been usually means of good; many Christians have blessed God for them; God sees we cannot live or do well without them; Paul gloried in the cross of Christ, took pleasure in distresses for Christ—and why then are we afraid of them, or would bargain to be secured from them? be ashamed of your nice and delicate spirits.

(2.) Some Christians are too apt to compound with God about these covenant mercies; † my meaning is, they can satisfy themselves without the whole series of covenant mercies, they are willing and content to be put off with some, and do not solicit all; they can apply some promises, not others—see a necessity of pardoning mercy, but do not plead and act faith for purifying, softening, quickening, enlightening mercies of the covenant. Consider, Christians, by thus doing,

[i.] You injure yourselves, you need all these covenant mercies; there is not one of the fore-mentioned blessings, that a Christian can live and thrive without; all are of great use, every one hath its peculiar excellency, a gracious soul cannot spare any of them; nay, it is a sin for it to be content with less than God hath promised; he that is not for all, is truly for none at all. The true owner will not divide; in one part of your life or other, you will want all covenant mercies; it is base unworthiness and ingratitude to slight any of them.

* Psalm cxix. 75, 67, 71.
† In closing with offers of grace, we must be uniform. Earthly things God is pleased to retail. All have some, none have all. But in the heavenly treasure, he will not break the whole piece, and cut it into remnants; if God would cut off as much as would serve men's turn, he might have customers enough.—*Mr. Gurnal's Christ. Armour, page* 310.

[ii.] You dishonour God, and disparage these mercies, as if God were not able to give you all, and pay the whole debt of his free and full promise ; as for example, suppose a rich tradesman owe you a sum of money, and you come to him and tell him you are willing to abate him so much, and compound with him, and take of him a shilling in the pound, or a pound in the hundred for the whole debt, he looks upon himself as disparaged, being a sufficient chapman, he will not have his ability or honesty questioned; but quickly answers, what do you think I am breaking? I will not be abated any thing, here is your money, I will pay you all. So God would not be compounded with ; he looks upon it as a dishonour to his free grace and faithfulness, and bids the soul open its mouth wide, and promiseth to fill it, Psalm lxxxi. 10 ; that is, ask great things, many things, spare not, ask what thou needest, ask what I have promised, I am neither sparing nor backward in giving, stint not thyself in asking, I shall not send thee away empty ; they that come for most, speed best ; and when thou hast gone to the utmost extent of thy reach in asking, " I can, and will give thee abundantly more than thou art able to ask or think."—Ephes. iii. 20. O Christians, chide yourselves for your sinful mannerliness and modesty ; and widen your contracted spirits for larger incomes of grace and mercy. Remember, these covenant supplies are all of mercy, not deserved; and they are mercies in the plural, containing large and liberal revenues to be communicated to indigent wanting souls.

(3.) God's children often do not live upon the mercies of the covenant; we blame them that have good estates, and live beneath them ; and well we may, for it is a base and a beggarly practice, when persons have enough, but want power to eat, take their portion, and enjoy the good of all they have; this is a sore evil, and a sad curse, and the contrary is good, and decent, a great blessing, and the very gift of God :* and O what a sad evil for the saints of God, the heirs of promise to live below their estates, none so rich as real saints, they are heirs to a vast inheritance; "God himself is their portion; yea, the portion of their inheritance, and of their cup, he maintains their lot;"† they have enough, and they cannot lose what they have. O at what a high rate should such rich heirs live! and what an unworthy degenerate spirit doth it discover to live in so beggarly a manner as most of us do! As,

[i.] To live so much by sense, and so little by faith; it is the gospel character of believers, to live by their faith; to walk by faith and not by sense, or sight, to see him that is invisible, to venture their all upon unseen grounds:‡ and O what a noble and generous, what a brave and a blessed life is the life of faith! and on the contrary, what a sorry and a sordid, what a beggarly and niggardly life is a life of sense! such a soul goes a begging, and craves a crumb of one, a morsel of another to make a meal of, and after all the soul's appetite is hungry and craving, and at the best, how quickly are such things gone! Alas, sirs, objects of sense will not carry you through the world; sense will sink with Peter where it cannot feel a bottom; it is faith only that will lift the head above water, and the heart above terror, when you must pass through a sea of sorrows in this tumultuous world. Christians, where is you faith? you are distinguished from others by this precious grace: the want of this undoeth us: hence it is,

[ii.] That God's children are so often at a loss, and

* Eccles. v. 18, 19. † Ps. xvi. 5.
‡ Hab. ii. 4. Rom. i. 17 2 Cor. v. 7. Heb. xi.

know not what to do; no wonder if they be at their wits' end, when they are at their faith's end. Many circumstances, yea, any affliction will throw a saint upon his back when he stands not upon the feet of faith, or leans not upon Christ by faith. This is the reason why in temptation we cry out, God hath cast me off for ever, and he will be favourable no more; and we give up the buckler, and yield to Satan's assaults and demands, which make us become our enemies' sport; yea, any little loss or cross dismays us, as though we were undone, or as though, with poor Jacob once, our life were bound up in a lad, or bag, or such like things. Ah, dear sirs, where is your delight in God?* where is your encouraging yourselves in God?† where is your rejoicing in the Lord with Habakkuk, when a cloud or curtain hath covered all your worldly enjoyments?‡ why do you not oppose one God to all the armies of evils that beset you round? why do you not take the more content in God, when you have the less of the creature to take content in? why do you not boast in your God? and bear up yourselves big with your hopes in God and expectations from him? do you not see young heirs to great estates, act and spend accordingly? and why shall you, being the King of heaven's sons, be lean and ragged from day to day, as though you were not worth a groat? O sirs, live upon your portion, chide yourselves for living below what you have; there are great and precious promises, rich enriching mercies; you may make use of God's all-sufficiency, you can blame none but yourselves if you be defective or discouraged. A woman truly godly for the main, having buried a child, and sitting alone in sadness, did yet cheer up her heart with this expression—God lives; and having parted

* Psalm xxxvii. 4. † 1 Sam. xxx. 6. ‡ Hab. iii. 17, 18.

with another, still she repeated—Comforts die, but God lives; at last her dear husband dies, and she sat oppressed and almost overwhelmed with sorrow, a little child she had yet surviving, having observed what before she spoke to comfort herself, comes to her and saith, " Is God dead? Mother, is God dead ?" this reached her heart, and by God's blessing she recovered her former confidence in her God, who is a living God. Thus do you chide yourselves—ask your fainting spirits under pressing, outward sorrows, does not God live? and why then doth not thy soul revive? why doth thy heart die within thee when comforts die? cannot a living God support thy dying hopes? thus, Christians, argue down your discouraged and disquieted spirits, as David did.—Psalm xlii. 5. But so much for that.

(4.) As Christians do not live upon, so they do not live conformably to these sure mercies of David, and that, in their frequently walking so

Unholily, unsteadily, uncomfortably and unfruitfully.

[i.] Many of God's children walk unholily, unspiritually, untenderly, not with that conscientiousness, exactness, and closeness they ought to do. If God's children lived up to their mercies and privileges, O how holy would they be, seeing that these things shall be dissolved, and seeing we look for such things as we do; nay, since we see and feel such things mystically already, even a new heaven, and new earth, after a sort, in this new covenant dispensation, " what manner of persons ought we to be? and O how diligent should we be that we may be found of Christ in peace, without spot and blameless!" 2 Pet. iii. 11—14. But O Christians, how far we come short, yea, how inconsistent are our lives with our privileges! how incongruous are our duties to our mercies! yea, how different are our spirits from our comforts! What sirs, heavenly mercies and carnal hearts, flat duties, earthly conversations! O shame yourselves before the Lord, blush, tremble to think of your unconformableness to covenant mercies! How far are you below these enjoyments! Doth not your unanswerable walking give just ground of suspicion, whether you have interest in these things or not? What sirs, are you saints and yet earth-worms? are you partakers of a heavenly calling, and yet walk so like the men of the world? Is it fit to see eagles on a dirty dunghill, or heaven-born souls in scenes of pollution? Either be better or quit your claim; you dishonour God, and discredit religion more than others. Alas friends, God will not be beholden to you for the mere title of being religious, he will not regard you unless you be really such. Mercies infer duty, and licentiousness is inconsistent with the nature and end of covenant mercies. You grieve God's spirit, cross his designs, wrong your own souls, sadden the hearts of the righteous, and open the mouths of wicked men. You little know what hurt you do by one visible act of sinning. Consider, that as the privileges of the covenant bespeak holiness, so the conditions of the covenant include holiness,* and how then come heirs of promise to be so unlike their heavenly Father? what are the children of light doing when tampering with works of darkness?

[ii.] God's children sometimes walk very unsteadily, that is, they are off and on, inconstant, have good moods and emotions, but they wear off, and decay, they quickly lose their lively impressions, and are constant in inconstancy; they are zealous and forward for God

---

* Qui bonus est et justus, et mundus et immaculatus, neque malum aliquid neque injustum neque abominandum in suo sponsali thalamo sustinebit.—*Iræn. adv. Hær. lib.* 4.

one while, at other times they are backward and indifferent. Ah sirs, is this a living up to these sure mercies of David, these constant, unchangeable, invariable mercies? This covenant is ordered in all things and sure, and so are the mercies of it. How comes it to pass then that covenanters are so often discomposed, disordered and unsettled? Sometimes they are for God, and sometimes not; they are halting betwixt two opinions; like drunken men, they are leaning sometimes to the right hand, at other times to the left; like Reuben, "they are unstable as water,"* and so shall not excel; like Ephraim,† a cake half-baked, hot and hard on one side, cold and doughy on the other; or resembling the same Ephraim's goodness, like a morning cloud, or early dew that tarries not long, but is quickly scattered by the violent storms of persecutions, or dried up by the warm beams of prosperity. These unstable Christians are like James's ‡ waves of the sea—like Jude's || wandering stars or flying clouds carried about of winds—or like Paul's § children, tossed to and fro; they are like locusts that move to and again—like grasshoppers that are still up and down in variable motions; the hearts of such are as a cart wheel, saith one, and their thoughts as a rolling axle-tree. I know, the best of God's children are incident to liftings up and castings down in point of feelings and enlargements, and this may be the effect of God's affording or suspending the influences of his grace; but I speak this of a Christian's remissness, and his inconstancy through neglect and carelessness, and want of stirring up in his soul the graces of God's Spirit, and so losing the liveliness which he feels sometimes; and again he may be warmed and melted, but afterwards returns

* Gen. xlix. 4. † Hos. vii. 8, and vi. 4.
‡ James i. 6. || Jude 12, 13. § Eph. iv. 14.

unto folly. This is often such a Christian's round, and how unsuitable is this for sincere believers? These stars are to be fixed in the firmament of the church, and are not to be wandering stars or meteors; these trees of the Lord's planting should be strongly rooted, and not like reeds tossed with every wind; they should be pillars in the house of God, and not feathers or weathercocks upon house tops; these living stones should not be round and rolling, but square and fixed, still settled upon the foundation.* If the testimony of Christ be confirmed in us, † we should hold fast our confidence firm unto the end, and pray hard for a more constant spirit, as David did, Psalm li. 10, that we may be like Jachin and Boaz, stability and strength; for if we be stable, we shall be strong, and so answerable to these sure mercies of David.

[iii.] It is a sad thing to see the heirs of this covenant walk uncomfortably. What, are you partakers and possessors of mercies, and yet sad? have you interest in sweet and sure mercies, and yet are you dejected? what will lift you up, if mercy will not? and what can interrupt your peace, when mercy waits on you to cheer your hearts? thou mayest lose estate, health, good name, relations, liberty; yea, thy life is in continual hazard, but as long as these mercies of the covenant are sure, thou hast no reason to complain. An ancient writer compares a Christian that is disconsolate for outward losses or crosses, to a man that hath a fine orchard, the trees whereof are richly laden with store of precious fruit, and because the wind blows off some leaves, the man sits down and takes on heavily; he weeps and mourns and cries out he is undone; why, what is the matter? why, the wind hath taken off some leaves, but the roots, and trees, and fruits are safe:

* Non vacillantes, sed tetragonoi.   † 1 Cor. i. 6.

should we not judge that a fond and foolish man? Just thus it is with the Christian; God and Christ, promises and gospel mercies are sure and steadfast by an inviolable gospel covenant. Yet the sinful, silly creature lies whining and complaining for the loss of some leaves of worldly comforts, which he may live well without. Ah, saith the poor soul, but these outward things are not the chief cause of my trouble and discouragement; did I know that those mercies were made sure to me, I should be comfortable—but, alas, I fear I have no share therein. I shall answer this doubt afterwards, at present I only say, lay thy hand upon thy heart, and deal ingenuously. Is this the ground of thy trouble? is not this only pretended? is not something else the real cause? the heart is deceitful; look again, see what comforted thee before this outward trouble came, and what cheers thee when thy present pressure is removed? But suppose it be jealousies about thy interest; yet, why shouldest thou be uncomfortable? hast not thou ventured thy soul on a sure foundation? what reason hast thou for discouragement? a faith of adherence brings some settlement as well as a faith of evidence. Every act of faith brings some comfort; "whom having not seen," (saith the apostle, with reference to a corporeal sight, so may I say of a kind of spiritual sense and assurance) " ye love; in whom though now you see him not, yet believing, ye rejoice with joy unspeakable and full of glory," 1 Pet. i. 8. Recumbency hath a kind of complacency; it argues want of faith to want joy, and unbelief is an aggravated sin, considering the assurances given us in the gospel; but more of this hereafter. But O consider, sirs, what wrong you do to yourselves by uncomfortable walking? you weaken and exhaust your strength and spirits. What discredit you bring upon the ways of God, rendering them gloomy and forbidding in the account of others! What opposition it expresseth both to many positive precepts, and to these sure mercies of David! Methinks I hear the God of heaven thus bespeaking the gracious, troubled heart: soul, what ails thee? what is it thou wouldest have? I have given thee many glorious gifts; pardon, reconciliation, adoption, ordinances, the benefit of all my works of providence, a title to the good things of earth whilst thou livest, and a free admission into heaven when thou diest; nay, I have given thee myself, my Son, my Spirit, and that by the surest marriage covenant—and will not all this revive thy fainting spirit? what wouldest thou have more? and what canst thou desire in order to make it surer to thee? speak but the word and it shall be done. Have I not gone beyond thy expectation? and why then art thou thus drooping and disconsolate? is thy heart revived when mortal, deceitful man makes thee a promise of some outward good? and canst thou now faint, when the eternal God hath taken all this pains to assure thy troubled heart of thy interest in these sure mercies of David? O Christians, shame yourselves for your uncomfortableness! Are the consolations of God small unto you? Thank yourselves for your discouragements, and let it be matter of trouble that you have so many needless, useless troubles in your souls.

[iv.] Another fault in the heirs of the promises, whereby they are not conformable to these mercies, is unfruitfulness; herein, they do not live up to these mercies, and are exceeding defective and imperfect, especially in two respects—the fruit they bring forth is both small and sour.

1. It is usually, but small in quantity, short of that abundance and ripeness that should come off so good a

soil as mercy is, especially when mercy is the tillage. God's vineyard is on a very fruitful hill,* so we read it; but in Hebrew, † it is the horn of the son of oil. I know the son of oil may import a very rich soil, as son of the morning means what is exceedingly bright and luminous; and so God's people were planted in Canaan, which was an exceedingly fruitful country, but the passage may, at least, allusively affirm of real saints, that they are planted in the horn of the son of oil, even in the Son of God, who was anointed with the oil of gladness above his fellows, and in whom true believers are planted, and from whom they may draw abundant juice and fatness, as branches do from the root of the olive-tree, Rom. xi. 17; moreover, what abundant pains doth God the Father, the husbandman, take, to make souls very fruitful; he " takes away such as bear no fruit at all," and " every branch that beareth fruit, he purgeth it that it may bring forth more fruit."—John xv. 2. O what mercies do the saints partake of! gospel privileges, promises, providences, ordinances, experiences, comforts, corrections, every thing that might make them fruitful in good works, in praying, reading, meditating, conferring, exact walking, doth God distribute; and where is their answerable fruitfulness? God expects more and riper fruit. Alas, how short and defective are we! how little glory do we bring to God! how little profit unto others, or comfort to our own souls! We should be filled with the fruits of righteousness; we should abound more and more, and bring forth fruits meet for sincere repentance, and be truly fruitful in every good work. ‡ But are we so or not? I much suspect it; and what

* Isaiah vi. 1. † בקרן בן שמן

‡ Phil. i. 11.   1 Thes. iii. 12.   Matt. iii. 8.   Col. i. 10.

a shame is it that we should lie under the warm influences of the sun of righteousness so long, and be so unfruitful! The God of heaven humble us for this!

2. I am afraid that the fruits we do bring forth are but sour and bitter, not so sweet and kindly as might be expected of the genuine fruits and products of these sure mercies. My meaning is, that the obedience and performances of believers too often flow from a spirit of bondage, fear and terror, and not from that filial child-like disposition, and the evangelical spirit of adoption that should be the principle and actuating cause of their spiritual obedience. I know legal fears and terrors are good in their tendency, to drive the soul out of itself, and unto Christ; but afterwards, a spirit of love best becomes a child of God; * hence, saith the apostle, Rom. viii. 15, " ye have not received the spirit of bondage again to fear, but ye have received the spirit of adoption, whereby we cry Abba, Father." A child-like boldness best befits a son. It is more acceptable to God to see souls attracted to him by silken cords of love, than scourged to him by severe lashes of wrath. Christ's soldiers are not so much pressed for his service by compulsion, as they are volunteers by a spontaneous movement. All our duties should be free-will offerings; but alas, sirs, how unwilling and forced are many of our performances! how grumbling are we in our actings for God! We go to God as though it were our burden, not with that delight and cheerfulness we ought. Consider sirs, how readily God offers us mercy! how freely Christ laid down his life for us! how acceptable a work it is to the blessed Spirit to apply these mercies to us! and be ashamed to be so reluctant and dull in your performances; yea, consider the dispensation you are under—a gospel covenant, made up of

* 2 Tim. i. 7.

mercy, and this should ripen our fruits to more sweetness and maturity than the Old Testament dispensation. As you know apricots and other fruit that are upon a wall, under the direct influence or powerful reflection of the sun beams, are sooner ripe, and sweeter when ripe, than such as are in the shade; so our fruits in gospel times should be better than theirs under the law; but, alas, how far do we fall short of David's warm spirit for God? or the holy acts put forth by him and other saints of God under types and shadows, when these sweet mercies were not so clearly revealed to them, and when the sun of righteousness did not shed his beams with so much warmth upon them! Ah Christians, if you would study mercies more, your spirits would be in a better frame for duty. David saith, " I will come into thy house in the multitude of thy mercies, and in thy fear will I worship toward thy holy temple."—Psalm v. 7. Observe it; the sense of God's mercy is an excellent ingredient in the worship of God; yea, it begets a holy awe of God, for these two are very consistent; and, indeed, nothing is so prevalent a motive to duty, and dissuasive from iniquity, and persuasive to the exercise of repentance, as a sense of mercy is. This truth, Scripture and experience will abundantly confirm. But I have been too long on this subject; only let God's children be humbled for their too, too legal disposition, and breathe after a more evangelical spirit by the studying of these mercies, rather than poring upon guilt and wrath.

CHAP. X.

THE SURE MERCIES OF DAVID DESERVE CONSIDERATION, AND SHOULD EXCITE IN ALL A SOLICITUDE TO OBTAIN THEM.

V. ARGUMENTS may be used to induce all classes of persons to look after their share in these sure mercies of David; and O that I had it in my power by any means to evince their importance! O what a mercy would it be, if by these sure mercies of David, and these discourses about them, some soul were enamoured therewith, and set, in good earnest, to make them its own. But shall I need to use many arguments to persuade any person to accept of mercy? Yes, certainly; the most part of the world forsake their own mercies by observing lying vanities; and they that can experimentally distinguish betwixt a gracious and graceless heart, find that it is the hardest thing in the world to close in with mercies in God's way. It is an easy thing for a secure sinner to presume upon mercy, to make mercy a pillow to sleep upon with ease, to build castles in the air, and feed himself with vain conceits of the mercy of God—this any one can do; but to be got off our own grounds of dependence, to despair of ourselves, to accept of Jesus Christ, to give up ourselves to God in covenant, to venture a troubled heart upon the promises of free grace. This is a high and hard work, an arduous and difficult undertaking; but this is done by every converted sinner, and a soul never obtains mercy till it be, indeed, savingly converted, 1 Tim. i. 13. If you be *lo-ammi*, not God's people by way of covenant, you are *lo-ruhamah*,* that is, persons that have not

* Hos. i. 6—9.

obtained mercy. O look after an interest in these sure mercies of David. Consider,

1. Nothing else in the world can be made sure; we live in an inconstant world; every thing is upon the wheel of change; sublunary comforts are like the moon, sometimes at the full, and sometimes in the wane— nothing continues in a fixed state; a man may be rich to-day and poor to-morrow, therefore the apostle calls them uncertain riches, or uncertainty of riches in the abstract. Now then, saith the apostle, Christians must lay up in store for themselves " a good foundation against the time to come."—1 Tim. vi. 17—19. Alas, riches were never true to any that trusted to them; the things of the world are like sand or smoke, with which you cannot fill your hand.* Who would be so fond of that which he knows he cannot keep? It is the part of a wise man to purchase such an estate as he may enjoy; friends, goods, honours, health, pleasures have their periods, but these mercies are sure and everlasting. O the vast difference! It is very deserving of consideration, that the things only that make us happy, can be made sure; but the things of this world, which cannot make us happy, cannot be made sure— and, indeed, whatever may be lost is not capable of making any truly happy. Now heavenly things are durable as well as suitable to the soul, therefore, let us all take the counsel of our Lord Jesus, Matt. vi. 19, 20, " Lay not up for yourselves treasures upon earth, where moth and rust doth corrupt, and where thieves break through and steal—but lay up for yourselves treasures in heaven, where neither moth nor rust doth

* Plato said, Οὐ πενία ποτε ἡ 'ὀλιγοχρηματία, ἀλλ' ἡ ἀπληστία· ἧς φροῦδης ὁ ἀγαθὸς ὢν και πλούσιος γ' ἂν εἰή.—Non est paupertas pecuniæ paucitas, sed insatiabilitas; quæ si recesserit, qui bonus est dives quoque fuerit.—*Clem. Alexand. Strom. lib.* 2.

corrupt, and where thieves do not break through nor steal."

2. Except you have an interest in these sure mercies, common mercies are accursed to you, nor indeed have you any real covenant title to any thing you enjoy, whatever right you may have before men,* yet, you are, in the court of heaven,† in a sense, usurpers or encroachers; you have forfeited all by actual rebellion, and have what you enjoy but as condemned prisoners or malefactors, to keep you alive till the execution of the righteous sentence of condemnation. O the woful condition of unconverted sinners! they are accursed with a gospel curse, and under a dreadful sentence of excommunication. ‡ There is a curse in their houses, on their actions, on their relations, as it respects them; there is a curse upon their very blessings, Mal. ii. 2; there is a plague in their apparel, poison in their meat, and, we may say, death is in the pot as to all their enjoyments—my meaning is, nothing is truly sanctified or perfumed with covenant mercy, and if God give a commission, whatever they enjoy may be their bane; whithersoever they go, a curse goes with them; whatever they partake of, a curse meets them in it; whoever they are with, a curse attends them. O fearful state! it was sad to be under the curse of a mortal man —Ham found his father Noah's curse heavy; but oh how heavy is the curse of Almighty God, who, with a word, can send the soul into hell, and follow his stroke into another world! Dear friends, who would live in this dreadful state another hour? On the contrary, whosoever hath these mercies of the covenant hath all blessings blessed; yea, and also crosses, and even curses are turned into blessings. Who would not be covetous of such a state? But to hasten,

* In foro humano.   † In foro Dei.   ‡ 1 Cor. xvi. 22. Prov. iii. 33.

3. Without these covenant mercies the soul is not accepted in its best duties: neither person nor performance is owned by God; it is only upon a covenant account that any are accepted; indeed in the covenant of works the person was accepted for the work's sake, but in the covenant of grace, God accepts the person first, and then the work; if the man be in Christ, then the offering is taken in good part, though it be but a turtle-dove or young pigeon, though but a sigh or groan; God takes a posy of flowers (of sweet-smelling graces) though mixed with offensive weeds and pricking briars of vanity and corruption, gathered by a child, and perfumed by Christ's mediation, and is better pleased therewith, than with the most odoriferous gifts of unconverted souls, where the heart is destitute of covenant graces. Alas, " the sacrifice of the wicked is abomination to God;"* the great and jealous God challengeth the wicked man that hath not covenant mercies in his heart, for taking covenant promises into his mouth: " What hast thou to do?" saith God;† as if he had said, thou poor, graceless sinner, thou profanest my holy name, and provokest the eyes of my glory in the works and worship by which thou thinkest thou dost most honour and please me: in the state wherein thou art, I cannot endure to look towards thee; I abhor thy offerings and performances, thy costly incense is a smoke in my nose; I can see thy inward deformity through thy painted beauty; thy gilded eloquence and rhetorical flourishes are no more to me than the roaring of bears or howling of dogs; get out of my sight, thou sorry whining hypocrite; all thy duties are ciphers, and signify nothing except the Mediator as the principal and only figure be set before them, and the Spirit of God write and indite them; which

* Prov. xv. 8.   † Psalm l. 16, 17.

are two of the greatest mercies of the new covenant. Ah sirs, God doth despise the most melodious tunes of wicked men, but " a broken and contrite heart he despiseth not;" * that makes sweet music in his ear, for a broken heart is a covenant mercy. These mercies are brave ornaments to believing souls, and render them lovely and amiable in the sight of God. Every penitent tear is a rich pearl; every prayer pierceth heaven and fetcheth down abundant incomes from the throne of grace. O what a difference do these mercies make in persons, performances, and acceptance with God!

4. Without these mercies you have no solid ground of peace, comfort, or satisfaction: for without these you are not only under a sentence of condemnation, but you have no real ground to hope that the sentence shall not be executed this very hour; it is a wonder to think that graceless souls should be so merry that are suspended over the pit of hell, but by the brittle thread of a mortal life. O how suddenly may this precarious thing be broken, and they are gone for ever! for aught they know, when they go to bed, God may say, (as once he did to one as rich and secure as they are,) " This night shall thy soul be required from thee." It is a wonder to me, how persons can rest quietly that are conscious to themselves, or have reason to suspect they are not in covenant with God; and so know not that they shall be another moment out of everlasting torments. But God leaves them to seared consciences; and Satan and the world join with their deceitful lusts to lull them asleep, till God awake them by true repentance or eternal vengeance. God, however, hath a time to shake the foundations of this bastard peace, and set the soul upon the sure bottom of covenant relation, and interest in Jesus Christ, which

* Psalm li. 17.

alone brings true content and comfort, peace that passeth understanding, joy in the Holy Ghost, and a sweet sabbath of refreshment to the agitated soul.* Here the assured believer may, as it were, terminate his desires, and make his strongest faculties expatiate upon his only portion—a covenant God; and thence will result continual ground of triumph and exultation, for these mercies are suitable and adequate to the desires of the immortal soul, and will support it under the greatest outward pressures, and in the hour of death; therefore I may conclude this exhortation with verse 2, of this chapter, —" Wherefore do you spend your money for that which is not bread, and your labour for that which satisfieth not? hearken diligently unto me, and eat ye that which is good, and let your soul delight itself in fatness."

5. These mercies of the covenant will render your condition safe whatever befals you; we little know what may befal us betwixt this and the grave—who knows what a day will bring forth? Man is born to trouble, a saint is born again to more; bad news may come as Job's messengers, treading in each other's steps; losses and crosses may occasion us sad discouragements. O but now to have a covenant God, a Saviour and all the fore-mentioned covenant blessings to solace the soul—what mercy will this be! when the true Christian can say, " I am my beloved's, and my beloved is mine; my flesh and my heart fail, but God is the strength of my heart and my portion for ever." Let the sea roar, men rage, heavens look black, and earth tremble, I lie at anchor in a sure port, I trust in

* Redite *prævaricatores ad cor,* et inhærete ei qui fecit vos: state cum eo et stabitis: requiescite in eo et quieti eritis. Quò itis in aspera? quò itis? bonum quod amatis ab illo est: sed quantum est ad illum bonum est et suave.—*Vid. Aug. Conf. lib.* 4. *c.* 12.

God, and fear no evil tidings from below; "God is my refuge and help, yea my present help in time of trouble;"* evils shall either miss me or mend me; all winds blow my soul nearer my haven, all dispensations hitch me a step nearer heaven, for all things work together for my good; my covenant God will teach me to profit by word and rod, by mercies and crosses, by ordinances and providences: God is my sun and shield, to enlighten me in times of darkness, to protect me in times of danger, he will command a guard of angels to attend me; yea, his wings shall cover me, his comforts shall refresh my soul; he will guide me here by his counsel, and afterwards receive me to glory. O happy man, that hath the God of Jacob for his God; and these covenant mercies for his portion: who can hurt such a person? But, oh the woful state of one that hath not the name of God as a tower or chamber to run unto when evils are approaching! how dreadful was Saul's state, when the Philistines were upon him and God had forsaken him! just such will be condition of a soul destitute of covenant mercies in the day of public or personal calamity; alas, all they bore up their carnal hearts with, is gone, and God is gone, and now their hearts either break with grief, or through despair they make themselves away, as Judas and Ahithophel. † Oh forlorn state of such as have not taken God for their God! sirs, think seriously of these things.

6. These covenant mercies will have a mighty influence upon your spirits in God's service, and in your conversation; an interest in the mercies of the covenant will make you fear God, and tremble to offend so gracious a Being; "there is forgiveness with him, that he may be feared," Psalm cxxx. 4; and fear to

* Psalm cxii. 7. Psalm xlvi. 1, 2. † Psalm lii. 7.

offend God is itself one great mercy of the covenant. These mercies will melt your hearts into tears of evangelical repentance for offending God, as you may gather from Zech. xii. 10; brokenness of heart is also one of the mercies of the covenant. Sense of these mercies will make your souls love God supremely, Luke vii. 47, while love to God is itself another of the mercies of the covenant; and so for the rest of the christian graces. There is not a useful disposition requisite to qualify us for God's service, but it is contained in the covenant; hereby we shall know God's will, be willing to obey it, and delight ourselves in God's service, as David did, Psalm v. 7, " I will come into thy house in the multitude of thy mercy, and in thy fear will I worship towards thy holy temple:" we shall then " sing in the ways of the Lord, and in the height of Zion, and flow together for the goodness of the Lord," Jer. xxxi. 12; that is, the goodness of the Lord will engage the saints to come with cheerfulness into God's presence, and thank him for an opportunity of enjoying the manifestations of his favour. Holy hearts delight in holy works; grace fits the soul for God; covenant mercies render a soul capable of and prepared for covenant duties; and the more you partake of these mercies, the more delight will you take in duty; the more like you are to God, the more delight will you take in God, and God will delight more in you, and so there will be sweet fellowship betwixt God and your souls. On the contrary, carnal spirits cannot endure spiritual exercises; they come to duties as a bear to the stake, and when they are therein, they are upon a rack: Lord, be merciful to such a soul!

7. These covenant mercies will not leave the soul till they have brought it to heaven. God's mercies are in the heavens, that is their proper element; and they

never cease moving and elevating the believer, till they they have raised him up into the highest heavens, where he shall " drink of the river of God's pleasures," Psalm xxxvi. 5, 8. *Now* covenanted souls do only taste that the Lord is gracious, but *then* they shall eat and drink abundantly, and shall be satisfied with marrow and fatness; yea, bathe their souls in " fulness of joy and pleasures for evermore," Psalm xvi. 11 ; these mercies will make you rich towards God, and rich with God to all eternity; if you die with covenant mercies in your hearts, you depart like old Simeon with Christ in his arms, you die in peace, and rest, with God. These sure mercies lead the van to eternal glory, which comes in the rear of a temporal life and spiritual graces; yea, eternal life is begun here, as the the Scripture testifies—how is that? why, no otherwise than by the possession of these spiritual mercies, and communion with God thereby : " this is eternal life, to know the only true God and Jesus Christ."— John xvii. 3. You lay hold on eternal life here, by laying hold on these best blessings and covenant mercies :[*] " he that hath the Son hath life," and by believing on the name of the Son of God, he may know that he hath eternal life, for " he hath the record in himself." See 1 John v. 10—13. What is the witness mentioned by the apostle? it is contained in some of these sure mercies of David. O, then, for a share and interest therein! On the other hand, he that hath nothing to do with these sure mercies, hath nothing to do with eternal glory ; such as are strangers to the covenants of promise, have no hope of a better life ; [†] " as the tree falls so shall it lie ;"[‡] and such as are found without mercies in their hearts at death, shall be found destitute of mercy at the great-day.

[*] 1 Tim. vi. 12, 19.   [†] Eph. i. 12.   [‡] Eccl. xi. 3.

There is one description of persons I would more particularly press to look after their share in these sure mercies of David, and those are the children of godly parents; and hence Solomon prays, " Remember the mercies of David thy servant."—2 Chron. vi. 42. So you that are the posterity of godly predecessors, be solicitous for and apply the mercies of your fathers; and there are two cogent arguments in the quality of these mercies which the text mentioneth, for here they are said to be sure; and you may consider, first, your parents found them sure to them; and secondly, the promise will make them sure to you.

1. Consider that your religious ancestors found these covenant mercies sure to their own souls. " Our fathers trusted in thee, cried to thee, they were delivered, they were not ashamed."—Psalm xxii. 4, 5. Heathens did pertinaciously adhere to the religion of their predecessors; and shall children of godly parents forsake their fathers' God? and such a God as never failed them. Moses in his song saith, " He is my God and I will prepare him a habitation; my father's God and I will exalt him."—Exod. xv. 2. Inquire and search, you that are the seed of his servants—had your fathers ever cause to complain of God? was he not as good as his word to them? did he not punctually keep engagements with them, and make good all his promises to them? did not your pious parents breathe their last with good speeches of God? did they not affectionately commend his service to you upon their death-bed? reflect upon their dying words; did they not proclaim to all the world, that God was a faithful covenant-keeping God to them? and did they not assure you he would be as good to you, if you embrace him and keep his ways? yea, cannot you bear witness for them, that their last words were employed in

speaking well of God, as Jacob and Joseph both did upon their death-bed? did they not in the faith and sense thereof commend you into the hands of their gracious God? as Jacob, Gen. xlviii. 15, 16, " The God which fed me all my life long unto this day; the angel which redeemed me from all evil, bless the lads" ——did they not express particular persuasions of some future mercy, as those blessed patriarchs, * " Behold, I die, but God shall be with you, and bring you again to the land of your fathers!" Yea, cannot you that are children bear your testimony for God, that he hath been and done according to your parents' faith and hope? Solomon could say, after David's death, " Thou hast shewed unto thy servant David my father, great mercy," or bounty——but that is not all, " and thou hast kept," saith he, " for him this great kindness, that thou hast given him a son to sit upon his throne."— 1 Kings iii. 6. And I question not but many of you can say as much for God, that God hath had respect to you in temporal things, because you were the seed of such as were dear to him. O follow their steps, and you shall fare as they fared.

2. Yet further, you who are the children of pious parents, lie directly under the influences of these sure mercies; the promise is made to believers, and to their seed, † Gen. xvii. 7. Acts ii. 38, 39. such promises bear up the hearts of God's poor expiring servants, concerning their surviving children. Well then, let children claim their interest, and plead this grant; none of you will lose your earthly inheritance for want of looking after it. If your landlord promise you a lease of your tenement after your father's decease, on condition you sue

---

* Gen. xlviii. 21. and l. 24.

† Isa. xliv. 3. and lix. 21.　Exod. xx. 6.　See 2 Sam. xxiii. 1—5. Acts iii. 25.

to him for it, and pay the accustomed fine, will you be so mad as to be turned out of your farm, and the heritage left by your fathers, rather than own your just and kind landlord according to the laws of the land? No man is so fond* in temporal things, and why should you be so foolish in spiritual? Ah Christians, look after your patrimony; despise not your birth-right; is it nothing to you to be born of believing parents? remember your parents' tears and prayers, their hopes and fears. O consider, how it comforted their hearts upon their death-beds, that they left you under a good covenant, and bequeathed to you a goodly heritage; and why should your parents be deceived in their hopes, and at the great day meet you strangers to God and Christ, to be set with filthy goats upon the left hand of the Judge? why will you barter, mortgage, or sin away this fair estate? why will you not in the court of heaven claim the privileges of this blessed charter for your own souls? God is as willing to make them over to you, as ever he was to bestow them on your parents; he is loth to cut off his kindness from their seed; he looks after you in your soul-destroying practices; and saith, as once to Israel who did so wofully degenerate, " I remember thee, the kindness of thy youth, the love of thine espousals, when thou wentest after me in the wilderness, in a land that was not sown. What iniquity have your fathers found in me?"—Jer. ii. 2, 5. " I remember the kindness that in former times there was betwixt thy ancestors, and me. O their zeal in running after me, the holy services they did perform to me! Thy father, or grandfather, and some former generations, maintained intercourse with me, and I with them; there was love of espousals betwixt us, and I am sure I was not wanting

* Simple.

to them; I looked carefully to them; all that sought to devour them, were my enemies, and did offend me, and I brought evil upon them; I pleaded their cause while they lived, and I took them seasonably to heaven, and if thou that art their offspring wouldest have put me to it, I would have done as much for thee; if thou hadst but laid hold of that covenant, those very covenant mercies should have been thine, but thou art gone back, thou wilt have none of me, but walkest after new upstart vanities; thou wilt not vouchsafe so much as to inquire after the God of thy fathers who was so faithful to them, and did so much for them: but let me ask thee since thou wilt needs leave me, what iniquity have either thy fathers or thou found in me? produce thy reasons, testify against me, did I ever do thee any wrong? have I not always done thee good? Oh how unhappy thou art, whithersoever thou goest from me, thou missest of such a God as thy fathers served."*
God seems in that scripture to speak after this manner: O hearken to the eternal God, if you will not heed the dying words of your mortal parents, that died in the Lord; though one would think those should move and melt your hearts into tears of gospel sorrow, why should your dear deceased parents rise up in judgment against you at the day of judgment? when it shall be inquired whether they did their duty, they must needs answer according to truth, that they did instruct, correct, counsel, admonish their wandering prodigal children, they brought them to ordinances, prayed for them, wept and travailed again for them, and yet could not prevail; and now must come in to bear witness against them, and must rejoice in God's just vengeance upon them. Oh what a sad case will these rebellious children be in! there is no pleading of privileges by

* A like Expostulation see in Mic. vi. 3, 4.

means of believing parents, at that day; the higher you were advanced therein, the lower will you be cast down to hell.—Matt. xi. 23. Oh how terrible will it be to see godly parents in heaven, and themselves " cast into outer darkness;" yea, to see strangers, or the converted children of heathenish parents, " come from east, and west, and sit down with Abraham, Isaac, and Jacob in the kingdom of heaven;" but " the children of the kingdom," the posterity of covenanted parents, " cast out into outer darkness." See Matt. viii. 11, 12.

Let me therefore persuade all graceless children to look about them; do you above all others beware of miscarrying; greater expectations are from you than others; the surviving friends of your religious ancestors look after you, and inquire what you do. O rejoice their hearts by walking in the steps of your predecessors; I shall bespeak you, yea charge you, in the words of the Rev. Mr. Bolton upon his death-bed, that none of you will dare to meet us at the great tribunal in an unregenerate state. Let every child of pious parents plead for covenant mercies; as once Solomon did, 2 Chron. i. 8, 9, " Thou hast shewed great mercy unto David my father——now, O Lord God, let thy promise unto David my father be established:" thus do you plead with God, and say—Lord, my parents embraced the covenant, it was thy free grace to choose them, and set thy heart upon them; and is that grace become weary? canst thou not own me with covenant mercy? nay, dost thou not call that mercy to Abraham by the surer name of truth unto Jacob? am not I a child of the promise?—Lord, cut not off the entail of covenant mercies from me or mine for ever.

But I must hasten—let all seek after a share in covenant mercies, you that are afar off, and you that are near, children of the good and of the bad; draw nigh hither, take hold of this covenant; here is mercy for you all, these mercies are attainable. " Let the wicked forsake his way and the unrighteous man his thoughts, and let him return unto the Lord, and he will have mercy upon him, and to our God for he will abundantly pardon."—Isa. lv. 7. They are mercies, fear not being made welcome; they are sure mercies, fear not disappointment: thou hast a tender of mercies, that is a mercy, yea, such a mercy as the fallen angels never had, nor ever shall have; and if thou refuse, thou dost not only neglect a great salvation, but the devils will rise up in judgment against thee: it is a wonder of mercies that thou hast run a wild course, yet there is hope if now thou come upon the call of mercy! all the condition God requires is acceptance of Christ and grace; you are invited, and if you wilfully reject mercy, what must save you? if you will perish, who can hinder you? you must thank yourselves for ever. The God of mercy stands waiting at your door, the Prince of peace purchased mercy at a dear rate, the Spirit of grace knocks and puts in his blessed finger at the hole of the door—will not your bowels yet move towards him? He that might with a word command you into hell, beseecheth you to be reconciled; and will you have no bowels of mercy towards your own souls? Ministers entreat, travail, study, weep, and earnestly beseech you for mercies' sake to come in:* and yet will you stand out? and must I after all this pains leave you short of mercy, these sure and sweet mercies? God forbid! however, remember you were warned.

* 2 Cor. v. 20. Rom. xii. 1.

CHAP. XI.

THE SURE MERCIES OF DAVID MAY SUGGEST VARIOUS DIRECTIONS.

VI. I SHALL proceed to offer some directions to sinners and saints, to which the consideration of the subject leads, and which may form a reply to the following inquiries :

1. What is a person to do that he may obtain an interest in these mercies ?

2. How a doubting Christian may be assured of these covenant mercies ?

3. In what cases may a believer improve covenant mercies ?

4. How a pious individual, that hath interest in these mercies is to behave himself ?

For the first, which concerns graceless characters, poor, unregenerate creatures; if any such inquire what they must do that they may have a part and portion in these sure mercies of David, I shall briefly propound these seven directions :

1. Make a strict inquiry into your state, diligently examine what title you have to the mercies of the covenant, practice this great and much neglected duty of self-trial—whether you have closed with the covenant ? whether Christ be in you, or you be in Christ ? * whether faith be in you, or you be in the faith ? Self-knowledge is a good degree towards saving grace. Autology or self-knowledge, is the first step to theology. A man cannot, will not look after mercy till he know his own misery ; they that conceit themselves to be something, deceive themselves ; therefore, " let every man prove

* 2 Cor. xiii. 5.

his own work."—Gal. vi. 3, 4. O how many thousands, with a vain hope, do descend into everlasting burnings! how many presume they have as good a title to mercy as any, and fall short of it! Mistakes on this point are dangerous and damning, therefore, sirs, try your title, be at a point concerning your state; some are children of wrath, and have not obtained mercy; yea, all are such by nature. That grace which changeth our title, changeth our dispositions, therefore deal faithfully with your own hearts. Ask them, whether they be renewed, changed, soundly converted? ask yourselves whether you be new creatures? Be not put off with silence or a slight answer; remember life and death depend on the resolution of this important question. You must be tried another day, you cannot evade God's impartial search; only consider, there is no returning back to mend the matter, as you are found at the great day, so must you abide for ever; but here, if you find a flaw in your title, you may have it well repaired; and this is the first step to amendment of what is amiss, therefore get a distinct knowledge of your state.

2. Work on your hearts the misery of a soul's being destitute of these sure mercies; yea, if upon serious examination you find that your souls have no interest therein, O consider what a dreadful, deplorable state your souls are in! you are, indeed, *lo-ruhamahs*, bond slaves of Satan, enemies to God, destitute of Christ, and have nothing to do with the good things of the gospel. Learn your state from the blessed apostle, or rather from the infallible dictates of the Holy Ghost: Ephes. ii. 12, " without Christ," whatever confident claim you may lay to him, however you may boast of him, " aliens from the commonwealth of Israel," that is, no members of the true church, though you may presumptuously

call and account yourselves the only sons of the church, you have nothing to do with the spiritual privileges, and sweet communion of saints; you are strangers from the covenants of promise, that is, you are not in this new covenant, but under that of works, and have not a right to any one promise, and so to no gospel mercy, consequently, without hope and without God in the world. The misery of a graceless sinner is inexpressible, yea, inconceivable; he is ready every moment to drop into hell; he must be shut out of heaven; God is angry with him every moment; Satan hath him in a string, leads him whither he list, and if he die this moment, he is gone for ever. O work on your hearts such sad thoughts as these! awake conscience, rouse up your affections, then cry out with the publican, striking on your breast, "God be merciful to me a sinner."* Woe is me, wretched creature that I am; what shall I do? I am undone, the guilt of sin is upon me, mercy is far from me; I have despised free grace, and now I may fear that mercy is turned into fury, that long forbearance will end in just vengeance. Oh is there any hope for a forlorn wretch? have not I worn out my day of grace? is there any hope for me? Surely, a little mercy will not serve my turn; I am a great sinner, yea, the chief of sinners; there must be a larger dole of mercy to me than others. Oh " what shall I do, men and brethren, what must I do to be saved?" Thus, sirs, bemoan your state. It is not a saying all are sinners, and God is merciful, that will serve the turn, but you must be sick of sin, then you will desire a physician, else you will slight and scorn both Christ and the covenant of God, with all the mercies thereof.†

3. Be thankful for, but be not content with, common mercies; they are good in their kind, and for their

* Luke xviii. 13. † Matt. ix. 12, 13.

use and purposes, but they are not suitable to, nor sufficient for, the soul. A Christian should be content with any thing in the world, yet content with nothing in the world ; the worst of the world doth please a believer along with God, the best of it cannot, should not please him without God ; you must look on these things as good in the way for a staff or bait, but not good as a centre or end, to terminate your thoughts upon. Remember, the worst of men may have the best of these blessings, yet have them with a curse, and may perish with them ; therefore, say as David, Psalm cxix. 132, " Look thou upon me, and be merciful unto me, as thou usest to do unto those that love thy name ;" and elsewhere he desires to be remembered with the favour of God's people ; * as if he should say, and every believer may adopt the same language : Lord, there are common mercies which fill the belly, clothe the back, supply outward wants, but these thou givest to the bad as well as good ; and though these are more than I deserve, yet more than these I desire ; these will only serve me the day and date of my temporal life, and will take their leave of me at death ; but Lord, thou hast better mercies to bestow than these, even such as will adhere to me in life and death ; mercies that concern the soul, such as thou bestowest on children, and on heirs of promise. O let me come in for a child's part of those, and put me not off with any else ; none besides will fit or fill my precious soul, or serve my turn. I must say, as once the children of Joseph said to Joshua, " why hast thou given me but one lot and one portion to inherit, seeing I am a great people?" † So must I say, if I were a brute creature, one lot of provender for this body would serve me, but seeing I am blessed with a noble, never-dying soul, that hath large capacious faculties, I must have a dou-

* Psalm cvi. 4. † Josh. xvii. 14.

ble portion, a single share is not enough—something that will live when this body is laid in the grave, and nothing is so fit for this immortal soul, as these sure mercies of David. O that I had my share thereof! more than these I cannot reasonably desire, expect, or enjoy, and less than these my soul is not content withal.

4. Cast out and cashier all sin, break off your sinful league with impure lusts. These sure mercies will not lodge in a foul breast; where Christ takes up his habitation, sin hath not dominion. God and sin go contrary ways—mercies mount the soul upwards, corruption pulls the soul downwards; you must be separate, and touch no unclean thing, if you would be received and embraced as children, and have God for your Father, 2 Cor. vi. 17, 18. Be you sure "the throne of iniquity hath no fellowship with God," and God will challenge such as hate instruction, and wilfully run into sin, and will say, "what hast thou to do—to take my covenant in thy mouth;"* do not think to yoke Christ and Belial, God will not be merciful to any wicked, persevering transgressor; do not think to divide mercies and faithfulness; make account to enjoy mercies only in the way of truth, that you may be able to say as David, Psalm cxix. 41, " Let thy mercies come also unto me, O Lord, even thy salvation, according to thy word;" as if he had said, O Lord, thou hast mercies to bestow, and thou hast told me, how and to whom thou wilt distribute these mercies; it is to such as fear and love and obey thee, and devote themselves to thee. Why, here I am, I have served sin and Satan too long, now I abhor the ways in which my soul hath delighted, I abandon works of darkness, I cut off a right-hand sin, and pluck out a right-eye lust, and now I am in the road of mercy, not as though this merited thy favour,

* Psalm xciv. 20. Psalm l. 16—18.

but as a condition absolutely necessary in the souls of such as obtain mercy, according to the precepts and promises of the word ;* and now though I cannot challenge mercy, yet I humbly plead thy promise for mercy, even covenant mercies ; I have forsaken my sinful ways and wicked thoughts ; " O be merciful to me according to thy word !" † O entertain me, and then I shall not lose but change my pleasures, the sensual pleasures of the flesh, for a solid, sacred, and soul-satisfying delight in Christ and grace ! Thus renounce sin, and you shall have what is infinitely better; but that is not all.

5. Renounce your own righteousness, and look after these sure mercies only for mercy's sake ; the wise merchant parted with all, not only his worldly enjoyments, but self-conceited thoughts of his own righteousness, for this pearl of price ; ‡ deny yourselves then, enjoy God, mercy is slighted when you dream of merit ; the poor Jews that sought to establish their own righteousness, would not submit to the righteousness of God, Rom. x. 3 ; they had something of their own to lean to, they scorned God's way of saving sinners ; they would not be beholden to God's mercy, and so went without. The poor publican was justified, but the proud Pharisee condemned ; come as importunate beggars, not as rich purchasers ; say as David, " save me for thy mercies' sake," Psalm vi. 4, as if he had said, Lord, I am a weak, worthless, wicked creature, if thou mark iniquity who can stand ? I am not worthy of one crumb of kindness, most worthy of thy fiercest displeasure ; if thou condemn me thou art righteous—if thou save me thou art infinitely gracious. Lord, when thy wrath is ready to wax hot, and justice prompts thy hand to strike the fatal blow, then reflect upon thy working bowels of

* Isaiah i. 16—18, and lv. 7.   † Psalm cxix. 58.
‡ Matt. xiii. 46.

tender mercy, and stop thy hand from a righteous execution of thy justly deserved sentence of condemnation, " Remember thy tender mercies and thy loving kindnesses, for they have been ever of old——Remember not the sins of my youth nor my transgressions, according to thy mercy remember thou me, for thy goodness' sake, O Lord." Thus a good man pleads with God, Psalm xxv. 6, 7, and thus do thou come empty-handed, " buy wine and milk without money and without price." Mercy were not mercy if it were bought at a valuable rate; but as that is not possible, so that soul which comes to purchase shall be dealt without, for all the good things of the gospel are of free and undeserved gift.

6. Close with Jesus Christ the root and spring of these covenant mercies. I told you in the doctrinal part, these mercies are made sure in and by Christ to all the heirs of promise. Would you then enjoy the benefit of these mercies, accept of Jesus Christ in the exercise of a sound and lively faith. You can expect no mercy but through a Mediator, " grace and truth come by Jesus Christ." * All mercy is laid up in Christ, as the great storehouse, and is to be fetched out by faith; those souls are under a dangerous and soul-destroying mistake that imagine God to be any other ways merciful than in Christ. " It is even dreadful," saith Luther, " to think of God out of Christ;" this is the only gospel way of obtaining mercy. God blesseth us with these spiritual blessings in Christ, and we are accepted in the beloved. † Well then, how have poor souls interest in Christ? This is only by faith, which is the soul's accepting of him upon his own terms. ‡ Here, I must not digress into the spacious field of that useful subject, saving faith; but must refer you to the large dis-

* John i. 17. † Eph. i. 3, 6. ‡ John i. 12.

courses composed on this radical, fundamental grace, and I beseech you, be not mistaken in this; here you have the hinge and vital source of religion, even in an entire, affectionate, voluntary, and universal accepting of Jesus Christ, as our King, Priest, and Prophet, to be ruled, guided, and saved by him in his own way. O sirs, if you do not this, you do nothing; if you believe, you shall be saved, but if you believe not you shall be damned,* that is plain English; and truly, my friends, all men have not faith, this faith of the operation of God, this precious faith. O, therefore, look after it, long for it; come with a broken heart to a bleeding Saviour; come weary and heavy laden, and lay your load on the Son of God; come with a troubled, humbled heart, wounded with a sense of sin, and look up to this brazen serpent for help and healing; reach out thy trembling hand and get hold of the skirt of his garment, or rather with old Simeon embrace Jesus Christ in the arms of thy faith, and then thou hast these mercies of the covenant.

7. Enter into a solemn covenant with the Lord; there is no way to be interested in the mercies of the covenant, but by entering into covenant. This, this is the work I would persuade your souls unto; this, indeed, is the life of religion, which is so called [*a religando*] from binding, because it binds, as it were, God and man together, and joins their interests in this blessed bond of the covenant. O, therefore, set yourselves to enter into a solemn engagement. † Give up yourselves to the Lord, openly profess that you are the Lord's, or else subscribe with your hand, and yield up yourselves to the Lord, to whom, of right, you do belong, and take God as your God; say, " the Lord our God will

* Mark xvi. 16.
† 2 Cor. viii. 5. Isaiah xliv. 5. 2 Chron. xxx. 8.

we serve, and his voice will we obey,"* as the people of Israel once did ; and thus do you make a covenant this day—lift up your hand to the most high God, as once Jacob did, who made a vow, saying, " if God will be with me and keep me in this way that I go——then shall the Lord be my God."—Gen. xxviii. 20, 21. Now consider, friends, hath not God done as much for you as Jacob here desires, or even more? and why should you not take God for your God? Say thus: I have heard of the Lord's goodness, nay, I have experienced a large share of his kindness and compassion; he hath done that for me, which none else could, and hath undertaken to do yet much more; and, therefore, God forbid that I should cleave to any other God all my days, as I would be wholly the Lord's, so I will have only the Lord, and as he is the only true God, so he shall be my God. This is that which the Scripture calls avouching the Lord to be our God, and if we avouch him to be our God, he will avouch us to be his people, Deut. xxvi. 17, 18, which imports the mutual conditions of this blessed covenant, even a reciprocal embracing and accepting each other; the saints take God to be theirs by the saving grace of faith, and God receives them by a gracious act of favour, love and condescension ; only be sure you remember that the articles of agreement are of God's own framing, and the soul must come up wholly unto his terms, else no engagement; God will not abate any thing of his appointed conditions, it must be sincere faith, though it be but weak, which empties the soul of sin, and self, and turns wholly to God, and doth resign up itself universally, voluntarily, and perpetually to be the Lord's ; and in the same manner the believer takes God to be his, and looks upon this as his mercy, as well as his

* Josh. xxiv. 24. 25.

duty—his highest preferment, as well as his greatest concern, and sweetest enjoyment. O, thinks a pious soul, that I could be more the Lord's than I am. I am too much my own ; but I will enter into the strictest engagement to be only for God, and not for another,* then I may expect he would be for me ; and O that I could take the Lord wholly for mine, and only as mine, and join no other lovers with him ; I need none but him, he is all-sufficient, and my exceedingly valuable and great reward. Upon this condition God takes you, and you shall gain by him, and the gospel covenant, and all the mercies of it ; if you be not willing to " forsake all for him, you are not worthy of him ;"† but I shall spend no more time about this, because so many have written on a soul's covenanting with God. See Mr. Baxter's Saint's Rest, part 1, p. 176—182, *et alibi passim.* Mr. Guthrie, Mr. Allen, and Mr. Vincent have prescribed directions and a form of words for a solemn covenant with God.

Secondly, How may a doubting Christian assure himself of these covenant mercies ? Many pious souls may have an interest in these, yet not be assured of their interest, which, however, is of great consequence and concernment, though not to the being, yet to the well-being of a Christian ; therefore, we are commanded to give diligence " to make our calling and election sure," 2 Pet. i. 10, not in respect of God, say interpreters,‡ with whom all things are firm and invariable, but in respect of others, say some, that those with whom we live may see the tree is good, because the fruits are good ; but I rather take it, that we must labour to clear these up to our own souls, that we may have some real, well-grounded assurance thereof in our hearts, and both these are mercies included in the gos-

* Hos. iii. 3.　† Matt. x .37. Luke xiv. 28, 29.　‡ Vit. Aret. in loc.

pel covenant. Only take notice that calling is before election, there we must begin, and so ascend from the work of grace in our hearts to the workings of grace in God's heart, for our love is a reflection of his love to us. Grace is a fruit of election; this, then, is a weighty case of conscience. Suppose a real Christian to be dark and doubtful about his state, and to be full of questionings and disputings whether these sure mercies of the covenant do belong to him. What must such a person do that he may be assured of his interest therein, and that they may indeed be sure to him? Now for answering this question, I shall propose these directions: *

1. Study the precepts, promises, and precedents in the Scriptures; be diligent in reading the word of God. O, of what use would this be! There you may find what God commands, how saints have obeyed, by what means they have manifested their integrity and interest in Christ; here you may find what are the conditions of the covenant, and upon what terms the mercies thereof may be enjoyed, and what are the infallible characters of such as have received benefit thereby; here you may find Christ the main and choicest mercy of the covenant; yea, for this end were the Scriptures written, that we might have comfort in God, and by consequence also, assurance of our interest in him. Rom. xv. 4. For this reason did Christ speak, and John write divine truths, † which are upon record, that the joy of our Redeemer might be in us; yea, that our joy might be full. An express text you have in 1 John v. 13, " These things have I written unto you, that believe

---

* See this point handled solidly in a Treatise called, " A Believer's Duty towards the Spirit," &c. on Ephes. iv. 30. Read 6th Direct. page 158—183. See Baxt. 32 Directions.

† John xv. 11. 1 John i. 4.

on the name of the Son of God, that ye may know ye have eternal life." The more you study the Scriptures, the more clearly you may read your names in the book of life; your hearts, if sincere, will echo to the word you read, because the law of God is written in your hearts, therefore read and study this blessed book; these words form a charter of your heavenly inheritance, food for your hungry appetites, glasses in which you may discern the complexion of your souls. O Christians, neglect not the Scriptures, look up for a right understanding, and due application of every passage therein, and then comfort yourselves, and one another with these words.—1 Thess. iv. ult.

2. Attend upon a lively ministry; here the terms of the gospel are propounded—the mercies of the covenant are displayed—true believers discovered and characterized; here you may meet with a Barnabas as well as with a Boanerges; yea, it may be, the hand that wounded may heal you. God usually makes the fruit of the lips to be peace,* and many times sends some choice interpreter to declare unto a man his righteousness, and clear up his integrity; † and therefore it is, that God directs all such as walk in darkness to obey the voice of his servants,‡ or rather gives this as their character that they do so; and God gives ministers a charge to comfort his people,‖ and lays up such comforts in their breasts to this end, that they may comfort such as are cast down. § O the reviving words, you may hear in the ministry of the word! Here you may have doubts resolved, cases of conscience proposed and answered, also hearts opened and anatomatized; here the Spirit of God is often conveyed which seals up the

* Isaiah lvii. 19. † Job xxxiii. 23. ‡ Isaiah l. 10.
‖ Isaiah xl. 1, 2. § 2 Cor. i. 4.

believing soul to the day of redemption. * The presence of God accompanies his institution, so that what the minister declares in the name and by the authority of Christ, according to the word he will ratify, second and confirm in heaven ; † and how many drooping heirs of promise hath God raised, satisfied, and encouraged about their title to covenant mercies by this ordinance ? O the advantage that many have got thereby! therefore wait on God in this ordinance. O look not upon it as one of the weak and beggarly elements, as some ignorantly and blasphemously call all ordinances. Make them not a matter of ceremony and formality, but prepare for them and attend on them conscientiously, and you shall see the delightful effects thereof.

3. Improve the seals of the covenant, both baptism and the Lord's supper. Circumcision is called the seal of the righteousness of faith,‡ because this sweet evangelical privilege, or marrow of the gospel covenant was signified, sealed and exhibited in that ordinance. O Christians, understand and improve the encouraging ordinance of baptism, it would be a spring of sweetness and satisfaction to your doubting, fainting spirits ; and then, for the Lord's supper, herein Christ's body and blood are particularly applied to us, to become our own; yea, verily and really, though not corporeally, but spiritually, exhibited to every worthy receiver; ‖ and hence, resulteth spiritual joy, solace and satisfaction, as in the passover in Hezekiah's days, " they kept the feast with gladness and there was joy in Jerusalem." § But be sure you examine yourselves, prepare your hearts, excite your graces, understand the covenant,

* Isaiah lix. 21.   Gal. iii. 2, 3.   Ephes. iv. 30.
† Isaiah xliv. 26.   Matt. xviii. 18.   ‡ Rom. iv. 11.
‖ 1 Cor. x. 16, and xi. 24.   § 2 Chron. xxx. 21—26.

apply these blessed mysteries to your own souls, open your hearts by meditation that the King of glory may come in, stir up your souls to God, and he will draw near to you; you will see Christ crucified before you,* you will enjoy a blessed feast of fat things, that will nourish and comfort your pining souls; here you will find pleasant apples and sweet flagons of the wine of his special love to refresh you and support your hearts in the day of your affliction, and sad desertion; and if you cannot enjoy that reviving ordinance, yet reflect upon your former enjoyments, meditate upon your crucified Redeemer, and represent his bruised body and effused blood to yourselves, and in due time you will cry out with Thomas, " my Lord and my God."

4. Frequent the throne of grace in the exercise of prayer; say as David, Psalm xxxv. 3, " O Lord, say unto my soul, I am thy salvation." God hath promised to make his people joyful in the house, or duty, of prayer. † Saints have found by experience the sweet and satisfying fruit of serious wrestling with God. Thus David prays, Psalm xxxi. 16, " make thy face to shine upon thy servant," and verse 21, he breaks out in thankfulness for an answer, " Blessed be the Lord, for he hath shewed me his marvellous kindness in a strong city." Yea, Christ himself commands us to ask that we may receive that our joy may be full, John xvi. 24, and is not a clear evidence of our interest in the covenant, and the mercies of it worth asking? therefore, plead with God; tell him thou preferrest covenant mercies above worldly enjoyments, and that thou wouldst rather have those mercies made sure to thee than to have a lease of thy life, for his " lovingkindness is better than life." ‡ Tell him the joy of the Lord is thy strength, and how much it will tend to thy

* Gal. iii. 1. † Isaiah lvi. 7. ‡ Psalm lxiii. 3.

furtherance in his service, if he will lift up the light of his countenance on thy soul; tell him he hath granted comfortable assurance to many souls, and thou needest it as well as they; thou art an humble suitor at the gates of mercy, and art resolved not to let him go, except he bless thee; yet once again, tell him, it is no more than he hath promised in his word, and Christ hath purchased by his blood; and, therefore, it is no arrogancy for thee to crave or expect, and when thou hast been pleading, conclude with that poor man in the gospel, " Lord I believe, help thou my unbelief,"* and he will say, " according to thy faith be it unto thee."†

5. Walk closely with God. As that is one of the mercies of the covenant, so it is an evidence of our interest in the covenant, and it is a notable means of obtaining and maintaining assurance; Psalm l. 23, " to him that ordereth his conversation aright will I shew the salvation of God." Close walkers have many choice discoveries. O the peace that such have as keep God's commandments!‡ O the sweet refreshment which results from a lively obedience! " The work of righteousness is peace, the effect of righteousness is quietness and assurance for ever."—Isa. xxxii. 17. If you keep constantly in the fear of God, he will discover to you the secrets of his covenant, he will cause the sun of righteousness to arise upon you; if you keep his commandments, you shall have a comforter, and he will manifest himself to you; ‖ but if you grow careless, and remiss in your walking, and step aside to any gross sin, no wonder if you have little assurance of these covenant mercies; for these do separate betwixt you and your God, you and comfort. This obscured David's interest

---

* Mark ix. 24. † Matt. ix. 29. ‡ Psalm cxix. 165.
‖ Psalm xxv. 14. Mal. iv. 2. John xiv. 16, and xvi. 13.

in God, and his inconsistent acts cost him many a tear, and sad thoughts of heart, which made him cry out of broken bones, and bitterly groan out his sad complaints for the want of the joy of God's salvation; yea, for one act of sloth and security, the church lost the sweet sense of divine love.—Cant. v. 6. O beware of sin, it is like a filthy vapour rising out of the soul, that causeth a mist, and such a thick mist between God and us, as will keep the light of his countenance from shining upon us—it begets jealousies, suspicions and uncomfortable fears in the soul whether God be ours or not, and, therefore, beware of sin, and walk humbly with God.

6. Be much in self-observation. Some have an interest in the covenant, but know it not for want of self-discovery; therefore, it were a good work to consider both your hearts and ways; indeed, the heart is deceitful, but you should have the candle of the word in the hand of conscience, and deal impartially with your hearts; seek into the obscure corners thereof, and it is possible, in some nook or other, you will find a covenant mercy. Canst thou not say as Peter in sincerity, " thou knowest that I love thee!"* or with Hezekiah, that you have walked before God in uprightness? † Dost thou not find in thy heart a care to please God, a fear to offend him, a desire to enjoy him, a hatred of sin, a love to the saints, poverty of spirit, a despising of the world, and low thoughts of thy best duties? Well now, a sound search, and clear discovery of the frame of your spirits will be an admirable way to confirm to yourselves your interest in these covenant mercies, and so proving yourselves, your rejoicing and satisfaction shall be from yourselves. ‡ If thou canst but

* John xxi. 17. † Isaiah xxxviii. 3.
‡ Gal. vi. 4. Prov. xiv 14.

find one saving grace in thy heart in truth, thou mayest gather some evidence thence ; God's children have taken comfort from their sincere love to the brethren, when they have scarce discerned any other grace, and so have assured their hearts before God that they were " of the truth," see 1 John iii. 18, 19 ; there is never a good work done, if it be right for principle, rule and end, but it will help us to a discovery of our state, that our work is " wrought in God," John iii. 21 ; therefore, let us be willing to come to the light, and try our hearts and acts ; so may we attain assurance of our interest.

7. Reflect upon, and recollect your former experience. This was David's usual method, to assure his heart of the truth of grace, and his interest in God, Psalm lxxvii. 10, " I will remember the years of the right hand of the Most High ;" also the " days of old ;"* hence " his songs in the night." † This course took Job, ‡ and many other saints; and the apostle bids the believing Hebrews " call to remembrance the former days, in which, after they were illuminated, they endured a great fight of afflictions, Heb. x. 32, and this was in order to the recovery of God's smiles, and the sense of his love. You will say, what am I better for remembering what goodness was in me in time past, which I am now fallen from and have lost ? I answer, much every way, chiefly because these mercies of the covenant are sure mercies, and though they may be obscured, yet they are never abolished, " where God loves once, he loves to the end."—John xiii. 1. The bud and blossom of comfort may be nipped, but the root of the matter and incorruptible seed remain in the heart ; ‖ a man in a swoon hath life though possibly

* Psalm cxliii. 5, 6. † Psalm lxxvii. 6. ‡ Job xxiii. 11, 12.
‖ Job xix. 28. 1 Pet. i. 23.

it is not discernible to himself or others; grace may be hid, yet alive, as the sap returns into the root in winter; want of comfortable sense and feeling is not a loss of grace—in this case search your records, and see if you cannot find some manifestations of God to your souls in former times. I have heard of a pious woman, who was wont to write down how God dealt with her heart, also time, place, and manner of her communion with God. A time of distress came, the comforts and counsels of ministers and friends were in vain; a good man gets her book, shews it under her own hand, which she could not deny, asserts and evinces the immutable love of God, constantly reminds her of it, and rivets conviction as it takes place. Thus she recovered her assurance; thus you may, and should recollect experiences.

8. Strengthen every grace. The greater any thing is, the more it is discernible; little grace is not so soon discovered as much grace; a greater measure of the graces of the Spirit carries a beauty and lustre along with it, and hath a self-evidencing testimony of the soul's sincerity. Christians, do you add to your faith, virtue, knowledge, temperance, patience, godliness, brotherly kindness, charity; for if these things be in you and abound, you shall both be fruitful, and they will help you to clear up "your calling and election."— 2 Pet. i. 5—10. These make the soul to resemble God, and the more God-like a Christian grows, the more certain will he be in reference to his state. Saints of the greatest attainments are usually more free from doubts than others; whilst sincere, yet weak believers, are much pestered with jealousies and misgivings; the more you get of these sure mercies into your hearts, the more sure you are of your interest in them; the faster hold you have of God, the surer you will be that

you have, indeed, hold of him; every step towards Zion will add new strength, stability and satisfaction to the holy pilgrim; increase repentance, and you increase assurance of the remission of sins; increase faith, and that brings on assurance of faith; strengthen hope, and you settle your anchor; grow in love to God and his ways, in courage and zeal for God, in humility and self-denial, and hereby you will evidence to your own souls and others, that these mercies of the covenant belong to you, for so saith the apostle, " the Lord make you to increase and abound in love——to the end he may stablish your hearts unblameable in holiness before God," 1 Thess. iii. 12, 13 ; if you have more grace, you may probably have more comfort.

9. Rest the confidence of your souls upon free grace. The more you mix any conceits of your own righteousness, the more you will stagger, and be disconsolate; let free grace be your foundation, and build upon nothing in yourselves, for your best graces, duties, and excellencies are imperfect and can afford you little solid satisfaction. Let Jesus Christ be all in all to you, be you nothing at all in yourselves. O how God loves to see a poor trembling soul, despairing of any thing in itself, accounting the world as loss and dross, flying into the outstretched arms of free grace, casting itself down at his feet, and resolving to venture every thing upon an all-sufficient Saviour, and though at present it walk in darkness, yet it will cast anchor in the dark, " and trust in the name of the Lord." * You shall see, in due time, the mists will be dispelled, and the soul's state clearly ascertained, and the troubled heart fully satisfied. Thus David † expected to recover the light of God's countenance, and banish disquieting thoughts, even by trusting in God, Psalm xlii. 5—12; mercy will

* Isaiah l. 10.   † See Psalm xxxiii. 20—22.

answer all your doubts and scruples—mercy will suit your necessities—mercy will revive and cheer troubled spirits; therefore, poor doubting Christian, though thou canst find no goodness in thyself, and therefore lookest on thyself as utterly unworthy, yea, incapable of interest in covenant mercies, yet hope in God's mercy. Let no muddy current of thy duties mix with the pure stream of free undeserved mercy, and as that will carry thy soul apace to the ocean of glory, so it will bring many sweet, refreshing streams of joy and peace into thy heart. We have instances of many in the word that judged themselves most unworthy of good, as in themselves, yet expected and received both mercy and assurance thereof for mercy's sake—as the "centurion, woman of Canaan,"* and others; because as mercy is free, so these covenant mercies are purchased and ensured by Jesus Christ, the mediator of the covenant, and therefore, though there be no goodness in men to procure these mercies, yet there is enough in their surety, and as their sins are made over to him, so what good is in Christ, is made over to the believing soul, 1 Cor. i. 30—here is the marrow of the gospel; and farther, the less goodness a humbled sinner finds in himself, the greater evidence hath he that these mercies belong to him, because he finds even such persons particularly invited and received.† Yea, humility, self-denial and poverty of spirit are mercies of the covenant, and do evidence interest.

10. Attend much to the duties which thankfulness prescribes, give God praise, and he will give you more grounds of praise; bury not his mercies in the grave of forgetfulness, especially bless him for covenant mercies. Alas, saith the soul, if I were sure I had an in-

* Matt. viii. 8, and xv. 27.
† Isaiah lv. 1. Matt. v. 3. Rom. iv. 5.

terest in these covenant mercies, then I could sing to God's praise, and be very thankful; but how can I praise him for that which I question whether it belong to me, or not? I answer, thou must bless God that there are such mercies in store for poor sinners, and that any have obtained an interest therein, and are carried to heaven thereby; bless God that you are under a call and capacity to enjoy these covenant mercies, that God hath not excluded, but included you in the universal tender of them; consider also, if you have not cause to bless God, that he hath been dealing with your souls in such a manner as he is wont to do with those whom he brings into covenant with himself. Hath he not humbled, broken, and brought your hearts off from your own grounds of dependence? Hath he not let you see a vanity in the world, and the excellency and necessity of Christ? Hath he not caused longings and pantings in your souls after these mercies? and doth not all this deserve your thankfulness? But know further, that thankfulness for what you have is a most effectual way to clear up your title and to beget assurance; praise raiseth the soul's faculties to a high pitch of joy and comfort; it is like David's harp, to banish away the evil spirit of disquietness or discouragement. Your praise should wait for God, and you will find God waiting to be gracious to you;* usually a thankful heart is a cheerful heart; you may sing yourselves out of your sorrows, as David did frequently: he made a song of these mercies of the covenant, even then when he could find little comfort in, or benefit from, these covenant mercies in many respects: compare Psalm lxxxix. 1. with verse 38, &c. Thus do you, Christians, sing yourselves into this blessed composure, and soul tranquillity. It is the

* Psalm lxv. 1. Isaiah xxx. 18.

fault of doubting Christians, that they pore all upon their sins, and forget their mercies, they think they can never be sufficiently bathed in the tears of repentance, or torture their hearts with doubtful thoughts, but consider not that a thankful commemoration of mercies is as well their duty as mourning and humiliation; yea, it is a sweet, heart-cheering, God-pleasing duty; therefore let Christians be much in this duty as a means of assurance. I shall add a word or two to excite all to press after a particular assurance of interest in these mercies of the covenant.

1. Christians may be assured of their interest, we are commanded to make it sure, many pious people have arrived at a plerophory or full assurance;* experience proves the truth of this; God himself hath promised joy and comfort to such as "ask it," it is the great office of the Spirit " to seal the souls of believers to the day of redemption;"† yea, the Scriptures were written to promote our comfort and assurance, seals of the covenant were instituted, ordinances and ministers were appointed for this very purpose—and shall we slight this infinite condescension of God who is so forward to help us? shall we use no means or endeavours to ensure these mercies to our souls? Oh ungrateful creatures! If it were a thing unattainable, we might be daunted; but how many gracious souls do we see and hear of, that do walk in the light of God's countenance, and triumph over all opposition in the sense of God's love? And one great reason why many of us are so full of doubts, is our neglect of God's appointed

* 2 Pet. i. 10.
† John xvi. 24. Eph. i. 13. Rom. xv. 4. It is promised—See Isaiah lx. 16. Saints have attained to it—Job xix. 25. Psalm lxiii. 1. Gal. ii. 20. 1 John iii. 14. and v. 19. Cant. ii. 16. Isaiah xlv. 24, 25.

means for the obtaining of assurance; for if it be attainable in the use of ordinary means, we sin exceedingly against God and our own souls in neglecting those means of assurance.

2. You cannot evidence the truth of grace, or your title to covenant mercies, unless you use God's appointed means to obtain assurance. It is an ill sign of a graceless heart to nourish doubtings and distrusts, and then to come in with such pleas as these:—" True faith is accompanied with doubtings; he that doubts not, doth not believe; a doubting faith is a good faith; let me have doubts and fears, I dare not be too confident, lest I presume." But I must tell thee, soul, a doubting faith is but a weak faith, and a Christian ought " to be strong in faith," * and make progress to a full degree and proficiency in grace, and endeavour to arrive at this full assurance, for this is the nature of grace to be pressing after perfection, and to "go from faith to faith," † even from a faith of adherence to a faith of evidence and assurance; yea, let such as slight means of assurance know this—that they live in a constant neglect of a known duty, in disobedience to a flat command, Heb. vi. 11, " And we desire that every one of you do shew the same diligence to the full assurance of hope unto the end;" as if he had said, if your faith and hope be of the right stamp, as it may seem to be, it will be working off all doubtings, anxious thoughts, and distrusting fears, and move to a further degree of confidence and assurance; else you may suspect the truth of it.

3. You cannot assure yourselves of creature enjoyments a day to an end, nor yet of immunity from crosses; and if you have not assurance of these covenant mercies, what have you to bear up your hearts in

* Rom. iv. 20. † Rom. i. 17.

an evil day? We little know what shaking times may come, that may tear from you whatever you account dear; and if you have not something above, oh the sad confusions that will seize upon you! but assurance of an interest in the God of heaven, and the good things of the covenant will be a guard to free your hearts from those numerous armies of tormenting fears that will beset you; this will be a cordial to drive away sick and swooning qualms from your troubled spirits; assurance of God's love will fortify your hearts against the fierce assaults of men and devils; Psalm xxvii. 1, " The Lord is my light and salvation, whom shall I fear?" destroying angels shall not come near any persons that are sprinkled with Christ's blood, and have the mourner's mark.* A day of danger, horror, and confusion may overtake us in the nation, in which we may be stript naked of all our enjoyments—surely then assurance of our interest in the best riches in the world, will stand us in stead, and when all things else fail, these will abide with us. But,

4. Consider the great advantages of assurance, I can but name them.

(1.) It will assure us that we shall want nothing that is good for us; " if God have given us Christ, then will he give us all good things."—Rom. viii. 32.

(2.) It gives a sweet relish to every comfort of life, and causes " delight in God's great goodness."—Neh. ix. 25.

(3.) It will sweeten the " bitterest cup of affliction." —Matt. ix. 2.

(4.) It encourages us to come " with boldness to the throne of grace," Heb. iv. 16, μετὰ παρρησίας, that is, with a liberty to say what we list if according to his will, and he will hear us.

* Exod. xii. 23. Ezek. ix 6.

(5.) Assurance helps the soul to despise the world; he that knows he is clothed with the sun, can trample the moon under his feet.—Heb. x. 34.

(6.) It strengthens the mind against the censures and reproaches of men,* no matter what men say when God acquits, Rom. viii. 33, 34; our conscience tells us we are not the men we are represented to be.

(7.) It enhances the reading of the word, and receiving of the sacraments, the promises, seals, and blood of the covenant: precepts of Scripture, ministers, things present and things to come, all are the believer's. —1 Cor. iii. 21, 22.

(8.) It enlargeth the soul in praise and thanksgiving; hence those hallelujahs in heaven: the more assurance, the more thankfulness.—Psalm ciii. 1—3.

(9.) It commendeth religion to others, makes God's ways lovely: " O taste and see that the Lord is good, come and I will shew you what he hath done for my soul," engageth many.—Psalm cxlii. 7. and lxvi. 16.

(10.) It helpeth on repentance, makes godly sorrow more kindly and evangelical; a look of love from Christ melts Peter's heart—this sun dissolves frozen souls.—Ezek. xvi. 63.

(11.) It engageth the soul against sin; manifestations of God are cords of love, which are strongest to an ingenuous spirit.—Rom. vi. 1, 2.

(12.) Assurance animates our performances and obedience; is any thing too much to do for God? yes, my God deserves all I am and have, his commands are not grievous.—1 John v. 3.

(13.) It deadens the heart to needless disputes and controversies; it settles the mind in an attachment to the truth, and fortifies it against the subtilties of seduc-

* 1 Pet. iv. 14, 16.

ing spirits, for " God's law is in the hearts of his people."—Heb. xiii. 9.

(14.) It representeth the glory of heaven, and is a blessed emblem of a soul's bathing itself in those rivers of pleasure that are at God's right hand, while it opens a Pisgah sight of the celestial Canaan.

(15.) It disarms the king of terrors, and plucks out the sting of death ; so that a gracious soul, assured of God's love, can triumph with Paul over this conquered enemy.—1 Cor. xv. 55.

And indeed none but an assured Christian can look death in the face without dread and amazement. Ruffling gallants may be prodigal of their lives, when they are far from any capacity of obtaining assurance, but those are more like brutes than men, who are guided by sense, not by reason, and consider not that their souls are immortal, and that they enter into eternity at death ; hence they have drowned themselves in sensuality, and consider not what they do. It is only the Christian that is upon good grounds assured of his good estate, who can in cold blood adventure upon death, yea, be willing to die, even desire " to be dissolved and be with Christ."

I have but hinted at these things, because it is an ordinary subject on which many have done worthily to promote endeavours to obtain assurance.

Sirs, what say you to these things ? is not assurance of interest in covenant mercies worth labouring for ? can you let these things lie without making your title clear ? doth not the new creature breathe after it ? doth not a rational soul desire it ? do not all wicked men catch at a certainty, and frame to themselves some kind of certainty ? do not worldlings take care to secure their money, goods, and estates ? shall they require bonds, seals, oaths, and sureties, and yet account all this too little, and shall we account any thing too much to secure these precious mercies without which we are undone for ever? Oh let nothing hinder your endeavours this way; let no objections make you delay or be discouraged; let not Satan deter you, or the world's conceits make you slight it as unattainable, nor a slothful unbelieving heart obstruct your diligence in this great and weighty case. Who of you would live at such uncertainties as the most do? who would have his life to hang in doubt on a mere conjecture? especially when it depends on this important case of conscience, whether the soul must live in heaven or hell? but most of all, consider that our very lives are so uncertain that the next moment we may step into eternity. The God of heaven awake the saints of God who have indeed an interest in these mercies, to use all means to know they have an interest therein, that, as the apostle expresses himself, 1 John iii. 19, " they may know they are of the truth, and assure their hearts before him."

Thirdly,—In what cases may a believer make use of, or improve these sure mercies of David?

In answer to this, I shall propose these seven cases wherein a gracious soul may and must have recourse to these covenant mercies.

1. In case of unsettling suggestions leading to atheism or unbelief. When reason begins to dispute the being of God, or the truth of the Scriptures, and shakes our confidence, or strikes at the foundation, then study and improve these sure undoubted mercies, and lean upon divine authority; if God speak it, the thing is out of doubt, his *ipse dixit* is beyond all demonstrations. Divines make distinctions relative to maxims in divinity, some of which are *partly* divine, others are *solely*

divine. In truths of the former class, reason may be made subservient—first they are believed, then understood ;* as a man believes the immortality of the soul, then he begins to ascertain the same truth from reason, only reason must not here come before faith, but know her place; for if she should offer to go before as an usher to make way for faith, we should never believe; therefore Schoolmen say, " Reasons going before faith weaken faith, but reasons coming after faith strengthen it :" † so that reason makes not the matter more sure *ex parte veritatis dictantis,* in respect of God the speaker, *sed ex parte intellectús dissentientis,* in respect of the weakness of our understanding. ‡ But now in things that are solely divine, and fall directly under faith, as the mystery of the Trinity, or of the incarnation, reason hath nothing to do but admire those hidden mysteries that she can never reach. O take heed of doubting or unbelief: gospel mysteries are without all controversy; here your way is not to dispute but believe; God's word is more than all the protestations, asseverations, bonds or obligations of all the men in the world. Consider what is said in the doctrinal part, and give your full assent to all revealed truths. You may better believe God than your senses: senses may deceive us, God cannot. Many men are brutish and will believe nothing but what is within the reach of sense; they are mere Sadducees about spirits and spiritual things; but, sirs, will you believe nothing but what you see? then surely you will not believe that there is such a city as Rome or Paris, because you have not seen them. But let me tell you,

* Primo creduntur, et postea intelliguntur.
† Rationes præcedentes minuunt fidem, sed rationes subsequentes augent fidem.
‡ See Weem's Portrait of Imag. Ep. to Read.

that that tempting spirit who persuades you now to doubt of the being of God, and the reality of divine things, cannot doubt thereof himself; for he to his cost feels the truth, though without any comfortable interest therein; " the devils believe and tremble."— James ii. 19. O therefore silence all unbelieving and disputing thoughts; doubt not after these clear revelations and demonstrations; * admit not this grand gospel sin of unbelief, this damning infidelity, but cry out as the poor man, " Lord, I believe, help thou my unbelief."—Mark ix. 24.

2. In case of guilt upon the conscience, and fears of acceptance, have recourse to these sure mercies of David. These are mercies, therefore mercy is working towards a poor sinner in misery; they are made sure by Christ to all heirs of promise, and though thou canst not sensibly apprehend him by faith at times, yet " whom he loves he loves to the end:" what though thy sins be many, yet mercy answers all demerits; it is not only mercy, but mercies, multitudes of tender mercies; he is plenteous in mercy, and will abundantly pardon; he doth not consult thy fitness, but his free grace: come then, poor guilty sinner, venture thy weary soul upon these sure mercies; he is meeting thee half way, as the prodigal's father, and ready to all upon thy neck, his bowels are yearning towards thy distressed soul; he is very free and liberal in distributing, be not thou backward and shy in entertaining these sure mercies, he waits to be gracious, do thou bid his gracious tenders welcome. Yea, but saith the troubled self-condemned sinner, " though there be mercies, yet I question whether they belong to me; I know they are sure to some, but it is a great question whether I be of that number?" and I reply, why not

* Non est disputatio aut dubitatio post evangelium revelatum.

to thee? What Scripture reason leads thee to suspect that thou art excluded? The grant is in general terms; "Jesus Christ came to seek and save what was lost," and thou art lost, and feelest thyself to be lost—doth not he bid weary souls come to him? If thou wert righteous, thou mightest justly fear thou mightest go without him, but thou sayest thou art a sinner, and thou knowest, "he came not to call the righteous but sinners to repentance;" thou art a sinner, suppose thou art a great sinner, even among the chief of sinners; and did not Paul look upon himself as such, and yet he obtained mercy? and consider if thou hast no interest in these mercies, whence then are all those fears, doubts, jealousies, complaints, and inquiries? Whence are these sad and dreadful apprehensions of thy sin and misery? these convictions of the nothingness of thy duties, and sufficiency of mercies only to relieve thy perishing soul? Whence are those meltings of heart for offended bowels of mercy? and strugglings against sin from the sense of mercy? What mean those prayers and tears, those tossings of thy soul betwixt hopes and fears about thy interest in mercy? and yet thou who thus complainest, wouldst not give up thy title, or quit thy claim to these covenant mercies, for a full possession of all the common mercies in the world. Thou art not content without these—thy inquiry is chiefly after these— thy expectation is most from, and dependance most upon, these covenant mercies;—these, and these alone are thy salvation and desire. But suppose the worst, that thou hast no interest as yet in these, why shouldst thou despair of future interest? shouldst thou not rather put it out of doubt by a present application of them by actual believing? Stand out, stand off no longer, take Christ upon his own terms, give up thyself to him, give him the glory of believing, remember all the ways the Lord hath taken to assure thee of these mercies; hence unbelief is the most unreasonable sin in the world *—this is the great damning sin; say not with Cain, thy sins are greater than can be forgiven; for is not the mercy of an infinite God beyond the demerits of a finite creature? Nay further, thou givest God the lie who is truth itself; he saith, "there is life for dead condemned sinners in his Son;"† thou sayest, "no, I have been to seek, and I want life, but there is none for me;" yes, yes, soul, there is life enough for thee, grace abounds, and you may have life in abundance, only shut not out yourselves by unbelief, but come to him and he will in no wise cast you off, for he is ready to forgive your iniquities, and give you these sure mercies.

3. In case of persecutions, afflictions, and temptations from Satan, the world, or any other quarter, you may then improve these covenant mercies, and find abundance of sweetness, solace, and satisfaction therein.— Were it not for these, the soul of a child of God would sink under his pressures; how often doth David profess that he would have perished in his affliction, had not God's word of promise supported him?‡ A covenant word will lift up the soul from the lowest depth, a covenant God will encourage a saint in the greatest straits; there is a divine art in a Christian's improving this stock to the best advantage, and affliction is a proper season to make use thereof; as supposing a man to be in poverty, there is enough in the covenant to make him rich; if in disgrace, covenant mercies make him honourable; if sick, one covenant mercy (even pardon of sin) will made him sound; if in prison, covenant mercies set him at liberty; if hungry or thirsty, why, covenant mercies are meat and drink to him; if

* John iii. 19. † 1 John v. 10, 11. ‡ Psalm cxix.

deprived of relations, still covenant mercies make up that loss, and give the soul to see better relations in heaven.* O Christians, your case can never be forlorn, as long as you have such rich mercies of the covenant to support and supply you, let all the men on earth set themselves against you, they can but storm the outworks, they can never surprise your citadel, or rob you of your best goods—these mercies of the covenant, which are made sure to you by a covenant of salt. O hold fast and embrace these mercies in such a time as this; when trade decays, your stock is safe; in a plundering time, none can divest you of your treasure and estate; you have something that all the devils in hell, and men on earth, cannot deprive you of; troubles will but drive these mercies into your breasts more firmly and feelingly, rather than keep them from you, or render you suspicious of your interest in them, for these are seasons wherein God communicates most of himself to the soul. Jacob's sad and solitary journey was attended with the choicest, heart-reviving discoveries; † heaven was opened and God shone upon blessed Stephen's soul through a shower of stones. ‡ O Christians, it is worth a world to have interest in God in the day of affliction, and it is your great work in such a day to bear up your hearts with what you have in the covenant of grace: beware of discontented murmurings under any trials, since you have a God that can and will be all in all to your souls, in the want of all comforts and in overflowing of sorrows.

4. You may improve these covenant mercies in a day of spiritual dearth, in the famine of the word,

---

* Isa. xxxiii. 24. Dei hominem et cultorem Dei obnixum spei veritate et fidei stabilitate fundatum, mundi hujus et sæculi temptationibus commoveri, negat.—*Vide Cypr. Tractat. cont. Demetr.* p. 273.

† Gen. xxviii. 10.   ‡ Acts vii. 56.

which is the saddest judgment, when means and ordinances fail, and the soul is in great danger of pining; then it is both safe and sweet to derive growth and strength from the spring head, even from God in a covenant way; these mercies nourish the languishing soul in a famishing season: Isa. xli. 17, 18, "When the poor and needy seek water, and there is none, and their tongue faileth for thirst, I the Lord will hear them, I the God of Israel will not forsake them. I will open rivers in high places, and fountains in the midst of the valleys: I will make the wilderness a pool of water, and the dry land springs of water." O blessed are the circumstances of believers, they have meat which others know not of, even hidden manna; God hath ways to convey marrow and fatness into their soul, when their ordinary provision is kept from them. I have read of a man, that was condemned to starve to death in prison; his daughter getting leave to visit him once a day, though not permitted to bring food, she notwithstanding preserved his life a long time by the milk which he sucked from her breasts. Oh how doth God preserve the souls of his children in prisons, by that good nourishment they derive from him in the breasts of the promises! he keeps them alive in famine; "bread shall be given them, their waters shall be sure;"* yea, he makes affliction and adversity both bread and water, therefore called in Scripture, "the bread of adversity and water of affliction,"† because souls are bravely nourished thereby: ordinances may for a season be removed, but influences of grace are still conveyed, grace is supported, and the soul supplied; as long as the spring remains free for a Christian's access he shall be provided for, though the channel be stopt, the streams cut off, and outward means much

* Isaiah xxxiii. 16. † Isaiah xxx. 20.

obstructed: therefore, Christians, when the word of the Lord is precious, and there is little open vision, make your addresses immediately to God, see what he will speak to your souls; own him in covenant relation, lay your souls at his feet, and tell him that you are cast in a thirsty wilderness, your graces are withering, and hearts failing; tell him you can scarcely meet with an instrument to receive a word of counsel or comfort from, but ask him if he cannot supply without as well as by the means; tell him, he sometimes stops the conduit that he may convince us where our refreshment lies, and whither we must have recourse for fresh supplies; tell him when you enjoyed the means, they could not work without him, and now you want them he can work without them, though he hath restricted us to the means, yet he hath not restricted himself to them; tell him once again, that the more immediate his communications are, the more evidential they are, and the sweeter emblems of heaven.

5. Amidst your backslidings and fears of apostacy, then, O then improve these mercies of the new covenant; you fall and miscarry and lose your hold of God, but God hath hold of you; you dare not venture to approach him again, but he calls and tells you he will heal your backsliding, and will not cause his anger to fall upon you, because he is married to you, and he hates putting away. ‡ The mercies of the covenant depend not on your mutable wills, but upon everlasting love—your souls are carried to heaven in the chariot of the covenant, which moves upon the solid axle-tree of free grace, which as it was not procured, so it is not continued by your merits or goodness. It is true, if you had carried the matter so towards men as you have done towards God, you might have expected a

* Jer. iii. 12, 14.

heavy sentence, but these are the sure mercies of an infinite God; the covenant is made in Christ, and made good in Christ; the Alpha and Omega, the Amen, the faithful and true witness is the surety and mediator of this blessed covenant. O Christians, place your confidence here; there is help laid upon one that is mighty to save, he can save to the uttermost, he is good at this soul-saving work; do not fear, he that hath begun this good work in your hearts will perfect it, you may be confident of it; you shall be "kept by the power of God through faith to salvation;"* though you be very weak, yet he is able to make you stand; you shall not depart from him, omnipotence is engaged for you:† exercise faith, therefore, upon the numerous and gracious promises of perseverance; though you have many "fightings without and fears within," though you feel averseness to good, and a tendency to sin, wants and weaknesses, burdens and breaches, snares and sadness, yet lift up your hearts, you stand upon better terms with God than Adam in innocency, or the angels in glory, who were not confirmed in their integrity, but are fallen by a dreadful apostacy. It were sad for poor believers, if their happiness did depend upon their mutable nature, or strongest resolutions; or if God should revoke his mercies, as often as they provoke his justice; but blessed be God for Jesus Christ, and the rest of the sure mercies of David. Triumph in this, O ye children of the promise, the covenant in which your souls are included, is ordered in all things and sure; heaven itself is engaged for you, the gates of hell shall not prevail against you, none can pluck you out of his hands, who is the Rock of ages, in whom is everlasting strength; you may confidently make bold and blessed Paul's victorious

* 1 Pet. i. 5. † Rom. xiv. 4. Jer. xxxii. 40.

challenge, " Who shall separate us from the love of Christ?"—Rom. viii. 35—39. Though your internal movements be often like Ezekiel's wheel,* intricate, confused and perplexed, as a wheel in a wheel, grace swaying one way and flesh another, yet if you be joined to the living creatures, and united to Christ in the bond of the covenant, you shall go straight on with constancy and uniformity till your souls arrive at glory. These mercies are not for a day, or week, or month, or year, but they run parallel with the life of God and line of eternity, for " with everlasting mercies, he will have compassion on thee." —Isa. liv. 7, 8.

6. In case of desertions, and God's withdrawment from him, the believer may and must improve these sure mercies of David. Now desertions are ordinarily distinguished into God's withdrawing, first, his quickening, and secondly, his comforting presence from the soul; in both these cases, the soul may improve them.

(1.) In case God suspend the gracious influences of his Spirit, and the heart be shut up under deadness, hardness, unbelief, and distractions, and the poor Christian cannot feel the lively springings of covenant graces in his heart, then let him have recourse to the promise wherein God hath engaged himself to give a soft heart, a new spirit, faith, love, repentance, the spirit of prayer, &c.—all habits of grace, the lively exercise of grace, assisting grace, quickening, enlarging, moving, melting manifestations are bound up in the gospel covenant; hence it is, that when David finds his heart dull and out of frame, he runs to God and cries out, " My soul cleaveth to the dust, quicken me according to thy word."—Psalm cxix. 25, 107 ; and he goes often over with that phrase, which imports, that David lay under the sense of some promise, which

* Ezek. i. 16, 17, 21.

God had made for the quickening of his heart, when it was out of frame, and accordingly he recounts the gracious influences of God's Spirit, and professeth that he will never forget his precepts, because by them he had quickened him, verse 93. Thus, lay your dead hearts at Christ's feet, and plead in this manner: Lord, my heart is exceedingly dull and distracted; I feel not those enlarging, melting influences which thy saints have felt, but are they not chief material mercies of the covenant? dost thou not promise a Spirit of illumination, conviction, and humiliation? is not holiness of heart and life a main branch of it? dost thou not promise therein to write thy law in my heart? to give me oneness of heart, to put thy fear within me, to subdue my corruptions, to help my infirmities in prayer? now, Lord, these are the mercies my soul wants and waits for, fill my soul with these animating influences, revive thy work of grace in my soul, draw out my heart towards thee, increase my affection for thee, repair thine image, call forth grace into lively exercise: doth not that gracious word intend such a mercy when thou sayest, thou wilt not only give a new heart, but "put a new spirit within me,"* to make my soul lively, active, and spiritual in duties and exercises? dear Lord, am not I in covenant with thee? and are not these covenant mercies? why then, my God, is my heart thus hardened from my fear? why dost thou leave me in all this deadness and distraction? remember thy word unto thy servant in which thou hast caused me to hope, and which thou hast helped me to plead; O quicken my dull heart, according to thy word. Thus improve these mercies in case of deadness.

(2.) In case of sadness and disconsolateness, and the

* Ezek. xxxvi. 26.

hidings of God's face from a troubled, drooping spirit, O make, then, much use of these covenant mercies, both as they are mercies and as they are sure mercies, they are as free and as firm as ever; if you see nothing but wickedness and wretchedness in yourselves, remember mercy prevents you; if you see nothing but justice and frowns in God's face, remember his faithfulness engageth him; he is faithful, he cannot deny himself— would he love you so as to make you his, and will he not now love you as his child? Consider, the covenant is certain, though there be a present suspension; your union to Christ is secured, though actual communion be intercepted; yea, real, genuine communion is continued, though sensible manifestations be obscured; for observe it, the soul holds communion with Christ by that which desertions cannot make void; salvation may be there, though the joy of that salvation be gone, covenant relation may continue without comfortable satisfaction; " why hast thou forsaken me?" saith Christ and David his type, " yet my God still." * Christians, you are not to trust to present feelings; David doth not say, make me to feel, but hear joy and gladness,† saith one, because sense or feeling is of no worth of itself, except first we hear it in a promise, that is a fancy which is felt and not heard from God, and we are to build upon a word of promise, even when we want the feeling of comfort; it is not safe altogether to lean upon former experiences only, though these are good secondary helps, yet our primary and principle foundation is God in a promise, as our God in covenant. Let a dark and troubled spirit read, study, and practice that choice instruction, Isaiah l. 10, " Trust in the name of the Lord," there is enough in God's name to answer all doubts, read it, Exod. xxxiv. 5—7; mercy there an-

* Psalm xxii. 1. † Psalm li. 8.

swers to our misery, grace to our unworthiness, long-suffering to our continued apostacy ; goodness answers our vileness, truth and faithfulness answer to our covenant breach and falsehood; God keeps covenant, though we break it, yea, God keeps covenant with us though we are apt to think he breaks it. David thought God's mercy was clean gone, and that his promise failed for evermore, but he was convinced at last that that apprehension was his infirmity, Psalm lxxvii. 8—10. Therefore let a clouded Christian in his blackest desertions, lift up his eyes and heart to these sure mercies, and ponder thus : " It is true my soul is dark, and God withdraws, it is a night of great affliction, but was it never day with thee, O my soul ? hath not the blessed day-star of grace risen in thy heart ? hath not God united thee to Jesus Christ ? did he never give thee the earnest of his Spirit ? didst thou never feel the stirrings of its graces, or the solace of its comforts ? Reflect upon thy former state, or rather study the freeness and fulness of gospel grace. What though I be without any sensible feelings of God's grace, or shinings of his countenance ? is not my life hid with Christ in God, even sometimes from mine own eyes as well as from others ? may not the sun be under a cloud ? shall I say my Father doth not love me, because he doth not always dandle me upon his knee, and evidence his love to me in sweet embraces ? I am resolved to cleave unto him though he kill me, and to believe in him though I cannot see him ; I will venture my weary soul upon his free grace in Christ ; the covenant is firm, its mercies are sure—there is hope in the God of Israel ; it may be he will cast a propitious look on a weary soul, how ever I am resolved to lie at his feet, and exercise affiance and dependence on his immutable promise, whether he ever shine upon my soul or not"—this will bring a good issue.

7. The last case wherein a Christian is to improve these sure mercies of David is in the hour and on the approach of death, when that grim serjeant looks upon us with his ghastly face, and arrests us with his cold hand, then mercy will stand us in stead, and sure mercies will be our sweetest cordial; these mercies remove the sting of death, perfume the grave, make way for the gracious soul to take its flight to glory, so that death is now become the Christian's friend and servant, rest and interest, conquest and crown. The apostle doth therefore reckon up death as one part of the saint's inventory, 1 Cor. iii. 21, 22, "All things are yours, whether Paul or Apollos, or Cephas, or the world, or life, or death, or things present, or things to come, all are yours———." This is the fullest, longest, surest title; here is a sufficient enumeration, nothing can be wanting either in the mercies ensured, or manner of ensuring, or the duration; it is to all eternity, and it is the best and clearest tenure, *in capite*, in the head, Christ; it is both by purchase and by conquest, nothing is wanting to make these mercies sure for ever, for death which dissolves all other bonds of relation doth more firmly and closely unite God and genuine believers; it is as a porter to let them into their Father's house; a divine limbeck* to purify and prepare them for glory; and a voice which calls to the believer, saying, come up hither; in this life souls are but espoused to Christ, after death they are presented to him, and the marriage is consummated;† here we are absent from our husband, while present in the body, but it is more desirable to be absent from the body and present with the Lord, and

* Alembic or Still.   † 2 Cor. xi. 2.

this takes place on a dissolution of the earthly house of this tabernacle; so that hereby death becomes again, and brings believers to their proper home;* and why should we be afraid of a stingless serpent, or helpful servant, that doth us the greatest kindness? why are believers afraid to die? why do they not rather say as a good man did, [*egredere, anima, egredere*] go forth, my soul, go forth, and meet thy dearly beloved. But we need go no further to prove either the immortality of the soul, or the advantage of death, than the subject we are upon, even these sure mercies of David; for they continue to David even when he is laid in the grave, therefore our Saviour proves the resurrection from the covenant with Abraham, Isaac and Jacob, because it is a perpetual covenant, a covenant of salt;† and thus runs the argument: God is the God of the living and not of the dead, therefore these patriarchs are living and have an existence, because he hath made a covenant with them;‡ otherwise if these arise not, then must the covenant, of necessity, cease; but the covenant endures for ever, therefore those with whom he makes the covenant must live for ever, since God calls himself their God, even after they are laid in their graves;|| therefore, let Christians rest in hope, when they are laying down their heads in the grave, for the Scripture saith, "the righteous have hope in their death;" the covenant abides firm still—the mercies thereof die not when the body dies. The heathens themselves saw this. Socrates saith, " the swan was dedicated to Apollo, because she sung sweetly before her death;" and the Romans, when their great men died, and when their bodies were burnt to ashes, caused an eagle to fly and mount aloft, to signify that the soul was immortal.

* 2 Cor. v. 1, 2, 6, 8. Phil. i. 21.   † Numb. xviii. 19.
‡ Matt. xxii. 31, 32. || Exod. iii. 6.

And shall not the children of promise sing cheerfully when their souls are ready to mount up to eternal mansions? I confess I am really ashamed when I read Cicero, that any who call themselves Christians should dispute against the immortality of the soul, when he brings such arguments and authors to assert it; but I am much more ashamed that any· real saints should shrink with fears of death, when even that poor heathen hath said so much to produce contempt of it.* Let Christians learn something from heathens. Many passages might be adduced for this purpose. I have subjoined a few; a world more of instances might be brought out of heathen authors to shame professed Christians, that have a higher sort of arguments against the fear of death, yet the sense of covenant relation is the strongest, and the sureness of covenant mercies is of singular use to mitigate those bitter pangs, when the king of terrors doth appear in the most formidable manner, and strikes his last stroke with the most terrible effect. Truly I may, with Mr. Dodd, call death the friend of grace, though it be the enemy of nature; our Saviour hath plucked out its sting and altered its very essence. I shall conclude

---

* *Cicero Tusc. Quæst. lib.* 1, *De Contemnenda Morte:* Maximum verò argumentum est, naturam ipsam de immortalitate animorum tacitam judicare, quod omnibus curæ sunt, et maxime quidem, quæ post mortem futura sint. Serit arbores quæ alteri sæculo prosint——quid procreatio liberorum, quid propagatio nominis, quid adoptiones filiorum, quid testamentorum diligentia, quid ipsa sepulchrorum monumenta, quid elogia significant, nisi nos futura significant, nisi nos futura etiam cogitare?——Nemo unquam sine magnâ spe immortalitatis se pro patriâ offeret ad mortem.—And against fear of death, he adds: Acherontia templa, alta Orci, pallida lethi, obnubila, obsita tenebris loca, non pudet philosophum in eo gloriari, quod hæc non timeat.——Itaque non deterret sapientem mors, quæ propter incertos casus quotidiè imminet et propter brevitatem vitæ nunquam longè potest abesse.

this branch with a poem of divine Herbert's called Death. *

> Death, thou wast once an uncouth, hideous thing,
> Nothing but bones,
> The sad effect of sadder groans,
> Thy mouth was open, but thou couldst not sing.
>
> For we consider'd thee as at some six,
> Or ten years hence,
> After the loss of life and sense,
> Flesh being turn'd to dust, and bones to sticks:
>
> We look'd on this side of thee shooting short,
> Where we did find
> The shells of fledg'd souls left behind,
> Dry dust, which sheds no tears, but may extort.
>
> But since our Saviour's death did put some blood
> Into thy face,
> Thou art grown fair and full of grace,
> Much in request, much sought for as a good.
>
> For we do now behold thee gay and glad,
> As at dooms-day;
> When souls shall wear their new array,
> And all thy bones with beauty shall be clad.
>
> Therefore we can go die as sleep, and trust
> Half that we have,
> Unto an honest, faithful grave,
> Making our pillows either down or dust.

Fourthly, An answer may be given to this question, How a believer, who is interested in these mercies, is to conduct himself? Though this be a necessary point, yet I must cut short on it, having insisted too long on the former particulars.

1. Believe and receive these mercies. "This is a faithful saying, and worthy of all acceptation, that Jesus Christ came into the world to save sinners."—1 Tim. i. 15. Is it the proposition only that is to be credited,

* The Church, page 180.

or embraced? Is it not Christ and the rest of the covenant mercies held forth in this precious maxim, which is the sweetest flower in the garden of Scripture, the choicest pearl in the word, and the most glorious star in the whole constellation of gospel promises? Who dares to doubt what God hath spoken? and who dares to refuse what God doth offer? He is so wise that he cannot be deceived, and he is so good that he will not deceive you; you may better believe God than your own sense;* give glory to him by embracing these mercies, deny or dispute no longer. Be not ungrateful for the grace of God, who has condescended so low as to give you evidence, on purpose that you may believe.

2. Improve these sure mercies, make use of them in all your particular necessities. If a man have a good spring he will make it serve for the convenient supply of many household wants, and convey it through several channels for a variety of uses; so a Christian must branch out the several mercies of the covenant to his diversified circumstances, as enlightening mercy for his darkness, enlivening mercy for his dullness, pardoning mercy in case of guiltiness, purifying mercy in case of strong corruptions—because God's grace is sufficient for us in all exigencies;† in all storms there is sea room enough in God's infinite mercy for faith's full sail; our God supplies all wants; ‡ religion is a spiritual bond to unite God and the soul together, and a Christian in the exercise of his religion singles out that in God which is needful for him on all ocsasions. The life of faith is a retailing of divine benefits; as the co-

---

* De iis, quæ cognovit futuris et quæ adhuc sub visum non cadunt, tam certam habet persuasionem cognitione præditus, ut ea magis adesse putet, quam quæ sunt præsentia.—*Clem. Alex. Strom. lib.* 7.

† 2 Cor. xii. 9.   ‡ Phil. iv. 19.

venant of grace gives a believer a title thereto, as it were, by wholesale. O let the heirs of promise improve these mercies.

3. Be content with these mercies. They are sufficient to make you happy; seek not further to eke out your contentment in the creature, as though you had not enough in having these. What a strange expression is that of good Abraham, Gen. xv. 2, " Lord God," saith he, " what wilt thou give me seeing I go childless ?" Give him! why had not God given him himself, and was not that an exceeding great reward ? verse 1; and could Abraham desire more ? O yes; all this is nothing unless God give him a child—he takes no notice of this in comparison of a son. This is just our case. Let God give us himself and covenant mercies, we can overlook all these in our distempered fits, and look upon them as of no worth if he deny us some outward comfort that our hearts are set upon; but this is our sin and shame—cannot God himself content us? can we go from covenant mercies to mend ourselves with common mercies? nay, do we not thereby weaken our interest, disparage our portion, and provoke God to withdraw his help from us ? Is not God a jealous God, and can he endure to have any rival in your affections.

4. Walk worthy of these sure mercies. O do not discredit them by your unsuitable carriage.* Live after the rate of heirs of promise; walk exactly, spiritually, self-denyingly and soul-resignedly; God hath given himself and these best blessings to you in mercy, O give yourselves and best services to God in a way of duty! if you give yourselves to God as a whole burnt offering,

* Cum id præstiterit gratia ut moreremur peccato, quid aliud faciemus si vivemus in eo, nisi ut gratiæ simus ingrati.—*Aug. de Sp. et Lit. c.* 6.

it is but a reasonable service, for he hath given you more than you can give back to him;* walk holily, steadily, cheerfully as becomes these mercies, do much for God who hath done so much for you; let nothing discourage or disquiet your spirits, since you have mercies, sure mercies to lodge in your bosoms. Why should that soul be sad that enjoyeth an interest in the Father of consolations, the Purchaser of salvation, and comforting Spirit? Sure mercies are calculated to create solid comfort and assurance for ever. O Christians, learn the lessons much inculcated, to walk worthy of your vocation and relation to God and his kingdom.†

5. Act as under obligation for these mercies. They cost Christ dear to purchase them, do not you think any thing too dear to do or endure for promoting or preserving of them; kindness is very endearing to a grateful heart; your pains cannot be spent to better purpose than in the cause of God; we must always be paying our debt, though we can never fully pay it, we must be behindhand with God, but let a soul under the sense of mercies spend and be spent for God. You sow not in a barren soil; as showers of mercy promise your fruitfulness, so an abundant crop of mercy will be your sure reward, and in your saddest seasons you shall have the richest harvest of mercy. If Christians knew what grapes of celestial Canaan they should taste in their wilderness sufferings for Christ, they would not be so afraid of them as they are. These mercies run most freely and sweetly when other streams run dry. Fear not sufferings, mercies will meet and support you.

6. Plead these mercies for your posterity; though you should leave your children thousands a-year, yet, these covenant mercies will be the best portion; you

* Rom. xii. 1. † Col. i. 10. Eph. iv. 1. 1 Thess. ii. 12.

cannot ensure your estates to your heirs, but these are sure mercies; so that if you take hold of God's covenant, plead it, and live up to it, you shall have the benefit of these yourselves, and some, at least, of your children and successors shall enjoy the same mercies, for God will remember these unto a thousand generations: though he be not bound to every individual soul of your natural offspring, yet the Scripture fully shews that this is the surest way to obtain a portion for your children; tell God they are more his than yours, you are but nurses for his children; tell the Lord that you must die and leave them, but he lives for ever, and entreat him to be their loving, everlasting Father; tell him that though you leave them something in the world, yet that is neither adequate nor durable; but these sure mercies will not fail them—and comfort your hearts for your house and family with the last words of David, 2 Sam. xxiii. 5. O labour to transmit to future generations, your title to the favour of God, as the two tribes and a half did to future ages by their altar Ed.—Josh. xxii. 24, 28. *

7. Breathe after a full possession of these sure mercies, they are from everlasting to everlasting; follow them to the spring in admiration and thankfulness, and follow this stream of covenant mercies to the ocean of eternity. Indeed, the streams are, in time, to the sons and daughters of men, but the origin is without a beginning in God's eternal thoughts of love, and the issue is without end in his everlasting embraces in heaven. O long to see the end: if these mercies be so sweet here, what will they be in heaven, in their proper element, as it were! O that blessed state, that paradise of pleasure, that joy of our Lord, Abraham's bosom, a house not made with hands, a city without foundations,

* See 1 Chron. xxviii. 9.

a crown, a kingdom! such things are the happy result of these sure mercies of David. Do these mercies bring forth such felicity? O happy lot, that my soul hath an interest in these sure mercies! but how long shall my soul be kept from the full possession of these mercies? when shall I come and appear before God? how long shall I sojourn in Meshech, and be detained from my Father's plenteous table above? shall a captive long for his deliverance, and a young heir for his full inheritance? and shall not my soul long to be with Christ above? shall my body be so weary, and hath not my soul more cause to be weary of its burden and absence from home? shall creatures groan, and shall not I, much more, to be delivered into the glorious liberty of the sons of God?[*] shall the Spirit and the bride say come, and shall not my soul that hears these things, echo, come? shall he say, himself, I come quickly, and shall I not answer, Amen, even so come Lord Jesus?[†] Come, Lord, I long to see the end of these wonders of grace; I much desire to enjoy those mercies which eye hath not seen, ear heard, or heart conceived, after another manner than here I am capable. Come, my God, I beseech thee shew me thy face; and because none can see thy face and live, let me die that I may see thy face, and be swallowed up in the ocean of mercy, whither these covenant mercies flow. Dear Lord, either come down to me, or take me up to thee; " make haste my beloved, and be thou like a roe, or a young hart upon the mountains of spices.[‡]

[*] Rom. viii. 19—23. [†] Rev. xxii. 17—20. [‡] Song viii. 14.

CHAP. XII.

THE SURE MERCIES OF DAVID ARE CALCULATED TO ENCOURAGE BELIEVERS, AND TO EXCITE THEIR GRATITUDE.

VII. FROM the subject which has been discussed, encouragement, comfort and refreshment may be derived. Here is an abundant spring opened to revive all the heirs of promise; but because I want room, and because much of that which hath been already delivered, tends this way, I shall rather improve it, to excite the people of God and heirs of promise to the great and delightful duty of thankfulness.

And here I might enlarge upon the nature, use, comfort and acceptance of the duty of praise in the account of God and men; but I must wave that, and only insist on some few particulars that concern the nature of these mercies, which may engage us to be thankful, which are these:

1. They are free mercies; they may be had without money or price, saith this prophet—free grace was the fountain, cause, and origin of these; he had mercy because he would have mercy; nothing moved his bowels of mercy on our part—free grace had no impulsive cause but itself. When you are to purchase these mercies, the price is fallen to just nothing—he gives liberally and upbraids not.* O what cause of thankfulness and admiration!

2. They are costly mercies. This doth not contra-

---

* Quanti, O homines, profiteremini vos esse empturos, si salus æterna venderetur? ne si Pactolum quidem, qui totus aureo, ut est in fabulis fluit fluento, quis dederit, pro salute justum pretium numeraverit.—*Clem. Alex. Adm. ad Gentes.*

dict the former—they are costly to Jesus Christ, but free to us ; they are purchased with the warmest blood in the veins of the Son of God ; yea, he thought his dearest heart blood well bestowed to purchase these sure mercies ; he sees of the travail of his soul and is well satisfied ; the fruits of his purchase are the joys of his heart ; he thinks these worth all his pains, pain and suffering; God the Father is well pleased and accounts these mercies a valuable fruit of his son's purchase—and shall not we be thankful?

3. They are extensive mercies, deep, high and broad, they have all the dimensions of greatness, Psalm xxxvi. 5, 6 ; these mercies can fetch up a drooping, despairing soul out of the grave, yea, out of hell—be the soul sunk as low as sin can depress it in this world, these mercies can recover it, and raise it out of the grave and pit of silence, and save to the uttermost.* O what a long arm of mercy hath been reached forth unto your troubled hearts in your low estate! and doth not this deserve thankfulness?

4. They are designed mercies, purposely designed, aimed and intended to set forth the riches of grace the infinite contrivance of the blessed God, to magnify the riches of his love to sinners. It is true, God intended to set off his power, wisdom, justice and truth, but he hath magnified his mercy above all the rest of his name ; it is beyond the greatest of his works, all the attributes of God are set very high, but mercy sits on the chief throne ; he declares to angels and saints what he can do for wretched man. O advance free grace.

5. They are dignifying mercies. Such honour have

* Aquæ quo sunt profundiores, eo sunt puriores, quoniam et crassa et terrea materia in profundum depressa est—hinc profunditatem aquarum bibere. Ezek. xxxiv. 18.

all his saints. O what a height doth God raise his covenant children to! he deals bountifully with them; by these covenant mercies was David raised up on high,* and therefore acknowledgeth, that God "regarded him according to the estate of a man of high degree," 1 Chron. xvii. 17; and truly it is the highest preferment in the world to partake of these sure mercies; we have, therefore, great cause of thankfulness.

6. They are sanctifying mercies. They season all other mercies, and make common mercies to become covenant mercies; yea, they make crosses, mercies; they perfume the most distressing grief, and are like Moses's tree that sweetened the waters of Marah. If you pour a pail of water on the floor, it seems a little sea, but pour it into the ocean it is swallowed up and seems nothing; so afflictions out of the covenant are intolerable, but as in covenant love they are inconsiderable, the depth of mercies drowns the depth of miseries—and is not this ground of thankfulness?

7. They are separating mercies. Hereby are God's children distinguished from all the people that are upon the face of the earth, even in their finding grace in God's sight, and having his presence with them, and making his goodness pass before them.* If there be any discriminating mercies for any of the children of men, as protection, provision, direction; these covenant mercies usher them in, and portion them out to the heirs of promise—and if you partake of them and find them to be good for you, then bless God.

8. They are sealing mercies; they signify, exhibit, and represent God's love to the soul. Wherever these mercies are laid up in the breast of a sinner, he is the Jedidiah, or beloved of God—they testify such a person's relation to God, and God's affection for him;

* 2 Sam. xxiii. 1.   † Exod. xxxiii. 16—19.

wicked men are strangers to covenant love. God's people are the proper subjects of these endeared thoughts of his heart—and are you of that number? O give God the glory of this mercy.

9. They are comprehensive mercies—they are exceeding capacious, and embrace all the heirs of promise, not a gracious soul, though ever so poor, is left out, yea, they reach every Christian's state, case, exigency, and necessity. Let doubts be what they may, let fears, falls, faults be sad, and soul overwhelming, yet these sure mercies will answer all; they are commensurate and proportioned to all conditions of soul, body, estate, or relation. O bless God for them.

10. They are diversified mercies; they have respect to all the good that God promiseth, or a soul needeth, peace and pardon, grace and glory, holiness and happiness, all our fresh springs are herein, the good things of this life and of a better: many are the precious things put forth by the sun of righteousness in a covenant way. O what cause have we to bless God and admire free grace, that hath not only given us the spiritual good things of his kingdom—righteousness, peace and joy in the Holy Ghost, but temporal good things by a sure and pleasing tenure; so that these sure mercies of the covenant ensure unto us the temporal things that are good for us; and also after another and better manner than any uncovenanted persons, though ever so great, can enjoy them; for, in a covenant way, believers do enjoy common mercies,

(1.) More refinedly, taken off the dregs of cares and sorrows, Prov. x. 22; a saint's bread, though never so coarse, is of the finest of the wheat, and he is satisfied with honey out of the rock;* yea, they come

(2.) More substantially: other comforts are but seeming comforts; as man walketh in a vain show, so what

---

* Psalm lxxxi. 16.

he enjoys is only a dream, but outward comforts coming through the blood of Christ are solid, substantial refreshments ;* again, they come

(3.) More agreeably : they have not those prickles and stings that worldly things have for natural men. O the peace and quietness that a Christian enjoys with outward comforts ; and further, temporal things come to a child of God,

(4.) More serviceably : the creature doth homage to its maker and master's children, so that what they have is for their good and doth them good ; and comforts also come,

(5.) More satisfyingly: a godly man is more contented with his little than the men of the world can be with abundance ; " a little that the righteous hath, is better than the riches of many wicked," Psalm xxxvii. 16 ; and then a child of God enjoys his comforts in a covenant way,

(6.) More safely : he needs not fear want, " bread shall be given him, his waters shall be sure," Isaiah xxxiii. 16 ; God is the Christian's purse-bearer, and it is in safer hands than in his own, and they are

(7.) More lasting : we shall have temporal mercies as long as we need them, and when we need them not, they shall be swallowed up in eternal enjoyments. O, therefore, let the saints of God be truly thankful—let the high praises of God be in their mouths ; this is the chief rent and reasonable tribute that God expects for these sure mercies ; sacrifice these sacrifices of thanksgiving, take this cup of salvation, and give God the praise that is due unto his name. Begin that work here in time, which shall be fully performed by the ransomed of the Lord to all eternity. This, this shall be the burden of the saint's triumphant song in the heavenly mansions; that glorious palace shall ring and

* Luke viii. 18. Psalm xxxix. 6.

echo with the blessed exclamation, Mercy! mercy endureth for ever! free grace laid the foundation, and grace only will bring forth the top-stone of saints' glory. O how will God be admired by and in all, who believe at that day! Well, sirs, begin those hosannas here, which will be seconded with hallelujah's hereafter; speak well of your gracious God, admire his new covenant design, and let him have all the glory of this blessed contrivance—so shall you accomplish God's end, and evidence your covenant interest in these sure mercies of David.

Thus, though these divine graces which adorn the temple of a Christian's breast do sometimes disappear, and sin costs the soul some tears, yet the gracious soul hath abundant ground of thankfulness on the whole. Take it as expressed in divine Herbert's Poem on the Church Floor.

> Mark you the floor? that square and speckled stone,
>   Which looks so firm and strong, is—PATIENCE;
> And the other black and grave, wherewith each one
>   Is chequered all along—HUMILITY;
> The gentle rising, which, on either hand,
>   Leads to the choir above, is—CONFIDENCE.
> But the sweet cement, which, in one sure band,
>   Ties the whole frame, is—LOVE and CHARITY.
>
>   Hither, sometimes, sin steals and stains
>   The marble's neat and curious veins;
> But all is cleansed when the marble weeps:
>   Sometimes, death puffing at the door,
>   Blows all the dust about the floor;
> But while he thinks to spoil the room, he sweeps.
>   Blest be the Architect, whose art
>   Could build so strong in a weak heart.

END OF VOL. II.

John Vint, Printer, Idle.